In the Pressure of the Moment:
Remembering Gerry McNeil

David McNeil

In the Pressure of the Moment
Remembering Gerry McNeil

Midtown Press

Midtown Press
7375 Granville Street
Vancouver, BC
V6P 4Y3 Canada

ISBN 978-0-9881101-8-2 (paperback)
ISBN 978-1-988242-01-9 (EPUB)
ISBN 978-1-988242-00-2 (PDF)

Legal deposit: 1st quarter 2016 (paperback)
Library and Archives Canada

Printed and bound in Canada

Editor: Louis Anctil
Assistant: Daniel Anctil
Copy editor: Heidi Petersen
Design and production: Denis Hunter Design

Library and Archives Canada Cataloguing in Publication

McNeil, David, author
    In the pressure of the moment : remembering Gerry
McNeil / David McNeil.

Includes bibliographical references and index.
ISBN 978-0-9881101-8-2 (paperback)

    1. McNeil, Gerry, 1926-2004. 2. Hockey goalkeepers--Canada--
Biography. 3. Montreal Canadiens (Hockey team)--Biography.
4. Sports journalism--History. 5. Mass media and sports--History.
I. Title.

GV848.5.M26M26 2015   796.962092   C2015-907080-5

FRONT COVER: Gerry McNeil kicks out a shot by Gordie Howe (detail). Detroit Olympia,
early 1950s. (Photo by James "Scotty" Kilpatrick. *Gazette* [Montreal], May 7, 2002, E3; and
Gazette [Montreal], Mar. 27, 2004, A2.) Copyright unknown.

BACK COVER: "Exclusive color portrait for *Sport* by International." [Although there is no
photo credit, this image is probably the work of Ozzie Sweet. "The Dirtiest Job on Ice," *Sport*
10, no. 2 (February 1951): 19. Article focuses on NHL goaltenders.] Copyright Macfadden
Publications (defunct) Macfadden Publications Inc., 205 East 42 Street, New York 17, NY.

This book is dedicated to all those players who are not enshrined in the Hall of Fame, but whose characters and feats underlie the greatness of others, and whose stories are an integral part of our fascination with sport.

Contents

Preface

WHEN GAME SEVEN OF THE 1954 STANLEY CUP FINAL BETWEEN the Montreal Canadiens and the Detroit Red Wings went into sudden-death overtime, most of the players involved felt a familiar mix of expectant dread and exhilaration. Detroit had won the Cup four years earlier in a seventh game against the Rangers that had also gone into overtime. On three occasions since, the Red Wings and Canadiens had needed extra time to decide a playoff game, the most recent being only a few nights before. When Montreal lost the Cup to the Leafs in '51, all five games in the series went into sudden death, and the Canadiens had two overtime wins against Boston—once at the Garden in the '52 Semi-final and again in the clinching game of the '53 Final. Gerry McNeil, the Habs goalie for Game Seven in '54, could take little solace in knowing that his stellar play had brought his team back from a 3–1 deficit. Few would remember the comeback, but everyone would remember the winning goal.

The pressures on goalies in the NHL of the early 1950s were unlike anything we know today. Just one goalie dressed for each team, so a substitution would occur only in the case of a severe injury. Goalies did not wear face masks and were expected to take the odd puck off a cheek from time to time. There was no hiding a subpar performance or escaping the tension of the situation. Years later McNeil would describe the feeling of losing that Game Seven on a fluky overtime goal: "It's like the end of the world!"[1] He didn't know it then, but it would be his last NHL playoff game. Another thing he didn't know was that no other goalie in NHL history could say that he had played in three overtime Cup-winning games. What he did know on that April night in 1954 was that there was a world of difference between victory and defeat, as there was between playing in front of a record-breaking crowd at the Olympia and where he had come from a little over ten years before.

This book pulls together two purposes. First and foremost, it tells the story of Gerry McNeil's short but remarkable NHL career, wedged as it is between that of two Hall of Famers (Bill Durnan and Jacques Plante). Second, it marks how our experience of the NHL has changed from the time of McNeil's career to the modern spectacle of today, roughly the last sixty-five years. This period includes what might be called the golden age of sports photography (the 1940s and '50s) and the beginning of the NHL on television.

The outline of the story follows a familiar pattern. Chapter 1 chronicles McNeil's long "understudy" role from his first NHL training camp in 1943 to his first chance at Big Time hockey in '47. The second recalls how he was called up to replace an injured Durnan at the end of the 1950 season and how he preserved the latter's last Vezina Trophy win. Chapter 3 traces his incredible streak of 218 minutes 42 seconds of shutout play against the best team of the time—the Detroit Red Wings. The climax of McNeil's spectacular rise is the focus of Chapter 4: the 1951 Final, when every game goes into overtime, the last one ending with Bill Barilko's famous goal captured by Nat Turofsky's equally famous photo. Chapter 5 deals with certain injuries and problems that McNeil, and other goalies, had to play through. In a time when concussions were not monitored as they are today, there was pressure on all players to shake off a bit of dizziness as if it were a bruise. McNeil's comeback to win the Stanley Cup in 1953 is the subject of Chapter 6. Chapter 7 looks at another playoff comeback and McNeil's subsequent attempts to retire from professional hockey. Nervous tension had exacted a cost, and it was time to plan a retreat back to a normal life. The last chapter traces the denouement of McNeil's post-NHL life and the new challenges that presented themselves.

Parallel to this story is an analysis of the development of sports media, specifically as it relates to Gerry McNeil's career but with an eye on more general elements. The early 1950s saw photography becoming part of popular culture via the magazine; McNeil's full-page colour portrait was featured in *Sport* magazine's article on NHL goalies in February 1951 (see back cover illustration). Canadians would gain access to the moving image with television in the fall of 1952 when the French CBC aired its first broadcast from Montreal; McNeil is the second player to be seen in the opening sequence after Gordie Howe. McNeil's presence in this history is almost Zelig-like insofar as his career remains virtually unknown, and yet unlike Woody Allen's fictional character, McNeil was actually there.

Chapter 1 contains commentary on the private and public sources upon which I have drawn, both photos and discourse. Since Gerry McNeil was my father, I had and continue to have access to a personal family history, much of it oral, that informs the public record as it exists in contemporary journalism and subsequent histories. Chapter 2 includes reflections on the aesthetics of sports photography—what we look for and what we marvel at. Skill and chance play essential roles. Nostalgia colours our reaction. Chapter 3 looks at a specific photo in some detail and examines its decorative and cultural functions as a private artifact. Chapter 4 analyzes some of the consequences that affected my father from being associated with Nat Turofsky's famous picture of Barilko's goal, a very public artifact. The chapter mentions a fishing trip that some of the Habs took that was the subject of a short publicity film and a number of rather unique photos. It also traces the beginnings of the popular sports magazine *Sport*, followed by *Sports Illustrated* with their pictorial formats.

Chapter 5 comments on the shift from the still to the moving picture or the feature film and how representations of events from the 1940s to the '60s were often based on extant photography. A scene from Charles Binamé's *The Rocket* is examined, as well as how an iconic image sets the stage for a particular scene. That certain famous photos served as points of departure for subsequent motion pictures is likewise discussed in Chapter 5. Chapter 6 deals with the beginning of televised hockey on the CBC, as well as the spontaneous versus the expected in the picture(s) of victory. In Chapter 7, I consider some of the newsreels of the era, along with Leslie McFarlane's remarkable 1953 film *Here's Hockey*. The more negative aspects of major sport as cultural spectacle are raised in Chapter 8, and these involve commercial interests, mechanical responses, and self-consuming gawking. This chapter also argues that the writing on hockey (look for those titles every fall in anticipation of the Christmas marketing season), insofar as it celebrates the game, may be seen in terms of MacAloon's idea of the festival surrounding a sport or sporting event.[2] The spectacle is not restricted to visual representation; in fact, its aural aspects are critical factors. The familiar radio voices of Foster Hewitt and René Lecavalier were part of the popular imagination long before the moving image; however, we now get to feast on the spectacle via digital technology. Hockey culture is as much noise as image; its engagement has as much to do with texts and voices as pictures.

Unlike other Hab goalies whose Hall of Fame stature makes it difficult to see beyond their statistics and fame (I refer to Patrick Roy, Ken Dryden, and Jacques Plante, and one could add Bill Durnan and George Vézina), Gerry McNeil is virtually unknown. His story, with all the multimedia accoutrements, can be enjoyed and the general significances noted without the noise of celebrity. An examination of his professional hockey career presents an opportunity to examine how different our experience with the sport is now. I have to say that it seems like yesterday when my father and I sat down and watched the Briston Films highlight reel of the 1954 Final. It was actually sometime in the mid-1990s, and what struck me most about the experience is that I was very conscious of the fact that my father was watching the action for the first time since it had happened forty years in the past. He was reliving the experience, and it was a miraculous moment—utterly unlike a regular game we had watched on television around the same time. In the latter, a controversial call had been made and we expected the team captain to appeal to the officials; what happened instead was that we were given a shot of the Canadiens' bench and every player seemed to be staring up at the rafters. "What are they doing?" we shouted. "The play was clearly offside!" What the players were doing, of course, was staring up at the Jumbotron, waiting for the replay. Showing replays in the arena itself had just started, and we couldn't help but think that this immediate reproduction stole some of the intensity from the moment itself.

It has been over ten years since my father passed away, and our experience of the NHL has become a moving feast of digital amusement and engagement. Twenty-four/seven access to all forms of representation is now in the palm of our hand. Some of us today cannot seem to walk down the street without being digitally connected, and we generally do not live as much in the moment as we did a half century ago. Moreover, fans born in the 1950s or '60s tend to feel nostalgically attached to events from the distant past, and especially so when access to reproduction in pictures or motion pictures is limited. In short, we always want what we cannot have. So this book speaks indirectly about how the live experience today does not have the same intensity or sense of exclusivity that it did sixty years ago. The link between Gerry McNeil's hockey career and the slice of sports media analyzed here has to do with depth of field and a bygone era.

As mentioned, the biographical subject is my father; my reconstruction of his hockey life is marked by points of reflection that were developed in the calm dusk of our adult relationship. Time for a hundred visions and revisions a half century after the fact. At times my focus is sharp and detailed; at times the angle gets as wide as my lens permits. The illusions, however, are always meant to instruct and delight.

1 Dick Irvin, Jr., *The Habs: An Oral History of the Montreal Canadiens, 1940–1980* (Toronto: M&S, 1992), 111.
2 See John MacAloon, "Olympic Games and the Theory of Spectacle in Modern Societies," in *Rite, Drama, Festival, Spectacle: Rehearsals Toward a Theory of Cultural Performance,* ed. John MacAloon (Philadelphia: Institute for the Study of Human Issues, 1984), 241–80.

1 An Understudy with the Royals

GÉRALD (SOMETIMES ERRONEOUSLY WRITTEN AS GERARD) "GERRY" McNeil came from the Limoilou section of Quebec City, or "the wrong side of the tracks," according to my mother. There was something telling about how the boy first started playing goal. A man by the name of Beaulne organized a bantam team in the late 1930s and early 1940s in Limoilou's Saint-Fidèle parish. In a game against a rival parish, McNeil, then a centreman, scored to give his team a 1-0 lead. Suddenly, the Saint-Fidèle goalie was injured, and the game began to look like a forfeit because nobody was willing to replace him. Not seeing any alternative, little Gerry went into the nets himself and ended up preserving the 1-0 victory. The goalie he scored on was Gerry Courteau. Years later the two Gerrys would face each other again in senior hockey: McNeil for the Montreal Royals, Courteau for the New York Rovers. Two of McNeil's best boyhood friends were the Schofield brothers, Allan and Stuart, who lived a street over. Allan remembers that Gerry got goalie pads for Christmas one year, and from then on he was always a netminder (see fig. 1). Those pads would only have been an inch thick, but unlike the bulkier equipment of today, they made it easier for goalies to go down and pop back up—a feature that lost its appeal with the "butterfly" style that came much later.

McNeil's career as a professional hockey player had an even more improbable beginning in the fall of 1943. As the story goes, Mike McMahon, a defenceman from Quebec City, had told the Canadiens management that he knew of this young goalie they might want to look at. McMahon had apparently seen McNeil with the Morton Junior Aces. Tommy Gorman, the general manager, took the tip seriously and sent the following short letter to "Gerry McNeil, esq., 162½ 11th Street, Quebec, Que.":

> *Dear Mr. McNeil: The Club de Hockey Canadien Inc. is starting training camp at the Forum on Sunday, October 17th. We would like you to report for same. Please advise us as soon as possible if you will be here October 17th, and we will make arrangements for your transportation. Reservations will be made for you at the Queen's Hotel.*[1]

Fig. 1 Gerry McNeil and teammates in Limoilou, Quebec City. Gerry is front centre with goalie pads. Allan Schofield to his right. One over to Gerry's left is Stuart Schofield, hugging his sister Phyllis. Coach Beaulne stands behind Stuart. (Photographer unknown. Late 1930s or early 1940s.) Photo courtesy of the author.

The McNeil family read the text over several times in disbelief. Eventually, they settled down to write a positive reply; Gerry, only 17, would need his parents' help.

That 17-year-old was my father. And so while most people were preoccupied with the war (this was eight months before D-Day), my father boarded a train with Mike McMahon for Montreal. He didn't remember ever having been away from home prior to this trip, and one can only imagine his wide-eyed wonder when he caught sight of Mount Royal and then Windsor Station. From there it would have been a short walk to the Queen's Hotel, located just across the street from the main post office on Peel Street.

The receptionist sent him up to a room where he was greeted by the gruff voice of Murph "Hardrock" Chamberlain.

"Whatta ya want?"

When my father told him that he was a goalie in town for the camp, Chamberlain seemed a little suspicious but eventually pointed to the bottom dresser drawer. "The top two are mine." My father was happy enough to be in the right place.

He had barely unpacked his bag when Chamberlain snapped at him again, "Come on, kid, we're going out."

I've never heard the full story of what happened that night. However, this much is known: Murph Chamberlain liked a good night out on the town. As a veteran, he probably felt that his place on the roster was safe. He had been around long enough to know that, come what may from the rookies, he would have his nocturnal fun. The story, as my father liked to tell it, resumes in the team dressing room the next day. Murph Chamberlain grabbed him by the arm and announced to the rest of the players as they were suiting up for the first skate since the previous spring: "The kid's okay. I took him out and tested him."

I shudder to think what a disaster the match-up could have produced. A 17-year-old kid in Montreal for the first time, away from his parents, in the hands of a seasoned reveller like Chamberlain—it was a wonder that McNeil stopped any pucks that first practice. His initial problem, however, was equipment: he didn't have his own. The trainer had to tell him to pick out some stuff from a pile in the corner. McNeil came away with a chest protector that seemed old then, but he ended up keeping it for his entire hockey career. Irvin wasted no time and used the teenager in nets for the first scrimmage. Since Bill Durnan was the only other goalie in camp, he had no choice. Bert Gardiner was supposed to report, but he had actually gone to Quebec City where the Bruins were training, thinking that Boston still owned his contract. He was not due in Montreal before the end of the week. In any case, McNeil made the most of the opportunity and Irvin was impressed with his "ability to block the hardest of shots." One report said he performed "like a little jumping-jack ... reminding many of Roy Worters and Jackie Forbes." His youthful face was pictured in the *Montreal Daily Herald* (probably the best English daily for sports in the city) the next day; the caption identified him as "Freddie McNeil, 17-year-old goal-keeping phenom ... [who] might even beat out such veterans as Bert Gardiner and Bill Durnan for the back-stopping job with Canadiens."[2] That chest protector is hidden under the sweater, of course, but clearly visible is a pair of elbow pads worn awkwardly outside his sleeves.

A second scrimmage the next night confirmed the positive impression made on day one. The headline in the sports section of the *Herald* read, "Canadiens See McNeil as Goaling Discovery ... Youngster May Be Flashiest Find since Johnny Mowers Broke In with Detroit."[3] Irvin wanted to put the kid to a real test, so he had him opposite the Punch Line of Blake-Lach-Richard. The result was that McNeil drew "rounds of applause from the hundreds of railbirds" by handling shots "with the coolness and ability of a proven National Hockey League veteran." Mervin Dutton of the NHL office and Lt. Gordon Savage, a former star player from the West, advised the Canadiens to "throw the kid in immediately; he will be a sensation."

After the third day and yet another scrimmage, Irvin would only say that he intended to give the young players a chance to show their stuff in the first exhibition game against Boston two days hence. Then Bert Gardiner reported and looked in good condition, so even though Irvin decided to take Durnan and McNeil to Quebec City, there was even more uncertainty about who would get the starting goaltender position. On the other hand, it could be argued that the Canadiens were really set on using Bill Durnan all along, that Gardiner was for insurance, and that McNeil was just a pleasant surprise. Durnan was a known and proven commodity, having played in the Quebec Senior Hockey League (QSHL) and at the peak of his ability.

The game against Boston was played in the old Quebec Colisée, and my father must have been proud just to be wearing the Tricolore uniform in front of a hometown capacity crowd of seven thousand. However, the fact that war was raging in Europe (the Allied forces were slowly making their way up the Italian Peninsula) would not have been far from the minds of those in attendance, as there was a pre-game ceremony to pay tribute to Alderman Hubert Simard, who died suddenly the day before, and his son, who was seriously injured in Italy. The plan was to use Durnan and McNeil in alternating periods, but Irvin stuck with Durnan for both the first and second periods, which finished with the Bruins up 4–3. True to his word, Irvin threw McNeil in for the final period with the game in the balance. The Bruins had the advantage of a week's more conditioning than their opponents and they pressed the attack against the kid goalie. McNeil drew a number of ovations with some sensational stops on 19 shots. Meanwhile the Canadiens scored three times to take the lead. A goal by Harvey Jackson with less than three minutes to play spoiled a perfect performance, but it was enough for the local paper to designate McNeil "star of the game."[4] Al Parsley of the *Herald* praised the teenager's "lightning fast" reflexes, his puck sense, and "acrobatic goaling."[5] He also claimed that the team would sign him if they could obtain the permission of his family.

What made that exhibition game special was that in the crowd was the coach who had cut McNeil from his local high school team, St. Pat's, the year before. Then there was Art Ross, who had to be a little disappointed that the Bruins hadn't known about the youngster, given they were training right in Quebec City and in dire need of a replacement for Frank Brimsek, who had joined the US military. It is also worth noting that this was the season that the NHL would adopt the red line and allow a forward pass from the defensive zone, changes that were designed to produce more scoring and that have long been taken to mark the beginning of the modern era.

The Canadiens returned to Montreal immediately after their game against the Bruins, and practices continued the next day. All three goalies were seeing action in the nightly scrimmages. With veteran goalies like Brimsek and Turk Broda doing military service, there was a keen interest in new and old talent. At least three clubs expressed a desire to get Gardiner. The Canadiens travelled to Cornwall for another exhibition match; this time they beat the Cornwall Flyers 7–3, and Durnan, looking very sharp, played the entire game.[6] Irvin was candid about his choice of Durnan for the Number One spot, but there was a catch: as of the day after the Cornwall match, Durnan remained unsigned. Irvin told McNeil to be ready to start the first game of the regular season that Saturday just in case.

In the meantime, the teenager had been speaking to the press. It was reported that his real name was "Gerard" (in fact it was Gérald) not "Jerry"—although he always wrote it as "Gerry," and "Gerry McNeil" is how it appears in all written records. His mother, Rose Dyotte, was French Canadian and originally from northern New Brunswick. He himself was bilingual and "proud" of it.[7] McNeil's ability to move between the English and French cultures of Quebec, especially the sports press, would prove to be a lifetime asset.

Durnan did come to terms with team President Senator Donat Raymond, chairman of the Canadian Arena Company, just hours before the opener on Saturday night.[8] So that part was set. In an ironic twist, the expendable Bert Gardiner was traded back to Boston, the team he had reported to ten days earlier by mistake. Gorman then offered his teenage sensation the standard Canadien contract of $3,200 (the elite players made $4,500) plus living expenses at the Queen's Hotel. They would also cover the cost of sending him to Montreal's Catholic High School. McNeil was to play for the Montreal Royals of the QSHL and practise with the Canadiens (see fig. 2). Although NHL teams only carried one goalie on their rosters, two were needed for scrimmaging in practice, and so my father was close to the Hab players all through the 1940s and watched the Rocket's rise. Obviously, Gorman was worried that if he didn't sign McNeil, somebody else would. The beauty of having him with the Royals was that they could follow his progress.[9]

But Gorman may have overplayed his hand. McNeil thanked the Canadiens for the training camp but said that he just wanted to go

Fig. 2 Montreal Forum Practice: Mike McMahon, Dick Irvin, Gerry McNeil. (Photo by Samuel Preval. January 1, 1944. Publication history unknown.) Copyright unknown.

home. Gorman probably thought the kid was trying to establish some leverage, but the truth was he was homesick.

Dumbfounded, Gorman called McNeil's father and explained the situation. "I just offered your kid here $3,200 to play for us this year, plus all his living expenses at the Queen's Hotel, and he says he's going home."

Pete McNeil, a foreman at the Anglo-Canadian Pulp & Paper Mills Ltd. in Quebec City, collected himself enough to do some quick math. "Did you say $3,200—a year?"

"Plus expenses."

Pete McNeil asked to speak to his son; Gorman handed the receiver to the teenager.

"Hi Dad."

"Gerry, you'd better think a bit about what they're offering you. I've been at the mill for ten years and I make $19 a week, which isn't considered too bad."

AN UNDERSTUDY WITH THE ROYALS

McNeil got the message—despite his longing for home, there were some things you weren't supposed to turn down. He hung up and asked Gorman where to sign.[10]

McNeil had fond memories of living at the Queen's. He got a real thrill out of ducking into the swanky dining room and ordering a shrimp cocktail from one of the waiters. The hotel was owned by Senator Donat Raymond so it was where sports teams tended to stay. Out-of-town players with the Canadiens, like Murph Chamberlain, had to pay their own expenses, so they'd make McNeil take their laundry and slip it in with his.

School was fine except that there weren't any math textbooks. In a bold move, McNeil told Brother Paul to order some textbooks and charge them to the Canadiens. About a month later, Gorman called him into the office.

"What's this?" He shook the invoice in the air.

"It's for the math books. I told Brother Paul that the Canadiens would pay."

Smiling, Gorman dismissed the kid.

According to Elmer Ferguson, Catholic High School had a number of good hockey players among its students: Tommy Bridell, Fleming Mackell, Bobby Newton, and Jackie Morrow. Because he played with the senior Royals, McNeil wasn't eligible to play nets for CHS except in the school league championship game, when he apparently "sparkled" as CHS defeated its Protestant rivals, Westhill High School.[11]

Needless to say, McNeil's first training camp experience was something that would not happen today.[12] Today a 17-year-old, as good as he might be at a pro camp, would know that he'd eventually go back to playing with other teenagers at the Major Junior level (the CHL). Today there is a more formal and tighter system governing how young talent comes to the Big Time—it is known as the NHL's amateur draft, normally held every June.[13] The higher the draft pick, the more likely one is to stick in the NHL. Of the select few who are picked, most will flounder in the second- and third-class professional leagues. It is easy to give youth statistical information on the chances of making it to the highest level, but there will always be that one undrafted or low-drafted kid who eventually makes it big (e.g., Martin St. Louis) and such cases give all hope of beating the odds.

My father never spoke about making it to the NHL when I was a kid playing the game. I'm sure he knew that I was a decent player for my age but nothing exceptional. He never had to lecture me on the long-shot odds of becoming a professional. When I was cut from a select midget team at the age of 14, the writing was on the wall. And so I think adults should simply let their children come to their own realizations about how the dreams of youth and the practical realities of life diverge. Just as many young boys in Canada have dreams of playing in the NHL, so do most of the same boys have memories of how it slowly sank in that they wouldn't. More prudent, I believe, are those parents who suggest that working toward a full athletic scholarship at a prestigious NCAA school is a more practical carrot to dangle. A free ride to Brown University, where a student-athlete could make friends and contacts that would set him or her up for life, seems a better goal.

There are odds and statistics and then there are those unexpected and marvellous circumstances that determine anyone's path in life. My father's opportunity came largely because so many hockey players, including goalies, were doing military service. However, he had to make the most of his chance at the Big Time to stay on the doorstep, and when he would tell me the story of how he plunged into adulthood as a 17-year-old sharing a room at the Queen's Hotel with Murph Hardrock Chamberlain, I got the impression that the wonder of the experience came from naïveté. Unlike many who play the game seriously as teenagers today, my father, and by extension his family, never worked up the prospect of the NHL before the fall of 1943. Tommy Gorman may have been happy to secure McNeil's services (be it only in reserve) at an early age, but unbeknownst to the Canadiens' management then, the downside would be that they would also lose him early.

McNeil's six seasons with the Montreal Royals (1943–44 to 1948–49 inclusive) were marked by a number of achievements: he was a QSHL First All-Star and winner of the Byng of Vimy Trophy for the most valuable player three years in a row (1947–49).[14] However, the achievement he liked to talk about is the Allan Cup win in '47. The Allan Cup, which is still awarded, goes to the best senior team in Canada, and in 1947 it was next in prestige to Lord Stanley's. What distinguished senior hockey from minor pro is that players in the senior leagues usually held other full-time jobs and weren't financially compensated to the same extent as those playing in the minor professional leagues. Since there was a general feeling that all had a responsibility to help with the war effort, senior hockey seemed to flourish in the first part of the 1940s (most players had jobs in munitions plants or some other industry that contributed to the military). Most of the Royals (including McNeil after he finished high school) worked at the War Assets department, which was very close to the Forum.

As part of the entertainment business, professional sports, especially the minor leagues, were a hard sell, not to mention that many of the athletes had joined the armed forces. However, immediately after the war, senior hockey, and particularly the Montreal Royals, became very popular. Their Sunday afternoon games at the Forum occasionally outdrew the Canadiens the night before.[15] All to the good of the Canadian Arena Company, which owned both the Canadiens and the Forum. A glance at some of the scoresheets of the QSHL reveals just how wide open the play tended to be; it wasn't uncommon for a team to win by six goals one night and then turn around and lose by a similar margin the next time out—not the kind of game usually favoured by goalies, but my father had fond memories of his years with the Royals (see fig. 3). Since a great majority of the players were local, senior teams garnered keen interest from fans who enjoyed the exciting offence often generated by skilled and flashy players deemed too small for the

Fig. 3 McNeil enjoys a bottle of Coke. (Photographer unknown.) Copyright unknown.

NHL. My father always claimed that there were many of the latter who never really got to stick in one of the hundred or so positions in the six-team NHL.

Among the skilled yet small players that excelled in the Quebec senior league was Tony Demers, a forward with the Sherbrooke Saints who could fire the puck with lightning speed and accuracy. Demers had played a few games with the Canadiens in the early 1940s, but trouble seemed to follow him and he ended up in the QSHL. My father admitted to me that he had felt a little cocky once when a reporter asked him what he thought of Tony Demers's shot. "Tony who?" he responded. The Royals would meet Sherbrooke in the 1949 QSHL Semifinal, which was oddly enough a best of three that year, and the Saints took the first game. The second game wasn't close, with Sherbrooke winning 7-0. Tony "Who?" Demers scored five goals, one of which was a blast from just over centre ice. The lesson was learned. Suffice it to say that McNeil never did forget that game (which would turn out to be his last in the senior league until 1956) or Demers's shot. It was all right to be confident, but you never wanted to say anything that could inspire the other team. A few months later (September 15 to be exact) an intoxicated Demers argued with his girlfriend and ended up kicking her out of a moving car. She died as a result of her injuries, and so did any hope that Demers (who was convicted of manslaughter) may have had of getting back to the NHL.[16] The year before he had been voted the most gentlemanly player in the QSHL.

To win the Allan Cup, a team had to first win their league championship (e.g., QSHL), then a regional contest (e.g., Eastern Canadian), before facing their opponent from the opposite end of the country. It was a gruelling campaign with as many rounds as the current Stanley Cup, and they often went longer into the spring than the NHL. The Royals had gone to the Eastern Canadian Final in '46 before losing out to Hamilton. The next year they managed to go up two games to one against Ottawa in the QSHL Final (one game had ended in a tie). Down 1-0 in Game Five with less than two minutes to play, Gerry Plamondon scored to tie it up, and the veteran Jimmy Haggarty notched the winner with fourteen seconds left.[17] Both goalies, McNeil and "Legs" Fraser were spectacular in Game Six; regulation time ended in a 1-1 tie, and then Plamondon played the hero role again by getting around the Ottawa defence and firing the puck home to win the series.[18]

The Royals then went up against Sherbrooke in Sherbrooke and stole the first game 8-3; however, McNeil injured his thumb and had to be replaced by Paul Leclerc in the third. Substitutions weren't made very often, so this move indicated how serious they feared McNeil's injury was.[19] McNeil did play the next game, but he probably wished he hadn't. It proved to be a good example of just how offensively explosive play in Quebec senior hockey could be. Leading comfortably 8–4 in the third period, the Royals began to self-destruct with a series of penalties. Sherbrooke took advantage and scored six consecutive times to win 10–8, much to the disgust of the twelve thousand packed into the Forum.

Seven of Sherbrooke's markers were tallied by their all-African-Canadian line of Ossie and Herb Carnegie and Manny McIntyre.[20] It has often been said that the Carnegie brothers would surely have been in the NHL if it were not for the blatant racism of the team owners.[21] My father concurred with this assessment and added that the racism in Quebec senior hockey was particularly sad given that most Montrealers were happy to see Jackie Robinson break the colour barrier in professional baseball when he was called up from the Royals to the Brooklyn Dodgers in April 1947.[22] Montreal was reputed to be more cosmopolitan than other North American cities, and Jackie and his wife felt especially welcomed in the French-speaking east-end neighbourhood where they rented an apartment.[23]

I met Herb Carnegie twice in my life. The first time was when I was allowed in the dressing room of the Quebec Aces Oldtimers for a practice sometime during the mid-1960s. My only memory of that Friday night experience is that Carnegie seemed to be a popular figure among his teammates, the centre of much attention when it came to jokes and comments. The second time came forty years later in 2006. Herb Carnegie was in Halifax to be inducted into a local hall of fame for black hockey players. I introduced myself when I got a chance.

"My father was Gerry McNeil," I said. "He told me how good a playmaker you were, and how you had to endure a lot physical intimidation. He also remembered that you usually avoided the hits and made other players look rather foolish."

"Did he? Well, your father was a very good goalie."

We exchanged a few more words, and the conversation took a sad turn when I informed Mr. Carnegie that my father had passed away a couple of years before. He then mentioned some of his own problems (he had lost his eyesight). Despite the sombre mood, I came away from the second encounter feeling that I had served as a conduit between two men who might have been rivals more than a half century earlier but who had also carried a sense of mutual respect for each other.

One final comment here. If you want to get a sense of the pain that Herb Carnegie felt as a victim of racial discrimination, you have only to read his autobiography, which has the unforgettable title *A Fly in a Pail of Milk: The Herb Carnegie Story*.

Since the 1947 series against Sherbrooke was a best of five, things did not look good for the Royals. Whatever problems McNeil might have had with his thumb, he got over them for Game Three. Playing brilliantly, he posted a shutout, and the Royals won 3–0. They closed the series out with another shutout, this time 6–0.[24] It was as if Sherbrooke had done all their scoring in Game Two and had nothing left. This meant that Montreal would face the team who eliminated them the year before, the Hamilton Tigers. The Eastern Final was to be another short series (best of five) so there was little room for mistakes.

For some reason, playoff hockey often features a goalie who is able to get in the "zone," so to speak, and carry a team. McNeil seemed to do this for the Royals in '47. Still hot from the last two games against Sherbrooke, McNeil led the way with his third straight shutout, and the Royals defeated the Hamilton Tigers in the opener of the Eastern Final 3–0. The game featured a brilliant end-to-end rush by the stalwart defenceman Jimmy Galbraith.[25] Clearly on a roll, the Royals dumped Hamilton in Game Two 3–1.[26] McNeil's shutout streak ended at 200 minutes and 13 seconds (little did he know then that he would beat this mark a few years later in the NHL). Hamilton retreated to Maple Leaf Gardens where, in front of ten thousand pro-Tiger fans, they prepared to make a last stand as Eastern Champions. It was not to be. The Royals finished them off 5–1.[27] There is a great team picture of the Royals celebrating in the dressing room that appeared in *The Globe and Mail*. Although there is no caption or credit, it was more than likely taken by Turofsky, who also took a single portrait of McNeil with his fist raised (fig. 4).

Examining the photo over a half century later, I pause to reflect on the special attractions of photography. First, my father looks so young and happy. His expression and dishevelled hair seem natural enough, but for those who knew him well, the square smile suggests that he had to perform for Turofsky's lens. I sense myself being drawn in by tactile associations of certain details. My fingers know the rough surface of the cinder blocks in the background, the wool fibres of his sweater, the canvas of his pants. It is almost as if I am magically touching history itself. Turofsky not only captures a small, albeit important, slice of one man's life; the sharpness of his photo can strike a nostalgic nerve in someone born in the 1950s or '60s, someone who remembers the tight pull of those wool sweaters. No secrets reveal themselves here, but the thrill of victory, one long gone and forgotten. There is something sad

AN UNDERSTUDY WITH THE ROYALS

Fig. 4 McNeil celebrates a win at MLG (probably the Eastern Canadian Championship) on route to the 1947 Allan Cup. (Photo by Nat Turofsky. May 1947.) Copyright unknown.

and beautiful about how the past recedes into oblivion, almost but for one picture. I start to feel that there is something sad and beautiful about how still photography can mark that process. This feeling is intensified when there isn't a film record, which is largely the case for senior hockey of the 1940s. If all that remains is the single frame, the act frozen in time, then the evocative power about what came before and after grows larger.

The Calgary Stampeders, Allan Cup winners from the previous year, repeated as the 1947 Western Champions and took the long train ride east with the same lineup they had the year before. The Final opened at the Gardens in Toronto on April 28th. A crowd of over eleven thousand was clearly on the side of the Stampeders, but the undaunted Royals would go on to win their sixth consecutive game by a 7–3 score.[28] Despite having the Torontonians on their side, the Calgary team were a long way from home and this had to be a disadvantage in the series. Games Two and Three were scheduled for the Forum in Montreal; Four, Five, and Six (the latter two if necessary), back at the Gardens in Toronto. A circus was booked in the Forum at the beginning of May, but the venerable old arena would be available if the series went to a deciding seventh game.

Russ Dertell, the Stampeder goalie, gave notice in Game Two that he could steal a victory himself. He blocked 30 shots and held the Royals to a single goal. Dunc Grant scored the winner for the Westerners with just over five minutes remaining.[29] Unfortunately for the Calgary team, Dertell could not hold off the high-flying Royal forwards two nights later, and his team fell 7–0 before an enthusiastic Forum crowd of 11,294. At the other end, the "classy" McNeil chalked up his fourth shutout of the playoff run, but it helped that Bunny Dame's close-in shot went from post to post and that Dunc Grant fired another one off the metal in the second. What distinguished this contest from the two earlier ones was the rough play; "16 penalties were dished out" leading up to a fierce fight between Galbraith and Shoquist with two minutes left.[30]

The Royals were a jubilant and confident bunch going back to Toronto. Eight and a half thousand fans attended, and many were not impressed by the sign in Dick Dowling's Gardens grill: "Closed for summer months." It was May 4th, the longest hockey season in the Gardens' history. The third period began with the Stampeders down 2–0, their drop-pass offence getting them nowhere. Then Syd Craddock scored, and only twenty-two seconds later the Gardens crowd erupted when the Westerners tied it up 2–2, Bob Brownridge converting a short pass from Dunc Grant. Pete Morin put the Royals back up, but the Stamps carried the play and tied it up a second time when Doug French and Archie Wider combined to beat McNeil. Montreal answered quickly again. Doug Harvey rushed up the centre, passed to Campeau at the blue line, and he beat Dertell. This time Calgary was not able to come back. The rough play continued from the previous game. Jimmy Galbraith took a punch from a fan in the second period while going

AN UNDERSTUDY WITH THE ROYALS

after Ken "Red" Hunter. He then grabbed the referee's sweater and ended up with a minor and a misconduct. Calgary's Joe Fisher caught Floyd Curry with a bodycheck that "almost tore Curry loose from his skates." Cliff Malone and Jacques Locas of the Royals suffered injuries, and their status was unknown for Game Five.[31]

Game Five saw both Dertell and McNeil shine. Hal Walker of *The Globe and Mail* reports that "the goaltending acrobatics of this lively pair and their hair-breath escapes... had the crowd in an up-roar." More brutal bodychecks were delivered, the best perhaps by Art Michaluk, who levelled Galbraith at centre ice. The difference was a late second-period goal by Brownridge, who took a pass from Hunter (Hunter having carried the puck into the zone and around the Royal net before setting his teammate up). McNeil got a piece of the shot with his arm, but not enough. The night really belonged to Dertell, who made a string of miraculous saves at the beginning of the third. According to Walker, "he did the splits, dived face first into shots and even swiped the puck away from Petey Morin with his pads when the latter closed in all by himself." The Royals outshot the Stampeders 20 to 9 in the third; trying to get off the ice for the extra attacker, McNeil was forced to stickhandle the puck himself away from a Calgarian.[32]

It seemed like a wintry night when another Garden crowd of over eight thousand saw the Stampeders roar out to a 2–0 lead in Game Six. Jacques Locas, back from his injury, scored twice in the second, but Calgary was still up 3–2 on Red Hunter's second goal of the game. Hunter completed the hat trick almost three minutes into the third. At this point, the Royals clearly lost their composure and started a pa-rade to the penalty box. Campeau cross-checked Michaluk after the latter hit him cleanly, and Harvey, having just finished serving a min-or, started exchanging punches with Brownridge. The momentum had changed drastically, and the Stampeders had reason to hope that they could complete the comeback against the undisciplined Royals right in the Forum.[33]

The temperature reached 70° F in Montreal on the day of the decid-ing game. Many of the eleven thousand plus fans who poured into the Forum that night were in shirt sleeves. A hard-fought game was antici-pated, but the Royals got off to a good start with some wide-open play and never looked back. With just over six minutes remaining in the second period, they held a 7–0 lead. The contest finished 8–2; Dertell may have run out of magic, but he still stopped 46 shots to McNeil's 21. When the game was finally over, the teams shook hands at centre ice, and the crowd cheered for three minutes.[34]

While praising McNeil's play in the opening game of the Final Series, Walker referred to him as "the unfortunate young man who has to wait until Bill Durnan retires to his slippers and fireside before he can play pro hockey for Canadiens."[35] When asked, McNeil always maintained that he was happy playing with the Royals and didn't have a burning ambition to unseat the man who seemed to have a lock on the Vezina Trophy (winning it six times in seven seasons). For "the kid" from lower town Quebec City, life in Montreal was better than good—it was exciting. He had married the one girl he had dated since his early teenage years, Theresa Conway, and they had started a family. He was making a decent salary and had everything he wanted: a car, friends, and a bright future. Practising with the Canadiens and getting game experience with the Royals allowed McNeil to mature slowly. He certainly didn't feel a lack of pressure competing for the Allan Cup; nor did

Fig. 5 Gerry McNeil weds Theresa Conway on July 27, 1946, in Quebec City. Photo courtesy of the author.

AN UNDERSTUDY WITH THE ROYALS

he feel neglected by the local press. He knew that he was part of a larger organization, the Canadiens, and was perfectly happy to fill the role the Canadiens wanted him to play.[36]

Professional athletes are no different than ordinary people in having to balance their work-related responsibilities with family or personal life. When Gerry McNeil and Theresa ("Teacy" or "Tee") Conway got married in 1946, they went to a lodge on Lake MacDonald for their honeymoon (see fig. 5). A car had been hired for the return trip to Montreal. It just so happened that a leading sportswriter for one of the Montreal newspapers was going back to Montreal at the same time, and so he asked to ride along with the newlyweds. That the sportswriter was intoxicated helps explain his insensitivity to the desire for privacy on the part of the young couple. McNeil, unaware of how intoxicated the man was, felt that he was obliged to accommodate the reporter. Not far from the lodge the reporter requested that the car stop so he could relieve himself. Urinating into a ditch by the side of the road, the reporter lost his balance and fell headlong into the mud. As much as he would have liked, McNeil couldn't just leave him there, so he had to help the poor guy back into the limo, and the party continued on their way into Montreal with an odious stench in the car. While an extreme example, the incident reflects just how much some people in the public eye will feel compelled to sacrifice a certain degree of individual privacy to adapt to media demands.

The Royals were a closely knit group; the many hours together in a bus or train had something to do with this. Some of McNeil's closest and longest friends were Royal teammates. Chief among these was Jimmy Galbraith, a defenceman, whose performances were always solid, and whose humble, even self-deprecating manner was perhaps all that kept him from making Big Time hockey (the 1940s euphemism for the NHL). For fifty years after their Allan Cup win, the Galbraiths and McNeils would routinely get together for a night of bridge and stories. Then there was Pete Morin, the flashy centreman, whose comical office antics were legendary. Morin had been a member of the Canadiens' Razzle Dazzle Line in 1941, but skill alone was not enough to keep him with the Habs, and so he had to settle for a career with the Royals. Harvey, Curry, and Riopelle rounded out this inner group, who were also brought together by the fact that their wives attended the games together and had themselves become good friends. Sometimes the wives and other family members would attend away games, since it was only a few hours' drive. The behaviour of the local fans could be crude, to say the least. Once at a QSHL game, Theresa alerted her father to an intoxicated fan who was pouring a cup of beer on her husband as he came out the passageway onto the ice. Her father had to point out that the "beer" had already gone through the fan's system.

The players themselves were sometimes guilty of wild behaviour. I remember coming across a page in an early family photo album that had been ripped out and reinserted, depicting the Royals at a festive party at a maple sugar camp. There were a half dozen or so pictures of men drinking or singing or carrying on in the woods. One player—it could have been my father (the coat and hat made it impossible to tell for sure)—was caught in a pose that suggested he was urinating into one of the sap containers; at least I have always wanted to believe that he was simulating the act. I believe this was the picture that drove my mother to rip the page out of the album (she admitted doing this). She never got around to throwing the page out, and somebody else evidently restored it to the album. I suspect this was my father, but he was reticent about it. My efforts to probe into the episode by trying to get my parents to talk about these photos reminded me of a comment by Martha Langford on the family photo album as a catalyst for recalling the past: "Our photographic memories are nested in a performative oral tradition."[37] And, as the case of my father suggests, our impulse to preserve the photos can operate even if we'd prefer that the memories stay in the nest.

I found evidence of more civil amusement in other, more public, photographs. Among my father's Royal memorabilia was a professional "souvenir" picture of the team at a New York nightclub (see fig. 6). Such pictures were a popular tourist service before the widespread use of personal cameras. After beating the Rovers 4–3 before "12,250 rabid hockey fans" at Madison Square Gardens (MSG), the team went to Leon and Eddie's, a restaurant and nightclub on 52nd Street that, according to Jerry Lewis, "was a mecca for nightclub comics."[38] Also the location of famous music clubs like the Five Spot and Birdland, 52nd Street was the heart of live entertainment in America, and since most people still had to "see" their entertainment in a live setting (i.e., this was prior to popular television), getting to 52nd Street held more significance. Jimmy Orlando, the nightclub manager and Royal defenceman, knew where to take the boys and show them a good time. Murph Hardrock Chamberlain may have initiated my father into adulthood, but it was with the Royals that he learned what adult fun was all about.

McNeil would have loved Leon and Eddie's, since his own fondness for pranks emerged at this time.[39] Dugger McNeil (no relation) remembers how the team was celebrating some victory on a yacht on Lac Saint-Louis near Dorval Island. "The guys got hungry, and Mac [my

AN UNDERSTUDY WITH THE ROYALS

Fig. 6 Members of the Royals at Leon and Eddie's in New York, Feb. 18, 1948 ("Souvenir Photo." W & L Concessionaires. NY. No. 12,487.) Photo courtesy of the author.

father's nicknames were "Mac" or "Maxi"] volunteered to go for some food. He picked up some live bait (i.e., minnows) and hid it in a selection of sandwiches he brought back. Some of the guys were feeling so good that they gulped them right down without noticing anything, but soon there was a scream, followed by much cursing, then finally laughter. McNeil was always up for stuff like that."

McNeil's routine would be to take the streetcar from his rue Saint-Dominique apartment (inherited from Mike McMahon, along with much of the furniture, when Mike was moved to Buffalo) south toward the Forum. Floyd Curry would join McNeil further down the route, and the two often travelled together. When the pair went by car, they'd use the parking lot across Atwater where the Alexis Neon Plaza now sits. Away travel was usually by bus, the Forum serving as the departure point.

While some of the Royal wives became close, it is understandable that there were other tensions surrounding girlfriends and bachelor behaviour. Orlando had a relationship with a flamboyant stripper who was famous for waiting until the game was ten minutes old before making a grand entrance through the Forum crowd. When I asked my parents about her, they had very different responses. According to my mother, her voice shrill with disgust, the wives wanted to boo the performer, and a number of them did threaten physical action. My father was only in the mood to confirm details: "Yeah, Orlando's girl, Lili St. Cyr; she played the Gayety." I almost expected him to give me the show times and tell me how much you had to tip the doorman. Very aware of my mother's reaction, my father gave me a look and fell silent. I sensed that the palpable tension in the room was something that went back almost half a century.

One can now access the dramatic art that was Lili St. Cyr via You-Tube. Her act might be described as an attempt at "classy," but taking off your clothes is still striptease no matter how you package it. In her autobiography, Lili St. Cyr claims that hockey was not her "*sport préféré*," but she also is clear on her attraction to Orlando (*"il avait un magnétisme qui le rendait irrésistible"*) and to athletes more generally.[40] As for attending games at the Forum, she only admits "*j'aimais tellement Jimmy que je passais des heures à le regarder évoluer sur la glace.*"[41] The woman who made an art out of being an object for the male gaze had her own admiration for hockey: "*Je ne pouvais m'empêcher de l'admirer quand il patinait avec l'aisance et la grâce d'un danseur virtuose.*"[42] Admittedly, it is hard imagining Jimmy Orlando as a *danseur virtuose*.

Retrospectively, Lili St. Cyr was conscious of holding a status in Montreal during the 1940s that was on a par with Maurice Richard, and so many of her nostalgic memories of the city—the clubs, arriving and departing from Windsor Station—run parallel to my father's.[43] In attempting to recover details about people from my father's past, I had more than once inadvertently touched a sensitive nerve, and Lili St. Cyr was one of those people. "The bitch!" I could hear my mother mutter as she left the room. In any case, Orlando's connections in the adult entertainment business (where dinner, vaudeville, and striptease mixed easily) helped spice up the social lives of many players.

Jimmy Orlando was still known as a "bad boy," a reputation that he earned while with the Detroit Red Wings. On November 7, 1942, he was involved in an ugly stick-swinging brawl with Cal Gardner, and the incident was captured in a famous photograph by Turofsky (it has been

AN UNDERSTUDY WITH THE ROYALS

erroneously said that the picture appeared on the cover of *Life* magazine).[44] In any case, 1942–43 would be Orlando's last season in the NHL. Orlando was from Montreal, and after a couple of years of military service, he finished his hockey career in the Quebec senior league, first with Valleyfield and then the Royals. My father remembered, somewhat shamefully, how Orlando was eager to try to rough up the black players whenever the Royals faced Sherbrooke.[45] However, before you could rough up the Carnegie brothers and Manny McIntyre, you had to catch them. No easy task.

Perhaps another reason for the strong camaraderie was that senior hockey didn't have big egos or star-status players who detracted attention from the team. The QSHL was a great holding tank of Quebec talent for the Canadiens, who were reluctant to see too many future players leave the area to play semi-pro elsewhere. That many such players were French-speaking made it more likely that they would stay in the QSHL. Jacques Beauchamp, a French sports journalist whose forty-year career started with *Montréal-Matin* in the early 1940s, was also a netminder and would sometimes get to practise with the Royals (and the Canadiens). This background (which may have allowed Beauchamp to develop a player's perspective), combined with a Québécois pride, seems to be behind his memory of how the Royals coach, Frank Carlin, inspired his team just before their 1947 run for the Allan Cup.[46] He called the players together and apparently said that he was told that the Royals would be a lot better if they didn't rely so much on local (i.e., Quebec) talent. Beauchamp suggests that the reverse-psychology "pep talk" had a lot to do with the team's success.

A story my father liked to tell exemplifies the communication difficulties that a unilingual French-speaking player could encounter outside of Quebec. Jacques Locas played with McNeil for a season in Cincinnati. The only menu item he could say in English was "ham an' eggs," and so he was getting rather tired of his limited diet. He asked Mac to help with his vocabulary, which Mac was happy to do.

"You can't go wrong with 'steak.' It's good and easy to remember."

The next time the waiter asked Locas what he wanted, he proudly answered, "Steak."

The waiter responded, "How would you like it?"

Locas stared back in silent confusion, so the waiter prompted, "Rare, medium, or well?" His Mohawk teammates remained silent.

Completely frustrated, Locas replied, "Ham an' eggs," and everybody burst out laughing.

Tommy Gorman and Dick Irvin must have realized the benefit of keeping the Big Time players a little on edge by having many of their hottest prospects playing right there in the same city. Not only did the Canadiens share the Forum ice with the Royals, but they had to share the sports page as well. Nothing could motivate a player like reading daily about the exploits of those who wanted to take his place. It was with this philosophy in mind that an exhibition game between the Royals and the Canadiens became an annual event. As one can imagine, they were bound to become grudge matches featuring those who had just made the Big club and those who were left behind. McNeil himself recalled how the bitterness of some of the Royal players would fester in the dressing room beforehand. Once the Royals actually won, and not surprisingly that was the last such contest. NHL teams going down to defeat at the hands of a senior or minor pro club were not unheard of. When the Allan Cup Champion Royals beat the Leafs in Kingston in October of '47, "Hap" Day, alluding to the twosome of Durnan and McNeil, remarked that the Canadiens owned the two best goalies in hockey.[47]

Although the plan was to keep McNeil in the wings until Durnan gave way, the agreement between the NHL and the CAHA (Canadian Amateur Hockey Association) prevented a player from the senior ranks from coming up for more than a three-game lend-lease. This may have been why the Canadiens brought Paul Bibeault up from the AHL for nine games when Durnan went down with an injury in January of '46. In any case it was a Saturday night in late November of 1947 when McNeil would get his first taste of regular NHL action. As was his routine, McNeil was in attendance at the Forum for a game between the Habs and New York. Five minutes into the second period, Durnan went down to smother a puck and his forehead was slashed open by the end of a skate (fig. 7). He was carried to the Forum clinic and a group gathered in the adjoining anteroom. Dick Irvin and Frank Selke looked pale. Gerry McNeil arrived, and then so did a group of reporters, who were held back by Andy Galley, the Royals trainer.

The gash was deep; Durnan could not continue. Irvin then whispered to McNeil to get ready. Galley said that he would suit up in the Royals dressing room and added, "Tell Ernie Cooke to send over a Canadien sweater." Murph Chamberlain, who apparently had been sitting in a clinic chair there all the time with his leg in a cast, picked up Durnan's catching glove and discovered a puck inside. "Whatta guy, that Durnan. He's knocked flat and badly cut and he still has the puck in his fist."[48]

The game resumed, and McNeil handled the first few shots easily. Then things started to go wrong. When Bill "The Beast" Juzda broke

AN UNDERSTUDY WITH THE ROYALS

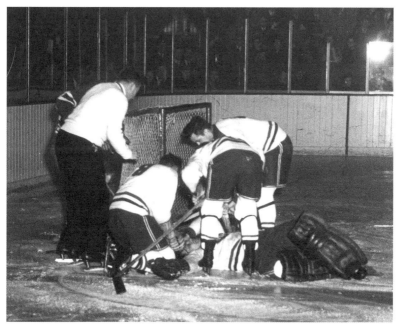

Fig. 7 Durnan suffers a serious head injury in November 1947 and must be replaced by McNeil. (Photo by David Bier. *Herald, Montreal*, Nov. 24, 1947, 24.) Copyright unknown.

in and knocked the puck in front of the Montreal net, Elmer Lach was there to clear it away; the only problem was that he cleared it right into his own goal. The second period ended 1–1. Richard gave the Canadiens the lead again at the beginning of the third, but it was not to last. The Rangers were soon on the counterattack; Laprade passed to Warwick, who tied the game. Then Buddy O'Connor, Don Raleigh, and Eddie Kullman scored in succession, putting the visitors up 5–2. Although McNeil certainly didn't shine, the defence seemed to collapse when Durnan went down. After the game, McNeil admitted to being nervous and hoped to play better in Boston.

This was the opportunity that many "spare" goalies of the 1940s would only get to dream about. Gerry Courteau, McNeil's neighbour from 11th Street in Limoilou, had been playing with the New York Rovers and attended many Ranger games at MSG just in case a goalie was injured. All he wanted at this point was to make an appearance in the NHL like his brother Maurice, who got to play six games for the Bruins back in 1943. He recalled having to get his equipment on four or five times to replace an injured Brimsek, McCool, and Lumley. Every time he did, the injured goalie reappeared before play resumed; he never got into the record book.

It must have been a long train ride down through Vermont that Saturday night for McNeil. He knew he had to play better if he was to keep his position of "man in waiting," let alone ever taking over from Durnan. It probably didn't help his nerves that the Boston goalie he would be playing opposite would be his childhood hero, Frank Brimsek. On the other hand, he remembered playing well against the Bruins in his first taste of the NHL four years earlier (i.e., the game that McNeil confused with this one—see above).

Boston Garden was rowdy, as the Bruins and Habs had developed a bitter rivalry. The first period was scoreless; Reardon put the Habs up 1-0 in the second. Going into the third, McNeil found himself in the same situation as the night before: having to protect a one-goal lead. So far in this game he was perfect. Nine minutes into the third, Dumart scored from ten feet out on a pass from Schmidt on the right boards. Like the Rangers, the Bruins seemed to smell the blood of a rookie goalie and kept the pressure on. When the puck rebounded off of Kenny Reardon's skate into the net on a behind-the-net pass by Joe Carveth, McNeil must have wondered if the gods just had it in for him.[49] Nevertheless, he hung in there and Lach set up Richard to knot the game again. The Boston fans screamed for the Bruins to finish off the Habs, but after a few rushes the siren sounded. The Canadiens salvaged a tie, and McNeil, knowing he had matched the performance of a goalie he had long idolized, settled into his seat on the train back to Montreal feeling much better than he did on the way down. It would be a few more seasons, however, before he would get another chance to take Big Bill's place.

When we speak of sports media today, we tend to minimize the importance of the written word (what we used to call print media) or old school journalism, and yet a good part of the informed commentary on hockey history still occurs in the books on the subject that appear every fall, well in time for the Christmas gift season. Our sports channels are full of spoken commentary, but with the exception of the "classic" games of the past, this discourse is all about current news. As a narrative, this book resembles what Don Delillo once called a "game in print"; the phrase is actually used by the narrator of *End Zone*, a novel that has generally been regarded as the best at representing football.[50] Delillo's narrator goes on to designate his text, "a form of sustenance, a game on paper to be scanned when there are stale days between events."[51] He identifies his exemplary spectator/reader as "the person who understands that sport is a benign illusion, the illusion that order is possible," and who needs detail "impressions, colors, statistics, patterns, mysteries, numbers, idioms, symbols."[52] Although Delillo's narrator claims that football best fulfills these needs, they can be translated into the detailed features of any sport. My "exemplary spectator/reader" will recognize that my "benign illusion" isn't a novel, but rather a fictionalized history, a history that I am constructing out of newspaper articles, a number of key photographs, oral stories, and—in only a minor way—film footage. (There are few archived radio broadcasts or video recordings from this period.)

This book is as much a tribute to sportswriters like Elmer Ferguson, Baz O'Meara, and Al Nickleson as it is to the players of my father's era. Their eye-witness accounts constitute the most accurate representation we have of hockey mid-twentieth century. Without the benefit of instant replay, they certainly felt the pressure of the moment—of having to concentrate hard on what was unfolding in front of them. Another important difference between the sports media of today and that of the 1940s and '50s is that the latter operated in relative isolation, whereas contemporary media are closely integrated despite geographic distances. What happened on a 1950 Saturday night in Montreal was not immediately known around the league, at least not with the same sense of detail. Not only did people live more in the moment, so to speak, they lived more in one place. Moreover, because of the restricted and primitive use of film, people may have heard or read about what happened in Montreal on a Saturday night, but their visual impressions were largely left to the imagination. In short, print media ruled perhaps in a way that the video operator rules today.

Generalizing about one man's life can be too easy at times, but I think it is noteworthy that my father only started playing goal because his bantam team needed someone to replace an injured boy. The way my father entered the NHL and the Canadiens had more to do with just being in the right place when a window of opportunity opened a crack, and then being happy to bide time when it took years to open all the way. He made the most of the 1943 training camp but didn't exactly jump at his first contract offer. Moreover, his admiration of Durnan allowed him to accept the role of understudy. He remembered being lured by Toronto (King Clancy was a fan) and not wanting to leave Montreal. Looking back on those years with the Royals, we agreed that hindsight didn't exactly view history objectively, but at least it provided more depth of field. McNeil's mindset, for lack of a better term, was one that was comfortable reacting to whatever happened to come his way as opposed to trying proactively to control his environment. Our culture might value proactive assertion to a fault. Being prepared to deal with those external factors over which one has no influence is an underappreciated mindset that is well-suited to playing goal. You have no way of knowing what you're going to face on a given day, and you have to be ready for anything—a deflected shot, a sudden surge from the opposing team, an unaccountable deflation in the play of one's teammates. You must go on regardless, and the best way not to be surprised by anything is to expect the unexpected.

1   Gorman to McNeil, October 6, 1943, personal collection of David McNeil. Mike McMahon would take credit for telling Tommy Gorman about the young McNeil; see Chrys Goyens and Allan Turowetz, *Lions in Winter* (Scarborough: Prentice-Hall, 1986), 65. *Lions in Winter* constitutes the best history of the Canadiens hockey club for the 1940s and '50s. See also D'Arcy Jenish, "1946–1955: Selke Builds an Empire," in *The Montreal Canadiens: 100 Years of Glory* (Toronto: Doubleday, 2008), 126–148.
2   "Canadiens Cut Ice First Time," *Montreal Daily Herald*, Oct. 20, 1943, 9.
3   "Canadiens See McNeil as Goaling Discovery," *Montreal Daily Herald*, Oct. 21, 1943, 10.
4   "Montreal Canadiens Trim Bruins 6–5 in Exhibition Tilt at the Coliseum; G. McNeil, 17, Stars in Victors' Nets," *Quebec Chronicle-Telegraph*, Oct. 25, 1943, 7. In later years, my father would confuse this game with the first time he replaced Durnan at Boston Garden in 1947. Consequently he often claimed that this first exhibition game pitted him against his idol Frank Brimsek and that it ended in a tie. See Irvin, *Habs: An Oral History*, 71, and Andrew Podnieks, *Players: The Ultimate A-Z Guide of Everyone Who Has Ever Played in the NHL* (Toronto: Doubleday, 2003), 573.
5   Al Parsley, "Canadiens Impress in Quebec… Irvin and Veterans Are High in Praise of Youthful Goalie," *Montreal Daily Herald*, Oct. 25, 1943, 10.
6   "Canucks Beat Cornwall 7–3," *Montreal Daily Herald*, Oct. 28, 1943, 9.
7   *Montreal Daily Herald*, Oct. 28, 1943, 9.
8   Irvin, *Habs: An Oral History*, 71.
9   On Gorman's cultivation of the Quebec Senior Hockey League as a source and holding tank of potential players, see Goyens and Turowetz, *Lions in Winter*, 64–66.
10 This was one of my father's favourite stories.
11 This according to Elmer Ferguson, "The Gist and Jest of It," *Herald*, Montreal, Mar. 13, 1950, 19.
12 There have been a number of popular studies of professional hockey that concentrate on how it affects the young lives of many men. For a good academic analysis, see Michael A. Robidoux, *Men at Play: A Working Understanding of Professional Hockey* (Montreal: McGill-Queen's University Press, 2001).
13 For the history of this draft, see Chris Tredree and Paul Bontje, "The NHL Entry Draft," in *Total Hockey: The Official Encyclopedia of the National Hockey League*, ed. Dan Diamond (New York: Total Sports, 1998), 285–348. For a concise expla-

nation of the system used for teams to secure the rights of players before the entry draft or prior to 1963, see Stephen Brunt, *Searching for Bobby Orr* (Toronto: Knopf, 2006), 53.

14 The Goaltender Homepage, accessed May 25, 2006. http://www.hockeygoalies. org/bio/mcneil.html. However, another source suggests that McNeil may have only won the Vimy in 1947; see Tredree and Bontje, "NHL Entry Draft," in Diamond, *Total Hockey*, 1678.

15 According to Irvin, Jr., *Habs: An Oral History*, 57.

16 Demers played forty-six games for the Habs in 1940–41. He was convicted of manslaughter and did half of a fifteen-year sentence at Saint-Vincent-de-Paul penitentiary. Goyens and Turowetz, *Lions in Winter*, 64.

17 "Montreal Defeats Ottawa, 2 to 1," *Globe and Mail*, Apr. 7, 1947, 17.

18 "Royals Champs of Quebec Loop, Beating Ottawa," *Globe and Mail*, Apr. 9, 1947, 19.

19 "Sherbrooke Seniors Bow to Royals in Opener, 8–3," *Globe and Mail*, Apr. 11, 1947, 18.

20 "12,000 See Sherbrooke Upset Royals," *Globe and Mail*, Apr. 14, 1947, 18.

21 For a discussion of racism against black players including the Carnegie brothers, see Cecil Harris, *The Black Experience in Professional Hockey* (Toronto: Insomniac Press, 2003). The often-told story is that Conn Smythe once said, "I'd give somebody $10,000 if he could make Herb Carnegie white."

22 Jackie Robinson was a popular player with the Montreal Royals, a kind of baseball companion to the hockey club and farm team for the Brooklyn Dodgers.

23 Arnold Rampersad, *Jackie Robinson: A Biography* (New York: Alfred A. Knopf, 1997), 151.

24 "Campeau Is Star as Royals Win, 3–0 Over Sherbrooke," *Globe and Mail*, Apr. 16, 1947, 16; and "Royals KO Sherbrookes and Enter Eastern Final Against Hamilton Tigers," *Globe and Mail*, Apr. 18, 1947, 20.

25 "Royals Triumph over Hamilton in Series Opener," *Globe and Mail*, Apr. 21, 1947, 22.

26 "Royals Best Bengals, 3–2, to Go Two Up," *Globe and Mail*, Apr. 22, 1947, 15.

27 "Royals Take Tigers, 5–1 and Win Eastern Title," *Globe and Mail*, Apr. 24, 1947, 17.

28 "Stampeders Beaten, 7–3 by High-Geared Royals as Senior Finals Start," *Globe and Mail*, Apr. 28, 1947, 19.

29 "Stampeders Beat Royals, Even Series," *Globe and Mail*, Apr. 30, 1947, 19.

30 "Stampeders Walloped by Flying Royals, 7–0," *Globe and Mail*, May 2, 1947, 19.

31 Hal Walker, "Montreal Royals Beat Calgary Stampeders; Need One More Victory," *Globe and Mail*, May 5, 1947, 19.

32 "Stamps Defeat Royals to Prolong Cup Final," *Globe and Mail*, May 8, 1947, 19.

33 "Stamps Stop Royals, Forcing Limit Series," *Globe and Mail*, May 12, 1947, 20.

34 "Royals Whirl to Title, Defeating Stamps, 8–2," *Globe and Mail*, May 13, 1947, 17. The members of that Allan Cup–winning team were Gerry McNeil, Ernie Laforce, James Galbraith, Doug Harvey, Claude Campeau, Cliff Malone, Pete Morin, James Haggarty, Floyd Curry, Bobby Pepin, Frank Carlin (coach), Gus Ogilvie (manager), Denis Casavant, Howard Riopelle, Jacques Locas, Andy Galley (trainer), Paul Raymond, Gerry Plamondon, and Eric Fleet.

35 Hal Walker, "Stampeders Beaten, 7–3, by High-Geared Royals as Senior Finals Start," *Globe and Mail*, Apr. 28, 1947, 19.

36 My father repeated this sentiment periodically over the course of his life. See Irvin, *Habs: An Oral History*, 72.

37 Martha Langford, *Suspended Conversations: The Afterlife of Memory in Photographic Albums* (Montreal: McGill-Queen's University Press, 2001), viii.

38 Jerry Lewis and James Kaplan, *Dean and Me: A Love Story* (New York: Doubleday, 2005). The Leon and Eddie's Souvenir Photo, February 16, 1948. Standing (left to right): Joe Lepine, Jimmy Galbraith, Gerry McNeil, Frank Carlin (coach), Grant Morisson, Bobby Pepin; sitting (left to right) unknown, James Haggarty, Gus Ogilvie (manager), Andy Galley (trainer), Ernie Laforce, Pete Morin, Denis Casavant. Having just notched a hat trick, Morin has reason to smile; "Morin Scores Three . . ." *Herald, Montreal*, Feb. 16, 1948, 20.

39 See Mike Wyman, "A Master Prankster: McNeil Legend Lives On," *Hockey News*, Collector's Edition, Fall 2005, 153.

40 Lili Saint-Cyr, *Ma vie de stripteaseuse* (Montreal: Quebecor, 2005), 157.

41 Ibid.

42 Ibid.

43 See Saint-Cyr, *Ma vie de stripteaseuse*, 158, 175, 271–75.

44 *Globe and Mail*, Nov. 9, 1942, 16. A picture of the incident appears on p. 17, but this is not the famous one by Turofsky that Podnieks erroneously claims appeared on the cover of *Life* magazine (see Podnieks, *Players*, 644). For some reason, the Turofsky shot of a stricken Orlando has attracted attention; it was selected for inclusion in the twentieth-century pictorial history *Canada: Our Century*, Sara Borins, Mark Kingwell, and Christopher Moore (Toronto: Doubleday, 1999), 235.

45 Al Parsley describes the "solitary" goal in a QSHL playoff game March 29, 1949, between the Royals and Sherbrooke and suggests how the All-Negro Line exploited the overly aggressive play directed at them: "It was Herbie Carnegie, of the famed All-Negro line who fashioned the solitary goal of the game when Jimmy Orlando and Bobby Marchessault tumbled his brother, Ossie, and let the black biscuit scot free near the Montreal cage." Al Parsley, "Sherbrooke Saints' System Baffles Crippled Royals," *Herald, Montreal*, Mar. 30, 1949, 23.

46 Jacques Beauchamp, *Le sport c'est ma vie* (Montreal: Quebecor, 1979), 219–20.

47 This comment is recorded by Elmer Ferguson, "Habs After Third Place...," *Herald, Montreal*, Mar. 9, 1950, 21.

48 The details in this paragraph and the following one are from Al Parsley's articles, "Durnan Back Soon" and "Sidelights," in *Herald, Montreal*, Nov. 24, 1947, 24.

49 "Habs Draw At Boston...," *Herald, Montreal*, Nov. 24, 1947, 23.

50 Don Delillo, *End Zone* (Reprint New York: Penguin, 1986), 111.

51 Delillo, *End Zone*, 112.

52 Delillo, *End Zone*, 111-12.

Taking the Torch from Bill

THE NEXT CALL UP TO THE BIG TIME FOR MCNEIL CAME AT THREE thirty in the morning on March 4, 1950, when Frank Selke finally tracked him down in Cincinnati. "Can you get yourself to Montreal for a game tonight? Durnan's in the hospital."[1]

McNeil had decided to turn professional at the beginning of the 1949–50 season, and so he joined the Cincinnati Mohawks, a new American Hockey League (AHL) franchise that was affiliated with the Canadiens and that was being run by King Clancy. Still under contract with the Canadiens, McNeil was lent to the team with the hope that he would encounter better opposition and continue to hone his skills. McNeil told Selke he would get to the airport as soon as he could; leaving his wife and child, he boarded a plane five hours later and hoped to arrive in time.

If he was anxious about getting his NHL chance, McNeil could have been paranoid about going to Cincinnati. The reason for such anxiety would be the probability that the Canadiens encouraged him to go to the Mohawks so that they could make room for the next in line— Jacques Plante. And sure enough while McNeil was finding his way back to Montreal, it was announced in the *Herald* that Jacques Plante, the youngster from Shawinigan who took over from McNeil as the Royals goalie, would replace Durnan.[2] It wasn't that the Canadiens had forgotten about their prodigy in Cincinnati, it was assumed that the Mohawks were somewhere on the road to Cleveland and hence incommunicado.

Clancy's laid-back style was the opposite of the sternness with which Dick Irvin coached the Canadiens, so Cincinnati offered McNeil a kind of refuge from the pressure of playing in Montreal. On the other hand, the inaugural season of the Mohawks was not one in which defence was emphasized; consequently, McNeil did see "a lot of rubber." One game officially had McNeil as having stopped 88 shots! Unfortunately, 9 others got by and so the Mohawks lost 9–0.[3] Rather than the friendly Forum, McNeil had to endure the boos of the Cincinnati fans, who had little tolerance for their last-place team. If the team attracted any press, it was usually negative. Such a situation could spell the end of a promising player's career. One could easily lose the desire to improve, to break into the Big Time.

McNeil's first game as a professional could be called a success even if it was a 3–0 loss. He stopped 30 shots; his Indianapolis counterpart, a guy by the name of Terry Sawchuk, had to turn aside only 14 for the shutout.[4] Nobody could anticipate that the goaltending that evening foreshadowed greater duels ahead. However, for McNeil things deteriorated from there. During a November road trip, he was shelled with thirty goals in five games, and Clancy had actually pulled him out of the starting lineup for Paul Bibeault.[5] Bibeault had been the Habs goalie before Durnan (1941 was his first year), and he had married Frank Selke's daughter.[6] Although few would have picked the older Bibeault to succeed Durnan with McNeil and Plante in the wings (in fact, it had been suggested that Bibeault wanted to retire), McNeil had reason to be worried. The American Hockey League has always been stocked with the guys either on the way up or down. McNeil still saw himself as in the former group, but Cincinnati was beginning to look like the burial grounds for would-be NHLers. Fortunately, Clancy gave him another opportunity, and over another five-game stretch in December McNeil yielded only eight goals for a GAA of 1.60. Early in January the Mohawks defeated the first-place team, the Providence Reds, despite being outshot 38 to 34, and McNeil is said to have made "three almost unbelievable saves during his team's closing stand."[7] Gerry was fighting to keep the Big Time dream alive.

As far as fan knowledge and support were concerned, Cincinnati couldn't have been more unlike Montreal. While professional hockey was well known in a number of American cities, Cincinnati wasn't one of them. All kinds of things were tried to publicize the team and the sport more generally. For some reason, goaltender equipment has been a perennial fascination among fans and sports writers. A Cincinnati newspaper published a full-page picture of my father squatting next to everything he would have worn: leg pads, pants, shoulder pads, socks, sweater, gloves, chest protector (the same one that was salvaged from a pile of old stuff at the Forum during his rookie camp in 1943), and stick.[8] Together it all weighed thirty-three pounds. Notably absent is, of course, the face mask. It would be another ten years before Plante would bring it into the game. The goalie skates are also missing. *The Boston Daily Globe* ran a similar picture in 1953 with the Bruin trainers kneeling next to the elaborate armour.[9] This time costs are itemized, as they would be twenty-one years later when Dave Stubbs did a similar piece for *The Montreal Gazette* (see Chapter 8).

Regardless of position, hockey players wear a lot of equipment compared to other team sports, and many are particular about each piece. The fit has to be just right. Whatever it is must be serviceable and yet almost unnoticeable. Hockey players typically hate having to upgrade or change an item. New leg pads for goalies might take an entire year to work in. Once familiar with the equipment and a routine about how it is donned, hockey players are loathe to alter the slightest detail—a strap here or tuck there. Nothing matches the fuss hockey players will make about their sticks—once it included sanding, now it is restricted pretty much to taping (what colour and where on the shaft as well as the blade). There are rituals about how to dress and prepare for a game that are followed obsessively, as if the need for certainty in this realm is supposed to make it easier to accept the absolute chaos and speed of the game itself. I wasn't around to observe any of this with my father (my only dressing room experience was limited to some Oldtimer play), but I do remember my father talking about it. I have also played enough hockey myself to know the concern about one's gear.

It is a sad but undeniable truth that opportunity for a professional athlete often comes out of another's misfortune. The story of how the little guy from Quebec City would eventually take the torch from Bill Durnan really began at Chicago Stadium on the night before Selke called him in Cincinnati. Durnan went down, trying unsuccessfully to block a shot by Jim Conacher, and ended up slashing his forehead open on the back of Conacher's skate.[10] The wound, very similar to the one he suffered two years previously, was closed with seven stitches, and Durnan finished out the game, a 5–2 loss. (Since the Habs were on the road, Plante wasn't available as a substitute.) Suddenly, Durnan's lead on Harry Lumley of Detroit for the Vezina Trophy was cut to four goals.

At this time, the Vezina was automatically awarded to the goalie who had started in the most games for the team that had the fewest goals against. In 1981–82 the criteria were changed and the award was adjudicated solely on the basis of performance "as voted by the general managers."[11] The team that gives up the fewest goals is now awarded the William Jennings Trophy—it actually goes to the team's goalkeepers who have played a minimum of twenty-five games. The change reflects a preference for adjudication, as is the case with the Hart (most valuable player), the Calder (best rookie), or Norris (best defenceman) as opposed to a determination based only on statistical information. While statistical information has become progressively more sophisticated (for example, save percentages are now calculated for goalies—i.e., percentage of shots stopped), numerical systems are imperfect in measuring distinctions in performance. The difficulty of a save as well as its context (e.g., did it come at a critical point in the game?) is key in assessing how important a goalie can be to a team. My father could never emphasize this point enough whenever we tried to compare players. That said, an obsession with statistical information characterizes many sport aficionados, especially those of baseball, a sport which seems to lend itself to statistical analysis. On the other hand, it must be admitted that adjudication is subjective and potentially biased—pitfalls that are somewhat offset by the fact that several votes are cast.

On the train back to Toronto after the Chicago game, Ernie Cook, the Canadiens trainer, told Dick Irvin that Durnan had a fever, and so Irvin wired the Leaf doctor, Horace McIntyre, asking him to meet the train at Union Station. Early Friday morning, Durnan was examined in Toronto and found to have a fever of 102° F. Fearing a serious eye infection, the medical staff recommended immediate hospitalization, but Durnan convinced them to allow him to continue to Montreal on the condition that he be hospitalized there.[12] And so, while Selke was arranging for an ambulance to meet the train, he was also looking up Clancy's number in Cincinnati.

We can now jump ahead again to Saturday afternoon. Selke sent Camil Desroches, the publicity director, to the Dorval airport to fetch McNeil. The plane finally landed at 6:15 PM, and after posing with Desroches for a picture on the disembarkment ramp,[13] McNeil was hurried into a waiting car. There was just enough time to get to the Forum for the opening faceoff. Having eaten only a sandwich that day, McNeil dressed quickly; he hadn't had the opportunity to read a Canadian newspaper, so he was unaware of the race for the Vezina. Chicago was an explosive team offensively; in three previous meetings against the Canadiens they had averaged five goals per game. As the Habs came out onto the ice there was a buzz in the crowd—*McNeil, not Plante, gets the start*. McNeil, for his part, felt good about being back on the Forum ice in front of supportive fans. Ironically, he would again face his boyhood idol Frank Brimsek, who had been traded to the Black Hawks.[14]

Maurice Richard gave the Canadiens a 1–0 lead, but it wasn't long before Bill Mosienko scored his 241st career goal to tie the game. The Meatball Line (Metro Prystai, Bep Guidolin, and Bert Olmstead) seemed to command the Montreal zone. At one point during the opening frame, McNeil made a brilliant save, leaping up to block a shot off his shoulder. Each stop drew a round of applause, and he seemed to gain confidence as the game progressed. In the second period, Prystai blasted a shot labelled for the corner until McNeil did the splits to kick the puck into the corner. Mosdell gave Montreal the lead when he banged home a rebound. The third period began with the Canadiens hanging on to a one-goal lead. Jack Stewart fired from ten feet out, and again McNeil made the save. Then Harmon sent a streaking Léo Gravelle in on a breakaway, and the "blond Gazelle," as he was called, deked Brimsek out and backhanded the puck into the open net. With the insurance goal, the edge was off and McNeil could breathe a little easier. Suddenly, the siren went, and the players came off the bench to congratulate the kid. Making only his second career start in the NHL, McNeil was chosen as the game's first star, and the newspaper headline on the first page of the Monday sports section read, "McNeil Steals Show as Canadiens Win."

McNeil was jubilant at the Royals game the next afternoon when he went to see his former teammates; he had just been told by Irvin that, because of Durnan's condition and the fact that Cincinnati was only playing five more games, the Canadiens wanted to keep him for the rest of the season. As the afternoon wore on and the time to board the train to Detroit drew near, his joy was replaced by a growing tension. Detroit led the league in offence, and they would be only too eager to help Lumley in his race with Durnan for the Vezina. Being back in Montreal was also like being back in hockey's pressure cooker. On the other hand, McNeil was reuniting with good friends from the Royals like Doug Harvey (see fig. 8) and Floyd Curry. He also felt confident; he had proven himself against Chicago and had actually increased Durnan's lead over Lumley by two goals since the Red Wings were clipped 3–2 by Toronto. His reflexes were sharp from having to withstand the offensive onslaughts that he faced with the Cincinnati team. So much of the mood of the athlete has to do with the latest personal performance or the latest performance of the team. With their victory over Chicago, Montreal was now tied for third place, having gained two points on the Rangers, who had lost. That the Leafs were only five points ahead was even more incentive, since the playoff match-ups would be first versus third, and second versus fourth. Montreal would much rather face New York than Detroit, the team bound to win the league title. And so the Habs felt good in the moment, even if they were headed to play the league's top team.

Although McNeil already had experience playing in New York's old Madison Square Garden (actually MSG III), since the Royals played an interlocking schedule with the Eastern Amateur Hockey League in 1947–48,[15] he was about to make his debut at the Detroit Olympia. The

Fig. 8 A young Gerry McNeil and Doug Harvey, once teammates with the Royals, now playing for the Habs. (Photographer unknown. Sometime between 1947–50.) Copyright unknown.

crowds at the Olympia were wild about their Red Wings, a dominant team with stars like Ted Lindsay, Sid Abel, and Gordie Howe. In fact, on this day in early March of 1950, these names were one, two, three in the scoring race. Many a team and many a goaltender had nightmare games in the Motor City, but McNeil would eventually put in some of his most spectacular NHL performances at the Olympia. Of course, he would not have known this when he skated out to face Howe and company that evening.

TAKING THE TORCH FROM BILL

Unlike today's rinks which are a standard size and equipped with identical retaining glass panels, the so-called "shrines" of the Original Six all had their own features. What made the Olympia distinct was its long oval-shaped ends; shoot-ins careened around the boards much more quickly than they did at the Forum (pre-1969), where the deep, sharp corners tended to slow the puck down. Today the corners in all NHL rinks conform to a standard radius.[16] Teams still adjust for what is sometimes referred to as "lively end boards," and the possibility of shooting the puck off a particularly sweet spot, but rink-specific strategies usually end there.

NHL rinks circa 1950 sported other variations. The Olympia had an iron mesh behind the net, rather than the retaining glass that had been installed in the Forum (and Maple Leaf Gardens). Chicago Stadium also had the mesh, and a puck tended to come off it erratically or to die somewhat. In both cases, these barriers only went a little way up the side boards; hence, fans and photographers could actually rest their elbows on the top of the boards and lean right into the playing area (these people were often referred to as "rail birds"). The defensive strategy of firing the puck high off the glass and out of one's zone didn't exist; teams were forced to be a little more creative, although they did use the boards, which tended to keep the rail birds alert. There were all kinds of instances of fans getting directly involved in altercations with players.

The Olympia, like Boston Garden, had two tiers, the upper hanging over a good part of the lower bowl (Chicago Stadium had three). Maple Leaf Gardens and the Forum did not have tiers, but the Forum, at least, had a rather steep rise that made viewers feel as if they were more on top of the playing surface than away from it (even though they might actually be the same distance from the action as a fan with a similar seat at the Gardens). Ultimately, there was significantly more intimacy between the players and fans in NHL rinks than there is today with all the protective glass and netting.[17]

The ice surface in Chicago, Boston, and New York was perceptively smaller than in the other three rinks. Fast skaters (like Léo Gravelle of 1950) like extra room, and this aspect of the game is still very much alive with the wider, European-style surface (many of which are now being built in North America). In short, the idiosyncrasies of the Original Six rinks gave a special character to the game that is now lacking in the NHL but very much alive in international competition.

Originally built in 1924, the Montreal Forum had been renovated in 1949 under the direction of Frank Selke, who had taken over from

Gorman a few years before.[18] In fact, Selke began making changes when he first arrived in Montreal in 1946. Chief among these was taking out the bleacher section at the north end of the building, which held four thousand—almost half of the seating capacity of 9,600. It cost fifty cents to get into "Millionaires Row," as the bleacher section was affectionately called, so the motive was financial, not altruistic as the 2005 film *The Rocket* seems to suggest. However, the big renovation came three years later when another floor was added, bringing the seating capacity to 13,551. Among other distinguishing characteristics of the pre-1968 Forum were its tight corners—the opposite extreme of the oval-like design of Detroit's Olympia.

To get a sense of what the interior of the Forum pre-1968 was like, one has to go to period photographs, especially those long shots that feature a bank of fans from ice level to the uppermost sections. The sports photographer who was best at capturing the full spectacle (i.e., the fans as well as the game) of professional sports from this period may well have been Hy Peskin. His most famous photo of this kind is of Ben Hogan taking a rare one-iron shot at the final hole at the 1950 US Open. What distinguishes the photo is not that Hogan is at a perfect follow-through stance, but that Peskin manages to get a near complete circle of fans lining the 18th fairway and hole.[19] The photo is not of a golfer or of golf; it is of the spectacle that is a major tournament. That Hogan would go on to force an extra playoff round and eventually win the Open, of course, provides the significant context.

In November of 1952, Peskin was sent by *Life* magazine to Montreal to get a photo of a record-breaking goal by Richard. Although he failed in his main assignment (see Chapter 5), Peskin did get one of his signature long shots of game action contained within the greater outline of a bank of fans. I saw the photo when it was part of the Getty Images online database. Unfortunately, when the licensing rights were transferred in 2012, the 1952 Peskin shots from the Montreal Forum were lost (at least the high-resolution versions of the images). One can still get a sense of Peskin's fondness for the distance photo by examining similar Peskin images featuring a baseball park or basketball arena. As a sports photographer, Hy Peskin had the ability to take a rather drab structure and make it look like a dramatic gathering of humanity when it was full of fans.

What Peskin was trying to capture from the Forum catwalk was an original angle. The subjects in sports photography, be they individuals or situations, remain largely the same for a stretch of time, so the true artist will search for some way to draw the viewer's eye. This mission was essentially what motivated Neil Leifer to install his camera eighty feet directly above the ring for the 1966 Ali vs. Williams fight. Only possible in the spacious Houston Astrodome, this contrivance led to the photo that Leifer himself considers his best (even better than his more famous Ali vs. Liston shot that *SI* voted most significant sports photo of the twentieth century; see Chapter 3).[20] The picture is a wonderful spectacle of framing and symmetry. Since it can easily be accessed at Leifer's website, I'll content myself with the traditional mode of *ekphrasis* (i.e., the narrative description of a visual object). The first straightedge frame consists of a two rows of journalists sitting behind their lined-up desks on all four sides of the ring. Then comes the canvas floor of the ring itself and the ring ropes that serve as the second straightedge frame, broken by the ringside photographers who poke their way underneath. Two wires suspending ring lights cut into this box from the bottom left and top right corners and lead the eye to the two principles of the contest. Leifer has snapped his remote at the precise moment when victory and defeat are demonstrably being registered by the combatants. In the bottom left corner is Ali, with his arms raised in the classic boxing champion position. In the opposite right upper corner is Williams laid out on the canvas in a perfect X. Leifer himself is in the blue shirt at 11:00. The photo does not convey the cultural significance of the Ali vs. Liston one, but its original bird's-eye angle yields a mesmerizing display of lines and balance. Aesthetically, it suggests perfection.

Like all art, sports photography is received for its cultural significance as well as its pure aesthetic qualities. However, the latter aspect of Leifer's favourite picture serves as an appropriate opportunity to introduce what may well be the most useful theory on how modern sport has become saturated with the spectacle. The social anthropologist John MacAloon proposes a series of frames (game; ritual; festival; spectacle) that allows us to understand the social function of spectator sports.[21] At the centre is the game itself; then moving outward we encounter the rituals surrounding the game (anthems, medal- or cup-presentation ceremonies); then the festival surrounding the official event (e.g., the tailgating parties, donning of team colours); and finally the spectacle itself that seeks to contain it all (now largely the televised game, but video reproduction has also permeated the arena itself). Substitute any of the major North American sports for the Olympics and the theory works just as well.

While Peskin had a knack for capturing a sense of cultural grandeur about professional sport in as much as it involved the crowd and venerable coliseum-like structures (the wide-angle subject), he also took wonderful pictures of individual spectators or groups thereof reacting to the action before them: Vicki LaMotta and Edna Mae Robinson at the Championship fight between their husbands Jake and "Sugar" Ray at Chicago Stadium on Valentine's Day in 1951.[22] One of these was also taken that November night at the Montreal Forum; the picture includes a section of fans frozen in their paroxysmal gestures and completely fixated on what is transpiring before them. Their high style and period dress are as expressive as their gestures. While everybody is mesmerized by the spectacle of the event, Peskin, in a simple act that can yield the most interesting subject, turns his lens back at the crowd. In Chapter 3 we shall examine some technical factors that resulted in spectators being present in the background of many hockey pictures from this era. For the moment, it is enough to acknowledge that the crowd as a deliberate primary subject or as a peripheral framing device defines Peskin's unique contribution to sports photography.

From this second Peskin shot we can easily note another difference from the typical NHL fan of today—dress. It obviously was much more formal (i.e., coat and tie, dress hats, etc.) in the 1950s. As late as the 1970s, I can recall always being amazed by how many suits I'd see at a Forum game. Some have said that this reflected the quasi-religious status hockey held in Quebec and a kind of Catholic emphasis on ceremony, but the formal dress can also be read in the fans at the Olympia and the Gardens. In fact, this was precisely what struck Richard B. Woodward about John Zimmerman's photo of Jacques Plante—the first hockey action shot on the February 17, 1958, cover of *SI*. Reproduced in both *SI*'s "Special Anniversary Issue, 1954–2004" and the *Anniversary Book*,[23] Zimmerman's photograph is unique for a number of reasons. First, the angle: it is a long, straight shot of the Canadiens goalmouth taken from an upper level at the opposite end of MSG III (i.e., a position above and behind the New York net). Most hockey shots are taken from the side and close to a goalmouth.[24] Second, Zimmerman's picture of Plante shows the Habs goalie crouching in a style that Sawchuk was famous for. The unprotected area of the six-by-four-foot net behind him looms very large. However, what caught the attention of Richard B. Woodward was "the tiers of white males in jackets and ties and fedoras": "It's a group portrait of a more formal era when people dressed up for a sporting event as if it were a Noel Coward play."[25] What I find fascinating about looking at the sea of faces behind Plante is that every one of them is intently focused on the play. With all the distractions of a contemporary arena and the benefits of video replay, one would be hard-pressed to find such mass attention any more.

TAKING THE TORCH FROM BILL

Today the crowd is full of people who prefer to wear team jerseys (or colours), face (or body) paint, and other festive accoutrements like puck-heads. Today professional sport is considered family entertainment; in the 1940s and '50s it was primarily for an adult audience who dressed the part. I like children (I've raised two of my own), and I understand that the approach here seems philosophically correct. Hockey is just a game; children play games; we should enjoy the arena by allowing it to bring out the child in all of us. Kids on the ice for the pre-game, the intermission, and even afterwards. Many of the paying spectators—kids. But I long for something more adult. Obviously it would be too much to suggest that people should dress formally: suits and dresses. Nevertheless, is it wrong to want the arena experience— professional hockey, to be precise here—to be taken more seriously? It isn't all about what rink has the best nachos. Maybe I want the kids to have to act more like adults, and the adults to act less like kids.

When the NHL moved out of the Original Six buildings (all of which dated back to the 1920s–30s) into huge bowl-shaped structures, seating capacities jumped from the 15,000–18,000 range to the 20,000–23,000 range. Despite the increased capacity, the new buildings sound at times more like mausoleums than sporting arenas. Fans are now courted to spend more time buying souvenirs and food, while watching live action is not nearly as important. Anybody who happens to miss a goal can view the replay on the Jumbotron, and this includes players and coaches. Caught in a bathroom or concession lineup, no problem— there are video screens everywhere. In 1950, fans followed the play much more closely and, although it is difficult to generalize, seemed to react more intensely.

The fans aside, sartorial elegance is something that has attached itself to the players. I glance through my father's scrapbooks and spot the same wide fedoras, double-breasted suits and haberdasher coats in the pictures of the players as are advertised elsewhere in the sports section. There were at least two Royals who went on to make good livings in fine men's clothing (Denis Casavant and Dugger McNeil). I clearly remember Dugger telling my father on a trip to Halifax that he purposely specialized in the "high end" because the profit margin was greater and the competition less fierce. In any case, I find it odd in the extreme that minor league hockey players as young as twelve are required to go to the rink dressed in a shirt and tie. Somebody once told me that the team rule about formal dress was to help the players get into the appropriate frame of mind for games. How formal wear assists anybody in mentally preparing for hockey is lost on me.

Some of us will remember the loud check blazers and leisure suits that hockey players gravitated toward in the '70s, but nothing is as notorious as the over-the-top clown patterns and colours worn by the sport's greatest media celebrity, Don Cherry. One could surmise that this cloak of formality that hockey cultivates off-ice and in public has something to do with disguising a primal brutality that underlies the sport, a sport that otherwise can soar with graceful motion and fine skill. Cherry's absurdly stiff collars and outlandish cuffs send a mixed message. On the one hand, they appear to be somewhat playful assertions that sport is a noble endeavour or that a gentleman's code operates. The game may get rough, but we are civilized. On the other, his dress is so excessively clownish that the whole idea of dressing up seems to be mocked. The game is rough, and to pretend otherwise is silly. However, irony is not part of Cherry's shtick; straight-faced dignity and respect are, which brings us back to formal dress as concealment.

Although it has never been as popular as the other major team sports, hockey has been featured in mainstream American publications going back to Eustace Tilley and *The New Yorker* of the 1920s and '30s.[26] *Life* magazine did run a few features on the sport in the '40s and '50s, and hockey ranks ninth in a list of sports to make the *SI* cover in a half century of publication (1954–2004).[27] A glance at *The New York Times Encyclopedia of Sports* (Volume 8), which reproduces a number of articles from the *NY Times*, confirms that hockey had a devout, albeit small, following in certain US cities—including Detroit, which first became known as "Hockeytown" in the late '40s and early '50s.[28]

Olympia Stadium happened to host "Sid Abel Night" the day of McNeil's first start there, which didn't help his nerves. There was an elaborate pre-game ceremony during which Abel was presented with a car, among other gifts. It became clear to McNeil that playing in front of the Olympia crowd was a world apart from facing the local fans in Shawinigan or Valleyfield. While the crowd seemed different, the work began to feel like Cincinnati. The Red Wings controlled the play, and eventually outshot the Habs 31 to 16 (Montreal got only a single shot on net in the third). However, the Canadiens held on for a 2–2 tie, which given the circumstances, was a positive result.

A few things made the game notable. McNeil got his first lesson at the hands of Abel and Howe when the former, showing his appreciation for the ceremony, took a pass from the latter, drew the rookie goalie out of his position, and then scored to tie the game 1–1 (see fig. 9). Meanwhile, Léo Gravelle was the hot forward for the Habs, getting both their goals, and Bert Hirschfeld, another recent call-up from Cincinnati, was

Fig. 9 Abel stands between McNeil and another Red Wing player. Note the oval curve of the boards and the sharp shadows on the ice (the latter obviously made by the flashlights mounted on the wire mesh at the Olympia). (Photographer unknown. Detroit Olympia, early 1950s.) Copyright unknown.

credited with two assists. McNeil did keep the Canadiens in front at the beginning of the third when he made superb stops on a high shot by McFadden and a close-in opportunity by Carveth. Eventually, Detroit evened the score when Pavelich surprised McNeil on a twenty-foot backhand. The Wings could have pulled out the victory when Babando got in on McNeil near the end of the game, but Mac made a good save to preserve the tie—the fifth straight deadlock between the two clubs, which goes to show just how close the teams were, despite Detroit being well ahead in the standings.[29] When José Théodore won the Vezina and Hart Trophies in 2001–02, I remember my father commenting that it was good for a goalie to play in close games, that it kept one's reflexes sharp. That clearly was the situation for the Habs in the 1949–50 season; the draw with Detroit set a new record of sixteen ties in one season.

The tie or draw is something else that has disappeared from hockey. NHL fans are now treated to five minutes of extra time and, if no one scores, a shootout. The shootout is something that was adapted from soccer as a means of determining a winner and loser when regular play seemed helplessly deadlocked. It certainly provides an added excitement to the game, and I wouldn't advocate going back to the official tie, but there is something to be said about its appropriateness and the sharing of a single point for each team based on a match that was evenly competed. American team sports favour the one-factor ranking (winning half your games is .500 or commonly referred to as "playing 500"), which demands a winner-loser decision. There are no shootouts in baseball or basketball. In any case, professional hockey prefers the clear decision, even if it is based on an artificial structure like the shootout. Any hockey game can be decided on the slimmest of margins—the puck that hits the post and stays out of the net—but the official tie or the recognition that play was equal seems to me an accurate representation that allowed for mutual respect. The tie allowed for the idea that sport is not *all* about winning and losing.

McNeil's popularity among the local fans was reflected in how he obtained 378 "Player of Distinction" votes for his debut 1950 performance. The leader was presented with the Lord Calvert Trophy at the end of the season; Maurice Richard remained clearly in the lead with 2,854 total votes.[30] In any case, the Canadiens travelled back to Montreal to get some rest before their next game the following Thursday at home to Toronto. Durnan was discharged from hospital on Thursday morning, but it would be at least a few days before he played again. It came as no shock that the game with the Leafs ended in a 1–1 draw. This time it was Billy Reay who came to the rescue and tied the game up with less than three minutes remaining. McNeil made two "particularly fine saves" in the third: one a block of Meeker's close-range shot, and a second off a "heavy slap-shot by Joe Klukay."[31] The Friday *Herald* featured a picture taken in the Habs' dressing room after the game: McNeil, half clad in his gear, is congratulated by a kneeling Durnan. Both men are smiling—Durnan's lead on Lumley for the Vezina had been stretched to eleven goals; there were only nine games left in the regular season.[32]

I found out about this story, like I did much of the detail about my father's career, by looking up contemporary accounts in the newspapers. In fact, I would say a good deal of what is recorded here owes itself to Elmer Ferguson or Dink Carroll, and the narrative that I am creating is largely based on their fiction. Reading newspapers from another era can give one a sense of passing through a doorway into the past. Before one gets to the sports section, one notices the major news story of the day (a battle in Korea, for example), the classifieds give one a sense of prices, but it is the advertisements that somehow bring a city and a specific time to life: what films were playing, what styles were popular—and there has always seemed to me to be something particularly glamorous about the 1940s and '50s—the men in their fedoras and gabardine suits, the female hosiery and lingerie.

I'm well aware that this sense of glamour is wrapped up in a Freudian nostalgia having to do with recollections of my late 1950s childhood (a colourful-patterned silk dress, somehow seen or encountered in my parents' bedroom, still swims in my memory). An expert on the subject, Fred Davis, has linked nostalgic romanticizing to an anxiety about the present; he also recognizes its connection to "mass spectator sports and commercial amusements," both of which are factors in this study.[33] The thing about someone my age reconstructing a history of the 1940s and '50s is that there is a certain tactile quality about the era; while I have no direct experience of the events, I can still touch the same people and places in my memory bank of the period immediately afterwards. I remember Jimmy Galbraith as robust and funny, his wife Shirley as blond and good-looking. Despite the Forum's makeover and eventual abandonment, some of the storefronts and buildings along Sainte-Catherine are the same now as they were a half century ago. One might walk over a patch of the same sidewalk today but be in a completely different world.

Since McNeil seemed to be doing well and Durnan needed a few days to regain his strength, it was announced that the rookie would be in the Canadiens' goal for the weekend: at home against the Bruins Saturday and in New York on Sunday. McNeil's routine for home games would go something like this: a light skate and equipment check at the Forum around noon hour, then home and a steak dinner around four o'clock, a post-dinner nap, during which McNeil may or may not have slept, a six o'clock summons, and finally the trip back to the Forum to suit up for the eight o'clock start. The Canadiens dressing room was on the Atwater or west side of the Forum, and the Habs traditionally protected the north-end net.

The Bruins had been on a scoring spree, having averaged six goals per game over their last four outings. If the Habs hoped to climb in the standings or have any success in the post-season, they would have to generate more offence themselves. Richard led the way by scoring forty-five seconds into the game. The Canadiens took command and outshot Boston 34 to 12 (16 to 2 in the second period); the final score was 5–0. McNeil preserved the shutout by robbing Kenny Smith, Dave Creighton, Paul Ronty, and Milt Schmidt, all in the third period. However, the game attracted more attention because of a "Pier Six" style fight between Richard and Fern Flaman in the third period. McNeil may not have seen the check that plastered Richard against the plate glass in the south end of the Forum, but he couldn't miss the fact that the twosome were soon rolling on the ice and then back up and punching again. Separated by the linesmen and some teammates, the pair wheeled around and re-engaged at least two more times.[34]

There wasn't much time to savour the moment. As soon as the players undressed, they had to hurry to the station to catch the train for New York. One could get the impression that travel in the 1950s NHL was glamorous, especially when it conjures up images of staying in some of the best hotels: the Leland in Detroit, Hotel LaSalle in Chicago, the Royal York in Toronto, or the Piccadilly in New York. However, the team rarely stayed over during the regular season. It was far more common to change quickly and then dash for the station for an over-night ride back home, or to Toronto if one was coming from Detroit or Chicago. Trips to Chicago were especially quick, with the team often only getting to the rink a half hour before game time. McNeil remembered the odd feeling of entering the stadium when the place was already packed with rowdy fans—what would they have done if they had known the visiting team wasn't even in the building yet? Immediately after the game, the team would race to catch the train back east.

If time did permit, the big attraction of Chicago was being able to do some shopping for items like golf clubs or sewing machines. When the Canadiens were in a train wreck on the bridge coming onto the island of Montreal in December 1950, many of these purchases came crashing out of the berths and resulted in some serious bruises. The contraband wasn't restricted to the players; both Selke and Irvin smuggled prize poultry back across the border on several occasions. The cages were hidden in with equipment bags and sometimes in hotel rooms.

Aside from playoff time, the players really lived on the train. They ate their meals in the dining car, slept in berths, and played countless games of gin rummy. In fact, card-playing would remain an extremely popular activity among hockey players and their wives from this era. There were no electronic amusements, so players tended to socialize more (even with reporters). When the players grew tired of cards, they tended to play pranks on one another. My father recalls one particular rookie initiation that got a little out of hand, and so the rookie took refuge in the bathroom. Frustrated that he wouldn't emerge, a few of the guys set fire to a newspaper and shoved it under the door. The Pullman cars of this era were elegantly finished in wood panelling and the fire, like the initiation itself, also got out of hand. Before the player could get it out, considerable damage had been done. As was the practice at the time, the team would receive the bill from the railway and simply pass it on to the players. It was customary for the players to divide the costs evenly per man regardless of who did what. Anybody joining the team would soon realize that such bills would have to be incorporated into the weekly budget. My father remembers that he often felt relieved to get his notice and know that "the damage that trip was only going to be $20 per player. That wasn't too bad." As for that rookie whom they attempted to smoke out of the bathroom, my father only said that "the kid was more afraid of riding on the train with the guys than going up against Lindsay and company in Detroit."[35]

The memory of many happy times socializing with other couples would be something that my parents referred to often later in life. Obviously playing in the NHL and feeling the pressure to win it all meant that the competitive atmosphere was a constant, but friendly get-togethers strengthened the bonds between players and their wives, as evidenced by a group photo taken at Butch Bouchard's cabaret (see fig. 10). Three of the couples are still in rather formal dress and, one assumes, were joined by the others later. Butch wears a pair of comic glasses and seems to be the centre of attention; the group is seated around a series of pushed-together tables, drinking beer. I'm intrigued to catch a glance at what these women looked like some twenty years before I would ever meet them. Kenny Mosdell at the back right with his arm around Lorraine, who would hold on to her all-American looks for at least another half century; Kaye Lach, the elegant blond, to her right; then I assume Paul Meger's significant other and Paul, of course; then the Richards, first Maurice and then the bubbly Lucille; Harvey at the head of the table with Ursula to his left; then the hosts, Marie-Claire and Butch; Elmer Lach; then my father leaning forward and grinning, my mother slouched back in her chair (she may have been a little concerned about the degree of festive involvement on the part of her husband); beyond, the Geoffrions, Marlene and Bernard; and

Fig. 10 A group of the Canadiens with their wives at "Butch" Bouchard's cabaret. Down the left side of the table: Ursula Harvey, Marie-Claire and Butch Bouchard, Elmer Lach, Gerry and Theresa McNeil, Marlene and Bernard Geoffrion, Lorne Davis and his date (?); back to front on the right side: Ken and Lorraine Mosdell, Kaye Lach, Paul Meger's date (?) and Paul Meger, Maurice and Lucille Richard, Doug Harvey. (Photographer unknown. Butch Bouchard's Restaurant [cabaret].) Photo courtesy of Émile "Butch" Bouchard family.

TAKING THE TORCH FROM BILL

finally at the far end I'm guessing Lorne Davis with his date. Many great years lay ahead.

With four successive games under his belt, McNeil would have begun to feel like *the* goaltender; even though everyone knew and expected Bill to return, it was McNeil who was riding the current streak, McNeil to whom media and teammates were looking as the guy back there. In "The Player of Distinction" race among Montreal fans, McNeil, with 1,110 votes, ranked second only to the Rocket for the games in which he took Durnan's place.

Montreal kept the offence rolling in New York, but they did come out a little flat in the opening period. The Rangers scored first on a two-man advantage, but the Canadiens scored four times in the second and added another in the third. McNeil blocked 26 shots to Rayner's 25, so the play was not as one-sided as it was against Boston the night before. Nevertheless, with five games played, McNeil continued his 1.00 GAA.[36] Five points separated the second- and fourth-place teams, but the Habs had a game in hand on the Leafs and Rangers. To be clear on the stakes involved, members of the team finishing in second place received an extra $500, those on the third-place team $350, while those on the fourth-place team had to settle for $150. These may not seem like grand sums today, but in 1950 they represented a range of roughly 8 to 17 per cent of the average annual salary. McNeil admitted that everybody was looking for extra money, and that he probably received some extra compensation that season but would have remained quiet about it.

Elmer Lach, injured in a collision with Bill Barilko a few games back, returned to the lineup in Detroit. McNeil made his second start at the Olympia in a little over a week. Since the six-team league played a seventy-game schedule in the 1950s, teams faced each other fourteen times. That meant that not only did players get more familiar with the unique characteristics of the original rinks (Montreal would play at the Olympia seven times during the regular schedule), but teams got to know each other rather intimately. There were only about a hundred players total in the NHL, so individual rivalries were often very intense and very personal. In any case, the results were not so successful for McNeil's second trip to the Olympia. The Big Line of Howe, Abel, and Lindsay figured into all of their team's goals as the Red Wings went on to a 4–1 victory. It was McNeil's first defeat since being called up. Abel drew four assists, Lindsay three, and Howe notched his thirtieth goal. Jack Stewart's goal actually went in off Kenny Reardon's skate. Although it was a rough game, only ten penalties were called; at one point in the third period, five players crowded into the penalty box at the same time.[37] (Unlike today, only one league official separated opposing players in the penalty box, which was designed to hold about three extra bodies maximum.)

While Lumley picked up three goals in the Vezina race, nobody now gave him a chance of catching Durnan, who remained ten goals ahead. After another weekend of play, Lumley and Durnan had identical 2.24 GAAS; the difference came in the games played by the substitutes: in six games McNeil posted a 1.50 GAA as opposed to Sawchuk's 2.28 in seven games. That my father never won a Vezina himself but helped another to that honour has struck me as perfectly in keeping with his character. He seemed to be a man who derived more pleasure from doing something for somebody else than he ever did from doing something for himself. If he happened to have tickets to a big game, he wanted you to use them. His replacement of Durnan in March of 1950 also reflects my father's essential contribution to the Tricolore dynasty. Although his NHL career wasn't long enough for him to be considered for the Hall of Fame, it should be remembered that secondary figures often play essential roles (something like Robertson Davies's "fifth business"); when his team needed him, Mac was there.

Durnan returned to the Montreal net for the second half of the home-and-home series. The Habs pulled out a 2–2 tie—their eighteenth of the season. On Friday, March 17th, it was announced that McNeil would return to Cincinnati, but only to pick up his car.[38] Paul Bibeault would finish out the Mohawk schedule and McNeil would stay with the Habs for the playoff run. My mother was quick to point out that a car was not the only thing Mac had left behind in Cincinnati. When McNeil drove back to Montreal, Teacy and toddler son, Ron, were with him. A late-season snowstorm hit as the young family stopped overnight in Toronto. The next day my mother remembers that two little tracks were all that marked the road to Montreal; she also remembers that her husband was determined to press on no matter what the conditions. Nothing would stop him from making the next Canadiens' practice.

McNeil's stellar performance to help the man he admired win his sixth Vezina was widely recognized. The front page of the *The Hockey News* leads with the headline: "Hab Sub Outdoes Old Master! Gerry McNeil in Nets for Durnan—Stingy on Goals."[39] Inside (page 9) one finds the "National League" feature story beginning with the text "Handsome, little Gerry McNeil" was a "unanimous choice for The-Player-of-the-Week and 'Schaefer Award.'"[40] I wonder how many NHL rookies have earned this honour or its equivalent in their first week.

TAKING THE TORCH FROM BILL

Finishing second with the fewest goals against, Montreal accomplished much at the end of the 1949–50 regular season, but it had come at a cost. The team went into the Stanley Cup playoffs with a number of injuries: Calum MacKay had an ailing knee, Billy Reay a deep slash in his foot, Hal Laycoe a broken nose, Butch Bouchard a pulled groin, and Kenny Mosdell a wrenched shoulder. At the end of the second game, Kenny Reardon joined the wounded when he crashed into the boards and dislocated his shoulder.[41] The goalie who was making a difference in the series was Chuck Rayner; he played magnificently as the Rangers won the first three games, twice coming from behind. As far as injuries were concerned, most of the hockey world was focused on Series A— the Semifinal between Detroit and Toronto and the recovery of Gordie Howe, who suffered a severe concussion after crashing headfirst into the boards. Only later did doctors admit that they feared for Howe's life. Worried about retaliatory brawling, the league assigned two referees for Game Two.[42] Meanwhile Series B followed an unusual home-away schedule, since a circus had been booked in MSG; the Rangers would have to play the rest of the series against Montreal on the road.

The story on the streets of Montreal before Game Four was whether the Canadiens could avoid the "ignominy of a complete white-wash" as Elmer Ferguson put it, something that had not happened since the NHL adopted the current playoff structure in 1936.[43] It certainly must have been a bit of a shock to see McNeil in the Montreal net; Durnan did not seem to have suffered any injury in the last game. After making two nice first-period saves off Stanley and Raleigh, McNeil was beaten by Pentti Lund, who banged home a rebound. The Finn, having scored a hat trick in Game Two, seemed to have discovered a magic touch. The Canadiens tied it up before the period finished, as little Norman Dussault got a breakaway, whirled in and crossed in front of Rayner before firing the puck past the Ranger goalie. Raleigh put the Rangers back up a goal halfway through the second, and that's how the score stood well into the third. The Canadiens tied up the game when Richard scored on a rebound from a point shot by Harvey. From then on the game was a thriller, full of dazzling speed and tense moments. McNeil dove flat to block a shot by Mickoski, and Rayner thwarted the Canadiens through the rest of regulation time.[44]

The fast pace continued in the overtime. Former Canadien Buddy O'Connor broke in alone on the wing, bobbing and deking to get the rookie goalie to move off the post. McNeil, pressed against the metal, held his ground, and O'Connor was forced to shoot. Years later McNeil would describe the need for a goalie to resist the "fake" or "move," which skilled players were so good at using. In such situations, doing nothing may be the hardest thing to do, yet a goalie needs to recognize the difference between a real move and a move that is only meant to draw the goalie out. Blocking shots is hard enough without beating yourself by reacting in an uncontrolled way to all stimuli. O'Connor had been part of the Canadiens' Razzle Dazzle Line in 1941–42 when he played with Pete (Pierre) Morin and Jerry Heffernan. McNeil had faced Buddy for years in practice and knew him as a finesse player, but few would believe that one-on-one experience meant anything at this point. In any case, holding the short-side position was the right strategy. O'Connor's shot hit the post, and the Canadiens were still alive.

A few second later, Charlie Rayner was in a similar situation with Elmer Lach breaking in on him. However, Lach came straight in and had more room to work with. He shifted to the left and Rayner went with him, leaving an opening on the right. Lach read the situation perfectly and fired a strike to the far right side. The puck hit just inside the metal and wheeled around the cage. The red light came on, and the Forum crowd exploded in jubilation. *Les Canadiens sont là.*

Elmer Ferguson recorded the post-game conversation in the Habs' dressing room. Lach claims that "Rayner stiffened on the play":

> When I swung in, he moved to meet me, but suddenly stiffened, as if he expected a high shot. Sort of tensed his upper-body. You don't have much time on these things. I just noted, in the flash of a part of a second that he had tensed himself for a high shot, so I shot low, and it whipped across his ankles. I guess I was lucky. Anybody's lucky to beat that Raynor [sic].[45]

The last comment is something that perhaps does not get mentioned enough. Fortune is often the deciding factor in a close competition. Writers and analysts are generally too quick to read motive and strategy into performances that owe themselves more to an unconscious action-reflex sequence. After congratulating Lach, the Canadiens were quick to praise McNeil's coolness in stopping O'Connor:

> Nearly everybody who came in told McNeil: "That was a great stop you made off Buddy O'Connor. That one saved the game." And to each of these, Gerry patiently responded: "I didn't stop that shot. Buddy tried to get me to move, but I didn't budge. So he had to throw it at the side he always shoots for. I had anchored myself to the post on that side, and his shot hit the post. I didn't stop it."[46]

Dick Irvin remarked that this was McNeil's first game action since March 15th, which made his accomplishment that much more impressive, since according to the Montreal coach's understanding of goalies: "Their reflexes are split second[;] they slow down in idleness."[47] There was a dressing room picture in the *Herald* the next day; it featured three smiling Canadiens, two of whom are in formal attire: a standing Kenny Reardon, the left sleeve tucked into the pocket as his shoulder is still in a harness, shakes hands with Elmer in the middle; to Elmer's immediate right sits Bill Durnan with his arm around the hero's back. One gets used to the postures of contentment in the sports section, but Durnan's smile in this picture sings out pure happiness and relief.[48] The Habs enjoy the victory while it lasts, but it didn't last long.

One of the delights of photography is coming across some unexpected detail that leads down a new path of discovery. A picture of McNeil stopping a shot from Dunc Fisher gives us a good wide-angle view of the MSG fans in the corner and behind the net (fig. 11). Prominent is a sign that reads "LANCIEN," a literal translation of which would be "the

Fig. 11 McNeil blocks a shot by Dunc Fisher at the MSG, probably sometime in 1950 when Jack Lancien (see sign) was in the Ranger lineup. Note the relaxed poses of the ushers in their white uniforms. (Photographer unknown. MSG 1950.) Copyright unknown.

former" or "the previous," but technically there should be an apostrophe after the L. Of course, it would be silly to expect correct grammar in such texts, but the lack of an apostrophe suggests that the sign may well have to do with a New York player by the name of "Jack Lancien," who got into a few Ranger games in the 1949-50 and 1950-51 seasons. Lancien came from Regina, and it is possible that either family or friends were in the MSG crowd that night and managed to hang the sign. This would have happened presumably in the spring or fall of 1950, when Lancien and McNeil happened to be playing against one another. Perhaps relatives or friends made the trip back east to see Jack in the Big Time. I cannot verify if this is so, but I like to think so and in this spirit would salute the efforts of all those who go to great lengths to see and support loved ones in such situations. Homemade signage conveys a sincerity, and often an originality (admittedly not in this instance), that completely outstrips the electronic imaging manufactured in most arenas today. For all its glamour, the life of the professional athlete usually involves leaving one's community and establishing a second home elsewhere. It can be lonely on the road, but change can also be exhilarating. Similarly, taking a picture or viewing one can yield unlooked-for surprises. We might be viewing McNeil taking a shot from Dunc Fisher of the Rangers, but we take more interest in noting the relaxed figures of the ushers sitting on the aisle steps in their white uniforms.

Unable to get to Rayner in Game Five, the Habs fell 3-0 and were eliminated.[49] Buddy O'Connor may have missed his chance, but he and the Rangers would have the last laugh. Still, it was a breakthrough game for Mac, who had demonstrated that he was ready for Big Time hockey. Not only does Elmer Ferguson give us the celebration in the dressing room after the Habs avoid being swept, he also relates the story of how Durnan passed the torch to McNeil.[50] It begins at Monday practice. Irvin noticed that his regular goalie hadn't gone out onto the ice; he knew that something was wrong but waited for Durnan to come to him. Durnan did.

"Dick, I think you should go back to the team of a month ago that only lost one in six."

Irvin answered that that was impossible, as Reardon was injured.

"It isn't Reardon," replied Durnan. "You need to make a change at Number One. I'm not playing up to the mark, Dick. My vision hasn't been really good since that accident in Chicago. Something has happened to my reflexes, to my nerves. It isn't fair to the boys that I should carry on. We've lost three straight and I don't feel . . . capable of going in there for a fourth game."

Irvin told him to sleep on it. The next day Durnan was there for the morning skate, but he wasn't getting dressed. Instead he sat in the anteroom smoking. He looked nervous, soaking wet. Irvin then told McNeil to get dressed to take a few shots because he would be starting in goal that night.

McNeil refused. "No, Mr. Irvin, I can't do that. I can't take Bill's job away from him. That wouldn't be right." Irvin then told McNeil exactly what had happened with Durnan. McNeil started to dress but quit again. "I can't do this. Bill is too fine a guy to have anyone push him out right in the Cup series. I won't do it."

Completely baffled, Irvin seemed lost for a solution. He went to Durnan. "Bill, it's up to you. You'll have to persuade Gerry to play in your place. I can't do it."

"Send him in here," Durnan replied.

McNeil went in and Irvin left the two alone for several minutes. They talked in low tones, and Irvin couldn't make out what was being said. Finally, he couldn't hold back any longer and entered the anteroom. "I'm darned if they weren't both crying. Tears were on both their faces."

At this point, McNeil did put on the rest of his equipment. As he finished, Frank Selke entered and talked to both goalies. According to Irvin, the coach and general manager then shed tears of their own, for they had seen how great Durnan was, and they knew that they had just witnessed the torch being passed.[51] What nobody in that room knew was how high McNeil would manage to hold it.

1   The story is related by Al Parsley, "Sidelights," *Herald, Montreal*, Mar. 6, 1950, 20.
2   Elmer Ferguson, "Plante Replaces Bill Durnan Against Hawks Tonight," *Herald, Montreal*, Mar. 4, 1950, 16.
3   Al Parsley, "Sidelights," *Herald, Montreal*, Mar. 6, 1950, 20.
4   Whitney Tower, "Crowd of 8,000 Sees Cincinnati Beaten, 3-0 by Indianapolis in Hockey Opener at Garden," *Indianapolis Enquirer*, Oct. 12, 1949, 28.
5   Whitney Tower, "He's Top Flight Now!" *Indianapolis Enquirer*, Dec. 31, 1949, 11.
6   Paul Bibeault played a total of 214 games in the NHL with Montreal, Toronto, Boston, and Chicago. He was always under contract with the Canadiens, who lent him to the other clubs. See Diamond, *Total Hockey*, 1609-10.
7   Michael J. Thomas, "Cincinnati Chills R.I. Reds, 3-2, as Goalie McNeil Stars," *The Providence Journal*, Jan. 11, 1950, 11.
8   The page is glued into a family scrapbook; the newspaper name is not visible. The picture appears on p. 4.
9   Jerry Nason, "Goal Tender's Job Toughest in Sports: Worse Than Catching," *Boston Daily Globe*, Apr. 7, 1953, 27.

10 "Durnan Gets Seven Stitches as Canadiens Lose to Hawks," *Herald, Montreal,* Mar. 3, 1950, 23, 25.

11 See Frank Orr, "NHL Trophies and Awards," in Diamond, *Total Hockey,* 99.

12 These details are recorded by Elmer Ferguson, "Plante Replaces Bill Durnan Against Hawks Tonight," *Herald, Montreal,* Mar. 4, 1950, 16.

13 See *Montréal-Matin,* Mar. 6, 1951, 23.

14 The details in this paragraph and the subsequent one are from Elmer Ferguson, "McNeil Steals Show as Canadiens Win," *Herald, Montreal,* Mar. 6, 1950, 19, 23.

15 The Rovers played at MSG III (also home to the NHL's Rangers from 1926–68) on 8th Avenue between 49th and 50th Streets. The interlocking schedule between the QSHL and the Eastern Amateur Hockey League also included the Boston Olympics, but these games were played at the Boston Arena (now the Matthews Arena).

16 For a description of a number of Original Six arenas and their distinguishing features, see Frank Orr, "The Other Guy's Barn," in Diamond, *Total Hockey,* 600–2.

17 For a classic study of the history of the sports spectator, see Allen Guttmann, *Sports Spectators* (New York: Columbia UP, 1986).

18 For information on the history of the Forum and its renovations, see Claude Mouton, *The Montreal Canadiens: A Hockey Dynasty* (Toronto: Van Nostrand Reinhold, 1980), 154–58; for specific descriptions of the building before its 1949 renovation, see Irvin, Habs: An Oral History, 44–45; and William Brown, *The Doug Harvey Story* (Montreal: Véhicule Press, 2002), 58, 65.

19 Many of Hy Peskin's photos can be viewed online.

20 For Leifer's comments on this and other memorable pictures, see Larry Berman and Chris Mahar, "An Interview with Neil Leifer," January 8, 2002. http://bermangraphics.com/press/leifer.htm. Leifer mentions both Hy Peskin and John Zimmerman as photographers whose work he emulated. The photo may be seen at http://www.neilleifer.com/ and in *Sports Illustrated 50: The Anniversary Book,* 66. The images, however, are reversed. Following comments by Leifer himself, I have based my description on the former.

21 MacAloon, "Olympic Games," in MacAloon, *Rite, Drama,* 241–80.

22 "The Robinsons and the La Mottas Go to a Fight," *Life,* Feb. 26, 1951, 19–23.

23 The photo (and all *SI* covers) can be viewed at SI.com. It appears in *Sports Illustrated,* "Special Issue—The Pictures: 50 Years of *SI* Photography," Apr. 26, 2004, 71. It is also reproduced in *Sports Illustrated 50: The Anniversary Book* (New York: Sports Illustrated Books, 2004), 52.

24 It is noteworthy that the two hockey pictures in *The Art of Sport: The Best of Reuters Sports Photography* (London: Reuters, 2003) are both of goaltenders (Tommy Salo, p. 45, and Curtis Joseph, p. 141); the second, featuring Curtis Joseph (then with the Toronto Maples Leafs) is also shot from this straight-on angle.

25 Richard B. Woodward, "Playing with Time," *SI,* Apr. 26, 2004, 78.

26 See Craig Monk, "When Eustace Tilley Came to Madison Square Garden: Professional Hockey and the Editorial Policy of *The New Yorker* in the 1920s and 1930s," *American Periodicals: A Journal of History, Criticism, and Bibliography* 15, no. 2 (2005): 178–95.

27 There were twelve hockey stories in *Life* between 1940 and 1972, three of which dealt with goaltending: "Ace hockey goalie" (Feb. 26, 1940), "Greatest Goalie— Terry Sawchuk" (Feb. 18, 1952), and "Hockey Goalies" (Mar. 4, 1966). Hockey subjects appeared on the cover of *SI* eighty-three times in the first fifty years of publication (1954–2004); see *Sports Illustrated 50,* 263.

28 See "Professional Hockey" in Gene Brown, ed., *The New York Times Encyclopedia of Sports,* vol. 8 (New York: Arno Press, 1979), 100–207, 211–15.

29 See "Canadiens Tie Wings Again, Hold Third by One Point," *Herald, Montreal,* Mar. 7, 1950, 19.

30 "Rangers Bid Tonight To Re-take Third Place," *Herald, Montreal,* Mar. 8, 1950, 19.

31 Elmer Ferguson, "Canucks Tie (17) Leafs, Rangers Gain Ground," *Herald, Montreal,* Mar. 10, 1950, 23.

32 Ibid.

33 See Fred Davis, *Yearning for Yesterday: A Sociology of Nostalgia* (New York: Free Press, 1979), 15–18, 128.

34 Al Parsley, "Richard, Flaman Brawl: McNeil's First Shutout," *Herald, Montreal,* Mar. 13, 1950, 19, 22.

35 For a brief description of the train travel by NHL teams during this era, see Don O'Hanley, "From Steel Rails to Jet Trails," in Diamond, *Total Hockey,* 87–88.

36 "Canucks Now in Third Spot; Score 10 Goals in 2 Games," *Herald, Montreal,* Mar. 13, 1950, 19.

37 "Champion Wings Meet Habs Again," *Herald, Montreal,* Mar. 16, 1950, 21.

38 "McNeil To Stay With Canucks," *Herald, Montreal,* Mar. 17, 1950, 24.

39 "Hab Sub Outdoes Old Master! Gerry McNeil in Nets for Durnan Stingy on Goals," *Hockey News,* Mar. 18, 1950, 1, 2.

40 "National League," *Hockey News,* Mar. 18, 1950, 9. Another picture of McNeil with his arm around a fellow Mohawk call-up, Bert Hirschfeld, appears on p. 9. In his *THN* column "Passing the Puck," Ken McKenzie also commented that McNeil "played exceptionally well" (p. 4).

41 "Dislocated Shoulder Ends Ken for Season," *Herald, Montreal,* Apr. 3, 1950, 21, 27.

42 See "Extra Referee in Leaf-Wing Game," *Herald, Montreal,* Apr. 1, 1950, 16.

43 Ferguson, "Gist and Jest," *Herald, Montreal,* Apr. 4, 1950, 19.

44 The details in this paragraph and the subsequent one are from Elmer Ferguson, "Lach Scores in Overtime, Keeps Habs in Cup Fight," *Herald, Montreal,* Apr. 5, 1950, 21, 23.

45 Quoted by Ferguson, "Gist and Jest," *Herald, Montreal,* Apr. 5, 1950, 21.

46 Conversation quoted by Ferguson, "Gist and Jest," *Herald, Montreal,* Apr. 5, 1950, 21.

47 Quoted by Ferguson, "Gist and Jest," *Herald, Montreal,* Apr. 5, 1950, 21.

48 Arless photo, *Herald, Montreal,* Apr. 5, 1950, 23.

49 "Canucks Face Shake-up after Loss to Rangers," *Herald, Montreal,* Apr. 8, 1950, 16.

50 Ferguson, "Gist and Jest," *Herald, Montreal,* Apr. 6, 1950, 29. Elmer Ferguson ranks as one of hockey's first, and perhaps best, reporters, having covered the NHL since just after WWI. His mode of fictionalizing conversations was generally accepted as a journalistic norm before radio and television interviews became common.

51 This anecdote is repeated in a number of places. Dick Irvin, Jr., gives the perspective of his father in *Now Back to You Dick: Two Lifetimes in Hockey* (Toronto: McClelland and Stewart, 1988), 53.

3 The Magician

MCNEIL PLAYED EVERY MINUTE FOR THE CANADIENS IN 1950-51. It was anything but an easy streak. In December, Ken McKenzie of *The Hockey News* reported that McNeil was in danger of losing some of his teeth after being hit in the face during the warm-up in Boston.[1] Vern Kaiser took the first shot and knocked the rookie unconscious. He was carried off the ice as the fans were arriving at the Garden but came to in time for the opening faceoff. Although Montreal did not have a winning season (managing only twenty-five wins versus thirty losses), the young goalie posted a respectable 2.97 GAA with 6 shutouts. Nevertheless, there were doubts about his holding down one of the six Big Time goalie positions; his small size was consistently raised as a liability which he could never overcome.

The Canadiens finished third with 65 points, well back of the still dominant Red Wings, who clinched first on March 17th with 101 points. The next day *The Detroit News* featured a photo with Tommy Ivan, Gordie Howe, Terry Sawchuk, and Jack Adams all standing around the Prince of Wales Trophy (awarded to the team that wins the league championship) and the Stanley Cup.[2] Having won both in 1950 and looking to repeat the feat with another successful run in '51, Detroit had every reason to be confident. There was no question that with the Production Line they had the offensive clout, and with Sawchuk coming within one goal of winning the Vezina, they could easily match any team on defence. Add to this the fact that the final game of the season against Montreal, their first-round opponent, ended in a 5-0 victory for the Red Wings, and one can easily understand why expectations in Detroit were high.[3]

However, it was not the perfect ending to the season. Despite the shutout, Sawchuk had still lost the Vezina to Al Rollins of Toronto by one goal on the last weekend. The Red Wings had given up three goals to Toronto's one on Saturday night; when both Sawchuk and Rollins registered shutouts on Sunday, the latter kept his one-goal lead. Irvin may have been playing mind games when he told the Detroit press that he felt the Wings had let their rookie goalie down, that the press made too much about four or five top stars, and that Detroit lacked team spirit.[4] He went on to say that Toronto was a more cohesive unit and maybe a better Cup choice. While Detroit had to like their chances, they weren't complacent; it was decided that the team would stay together in Toledo for their home playoff games in order to be isolated and undistracted. The Canadiens, by contrast, would stay in their usual Detroit home, the Leland Hotel, located downtown.[5] McNeil recalled the spectacular lobby and marble floors, and the pleasure his teammates took in hanging out in the lobby and joking with one another.

As mentioned earlier, Mac was known as a prankster. Perhaps that is how he coped with the pressure. He once went to the front desk of the hotel claiming to be Skippy Burchell (an old friend who was twice called up to the Canadiens for a couple of games). "I'm on a special medication," he told the clerk. "Could you please call my room every hour on the hour to remind me to take my pill? I'll probably be quite angry when you wake me up, but it's important that I take my pill, so just keep calling." The next day Burchell was exhausted at a team meeting. When the rest of the guys started teasing him ("Skippy, what's the matter? Didn't you sleep last night?") he got angry but eventually joined in the laughter himself. Skippy and Mac would both enjoy telling the story for years afterwards. Another time, Mac slipped a box of pink dye into the underwear wash. However, he forgot to include his own pair, so when the guys were handed their "pinks" before the next game it was clear who the culprit was. Anything to break the tension.

Detroit came out strong in the opening game, and Montreal seemed to fall back into a defensive posture. Howe, taking a long rebound, backhanded the puck into a tiny opening and gave the Red Wings the lead. Telenews footage of the goal shows McNeil out of position after having gone down to stop a shot by Abel.[6] Less than two minutes later, Bouchard scored on a long drive from the corner that somehow made its way through a crowd and looped over the Detroit goalie's shoulder; it turned out to be the only official Montreal shot of the entire period. Hence, while McNeil was credited with 14 first-period saves, Sawchuk didn't have any.[7] There was a dramatic shift in momentum in the second period when the Canadiens came to life and the game suddenly got physical. Referee Bill Chadwick made few penalty calls, but he and his linesmen were quick to step in and break up any scuffles. He was also at the centre of a rather comic moment when, in an attempt to get out of the play, he jumped up on the boards and ended up going right over into the first row of seats. Play continued until Chadwick stood up among the spectators and blew his whistle.[8] It became obvious that a number of "extra" whistles could be heard, and Clarence Campbell,

THE MAGICIAN

in attendance for the league, criticized this practice among Detroit fans who wanted to see penalties called whenever one of their own went down. Later Chadwick called penalties on Richard and Lindsay, and the twosome were still in the box at the beginning of the third when Howe carried the puck in and left it for Abel who, in turn, made a nice pass to Reise. The defenceman skated down the centre and beat McNeil from twenty feet out. The Olympia exploded into cheering. Just after the nine-minute mark, Goldham blocked a shot from Richard, but Olmstead was there to fire the rebound into the top corner. Richard had a chance to win the game in regulation time, but Sawchuk made a sensational glove save.[9]

The first overtime period saw both teams with excellent chances to win the game. Sawchuk robbed Richard again when the latter stole the puck from Marcel Pronovost and skated right in on the Detroit net. Then Bud Macpherson shot through a maze of players from the blue line and again Sawchuk stopped the puck sharply. At the other end, Howe took a pass from Red Kelly just inside the blue line and streaked in on McNeil.[10] McNeil would later describe to Elmer Ferguson how he sensed that Howe wanted him to move, how he held his position and made a pad save.[11] It was the play that the Habs goalie singled out later as giving him the biggest thrill of the game, for he remembered thinking that it helped challenge the opinion that Howe was a better player than Richard. He then snagged a fifteen-foot shot by Lindsay. The game became a battle of the netminders. Who would make the fatal mistake or get beat?

There is a photo of my father kicking out a shot by Howe that might well be the save he mentioned to Elmer Ferguson (see fig. 12). He was obviously proud of it, because I remember it as the one hockey picture that my father made sure to hang in some prominent position in the house. The image lurked in the background of my childhood. Many times as a youngster, and then even later when I was older, I paused to inspect the expressions it featured. On the left is my father with his familiar panicky expression, foreboding some disaster. That look I knew so well whenever he noticed that I, and years later my children, had left a glass of milk too close to the table's edge. "That's going to get knocked over. I can see it coming." (My father sometimes spoke as if he had

Next pages
Fig. 12 Gerry McNeil kicks out a shot by Gordie Howe. Detroit Olympia, early 1950s. (Photo by James "Scotty" Kilpatrick. *Gazette* [Montreal], May 7, 2002, E3; and *Gazette* [Montreal], Mar. 27, 2004, A2.) Copyright unknown.

some kind of extrasensory power, especially when it came to household disasters. In any case, the ability to "see it coming" was not a bad thing for somebody whose major life occupation was goaltending.) On the right in the photo is Gordie Howe, staring ahead in sheer awe at the goalie thwarting his effort. Howe also looks so incredibly young; my father, not so much young as frazzled. In the background between the two adversaries, one can see the expressions of a number of fans. There is a woman who appears behind my father; she looks as though she could be a little bored with what's going on in front of her, either that or she just isn't following the play. Another man sits in the middle of the principal adversaries; he leans forward, enthralled by the action.

The photo had to have been taken near the beginning of a period because the surface is still quite shiny. This condition is responsible for another special feature, which is the reflection of the end red line painted on the boards which just happens to run across the ice dividing the space between the shooter and the goalie (the actual red line painted under the ice is there on the left but not visible); this division lends the scene a mano-a-mano quality. The puck is in clear view in the centre, having just been kicked out by my father's right pad. A definite point of aesthetic distinction about the sports photo is the importance of having the puck or ball in the frame. It gives meaning to the bodies in motion, a clue as to what has just happened or is about to happen.[12]

So much nostalgic history may be read in the sticks alone. Howe's, from which the shot obviously originated, reveals a perfectly straight blade, emblematic of a simpler era when equipment was less sophisticated and team allegiance more pronounced. It cuts diagonally across his half of the picture from the middle right to the lower left and is offset by the goalie's stick on which one can tease out the words "Raymond Hardware" (the main supplier of sticks in Quebec), which crosses the left half of the picture, centre to bottom right.[13] So the game was played by our ancestors—the sticks as bygone as everything else in the frame.

None of these details, of course, was composed by the photographer, James "Scotty" Kilpatrick of *The Detroit News*. Kilpatrick had made a name for himself when in May 1937 he managed to get some shots of a fight between striking auto workers and management-hired security guards. The incident, known as the Battle of the Overpass, ranks as a significant event in the labour history of the United States, and, on the basis of Kilpatrick's photos, the Pulitzer Prize Committee decided to institute an award for photography.[14] The only thing one can say about Kilpatrick is that he knew where to position himself and he got results.

THE MAGICIAN

Cultural context means everything in how a photo is deemed significant. The best known mano-a-mano (or defeat-victory) image is, of course, Neil Leifer's shot of Ali standing over a prone Sonny Liston and taunting the older fighter to get back up. *SI* voted it the sports photo of the century,[15] and Leifer himself, who personally thought that his shot of Ali vs. Williams was technically better (see Chapter 2), understood why. He pointed to the fact that the photo didn't make the cover of *SI* at the time, only when it was selected in 1999; instead, the magazine chose a shot that featured both fighters still on their feet.[16] The Ali vs. Liston photo has grown with time to represent an iconographic moment not just in Ali's career or the history of sports, but in the history of the civil rights movement in the United States.[17] Leifer was well aware that luck has to co-operate for composition elements to come together in an aesthetically pleasing fashion—all the photographer does is make the most of fortuitous opportunities. Perfectly visible between Ali's legs is the face of the other *SI* photographer, Herbie Scharfman, helplessly positioned to see little else but Ali's back. (But even this combined sense of achievement and failure was part of the overall successful *SI* strategy to ensure that Leifer and Scharfman were on opposite sides in order to maximize the chance of getting a good shot.)

What all these photos have is a timeliness about the drama depicted. In some cases, photographers can anticipate where the opportunity will be to capture this timeliness, and in others, it is simply fortuitous. Moreover, as Leifer's famous photo demonstrates, just as individual moments in a game must co-operate to make a particular photograph significant (i.e., the "turning point"), so events over a much longer period of time must co-operate to make a single game or match significant. If one accepts that the main purpose of competitive sport is to produce this liminal or threshold moment when victory and defeat are determined, then it is possible to associate this purpose with another theoretical aspect of the spectacle. Victor Turner, a cultural anthropologist, pointed to the liminal and ritualistic in human activity (including sport) and argued that performances, such as the singing of the national anthem, both reflect the social system and offer a possible critique of it.[18] Have the elaborate laser, smoke, and video pre-game shows gone so far as to be self-parody? Perhaps, but what always sustains our interest—now more than ever, with the highlight cable channels repeating the same video clips every hour—is the scoring play deemed to be decisive in the outcome of the game. Sports photography loves to depict "the thrill of victory and the agony of defeat," sometimes together and sometimes in isolation.

Kilpatrick's photo of my father kicking out a shot by Howe is devoid of any cultural significance beyond familial history, but that it was my father's favourite picture and the one that always hung somewhere in the house does hint at why a particular image has particular meaning. Moreover, there are greater technical issues involved. The clarity of some of the faces in the crowd is especially noteworthy, and I am forever amazed at being able to see both the hinges in the door along the boards and the knit in my father's socks. Sports photographers of this era were still using large-format cameras, the most popular being the Speed Graphic.[19] Because of the large negative size ($4'' \times 5''$) and the use of strategically mounted strobe lights, shots taken with a Speed Graphic tended to capture a richer depth of field and far more detail (approximately thirteen times) than that of a 35-mm picture.[20] With the subsequent widespread use of 35-mm and the telephoto lens, we still have sharp action shots, but content is sacrificed for convenience: we get a slice of the action but little else.

Sports photography of the 1940s and 1950s includes the crowd as a subject in a way that was subsequently lost for decades, or at least restricted to a few special shots in *SI*. I am not talking about the deliberate crowd-as-primary-subject found in Hy Peskin's work (see Chapter 2), but as a peripheral inclusion. Technological advances have now brought detail and depth of field back; the megapixel levels and options on digital cameras provide rich creative capabilities. As for the moving images, here too we now have high-definition (HD) detail and sharpness, not to mention more possible angles with net- and cable-cams. What is utterly different is that a photographer can easily take thousands of shots of any one event; just aim and hold a finger on the shutter. In the 1950s era, the norm was for a photographer to return from a game with maybe a dozen shots. The technology just didn't allow for much more than that. Working with these limitations, photographers learned to be selective when it came to quality shots. Finally, as permanent records the photos themselves took on a sense of importance that came from the simple fact that there weren't many of them—that and the fact that film footage was extremely rare. We still feel this importance in 2015; we marvel at this shot of Gordie Howe in a way that we don't for a similar shot of a star player today.

Kilpatrick was in the exact same location that he was for the picture he got of McNeil and Howe when he captured Terry Sawchuk going down to smother the puck, an image that *Life* magazine used in its profile of the Red Wing goalie.[21] How my father came to possess his Kilpatrick photos remains a mystery (he couldn't recall), but it is likely that Kilpatrick must have done what a number of photographers did at the time—given prints of his photos to the people captured in them. What makes his prints special is their size. The McNeil and Howe shot is one of two 12″ × 9½″ glossies; another goalmouth shot featuring Butch Bouchard as well as my father measures 14″ × 11″ (see fig. 22). Most press prints that I have seen from the 1940s and '50s are 8″ × 10″ or smaller. Kilpatrick used special film techniques to enlarge his photos. It may well be that the photos were done for a December 23, 1950, issue of *The Hockey News.* Although the five-column photograph that was used on the front page appears without a credit line, it depicts another shot on McNeil by the Red Wings at the Olympia, and one of my father's glossies had "5 col cut The Hockey News" scribbled on the back. Another possibility is that it was one of a group that was used in a special feature on my father that appeared in the weekly magazine *The Standard.*[22]

Retired photographer Dick Van Nostrand, who remembers talking with Kilpatrick in the 1960s, writes that he "rigged Olympia Stadium with some of the first strobe lights and had them controlled by switches so he could change lighting effects. He also experimented with developer and film combinations so he could enlarge small sections of the negative shot with Hasselblad and Rollei cameras and make nearly grain-free enlargements. As a teenager I fought my dad for the paper so that I could see his photos."[23] Although his name might not be as well known among hockey historians as David Bier and Roger Saint-Jean (Montreal) or Lou Turofsky and Harold Barkley (Toronto), Kilpatrick was at the top of the sports scene in Detroit and his work can be compared to that of David Klutho (*SI*) today.

We now tend to dwell on the video replay of a sporting event, for it is the sequence of action that really matters or seems to reproduce reality. The frozen still is anomalous insofar as life never stops; perhaps it would be more accurate to say miraculous: to hit the pause button on reality and then to scrutinize that split second moment with all the leisure we want—not exactly a hundred years for each player, to paraphrase Marvell, but at least a half century, as far as our cultural memory of 1950 is concerned. I exaggerate, of course, but the details in Kilpatrick's image of Howe and my father have slowly entered my mind over the years and now seem permanently fixed. Look at the photo and then watch the moving image at regular speed. In time, the former is almost the equivalent to the molecular structure of space—a visual image so precise, so short that the natural eye never sees it except in the photo. In this respect, we may recognize the otherworldliness or even magical quality of photography over video.

Back at the Olympia at the end of the second overtime period, Irvin ordered his players to change into dry underwear, which sounds like a good idea until you consider the time and effort required.[24] Since goalies had more equipment to remove, McNeil was excused. It will shock some readers to know that the usual between-period ritual that my father would later remember was having a cigarette. As the goalie, he was the only player allowed to go into the anteroom off the main dressing room at the Forum to find some relief with a smoke. The other players would sneak in because they knew they could count on Mac to give them a few puffs. Once in a while Irvin would march into the dressing room to give the squad directions, only to find most of the guys crammed in with McNeil.

As the players hurried to go back out, Butch Bouchard said that he had seen in a crystal ball that Richard was going to get the winner.[25] At first his prediction seemed doubtful, as Detroit regained control in overtime periods two and three, outshooting their opponents 14 to 6 and 13 to 7 respectively. McNeil made a great save on Abel's try right at the crease. He then used his body to stop Lindsay, who had left Tom Johnson and Butch Bouchard sprawling on the ice before breaking in alone. *The Detroit News* published a picture of Lindsay going airborne over McNeil's body, which stretches across the crease.[26] Roy Rash took the same picture from the reverse angle getting Lindsay from the front, and it appeared in *The Standard* (see fig. 13).[27] Rash's photo is the better of the two, especially for how it features Lindsay in a classic pose sailing at least a foot off of the ice. One can easily read the Northland pro label on his stick as the forward looks back to find the puck, and the goalmouth focus gives it a definite Kilpatrick look. Montreal's best chances came from Ken Mosdell, who seized upon a Richard rebound only to fire it high, and MacKay's breakaway, which was stopped by Sawchuk. The game was now beyond a goaltending contest; it started to take on a sense of eternal life and became a bizarre spectacle of endurance. People were now leaving the Olympia or turning off their radios at home.

A minute into the fourth overtime period, Richard stripped the puck from the Red Wing defenceman Red Kelly and broke toward the Detroit net. Sawchuk made the mistake of going down before the shot; Richard had a split second to register the move and fire high over the goalie's shoulder. The puck bulges the mesh—finally, game over, at 1:12 AM![28] The third longest game to that point in NHL history. The existing footage of the play catches only the moment immediately after the goal. Richard has already pivoted and glides backwards, arms outstretched in victory. A second later he is mobbed by teammates.

THE MAGICIAN

Fig. 13 Ted Lindsay goes airborne over McNeil, who stops the puck to prolong the overtime. Detroit Olympia, March 28, 1951. (Photo by Roy Rash. *Standard* [Montreal], Mar. 30, 1951, 9.) Copyright unknown.

The Sawchuk-McNeil duel in Game One of Series A was definitely a classic, and no doubt McNeil must have felt a great deal of satisfaction knowing that he had bested Detroit's sensational rookie. Paul Chandler of *The Detroit News* attributed the Montreal victory to their goalie who, prior to the game, was given little respect from the Detroit press ("least valuable in the entire National Hockey League").[29] The Montreal goalie had gotten off to a slow start at the beginning of the season, and this negative initial impression followed him throughout the regular campaign. At any rate, it was after the heroics of Game One that Chandler nicknamed McNeil the Magician.[30] The fact is that *Montreal Star* reporter Baz O'Meara had referred to the "McNeil magic" some months before, when the little netminder posted his first shutout of the year (a 4–0 revenge blanking of the Rangers, who had eliminated the Canadiens from Stanley Cup play the previous spring).[31] It was his small size that made the association appropriate. The larger the body the less need for reflex action to get in front of the puck. It was McNeil's lightning-fast reactions and an instinct about where to position himself when he couldn't see the puck that gave his performance a sense of the paranormal or of the "unseen hand."[32] Someone in the press box had counted 16 screened shots on the Montreal goalie, all of which in a miraculous fashion he had blocked.[33] (Needless to say, it would have been very difficult to determine a screened shot from the perspective of the press box.) A study of the existing footage of his performances reveals that McNeil was most definitely a stand-up goalie, at least as far as the first shot is concerned.[34] However, if the situation required it, he would dive face-first into the fray. His movements, while spectacularly fast, were also measured; he consistently positioned his body to cut down the angles, to reduce the distance he must move.

Another characteristic that O'Meara commented on was his nervous disposition. McNeil was apparently known as "Jittery Gerry… a worrier who gets tense and taut before each game."[35] Irvin claimed to have noticed this, and a tendency to brood, which gave the Canadiens coach the idea of rooming with his goalie for the playoffs. It is hard to think that this move would have had a calming effect on Mac (especially if Irvin happened to be keeping some prized pigeons in the room), as Mac was used to sharing quarters with his old Royals friend Floyd Curry. It did, however, give Irvin a chance to get to know his goalie better, and one thing he did discover was that McNeil seemed concerned about recognition. Irvin would tell Dink Carroll of *The Gazette* that when the Canadiens defeated the Rangers 6–3 earlier in the season, McNeil felt slighted by the press, who commented that the home team would have scored more had it not been for Rayner's spectacular play in the Rangers' net. He thought he had saved "some tough ones" and that Rayner had fanned at least three times: "What do you have to do to get a little recognition anyway?"[36] Well, McNeil certainly could not complain that he wasn't getting recognized now. Whether from Montreal or Detroit, the press was lavish in its praise of the Habs' goalie.

Fig. 14 "Clipping Detroit's Wings." (Cartoon by John Collins. *Gazette* [Montreal], Mar. 29, 1951, 18.) Reproduced by permission of *The Gazette* / Postmedia Network.

The first John Collins cartoon (see fig. 14) about the series appeared in *The Gazette* March 29th. It features an image of McNeil, bird (i.e., Red Wing) in one hand, a pair of scissors in the other. In the middle left-hand side is a man half asleep next to a radio: "Must be time for breakfast." One of the text balloons reads: "Rollins and Sawchuk got all the headlines all season, but Gerry came through when the chips were down."[37] This comparison was echoed by Jack Adams, the Detroit general manager: "Why is there so much argument about who is entitled to the Vezina Trophy, between Sawchuk and Rollins?... they're arguing about the wrong guy... McNeil is great." One has to go to extraordinary lengths to earn such compliments from those against whom one competes. Adams summed up his assessment: "It was like running into one-hit pitching your first time out.... The greatest goal-keeping this team has ever faced."[38] *The Detroit News* recorded that McNeil made 56 saves to Sawchuk's 40.[39] (Camil "Cammy" DesRoches, the Canadiens' publicity man, revised this shot-count, claiming that it was more like McNeil 69, Sawchuk 49.[40]) Trying to explain their lack of success, some Detroit players emphasized the good fortune of the Montreal goalie. Ted Lindsay referred to him as "That lucky stiff, if he fell down the sewer he'd probably catch a fish."[41] Marty Pavelich said, "He won't play that kind of game again";[42] it was a comment that came back to haunt him.

While Dick Irvin didn't want to single out any individual Habs, O'Meara claimed that "tears of joy were streaming down his face," as he congratulated his new roomie. Irvin's official line still emphasized team spirit—that his club had no less than ten first-year players. In addition to McNeil, there were Paul Meger, Boom Boom Geoffrion, Tom Johnson, Sid McNabney, Paul Masnick, Bud MacPherson, Vern Kaiser, Claude Robert, and Ross Lowe. A group of reporters milled about Richard in the dressing room; he shrugged off their praise and nodded toward McNeil: "Never mind me.... Congratulate that little guy over there. The kid is the one. I got a break."[43]

As for McNeil, he reminded people that only a week earlier he had read in a newspaper that he was going to be traded to Chicago next year.[44] Before the game Elmer Ferguson asked the Black Hawks president and former goalie, Bill Tobin, if there was any truth to the rumour that the Canadiens would be trading for the veteran netminder Harry Lumley. "No, and why should there be?... in my opinion [the] Canadiens have the greatest potential goaler in the person of McNeil."[45] Marshall Dann apparently commented that McNeil's work was the best in playoff history. Baz O'Meara made a more reasonable claim in writing that the game had been the finest in the young goalie's career, amateur or pro. However, sensing an historical significance to the event, he would also suggest that Game One resembled the night in 1935 when Alex Connell of the Maroons stopped a barrage of shots from the Leafs, Charlie Conacher in particular.[46]

Needless to say, the early dawn light was visible as the players took cabs down Grand River back to the Leland. Doug Harvey broke everybody up when he turned to Irvin, "What time this morning coach, for practise?"[47] The game and post-game press scrums had only raised their adrenalin, and so a group played gin rummy until 8 AM.

That day a Detroit sports editor, Bob Murphy, phoned to get McNeil on his television show. The goalie tried to put Murphy off, claiming that he didn't know what his schedule was. Murphy found his non-committal attitude strange, as most American athletes jumped at such offers. According to Elmer Ferguson, a third party called Murphy back, "I'm here with Gerry McNeil, and he says he'll go on the television show only if he can have his friend Floyd Curry go on with him."[48] Murphy agreed, and so Mac made his first television appearance with "Busher." The Canadiens goalie explained to Dink Carroll, "I need some help out there in front of me all the time."[49]

One game does not determine the momentum of a best-of-seven series, and the Detroit players and press still had reason to be confident about their ability to prevail. Stay the course seemed to be the thinking in the Red Wing camp. McNeil's performance in Game One, while praised in the papers on Wednesday, was characterized as "unconscious" (i.e., read "lucky") on Thursday. *The Detroit News* ran a story about McNeil's weaknesses: one, he had slow reactions and played most shots from a standing position (a weakness?); and two, he was awkward on high shots.[50] The same article made reference to the goalie's successful debut at the Olympia the previous spring and conceded that none of the aforementioned weaknesses were present Tuesday night. Nevertheless, the thinking was that the team with the dominant Production Line would break through; there was no reason to panic. Meanwhile, McNeil must have felt a tremendous boost from that first game. It was a complete turn-around from the final season contest in which Detroit scored five times and muzzled the Canadiens' attack. If he felt he had done well enough to merit respect, then he also knew that the job wasn't complete, that things could shift quite quickly. He could still be the goat; there was no release from the pressure of the situation, and the situation was now beyond his control. He would have to play Game Two and play well to be able to hold his head up among his teammates.

The team bonded together during the road trips. Harvey was responsible for doling out expense money to the rest of the guys; my father remembered a $7 per diem, which would have to include cabs as well as food. If a group of players went out together, the bill would be divided evenly no matter what individuals had ordered. "It probably wasn't the best system," McNeil said years later, "because it encouraged you to order 'big.' You were going to have to pay anyway." Nevertheless, it was strictly adhered to, and the players felt like they belonged to one big family. This strong sense of club loyalty eroded years later with free agency and the Players Association.

However, the downside was an intractable animosity between teams and players: the Canadiens and Detroit, Richard and Lindsay. The trains that ran back and forth from Montreal and Detroit would carefully make sure that each team's car was separated by the dining car, and that each team had their own schedule for using the dining car. My father often spoke about the police who would be at Westmount Station (not far from the Forum) in Montreal after a Saturday night game to ensure that the teams boarded without incident. Otherwise, the risk of an all-out donnybrook was very real.

It is ironic that Ted Lindsay was a target for other teams, since he would be so instrumental in efforts to establish an association of NHL players. In retrospect, other players from this era admired Lindsay for being bold enough to challenge team owners. I once heard these subjects being discussed by my father and some of his hockey pals, and they brought up the tendency of current NHL players to fraternize in the off season. "Can you imagine the Rocket and Lindsay working at the same hockey school?" There was a slight pause as an image formed in everybody's mind; then howls of laughter filled the room.

For a goalie who played only four seasons in the NHL, McNeil had many "dream" games. One of them was played on Thursday, March 29, 1951. A number of Red Wing fans crowded outside their team's dressing room to cheer their walk to the ice. The teams were apparently slow to warm up, perhaps fatigued from two nights previously. However, when they did "find their legs," the game became as wide open as the best of the play two nights before.[51] Richard was derisively cheered as he touched the puck for the first time, and when Kelly and Reise knocked him flying, the cheering went up several decibels. Howe got off a twenty-five-foot blazer that beat McNeil but not the goalpost. At the beginning of the second, George Gee moved in close on McNeil twice, but the Canadiens netminder was brilliant on both attempts. Apparently Montreal's best scoring chance to this point in the game came from one Sid McNabney; Sawchuk handled his drive easily.

From here on the game was once again a duel between the two goalies. The best offensive chances came on the power play. First Detroit. Skov missed an open corner, Howe's shot was blocked, Abel was robbed on the doorstep, then Howe shot over the crossbar. Then Montreal. Curry stole the puck from Howe and got a breakaway only to be pulled down by Lindsay—a "good" penalty if ever there was one. With Lindsay penalized again, Montreal had great opportunities, but Sawchuk pulled off unbelievable stops on Richard, Lach, and Olmstead. At the end of regulation time, McNeil had made 25 saves to

Sawchuk's 21. The muggy conditions combined with the crowd and length of the game produced a slight fog over the ice.[52] This was common enough when arenas were not air-conditioned, and the play-offs stretched into the warming weeks of spring.

Howe had three excellent chances early in the first overtime, but McNeil met the challenge each time. Abel had an opportunity to put away the rebound on Howe's third try, but again Mac the Magician got a pad on the puck, which danced crazily in the crease before being swatted away by a Montreal defender. At the other end, Richard looked to repeat his game-winning play of Game One when he beat two men and broke in on Sawchuk. Suddenly Reise made a terrific defensive play by diving just at the right moment to poke the puck away.

When the second overtime started, it seemed as if the Olympia crowd could sense imminent victory. Nobody was leaving as was the case in the first game. It looked for a moment that their intuition was correct. Abel and Stewart both had chances to finish the game, but McNeil somehow thwarted their efforts. Then Leo Reise looked like he would be the hero in a mad scramble at the net, but the puck stayed out. Meanwhile Sawchuk worked some magic of his own by stopping Paul Masnick on a pair of chances. At the period's end, Howe and Harvey were sent off for roughing.[53]

Many players can remember being in an overtime marathon, but few could say that they played in two consecutive ones. Not only were both teams dead tired, their equipment was soaking wet, making it heavier. This was particularly true of leather-felt goalie pads that never completely dried out between October and April. That the Olympia clock had mysteriously stopped working in the very first period (officials were forced to make use of a stopwatch[54]) seemed an eerie symbol of the athletic contest itself being frozen in time.

The third overtime period began. The play was in the Montreal zone and the Canadiens "reversed" the puck, that is moved it up the opposite side from where everybody seemed to be playing. According to Billy Reay, Bud Macpherson passed it to him just before the blue line.[55] Reay spotted Reise covering Olmstead on the left wing, so he decided to gain the neutral zone himself. As Red Kelly, the Detroit defenceman, moved to the middle to challenge Reay, Richard put on a burst of speed and got behind Marty Pavelich. Reay faked a pass to draw Kelly into a blocking posture and then sent the real thing to his right winger, who was now in the clear. Richard, a left shot playing the right side, claimed that he carried the puck for only about five feet before releasing a backhand shot to the far corner. He also claimed that he wanted to keep the puck

on the ice, but it had risen about five inches.[56] Another account suggested that the puck never left the ice.[57] In any case, Sawchuk seemed
frozen for a second. Perhaps he wasn't expecting a backhand; perhaps
fatigue had momentarily robbed him of his reflexes. The puck went in
the goal into the far corner. Richard had done it again. The Olympia
crowd was stunned, while the listening radio audience back in Montreal could hardly believe their ears. Was it possible? The Canadiens up
2–0 coming back to Montreal? Celebrating began, prematurely.

There have been a number of left-hand shots who played the right
wing, but none so famously as Richard. In the 2005 feature film *The
Rocket,* there is a scene in which actor Roy Dupuis is depicted practising his backhand—the lone player on the ice—by firing a number of
pucks into an open net. Richard's special dedication was something
my father, who practised with the Habs all through the '40s, remembers
well. To be at all effective playing the "off wing,"[58] hockey players must
develop their backhands to the point where they are as comfortable
in that position as they are on the forehand. The only way to achieve
this is to practise the moves (shooting and handling the puck) over and
over again. What a player gains by playing the off wing is a much better
angle at the net on the forehand—an advantage that can only be realized when one has a strong backhand.

As anybody involved in sport knows, the pure joy of winning is most
intense right after the competition ends. The visitors' dressing room
at the Olympia did not have a crowd of fans outside, but it did have a
number of reporters and photographers inside. A couple of shots were
taken of the two Canadiens players who were at the centre of the team's
success in Detroit: Maurice Richard and Gerry McNeil. The photo reproduced as figure 15 appeared in *The Montreal Star.*[59] The two men
are seated, locked in a half embrace; expressions of content parallel
the matching Canadiens insignias. For a second or two, the victory
belongs to them. They look at each other, connecting in their mutual
satisfaction and joy as only teammates who have known each other for
some time can connect. McNeil bursts with a boyish smile; Richard,
the senior, has his hand on McNeil's head and gives his goalie a look
of approval, as if to say, "if it weren't for you, I would never have had
the chance." The twosome would go on to win and lose Stanley Cups
together, but this moment of mutual achievement against the league's
top team would be shared only once.

Richard and McNeil were together for a less pleasant incident
earlier that year. The Canadiens had just arrived in New York after having played in Montreal the night before. In that game referee Hugh

THE MAGICIAN

Fig. 15 Gerry McNeil and Maurice Richard after winning Game Two of the 1951 Semifinal in the fourth overtime period. Detroit Olympia, March 30, 1951. (Photographer unknown. *Montreal Star*, Mar. 31, 1951, 44; and Detroit News, Mar. 30, 1951, 57.) Copyright unknown.

McLean had given Richard a game misconduct when the Canadiens star wouldn't quit protesting the lack of calls. (The Rocket had felt that the opposition was getting away with all kinds of infractions.) Richard, McNeil, and a few other players were apparently exiting the Piccadilly Hotel, on their way to Saint Malachy's church a few blocks north on 49th Street, when McNeil spotted MacLean in the lobby. McNeil turned to Richard and said something like, "did you hear what he said about you?" Prompted to action, Richard confronted McLean, and after some hard words the fiery Rocket struck the referee and knocked him down a few stairs. Paul Raymond, the Canadiens' treasurer, and Camil DesRoches rushed in to break things up, but it was too late. League President

Clarence Campbell fined Richard $500 for the incident, not an inconsiderable sum for the time.[60] Looking back on the episode almost thirty years later, Richard remembered McNeil as being the instigator: "The real culprit... was Gerry McNeil.... Nothing was gonna happen except that, when we got outside, Gerry McNeil asked me if I heard what McLean said about me when I passed, I didn't know he was kidding. So I ran back in and grabbed McLean."[61] McNeil for his part didn't deny this characterization; he only added that he remembered the players praying with greater fervour than usual when they got to church.

The Detroit press tried to make something of the Richard-McLean altercation when the playoffs began. Baz O'Meara quoted Paul Chandler of *The Detroit News* as noting a "mental question... there is widespread notion within the N.H.L. that Richard has been in a mental turmoil since being fined $500 for his brawl with a referee in a New York hotel lobby."[62] The suggestion was hotly denied by Dick Irvin, who must have been annoyed that the opposition was playing mind games, a tactic for which he himself was notorious. After the first two games in Detroit, it was clear that the Rocket wasn't suffering any mental turmoil; however, his problems with Campbell would only get worse—much worse. The fight with McLean became part of the "history" Campbell took into consideration the next time Richard would get in trouble with the league in 1955 (the season suspension that led to the famous "Richard Riot"). Whenever I teased my father as having unwittingly played a role in starting Quebec's Quiet Revolution, he'd shake his head and chuckle, "It's funny, *now*."

As far as Richard was concerned, my father would always be something of a shit-disturber. The reputation resurfaced as late as the 1990s on a visit to the Mosdells, who had a rural home in upper-state Vermont. My father was responsible for operating the tender to conduct everybody from a sailboat to the wharf. Richard was the last person left aboard, and just as the storm clouds were looming ever closer, my father apparently commented that he thought he would go for a drink and fetch him later. "You could hear the Rocket screaming something across the lake about how I was up to my old tricks."

There was another story about the Rocket that my father enjoyed telling. Everyone on the team knew that the one thing that made Richard lose it in a game, or any place for that matter, was the sight of his own blood. God help the person who might inadvertently cut him with a high stick in practice. Once the team was coming back after winning an important game in Detroit. Euphoria and celebration filled the car. The wives had been called in advance, and the plan was for them to meet the train when it got into Windsor station. "Dress up," was the directive, "we're going to take you girls out to a nice restaurant to celebrate." Getting ready for bed, Billy Reay was moving a spittoon and he happened to catch the Rocket right on the forehead with a sharp edge. It started to bleed. Profuse apologies were not enough; the Rocket responded impulsively by throwing what he assumed were Reay's pants off the train. The pants belonged to another player, who was warned that he'd look pretty silly the next day when they got back to Montreal. Everybody laughed, but the player in question then tossed Richard's shoes. The laughter stopped and things quickly got out of hand. Everybody was grabbing whatever they could lay hands on and pitching it into the night. Somewhere along the southwestern Ontario tracks the next morning was a trail of men's clothing. When the train arrived in Montreal, the guys were a pitiful sight. Butch Bouchard stepped out onto the platform wearing nothing but a trench coat that was three sizes too small. The wives, dolled up in their finest, stared at their husbands in disbelief. The celebratory dinner was postponed.

The post-game discussion to Game Two again brought up the question of nerves. McNeil denied that he was overly tense. Dink Carroll would only say that a glance at McNeil's "fingernails belies that statement."[63] He described them as "chewed right down to the nub" (which incidentally is how they would remain the rest of his life). Taking stock of the situation, Carroll facetiously allowed that McNeil might have been sincere: "A nervous goalkeeper would likely bite his fingers off without quite realizing what he was doing." Collins published another cartoon in *The Gazette*.[64] This one emphasizes the one-two punch of Richard and McNeil. The former holds a shotgun, which is aimed at the "Red Wing" bird. Around the bird's neck is what appears to be a life preserver with the caption: "Gerry's Horse Collar." The bird exclaims, "Flying? I can't even get off the ground!!" What makes any 1–0 game special from a goaltending point of view, let alone one that had three extra periods, is that both netminders are obviously getting the better of the forwards. What makes a game exciting is not scoring, but scoring chances. There were plenty of the latter in Game Two, but whoever did break through would inevitably receive attention. In the spotlight, Richard was all humility.

The year before, McNeil felt as if he had proven his worth, that he belonged, but every team player wishes for more, wishes to be the one to move the team forward. Not only does this require the acknowledgement of one's peers, it must include an endorsement from management or the coaching staff. Dick Irvin publicly congratulated McNeil

Fig. 16 Dick Irvin, Gerry McNeil, and Maurice Richard after winning Game Two of the 1951 Semifinal in the third overtime period. Detroit Olympia, March 30, 1951. (Photographer unknown.) Copyright unknown.

in the dressing room after the second overtime win; this moment was captured in a photograph that features McNeil between Irvin and Richard (see fig. 16).[65] This shot was probably taken within seconds of figure 15 (same spot on Richard's left cuff); the focus, however, is sharper. McNeil and Richard have their arms around each other. McNeil's right hand rests on Irvin's knee, while Irvin pats the goalie's head. The three smiles are all genuine enough, but Richard's and Irvin's are directed toward the face of youthful exuberance in the middle. McNeil beams with sheer joy.

The caption reads as follows: "Toast to Gold Dust Kid: Gerry McNeil's offered by tea-totaller, Dick Irvin. Coach Irvin has always said goaltending means 70% to a team in the playoffs." It sounds cliché to talk of the importance of a "hot" goalie in the post-season, but that is only because the talk reflects a truth. Since situations repeat themselves naturally in the artificial and arbitrary construction of athletic competition (e.g., an elimination game), commentary cannot escape the cliché (e.g., "backs against the wall"). This shouldn't prevent those who write about the sport to emphasize what they feel is true about the way

THE MAGICIAN

it is played. Even Wayne Gretzky, the Great One, who should know something about the subject, has written about the hot goaltender's potential to determine a playoff round.[66] A Ken Dryden, Patrick Roy, or Martin Brodeur; in 2006, Cam Ward.

Oddly enough, the Canadiens remained in Detroit an extra day, working out at the Olympia again on Friday.[67] The plan was to reduce the mobbing by well-wishers and autograph-seekers who would now be out in force in Montreal. Riding the emotional highs and lows that follow the sporting event is part of the daily lives of athletes. The entire Canadiens team could not help but be happy as their train-car snaked home. The card-playing was interrupted more frequently with mocking tales and gibes, and Irvin knew that he had to leave the boys their time to feel the sweetness of winning, of getting a tough job done. He also knew that the Red Wings were far from finished, that pride alone would drive them in the next game. And so he waited, and when he thought the voices had grown shrill enough, he sharply cut in with a reminder about how small their margin of victory was, about not being too confident. By the time the train reached the Quebec border, the players had settled down for some badly needed sleep, but if they did manage to nod off, their rest was periodically disturbed by the knowledge that Detroit would surely come out strong for Game Three.

After the second game, the Detroit press continued to praise McNeil's success, but attention was also given to the failure of the Red Wing stars to score: "The Production Line (Abel, Lindsay, Howe) has been throttled."[68] McNeil had not given up a goal since Reise scored at 1:10 of the third period in Game One which, when added to the 1-0 marathon of the next game, was a total of 182 minutes 19 seconds and counting. No wonder the Red Wings, unlike their opponents, were anxious to get out of the Motor City. They actually arrived in Montreal on Friday and then headed directly to a hideaway in Granby, about an hour away in the Eastern Townships.[69] It is noteworthy that McNeil's shutout streak, while not a league record, was racked up against the league's most powerful offensive team. Nevertheless, McNeil didn't recall being conscious of the streak; he did recall being conscious of the awesome power of the Detroit team and of the need for him to continue his play if the Canadiens were to prevail.

Playoff fever hit a high in Montreal. Some one thousand seats and another three thousand standing room tickets went on sale Saturday morning; fans stayed out in the rain all night to get into the Saturday night game.[70] But it wasn't only Montrealers who were getting caught up in the excitement. Two unidentified youths from Pontiac, Michigan, were found hiding in the Forum on Friday; they apparently offered an usher three dollars to let them stay in the building for the game Saturday night. The total attendance for Game Three of the 1951 Semifinal was close to 15,400. The Forum staffers believed that they could have sold fifty thousand tickets. Scalpers sold $2.75 seats for $15; a pair of choice box seats went for $50.[71] No need for laser lights and artificial sound. The building buzzed with anticipation as the officials came on the ice. Then when the white uniforms of the Tricolore were seen emerging, there was an explosion of cheering and the brick walls seem to vibrate. This was for the first two games, for Richard and McNeil, and for earning the respect of all hockey fans.

The first period continued the scoreless play that had characterized so much of the series thus far. Then, well past the midway point of the second, Callum Mackay (assigned to shadow Howe) went to the bench for a substitution. Meanwhile, Bob Goldham was weaving up the centre from his own end; he spotted the open Howe and sent him a long pass, allowing the Red Wing star to break in all alone. Howe feigned a shot, cut across the goal, and brought the puck to his backhand. The picture in *The Montreal Daily Star* captures this exact moment.[72] McNeil is still up miraculously on the tips of his skates, still in a position to make the save. Howe, however, held onto the disk for another moment as McNeil started to go down. His backhand was quick enough to find the right side. In *The Gazette* is a picture of Howe, stick upraised, just as he realizes that he has scored.[73] McNeil lies on the ice, right leg still up in the air, his head looking back into the net. Finally, Detroit broke the spell.

The scoreless streak ended at 218 minutes, 42 seconds. Nobody seemed to know whether the streak was a record; it wasn't. There were three longer streaks (i.e., for the longest shutout stretch in the playoffs) that all date back to the 1930s: another Montreal goalie, George Hainsworth, has the longest at 270:08 (1930), then comes Dave Kerr of the Rangers with 248:35 (1937) and just three seconds behind Kerr was Detroit's Norm Smith with 248:32 (1936). However, McNeil's feat came in the face of the most powerful offence in the league, and almost half of the 218:42 (or 103:29) was racked up during overtime, when the will to score is highest.

It was almost surpassed by Jean-Sébastien Giguère of Anaheim in 2003. In fact, my father had come to visit me in Halifax that spring, and we were still in our pyjamas, sitting out on the deck, enjoying the sun and our morning coffee, when my neighbour Peter James walked into the backyard with the Sunday paper in hand. He drew our attention to a story on Giguère's streak (217:54) which mentioned that it was the "longest since Gerry McNeil's in 1951." For a moment we basked in the sun and playoff history, and the coffee seemed to taste better.

Giguère actually came within a minute of surpassing my father's, and I well remember not being able to watch the crucial game, since I knew that he was within five minutes of setting a new mark. Minnesota's attack had looked so inept that it seemed inevitable that the position my father had held for over fifty years would be passed. When I saw on a sports network tickertape that the Wild had actually gotten a puck by Giguère at 4:37, I couldn't do the math because I simply did not know the exact numbers involved.[74] I knew that it would be close, and I tried to take solace in the fact that, even if my father's mark had been surpassed, just holding it for over half a century was a great achievement in itself. But, as the cliché goes, a record is set to be broken.

Although my father's mark was not strictly speaking a "record," it was the longest playoff shutout span for over fifty-five years in what is generally referred to as the modern era (post-1943) or the introduction of the red line. And I got to enjoy this fact for another three years. Then, one Monday morning I heard a radio report about another Duck goalie, Ilya Bryzgalov, going 229 minutes and 42 seconds without allowing a goal. The same sun was shining on the same deck, but my father was no longer around. There was no coffee or visit from the neighbour. This time I had to take solace in the thought that my father would have at least enjoyed having his mark surpassed by a relatively unknown goalie from Togliatti, Russia, playing in his first playoff series.[75]

The Canadiens couldn't get their own attack going in Game Three. In the latter part of the third period Howe set up Abel, who fired a shot from twenty-five feet that found the net. The insurance goal; Habs lose 2–0. *The Detroit Free Press* headline the next day read "Still Abel—and Howe! Wings Win at Last."[76] Despite the loss, McNeil was said to have "retained enough of his magic to stop at least a half dozen other shots which could have been goals."[77] The roller-coaster ride that began at the Olympia was now over. With a taste of success, the Red Wings would be hungry for more. The Canadiens left the Forum and headed north for their own hideaway in Val-David.

Exactly where the Canadiens stayed in Val-David was, of course, kept a secret, lest the "ticket-kibetzers, autograph hounds and the hordes of well-wishers … ruin the peace and mind of the tired athletes." However, Al Parsley identified Roger Puvilland, one of the best twenty-five chefs in all of Quebec, as the person in charge of the kitchen.[78] Parsley also wondered if culinary expertise was necessary to prepare steak-and-potato meals. Rain kept the players inside, and so they amused themselves with ping pong and shuffleboard; at night there were movies. *The Gazette* features a photo of a group of Canadiens gathered around a piano, and another of McNeil and MacPherson pretending to be cooks.[79]

Game Four brought more pressure than Three. Up two games coming home was too great a lead to squander. However, early on it looked like Montreal was going to do exactly that. Leo Reise, the big defenceman who had been playing well for Detroit, took the puck up ice and put the Red Wings in front 1–0.[80] Then it was the third line of Metro Prystai, Gaye Stewart, and Doc Couture that delivered: first Prystai, converting a nifty skate-pass from Couture, then Couture himself drilling the puck into the top corner. Finally, it was Abel scoring to put the game away in the third. Lach got credit for the lone Montreal goal when Harvey's second-period point shot went off a number of bodies (including Lach's) and behind Sawchuk. The Habs looked listless in the first and third periods and were outshot 28 to 23. According to the Detroit press, the universe was simply unfolding as it should. In the words of Marshall Dann, "Gerry had lost his magic."[81] Meanwhile, the Red Wings had not just pulled even; they had clearly stolen the momentum and re-established themselves as the odds-on favourites. And so the mood was very different for the Montreal team on the train back to Detroit. They once again found themselves in the position of having to prove something.

Another sellout crowd of 14,221 packed into the Olympia to see their team reassert itself against the insurgent Habs, and they weren't disappointed with the first period. Abel scored after just a minute, and Howe added a second. The Wings took a 2–0 lead into the dressing room, and everyone assumed that they were well on their way to the Final. The mood in the Canadiens' room was desperate; the series was slipping away. Who would have thought so after Montreal jumped out to a 2–0 lead in games? Added to the score was the fact that Richard had just received a major penalty for punching Lindsay. The Red Wing power play could finish the Habs—but things turned around in the second: the Canadiens scored three unanswered goals. The Wings seemed lackadaisical and went on to lose 5–2.[82] The Detroit newspapers were extremely critical of their team; the consensus was that they were not hungry enough. In a statement that seems to endorse violence, Irvin attributed his team's comeback to Richard's unanswered punch[83]—was he right?

Saturday night back at the Forum. The third Collins cartoon depicts Irvin and Selke trying to disguise the Forum as the Olympia.[84] It was

Fig. 17 The Canadiens raise bottles of 7 Up (for some reason the NHL's celebratory drink of choice during the 1940s and '50s) after their defeat of the Red Wings in the 1951 Semifinal. (Photographer unknown.) Copyright unknown.

suggested that part of the reason for the poor showing at home was the large number of rookies who strained under the possibility of failure in front of friends and family. Athletes cannot excel when they fear making mistakes; rather they tend to find excellence when they lose themselves in the moment. Game Six was wide open, up and down, and scoreless for two periods. Bill Chadwick, officiating for the third time in the series, decided to let the teams play (i.e., he didn't call a single penalty), and as a result the pace was frantic. Almost seven minutes into the third period, Billy Reay managed to deflect a shot from Geoffrion and the Habs went up by one. Then McNeil blocked a shot by Howe, but Abel was there to put home the rebound. A couple of minutes later Richard gave the Canadiens the lead again on a wraparound goal, and Mosdell tallied the insurance marker when Curry hit him with a perfect pass. The Wings pressed in the last minute; McNeil turned away shots by Lindsay and Abel but was unable to stop the former on another rebound. The last forty-five minutes were "packed with drama," but the Habs held on to win.[85]

The mighty Red Wings were eliminated. As the Habs mobbed their goalie, McNeil threw his stick up in the air and it almost hit Chadwick on the way down. The teams shook hands, and the fans saw something quite unusual: Sid Abel with his arms around the Rocket. A celebratory team picture is taken back in the Canadiens' dressing room (fig. 17).[86] Even Senator Raymond joins the group (the white-haired man, third from the right). Partially visible in the newspaper versions is the inspirational sign on the wall behind the players: "No substitute for work: it's the price of success." The narratives around sport contain little else beyond the cliché. Jack Adams said that it was a shame—his team finished the regular season 36 points ahead of Montreal. However, one truism, universally acknowledged, about the fascination of sport is the ever-present possibility of an upset. A second has to do with why upsets occur: superlative performances, work, fortune? On this subject, the comments of the Wings coach, Tommy Ivan, were unequivocal: "Gerry McNeil was the difference. He was terrific in their net."[87]

1 Ken McKenzie, *Hockey News*, Dec. 23, 1950, 6. Kaiser's shot hit McNeil on the left side of his face cutting him for three stitches and "loosening as many teeth"; see "Staggering Canadiens Bow to Bruins," *Globe and Mail*, Dec. 11, 1950, 21.

2 "Red Wings Clinch Title, Now For Playoffs," *Detroit News*, Mar. 18, 1951, 2–1.

3 Marshall Dann, "Shutout Not Enough for Sawchuk," *Detroit Free Press*, Mar. 26, 1951, 24.

4 "Irvin Speaks: Raps Wings for Failure of Sawchuk," *Detroit Free Press*, Mar. 26, 1951, 24.

5 "Olympia Ice Cold Indeed to Montreal," *Detroit News*, Mar. 26, 1951, 21.

6 "Wings Upset," Sports Flashes, Telenews, Mar. 28, 1951. I am indebted to Paul Patskou for locating this sequence at the Research Centre of the HHOF.

7 The details of Game One are taken from a variety of sources: Paul Chandler, "While a City Sleeps, Wings Lose: League's Ignored Goalie Is 'Magician,'" *Detroit News*, Mar. 28, 1951, 57; Marshall Dann, "Montreal Nips Wings, 3–2, in 4-Overtime Opener: Richard Scores on Breakaway," *Detroit Free Press*, Mar. 28, 1951, 32; Elmer Ferguson, "61.09 Minutes Overtime: Rocket's Goal Wins for Habs: McNeil Shares

Glory," *Herald, Montreal*, Mar. 28, 1951, 1.24; Baz O'Meara, "Fourth Overtime Goal Cools Favored Detroit: Rocket's Blast Breaks up Brilliant Stanley Cup Duel–McNeil Sensational," *Montreal Daily Star*, Mar. 28, 1951, 31, 32; Dink Carroll, "Goal by Richard in 4th Extra Period Beats Wings 3–2: Rocket Provides Thriller Finish for Canadiens Win," *Gazette* (Montreal), Mar. 28, 1951, 18; "Richard's Goal in 4th Overtime Beats Wings," *Globe and Mail*, Mar. 28, 1951, 15.

8   "Referee A 'Sketch,'" *Detroit News*, Mar. 28, 1951, 60.

9   Marshall Dann, "Montreal Nips Wings, 3–2, in 4-Overtime Opener," *Detroit Free Press*, Mar. 28, 1951, 32.

10 Ibid.

11 Ferguson, "Gist and Jest," *Herald, Montreal*, Mar. 28, 1951, 21.

12 I cannot find any evidence of the photo having been published in the early 1950s, although I am still looking. It has, however, been published twice in recent years to accompany two articles that Dave Stubbs did on my father. See Dave Stubbs, "McNeil's Win Only Part of Story," *Gazette* (Montreal), May 7, 2002, E3; and "A Slice of Netminding History," *Gazette* (Montreal), Mar. 27, 2004, A2.

13 On this specific subject one can consult Bruce Dowbiggin, *The Stick: A History, A Celebration, An Elegy* (Toronto: Macfarlane, Walter & Ross, 2002).

14 "The Battle of the Overpass," *Detroit News*, Review Mirror. See http://info.detnews. com/history/story/index.cfm?id=172&category=events, accessed 26 May 2006.

15 See *SI*, July 26, 1999.

16 See *SI*, June 7, 1965. Ali lands a blow to Liston's head, but both fighters are on their feet. The caption reads, "The Fight You Didn't See."

17 Leifer alludes to this in the Berman, Mahar interview, accessed 10 July 2006, http://bermangraphics.com/press/leifer.htm.

18 See Victor Turner, "Images and Reflections: Ritual, Drama, Carnival, Film, and Spectacle in Cultural Performance," in *The Anthropology of Performance* (New York: PAJ Publications, 1986), 21–22. Richard Schechner's introductory essay to this collection, "Victor Turner's Last Adventure," is a good place to find a summary of Turner's main ideas.

19 The Speed Graphic used a negative size of $4'' \times 5''$, the smallest in what is known as "large-format." For a basic introduction to the subject, see "Large Format" in *Wikipedia*, accessed May 26, 2006. http://en.wikipedia.org/wiki/Large_format. For a brief, albeit eloquent, history of sports photography, see Richard B. Woodward, "Playing with Time," *Sports Illustrated*, "The Pictures: 50 Years," Apr. 26, 2004, 75–82; and Simon Barnes, "Introduction," *Sportscape: The Evolution of Sports Photography* (London: Phaidon Press, 2000).

20 See "Large Format primer, basics," accessed May 26, 2006, http://www.large-formatphotography.info/why.html; for more technical detail, "The Graflex Speed Graphic," accessed May 26, 2006, http://www.graflex.org/speed-graphic/FAQ.html.

21 "Greatest Hockey Goalie Ever," *Life*, Feb. 18, 1952, 103.

22 See Andy O'Brien, "Why It's Different in the NHL," *Standard*, Feb. 3, 1951, 13. Although the main photo in the feature resembles a Kilpatrick (i.e., same angle at the Olympia), it does not bear the Kilpatrick stamp.

23 This quotation is from the bulletin board "Sports Shooter," accessed April 12, 2004, http://www.sportsshooter.com/message_display.html?tid=8831. Van Nostrand has confirmed these details directly with the author.

24 Dink Carroll, "Playing the Field," *Gazette* (Montreal), Mar. 30, 1951, 22; and Ferguson, "Gist and Jest," *Herald, Montreal*, Mar. 29, 1951, 21.

25 See John Walker, "I Told You So," *Detroit News*, Mar. 28, 1951, 57; and Baz O'Meara, "The Passing Sport Show," *Montreal Daily Star*, Mar. 29, 1951, 44.

26 *Detroit News*, Mar. 28, 1951, 57. The caption reads, "Ted Outskates Sprawled Canadiens but McNeil Saves."

27 *Standard*, Mar. 31, 1951, 9.

28 Elmer Ferguson, "Rocket's Goal Wins for Habs: McNeil Shares Glory," *Herald, Montreal*, Mar. 28, 1951, 1.

29 Paul Chandler, "League's Ignored Goalie Is 'Magician,'" *Detroit News*, Mar. 28, 1951, 57.

30 The headline reads "League's Ignored Goalie Is Magician."

31 Baz O'Meara, "McNeil Magic Frustrates Rangers with 4–0 Shutout," *Montreal Daily Star*, Oct. 20, 1950, 44.

32 The "unseen hand" was a favourite expression of Irvin's. Dick Carroll quotes it in "Playing the Field: McNeil's Greatest Game?" *Gazette* (Montreal), Mar. 29, 1951, 18.

33 Baz O'Meara, "Fourth Overtime Goal Cools Favored Detroit: Rocket's Blast Breaks Up Brilliant Stanley Cup Duel—McNeil Sensational," *Montreal Daily Star*, Mar. 28, 1951, 31.

34 I have viewed all the existing footage of McNeil's play held by the Hockey Hall of Fame; thanks to Paul Patsku for compiling the videotape.

35 Baz O'Meara, "The Passing Sport Show," *Montreal Daily Star*, Mar. 29, 1951, 44.

36 Quoted by Carroll, "Playing the Field," *Gazette* (Montreal), Mar. 31, 1951, 8.

37 John Collins, "Clipping Detroit's Wings," *Gazette* (Montreal), Mar. 29, 1951, 22, cartoon.

38 Quoted by Dink Carroll, "Jack Adams High on McNeil's Play," *Gazette* (Montreal), Mar. 29, 1951, 19; and Chandler, "League's Ignored Goalie," 57.

39 Chandler, "League's Ignored Goalie," 57.

40 According to Ferguson, "Gist and Jest," *Herald, Montreal*, Mar. 29, 1951, 21.

41 Quoted by Carroll, "Playing the Field," *Gazette* (Montreal), Mar. 29, 1951, 18.

42 Quoted by Baz O'Meara, "The Passing Sport Show," *Montreal Daily Star*, Mar. 29, 1951, 44.

43 Quoted by Baz O'Meara, "Fourth Overtime Goal Cools Favored Detroit," *Montreal Daily Star*, Mar. 28, 1951, 31.

44 Carroll, "Playing the Field," *Gazette* (Montreal), Mar. 29, 1951, 18.

45 Quoted by Ferguson, "Gist and Jest," *Herald, Montreal*, Mar. 29, 1951, 21.

46 All of these comments are recorded in Baz O'Meara, "The Passing Sport Show," *Montreal Daily Star*, Mar. 29, 1951, 44.

47 Quoted by Ferguson, "Gist and Jest," *Herald, Montreal*, Mar. 29, 1951, 21.

48 Ferguson, "Gist and Jest," *Herald, Montreal*, Mar. 30, 1951, 29.

49 Quoted by Carroll, "Playing the Field," *Gazette* (Montreal), Mar. 30, 1951, 22.

50 Paul Chandler, "Wings Eye Soft Spots: Hope to Crack the Great McNeil," *Detroit News*, Mar. 29, 1951, 57–58.

51 Marshall Dann, "Canadiens Beat Wings 1–0, in Third Overtime: Richard Gets Big One Again," *Detroit Free Press*, Mar. 30, 1951, 27.

52 Dick Peters, "Overtime Games No Novelty to Wings," *Detroit Free Press*, Mar. 30, 1951, 27.

53 Dink Carroll, "Richard Nets Playoff Goal as Canadiens Edge Detroit 1–0: Rocket Decides Stanley Cup Game in 3rd Overtime—McNeil Stars," *Gazette* (Montreal), Mar. 30, 1951, 22.

54 Dick Peters, "Overtime Games No Novelty," 27.

55 Billy Reay as told to John Walker, "Chances Only 28 to 1 for Wing Comeback: Rocket Describes Second Winning Shot," *Detroit News*, Mar. 30, 1951, 57.

56 Maurice Richard as told to John Walker, "Chances Only 28 to 1," 57.

57 According to Marshall Dann, "Richard Gets Big One Again," *Detroit Free Press*, Mar. 30, 1951, 27.

58 "Off wing" refers to a right winger playing the left side, or vice versa. See Andrew Podnieks, "Glossary of Hockey Terms and Phrases," in Diamond, *Total Hockey*, 618.

59 A smaller version of the photo (i.e., just the faces) appeared in *Detroit News*, Mar. 30, 1951, 57; the full shot was published the next day in *The Montreal Daily Star*, Mar. 31, 1951, 44.

60 The details of this incident are taken from McNeil himself and two print sources. See Bernard Geoffrion and Stan Fischler, *Boom Boom: The Life and Times of Bernard Geoffrion* (Toronto: McGraw-Hill Ryerson, 1997), 24; and Milt Dunnell, "Only for Charity . . . ," *Toronto Star*, Mar. 24, 1980, B.1.

61 Quoted by Dunnell, "Only for Charity . . . ," B.1.

62 Quoted by Baz O'Meara, "The Passing Sport Show," *Montreal Daily Star*, Mar. 28, 1951, 31.

63 Carroll, "Playing the Field," *Gazette* (Montreal), Mar. 31, 1951, 8.

64 John Collins, "Flying Low," *Gazette* (Montreal), Mar. 31, 1951, 8, cartoon.

65 The picture was reproduced in *Montreal Daily Star*, Mar. 31, 1951, 20. However, Richard was cropped out and so was the bottom of the picture.

66 See Wayne Gretzky, "The Hasek factor: Goaltending Is the Difference between Winning and Losing the Stanley Cup . . . ," *National Post*, Apr. 8, 2000, A17. This and a number of other *National Post* articles from 2000 supposedly by Gretzky were actually written by Roy MacGregor.

67 According to Dink Carroll, "Visitors Makes Headquarters at Granby; Locals Stay in Detroit before Third Playoff Game," *Gazette* (Montreal), Mar 31, 1951, 8.

68 Paul Chandler, "Production Line Throttled," *Detroit News*, Mar. 30, 1951, 57.

69 According to Elmer Ferguson, "Fabulous Prices Offered for Habs Ducats," *Herald, Montreal*, Mar. 31, 1951, 1, 16. A file headshot of McNeil appears on the front page.

70 Marshall Dann, "Montreal Hockey-Mad, Giving $50 for 2 Ducats," *Detroit Free Press*, Apr. 1, 1951, C.1.

71 According to Paul Chandler, "Scalpers Do Big Business in Montreal," *Detroit News*, Apr. 2, 1951, 2.1.

72 "Gerry's Long Holdout Siege Succumbs to Game's Big Gun," *Montreal Daily Star*, Apr. 2, 1951, 33.

73 Photo by Davidson, "Howe Waves Stick after Goal to End McNeil's Shutout String," *Gazette* (Montreal), Apr. 2, 1951, 22.

74 Giguère's streak was stopped by Andrew Brunette, who deflected a puck past the Anaheim goalie after his team had gone scoreless for 217 minutes and 54 seconds. See "Duck Gets Rest after Sweep: Giguère's Scoreless Streak Ended at 217 minutes 54 seconds," *Sunday Herald*, May 18, 2003, D2.

75 Bryzgalov's shutout streak was stopped at 249:15, which put the Russian goalie second on the list. McNeil dropped from fourth to fifth.

76 Marshall Dann, "Still Abel—and Howe! Wings Win at Last: Sid, Gordie Cut Montreal String, 2-0. Goal Famine Ends after 218 Minutes," *Detroit Free Press*, Apr. 1, 1951, C.1.

77 Dann, "Still Abel—and Howe!" C.1.

78 Al Parsley, "Sidelights," *Herald, Montreal*, Mar. 31, 1951, 17.

79 "Habitants Enjoy Country Life While Awaiting Game With Detroit," Dink Carroll, *Gazette* (Montreal), Apr. 3, 1951, 20.

80 Marshall Dann, "That's More Like It: Wings All Even: Montreal Slapped Down, 4–1; McNeil No Mystery as Mates Lose Touch," *Detroit Free Press*, Apr. 4, 1951, 20.

81 Dann, "That's More Like It," 20.

82 Dink Carroll, "Canadiens Overcome Early 2-Goal Deficit . . ." *Gazette* (Montreal), Apr. 6, 1951, 20; Baz O'Meara, "Canadiens Back in Favored Role After Win at Detroit," *Montreal Daily Star*, Apr. 6, 1951, 31.

83 "Prystai," *Detroit News*, Apr. 6, 1951, 54.

84 John Collins, "At Home Away from Home," *Gazette* (Montreal), Apr. 7, 1951, 9, cartoon.

85 All details in this and the subsequent paragraphs are taken from Dink Carroll, "Canadiens in Stanley Cup Final with Leafs by Defeating Wings 3–2," *Gazette* (Montreal), Apr. 9, 1951, 22.

86 See Carroll, "Playing the Field," *Gazette* (Montreal), Apr. 9, 1951, 22; and "Jubilant Canucks Let Out Victory Roar," *Montreal Daily Star*, Apr. 9, 1951, 30.

87 Quoted by Carroll, "Playing the Field," 22.

THE MAGICIAN

The Goalie in the Barilko Picture

IT IS IRONIC HOW POPULAR HISTORY CAN FOCUS ON A SINGLE moment in a player's career with the result that it seems to haunt that player for the rest of his life, yet this is what happened to my father, who was most often remembered as the goalie who let in the Barilko goal. When Bill Barilko scored the overtime goal to win the 1951 Stanley Cup for the Leafs, he had no idea that it would become one of the most legendary feats in NHL history, not to mention the subject of one of the best-known photographs in sports journalism. Unfortunately, Barilko had only a few months to enjoy the glory. The following August he was on a fishing trip up north and made the decision to fly back in bad weather. The small plane disappeared sometime after takeoff, and the wreckage wasn't discovered until eleven years later (1962), which just happened to be the next time the Leafs would win the Stanley Cup.[1] Barilko was robbed of a lifetime to reminisce and relish the goal, and the Barilko phenomenon that survives among Leaf fans today (e.g., The Tragically Hip's "Fifty-Mission Cap") owes itself to the circumstances of his tragic disappearance.

In contrast, McNeil capitalized on his role in the game that led to Barilko's heroics. Several times he was paid to appear at autograph sessions in Toronto where fans, for a fee, could get their hockey cards or photographs signed. Once he was even billed not by his name, but as "The Goalie in the Barilko Picture." At one time, this focus on a single goal did bother Mac, but he learned to accept it as an opportunity to let fans know about other highlights of his career. Moreover, he never thought it shameful to have played for the Stanley Cup. The appearance of the Canadiens in the Final of '51 was the first in a run of ten straight Cup Final appearances for the team, a mark that may last longer than the five straight Cup victories in the latter half of the 1950s. McNeil was also quick to point to the need to look beyond the spectacle moment, to look past Barilko's goal to what happened earlier that game, or earlier in the series.[2]

Although many NHL enthusiasts are familiar with the Barilko goal and Turofsky's picture thereof, few know that the 1951 Cup Final stands as the only playoff series in which every game went into overtime.[3] The amount of stress on the goalies in the series was particularly high since the winning goal could be expected at any moment. What for many years used to be known as sudden-death overtime is now referred to as "sudden-victory" overtime.[4] Call it what you like, the essential role played by the goalie is to give the team life, the chance to win. For many years, NHL hockey was *the sport* for overtime entertainment, the only game that had that magical feeling, familiar to the sport enthusiast, that within a few seconds either way any team could win. Baseball has half of that feel insofar as the home team batting in the bottom of the 9th inning, or any inning after the 9th, could win at any time. Soccer has rarely used sudden death; for most of the twentieth century it was content to have a complete extra period to decide a match (or penalty kicks), as was the case in the 2006 World Cup. The NFL brought sudden-death overtime into play for the regular season a while ago, but, because this usually means a field goal kicked from a predictably successful distance, the feeling isn't that of fate teetering in the balance but of the possibility that the poor kicker will choke (i.e., the game is expected to end). It could even be said that the same feeling extends to the penalty shot or kick.

In 2005–2006, the NHL adopted the shootout, which resembles soccer's penalty kick insofar as a series of offensive players confront the goalie in one-on-one duels. While this innovation seems to have been a popular move, there are some purists who still believe that only the game should determine the outcome, and that there is nothing ignoble about a tie. As mentioned in Chapter 2, I tend to feel more affinity with the latter position, although I do admit that the shootout provides great entertainment. For me what determines the outcome should dignify the athletic competition. As soon as one introduces something other than the "game" (five skaters and a goalie versus five skaters and a goalie), something about the sacredness of the "game" is lost. Why not settle a draw by declaring the team with the most shots on net the winner, or by having two-on-two? Why not allow ties, and reserve sudden-death overtime for playoff games or when a league title (or tournament) needs to be decided? I realize that the majority of sports fans want a decision—a winner and a loser—but is this distinction even appropriate for an evenly fought contest? Are we more interested in arbitrary designations or in the nobility of the sport itself? I would say the former; there are all kinds of examples of a team getting outplayed by an opponent but still managing to win the game. In hockey and soccer, this usually has to do with a wide differential in shots on goal. In baseball, it has to do with hits (versus runs). Football, yardage gained versus points. I would hypothesize that most sports fans are drawn to a particular team that they want to see *win* any way possible. Some want to see what they call "a good game," by which they usually mean a closely fought contest. Ultimately, I would like to suggest that if one of the things that makes sport so popular is its metaphorical representation of life, then sudden death provides the most dramatic, and unambiguous, spectacle.

When a hockey player goes in for a penalty shot, the chances of success are roughly fifty-fifty. In soccer, the penalty kick is supposed to go in, so the exercise goes on until the goalie guesses right or the kicker blows his kick. In the extremely rare situation when the playing time runs down in a basketball game just as a shooting foul is called (I once saw this), the expectation is again that the shooter will make his shot (success averages are always above 50 per cent) and so the mood is all about choking. The magical feeling of sudden death in hockey is a unique feature that derives from the rules of the game and its established dimensions.

What I do like about the shootout in hockey is that it retains this feeling of even odds that lies behind the ultimate entertainment of any sport; winners and losers can be determined by a great offensive move or defensive save. A lover of baseball once said that ninety feet between the bases was the closest thing to perfection in life; perhaps, but the four-by-six-foot hockey goalmouth may come close, too. Anyone who follows hockey knows that what has changed is that goalie equipment kept getting bigger until 2005–2006, when restrictions cut it back. On the other side, it could be argued that improved stick technology has enabled players to shoot harder. Some dimensions in sport are sacred despite changes in equipment and the fact that players now are bigger and more athletic. Nobody is really serious about raising the rim in basketball despite the fact that players now seem to have a greater vertical leap (and perhaps better shoes). Keep the goalmouth four by six feet, and restrict the goalie equipment. Keep that magical balance that epitomized the Stanley Cup Final of 1951.

If few fans know that the '51 Final was the only series in Stanley Cup play in which every game went into overtime, fewer would know that Bill Barilko saved Game One with a first-rate defensive play.[5] In any case, nobody could have guessed that the series would be as close as it was. While the Canadiens had ousted the favourite Red Wings, Toronto had disposed of the Bruins. Both series went six games, but Toronto certainly had momentum. They were able to rebound from the season-ending injury to their Vezina Trophy winner Al Rollins to go on to win four straight. The 36-year-old veteran Turk Broda came on in relief and posted 2 shutouts. The series win was capped with a 6-0 rout. Many of the veteran players from the three successive Cup wins in '47, '48, and '49 were still with the Leafs, and finishing the 1950-51 season with 95 points, the team was a close second to Detroit, who had 101 points. Now that the Red Wings were out, Toronto was the clear favourite. Furthermore, Montreal could only manage two wins in the fourteen games against the Leafs that season.[6] Recalling the '51 Final, my father once commented reflectively, "you don't always win when you play your best."

However, when Game One started, McNeil didn't look his best. The puck was no sooner dropped when Tod Sloan took it into the corner, fought off both Bouchard and Johnson and then passed to Sid Smith in front. Smith beat the Habs netminder, and the game was 1-0 at fifteen seconds—the fastest goal scored in an NHL playoff game! Later in the first period Richard knocked down an attempted outlet pass and broke in on the Toronto net. Broda dove and took down the Rocket at the same time; neither player seemed to touch the puck as it slid to the back of the net. Only fifteen seconds later, Toronto was back in front when Sloan banged home Mortson's rebound. Montreal pulled even in the second period when Billy Reay won a faceoff and passed the puck back to the rookie Paul Masnick. Masnick manoeuvred around and let a backhand go that found the short side. At 7:56 of the third Gus Mortson scored on a long shot, but referee Bill Chadwick disallowed the goal claiming that Cal Gardner was in the crease. Regulation time ended with the score still 2-2.[7]

The overtime was fast and exciting. Broda poked the puck away from Lach, who was positioned to deflect a MacPherson shot in. At the other end McNeil stopped Mortson with a pad save, and Meeker was unable to score in a goalmouth scramble. Montreal threatened again when Richard eyed an open corner and drilled a shot. However, Barilko made a game-saving play by diving in front of the open net and deflecting the puck over the boards. Moments later Floyd Curry almost ended it, but the puck hit one post and came out off the other. Back in the Canadiens' zone, Sloan got the puck from Harvey and MacPherson behind the net and passed out to Smith, who backhanded the winner, his second goal of the game. A picture of it was on the front page of the Toronto *Globe and Mail* the next day just under a headline about Truman having fired General MacArthur.[8] Harvey appears panicky as he moves out from behind the net; McNeil looks back and down at the puck, which presumably has just crossed the line. The *Herald* photo,

Fig. 18 Sid Smith and other Leaf players celebrate Smith's overtime goal while McNeil skates off dejected. Star caption reads: "Canadiens' Good Little Goalie Shown Leaving the Ice After He Was Beaten by Sid Smith's Overtime Goal Last Night at Gardens. Leafs who can be identified, left to right: Klukay, Mortson, Mackell, Smith, Watson, Broda, Meeker, Barilko, Thomson, Sloan and Timgren." (Photo by Harold Barkley. *Toronto Star*, Apr. 12, 1951, 25. Reprinted *Gazette* [Montreal], June 19, 2006, C2.) Reproduced by permission of "Harold Barkley Archives."

taken from a different angle and a moment later, makes Smith look like he has barged into the netminder, whose only consolation would be to read Jim Vipond, the sports editor for *The Globe*, the next day on how the Leafs had outshot Montreal 14 to 5 in the first, "only Gerry McNeil's net mastery prevent[ed] a first period deluge of goals."[9] Still, a loss was a loss.

Red Burnett wrote a similar assessment in the *Toronto Star*; it was titled, "Credit McNeil's Magic for Carrying the Leafs to Overtime."[10] Sitting on top of his column is a page-to-page photo by Harold Barkley, which shows a long line of Leafs skating off the ice just after they have mobbed the crewcut, Toronto-born "Smitty" (see fig. 18). To a man, the Leafs wear grins of sweet jubilation and exhausted satisfaction.

The caption lists the identifiable: "Klukay, Mortson, Mackell, Smith, Watson, Broda, Meeker, Barilko, Thomson, Sloan and Timgren." The lone Canadien in the foreground is Gerry McNeil, holding his goal stick in both hands with his eyes fixed on the ice. A greater contrast between the thrill of victory and the agony of defeat, of team joy and individual regret, is hard to imagine. Barkley, whose hockey photos would become almost as famous as those of the Turofsky brothers, has captured the perfect moment when winning and losing registers in a single image.

Barkley's picture also expresses the essential isolation that every goalie feels. While everyone who plays a skating position is constantly involved in moving with the action, taking and receiving passes, engaging opposing players all over the ice, exchanging views about the game with teammates on the bench, goalies are by themselves and relatively stationary in their crease (this was especially true of goaltending pre-Plante). In games, they are pretty much out there by themselves, and in practice they must face their own teammates' shots, which tend to come harder when the team is struggling. When McNeil met Théodore in the spring of 2004, one thing that both goalies realized hadn't changed was how some players actually take out the frustrations that build up during games in practice.[11] A goalie had best beware the practice or warm-up when the team isn't winning. Hence, it shouldn't surprise people to learn that some of the worst goalie injuries come in team practices. In any case, somebody sent the *Toronto Star* page with Barkley's photo to my father, and it ended up in his scrapbook where I first saw it as a child. It would not be inaccurate to say that I have been continually fascinated with it ever since. To enjoy the full happiness of victory, one must remember what it feels like to lose.

For years I tried to locate a glossy print of Barkley's photo. It wasn't in Mike Leonetti's *The Game: Hockey in the Fifties,* the first collection of Barkley photos to be published.[12] Imagine my delight when I mentioned my futile search in a phone conversation with Dave Stubbs and the reporter responded by saying, "I think I actually have the negative of that picture." It turns out that Leonetti had lent Stubbs the negative when Stubbs was working on another article about my father. With Leonetti's permission, I got to examine the $4'' \times 5''$ negative and get glossies printed. There is a surreal quality about the shot insofar as the faces seem sharp in detail but the background is rather blurry.[13] As it turns out, I was not the only one mesmerized by Barkley's picture. In 2008 I noticed a Carleton "Mac" McDiarmid artistic reproduction of it in the "Jacques Laperriere" Classic Auction catalogue, where the scene was erroneously identified as having occurred after the last game of the Final.[14]

After the initial shock in the dressing room, McNeil sounded more positive: "I guess it's the law of averages. We won two tough games, and we couldn't win them all."[15] On the goal itself, he didn't give up much: "I'm not making any alibis but it was a mighty lucky goal that Sid Smith scored to break it up. He fell coming out from behind, tried to hook the puck across the cage to a teammate, but it took what was for the Leafs a lucky curve and went into the cage on the far side." Dick Irvin was short-tempered with a reporter who asked him what he expected in the rest of the series: "Why should you ask me to make predictions? You predicted we'd finish last, then you predicted Detroit would mop us up. So go right on predicting." The Canadiens returned to the Royal York Hotel and tried to rest for Game Two.

There was a lot of talk in the press about the use of film and the disallowed Leaf goal in the third period. Conn Smythe, the Toronto general manager, invited the press to a film viewing at the Gardens the next day, the result of which was a story in *The Globe and Mail* claiming that Chadwick had screwed things up. Cal Gardner might have been in the crease, but it was alleged that the film clearly shows Bud MacPherson holding him there with his stick. The rule stated that if a player "has been deliberately pushed into or is deliberately held in the goal crease by an opponent" the goal should stand.[16] Although the league was nowhere near using such footage to review plays, the incident was an example of how film could be used to pressure the officials. It is now taken for granted that video replay is an indispensable part of officiating. In the early 1950s things were much different. There still wasn't any television coverage of the games, forget slow-motion replays and multiple angles. Referees, like fans, paid attention to the live action in ways that we cannot even understand psychologically. While I agree that video replay usually results in better decisions, it must be admitted that it also creates a luxurious sense of second opportunity. No need to be so fixated on the live action when it can always be endlessly replayed. On the other hand, the visual experience only included a small portion of the audience; for most fans in 1951, paying attention meant listening to the live broadcasts on radio.

Another capacity crowd of 14,567 was at the Gardens to watch Game Two. Dick Irvin promised some changes, but few believed his strategic pre-game comments. Apparently, Doug Harvey had an injury and would not be used much. Harvey, it turns out, played more than the norm. The second change was for real. Irvin put together a Kid Line, consisting of Paul Masnick at centre, Paul Meger on left, and Boom Boom Geoffrion on the right side. The rookies actually produced the first Montreal goal when Meger won a behind-the-net battle for possession and set up Masnick in front. The young centreman beat Broda. Halfway through the second, the Canadiens went up 2–0 on a beautiful around-the-goal passing play, Richard to Olmstead to Reay, that left the Leaf defenders standing still like "totem poles."[17] The Leafs got on the board six minutes later with a pretty play of their own. With MacPherson off for tripping, "Teeder" Kennedy got the puck behind the Montreal net and sent it quickly to Max Bentley in the slot; Bentley then slid a short pass to Sid Smith, who scored his third goal in two games. The tying goal came in the third on another Leaf power play, although this one was not so pretty. Richard was in the penalty box when Kennedy picked the puck up in his own end and fought his way down the left wing. He passed to Sloan, who fired a shot; the puck bounced off McNeil's pads, then off Kennedy's knee and into the goal. The Canadiens protested vociferously to referee Gravel; some even grabbed his sweater, and Harvey, in particular, was said to have made a degrading gesture.

While the Canadiens seemed better than in Game One, Toronto still dominated the game, outshooting the Habs 36 to 24. Jim Vipond commented on how McNeil made some "astounding stops"; one was against Max Bentley, who tried unsuccessfully to deke the goalie out. McNeil coolly stood his ground and watched the puck go off his pads. Having recovered from a shoulder injury, Harry Watson rejoined his linemates Cal Gardner and Howie Meeker; the threesome seemed to get all kinds of chances, but they either muffed the shot or simply could not beat McNeil. It seemed as if a hex had been placed on them.

The overtime winner came fast. Doug Harvey had the puck at his own blue line as the Leafs were changing on the fly. He spotted an open Richard just before the opposite blue line and hit him with a sharp pass. Richard sidestepped a defenceman and seemed to be moving in on Broda at top speed. He somehow drew the Leaf goalie out and fired the puck into the open side. It was his third overtime winner in the 1951 playoffs, a record that remains unsurpassed despite the fact that the playoffs now consist of two extra rounds. It was also described as being one of the prettiest goal-scoring plays in playoff history. The stunned crowd at the Gardens could hardly believe that Richard was onside. There is something quintessentially spectacular about such plays, like hockey's blue-line pass, or the sideline pass in football, or baseball's corner strike-zone pitch, that involves pushing the limits, or going all out while staying within the rules of the game. The press-box consensus was that the play was good, but again mention was made of film to confirm visual impressions. Given the time necessary for advancement, this possibility would not be feasible for another half century.

The game was not the only thing the Leafs lost. Fern Flaman, their stalwart defenceman, was out for the rest of the series after pulling his groin toward the end of the second. And so the momentum of the series, which in the opinion of all had been terrific thus far, seemed to shift.

Back in Montreal a pair of tickets fetched seventy-five dollars on Sainte-Catherine Street. By Monday afternoon, there were five hundred people lined up outside the Forum box office, which only opened at 10 AM the next day.[18] Taking pity on the faithful, Forum officials allowed the crowd inside the lobby where sandwiches were sold and free coffee distributed. Richard had restored hope, and the city could hardly wait for Tuesday night.

Al Rollins, the rookie netminder who was injured in the Semifinal against Boston, returned to the lineup for the Leafs. The Forum crowd had barely just settled into place before Chadwick called a penalty on Tod Sloan for holding. Just after Richard got knocked down at the blue line, Bert Olmstead broke in on Rollins and fired a shot that bounced out into the slot area. Gus Mortson was there to clear the rebound, but somehow Richard had meanwhile gotten back up and streaked to the front of the net—just in time to beat the defenceman to the puck and bang it home. The Forum faithful poured forth their cheers. It was Richard's sixty-second goal in fifty-five post-season games, which tied him with his former linemate Toe Blake for the most playoff goals. Richard, playing with Olmstead and Lach, and the Kid Line of Masnick, Meger, and Geoffrion kept the spectators enthused by looking dangerous. Both sides had good shots on net in the first period; there was no other scoring.

Harvey got called for high-sticking in the second period, and Toronto went to work on the power play. Sid Smith took a drop pass from Bentley, shot hard knee high and found an opening on the short side. The game was tied 1–1. Toronto definitely dominated the second period. Sloan, Kennedy, Smith, Bentley, Meeker, Gardner, and Watson all had excellent opportunities, especially on the power play, to put the Leafs ahead, but once again McNeil made a number of miraculous saves. Rollins was equally good at the other end, stopping "Baldy" Mackay twice. The Canadiens reasserted themselves in the third but could not regain the lead.

Overtime for the third straight game. At first the Habs dominated and the crowd sensed victory. Richard and Geoffrion fired pucks that Rollins stopped but had to scramble to clear away. Then Mosdell shot again; Rollins blocked it, but the puck dropped down into the crease. Out of nowhere came Kennedy to clear it away and relieve the pressure. Bill Juzda moved the puck into the Montreal zone. A wild scramble ensued, and Mackay's attempt to clear landed the puck right on Sloan's stick. Sloan to Kennedy, and it's game over. Coach Joe Primeau and the other players jumped over the boards to congratulate their team captain, who saved the game at one end and ended it at the other. Back in the Leaf dressing room, Broda was among the first to congratulate Rollins on his successful return.

Although the Habs were able to manoeuvre more offensively, the Leafs still outshot them 29 to 25. A sense of the paranormal came up again in Vipond's assessment of McNeil's play in Game Three: "McNeil had the area around his goal hypnotized by his presence. For a couple of minutes it appeared as though an invisible wall was turning shots aside."[19] However, the pressure now shifted to the Canadiens to win Game Four and even the series. To fall to 1 and 3 would spell almost certain defeat. More difficult was the sense that the Canadiens should have won Game Three, but there wasn't time to dwell on the "shouldas" or "couldas." Practice for both teams was scheduled for early the next day, after which the Forum wrestling ring would be set up for Togo the Mad Jap.[20]

That all three games went into overtime got noticed in the press. Game Four began like a reprise of One. It was only seconds after Barbara Ann Scott, Canada's figure skating queen, dropped the ceremonial faceoff that Ted Kennedy stole the puck from MacPherson behind the Canadiens net and set up Sid Smith in front. When Smith's quick shot bulged the twine, he not only gave the Leafs a 1–0 lead but killed the initial enthusiasm of the Forum crowd. Before the end of the first, Harvey passed the puck to Reay who relayed it to Richard. Richard, experienced at playing his off wing, used his finely developed backhand to beat Rollins to the far side. The Forum crowd came back to life when Richard almost put the Canadiens in front with a great burst of speed. Mosdell sent Curry in on another good scoring opportunity before the period ended.

The Habs failed to build on the momentum as the second period began. Watson passed to Meeker at the goalmouth and the latter tipped the puck behind McNeil. Toronto led again by a goal, and Meeker ended the jinx that seemed to have foiled a dozen sure goals up to this point. In the third period, the Canadiens were swarming the Leaf net. Rollins made several sensational saves to hold Montreal off. The stop on Curry was breathtaking. Then Bouchard to Richard to Lach and suddenly the puck was behind Rollins. The Forum delirium was ear-splitting. Soon the ice was covered with newspapers, programs, and rubbers. It took several minutes for the maintenance crew to clear the debris, which probably helped the Leafs since the Habs had time to cool off. For the fourth straight time the teams went into overtime.[21]

Montreal had the best chances early. Olmstead came down the left side and failed to spot Richard all alone on the right. Rollins easily handled Olmstead's shot. Then Richard intercepted a breakout pass by Gardner and passed over to Reay, who fired at the Leaf net. Again Rollins was solid. Moments later a roar began as Geoffrion headed up ice from the Canadiens zone. The Leafs had been caught on a line change. But suddenly Max Bentley went down on one knee to strip Boom Boom of the puck. Bentley followed through on his sweep, and the puck went right over to Watson, who beat Harvey before firing the winner past McNeil. The sound of silence was deafening. Never before had there been four consecutive, overtime playoff games. Not since 1933 had there been three.

I mentioned in the previous chapter that the use of the flash was a standard part of interior photography for this period, and modern films love to mimic the explosive sounds they would make. Sometimes equipment failures actually contributed to spectacular effects, as was the case in Montreal for Game Four. A photographer took a picture of Tod Sloan getting a shot on net; however, his flash didn't fire. All was not lost, because another photographer on the opposite side of the rink clicked at exactly the same time. The flash from the opposite side lit up Sloan's head like a halo (see fig. 19). The picture was published on Saturday in *The Standard* with a caption that read in part, "this photo typifies much of hockey's whirring glamor."[22] Such occurrences happened more often than one might think—another such picture appears on the back page of *The Hockey News* on December 23, 1950.

As if overtime weren't enough, there were other pressures on McNeil. Theresa, his wife, was due to give birth any day. When he left her Thursday night for the Val-David hideaway, she was in acute pain. Before boarding the train for Toronto on Friday, Gerry rushed Teacy, now in labour, to the Catherine Booth Hospital. There was no question that he would make the trip to Toronto and play the next night, but there was also reason to think that the little netminder would be distracted. Fathers tended not to be present at births in 1951 in the way

Fig. 19 Gerry McNeil makes the save off Tod Sloan of the Toronto Maple Leafs during Game Four (April 19th) of the 1951 Stanley Cup Final; Floyd Curry is the player attempting to check Sloan. Photo is distinguished by the simultaneous flash of another camera on the opposite side of the rink, which produces a halo effect around Sloan's head. Note also the number of other cameras along the boards. These photographers were close to the action and weren't shooting through protective glass. (Photographer unknown. "Hockey Photo of the Week," *Standard* [Montreal], Apr. 21, 1951, 11.) Copyright unknown.

they are now, but obviously they still wanted to stay close to the action. By press time Saturday morning, it was known that Teacy had given birth to a healthy girl. The twist that was given this tidbit of behind-the-scene news was that it should inspire Gerry's teammates to provide a "stone wall of defense" in front of their goalie.[23] After witnessing McNeil's performance in the Semifinal against Detroit (see previous chapter) and now against the Leafs, Frank Selke, the general manager, made a comment to the press that seems designed to calm his goalie: "The only department in which we feel absolutely satisfied for future Canadiens' planning lies between the goal posts; McNeil has a frozen lease on the spot."[24]

THE GOALIE IN THE BARILKO PICTURE

Toronto was hungry for another Stanley Cup; if the Leafs came through that night, it would be four in five years. Enough for the team to earn a "dynasty" place in Cup history. Al Nickleson wrote that "it has been a magnificent spectacle, this Stanley Cup series of heart-hammering excitement."[25] A Cup win would also complete the trophy case of Joe Primeau, the Leaf coach, who could already boast Memorial and Allan Cup victories. From their St. Catharines hideaway, the Leafs made the expected statements about having to come out strong and not wanting to return to Montreal. Selke admitted that his team was down, but pointed out that they had won in Toronto before. Dick Irvin, always using the press to play mind games with his team and the opposition, sounded as if he were surrendering: "There really wasn't much use making the trip here. We've given our best and the Leafs are ahead. I guess the Semifinal with Detroit took too much out of us."[26]

Just after the opening faceoff, Kennedy went down and looked to have seriously injured his back.[27] Taken off on a stretcher, the Leaf captain made a dramatic return to the bench a few minutes later. The Leafs were on fire in the first period and outshot the Canadiens 14 to 4. Their dominance was so complete that everyone agreed they had rightfully earned the Cup. The only problem was that the period ended scoreless, thanks to the acrobatics of Gerry McNeil. He robbed Meeker, Watson, Bentley, and Klukay. Bob Dawes, one of the Montreal rookies, seemed to be doing a good job of checking Kennedy until he hit the boards in a scramble. He writhed on the ice in pain, his broken leg twisted grotesquely. Nobody in the Toronto camp was worried until almost halfway through the second; MacPherson hit Richard with a pass while the latter was floating in the neutral zone. Thomson immediately went to check the Habs star, but the Rocket somehow continued with the puck and, when Rollins went down, found an open net. Suddenly, there was concern on the Toronto side. Had the momentum swung to Montreal? Just four minutes later Kennedy carried the puck up ice and slid a pass to Sloan. Sloan powered toward the net with Harvey attempting to nullify the play. The Leafs finally scored to tie the game. The second period was rather even with Montreal actually outshooting Toronto 6 to 5.

Early in the third, another Montreal rookie, Paul Meger, took a pass from Harvey and avoided Klukay. He actually pulled up and fired behind Klukay to beat Rollins on the short side. The sense of hope on the Canadiens bench, having gone from faint in the first to something more in the second, now grew stronger as the third period counted down. Barilko and Johnson got into a shoving match. When Chadwick sent both of them off, Reay started to protest loudly—too loudly—and ended up getting a ten-minute misconduct. This left the Habs short-handed at centre for the rest of regulation time. The Leafs dug deep; experience told them that the odds of their winning three consecutive times in Montreal was remote. Their best chance was right now.

With a minute and thirty-three seconds left, Joe Primeau called Rollins to the bench for the extra skater. Even though Kennedy had just finished a shift, Primeau left him on for another. He also sent out the "hot" men of the series: Smith, Sloan, Watson, Bentley and Mortson. Irvin countered with his good checking line—Mosdell, Curry, Mazur—and Johnson and Bouchard on defence. The faceoff was in the Montreal zone. Mosdell kept moving toward Kennedy and got waved out. Curry came in to take the draw. This one soon became a pileup and the whistle went again. Irvin sent out Lach, then called him back.

Mosdell got the puck out and fired it toward the Toronto net, but Watson hustled back to intercept. He circled the Toronto net and headed up ice. The play was called (offside?). Now only a minute left, with the faceoff just outside the Canadiens' end. Rollins went back in for this one. Some Leaf fans voiced their disapproval, but Kennedy won the draw and sent the puck into the Montreal zone. Rollins raced back to the bench as the puck was frozen against the boards. Kennedy remained on the ice for another faceoff with Lach. Harvey replaced Johnson. This one was to McNeil's left.

Kennedy managed to knock the puck toward the boards. Lach was in pursuit but fell. Bentley had control at the point; he skated niftily toward the centre, "Joliat-like in his finessing" wrote Baz O'Meara.[28] He shot through a maze of players toward the net; the puck bounced to Smith, who whacked it at McNeil. It hit the far post, and Sloan was there on McNeil's left, unguarded. He tapped it over the red line. Half a minute left. The Leafs had tied it up—the Garden exploded. When the action resumed, there were no further scoring opportunities and regulation time came to an end with the building still abuzz about Sloan's goal.

While the talk was positive in the Canadiens' room, emotions sank with the feeling that victory was slipping away. In contrast, the Leafs were anxious to finish a game they felt they had dominated. The difference was immediately apparent in the play as the overtime began. Montreal was unable to get the puck out of their zone, let alone make an offensive play. Meeker gained the puck along the boards before it got over the blue line and fired it in at the Montreal net. Following his own shot, Meeker grabbed the puck to the left of McNeil and tried what today would be called the "wraparound." McNeil wasn't fooled, but he went down to make the stop. Before McNeil could get back to his feet, Meeker managed to pass the puck out in front to Watson who redirected it at the net. At this point, it is impossible to know exactly what happened, but my father did not remember the puck hitting him. The only plausible theory is that it hit Butch Bouchard and landed to McNeil's right. The goalie did not have time to get back up, but he instinctively tried to move across the crease. Barilko, however, sensing that such an opportunity might present itself, had moved in from his blue-line position. Fortune could not have favoured him more. He wasted no time in shovelling the rebound at the net. The puck sailed high and beat McNeil to the right.

The roar that erupted in the Gardens could be heard blocks away on Yonge Street. For the fourth time in the series the Leafs would swarm their goal-scoring hero—this time the defenceman Barilko, whom Smythe had threatened to tie to a clothesline to prevent his pinching in. In 1951 there wasn't even a phrase "pinching in" to describe what Barilko was known for. When a defenceman ventures deep into the offensive zone, he risks not being there to defend against a breakout by the opposing team. And yet there is an adage about risk-takers being successful—fortune favours the brave. It is certainly true that you miss all the shots you don't take. Barilko would take another risk that summer in flying back from his fishing trip in bad weather. That time he would not be so lucky.

The thrill of a Stanley Cup victory is more exhilarating when it comes in sudden-death overtime. There is no anticlimactic countdown to a final win, no playing out of the clock. It is all on the line up until the very last second. When Barilko scored his final goal, Joe Primeau may have been the first over the boards to congratulate him. Al Rollins quickly skated the length of the rink to join in the mobbing. For the losing team, there is nothing to do but try to endure the moment, which seems to last an eternity. One must somehow contain one's own sense of defeat while witnessing the celebration of the opposition. The game is over, but it is difficult not to see the other team as anything but the hated opposition. The Canadiens of the early 1950s had a hard time accepting defeat. One could have pointed to the Semifinal loss to New York the year before, and Doug Harvey's refusal to shake hands afterwards. Other players started to follow Harvey off the ice without the customary congratulation to the winning side.

Harvey always maintained that the handshake was hypocritical, disingenuous. That to expect an athlete to transform suddenly from the vanquished opponent to noble well-wisher is to ask for a lot if not the impossible. We believe that we have gotten beyond the uglier side of competitiveness in sport, yet so much of the post-game congratulation today (especially at the minor league levels) is perfunctory. Whenever an action becomes expected, as opposed to spontaneous, it is an empty form and teaches little that has to do with the ideals of sport. (How genuine is the routine glove-touching that happens now between all players on the ice and those on the bench after every goal is scored?) Nat Turofsky, who had just taken his famous picture of the winning goal from the east side of the Gardens, took another shot a few seconds later. This one shows Meeker offering congratulations to my father who is by now back on his feet. I do not know, and my father didn't remember, if he was still on the ice when Ted Kennedy, the Leaf captain, called for a cheer for his counterpart Butch Bouchard and "his gallant Canadiens," but one can point to Kennedy's gesture as one that seems to have been a sincere act of sportsmanship. McNeil did remember that all he wanted to do was somehow escape the sick feeling of defeat, to numb his emotions.

While the on-ice speeches and celebration continued, the Canadiens made their way to their dressing room on the west side of the Gardens. Beneath the roar of the crowd they quietly found their stalls and tried to lose themselves in muted oblivion. For a reporter, the hard assignment is to enter the dressing room of the losing team to get the story from the other side. It is especially hard when one enters as a reporter from the other city; such was the case for Al Nickleson and Jim Vipond of the Toronto *Globe and Mail*. Nickleson's words speak for themselves:

> In a room just a few feet off the ice from where the Leafs were shouting and embracing there was a death-like silence broken only by the sobbing of strong men wearing sweat-soaked Canadien uniforms. That few feet of difference between laughter and tears represented the closeness of the thrill-filled and fantastic five overtime games of the finals....
>
> We thought that the Leafs could have won by two or three goals in regulation time but for one thing. That thing was the marvellous mite, Gerry McNeil, who cried as did Rocket Richard in the dressing room while the roars of the victors rang and rang outside.
>
> As we watched him, lump in throat, we decided that we never had seen such amazing goaltending in a series and particularly in the game just over. How he kept out some of the 41 shots we'll never know.[29]

Such eloquence and respect mark the best kind of sports journalism. One thing the Canadiens organization has been known for is its heart.

THE GOALIE IN THE BARILKO PICTURE

Just as McNeil and Richard had shared the bond of victory over Detroit in the Semifinal, so here they shared tears of defeat. Boom Boom Geoffrion provided an insider's view of the team's emotional state after Barilko scored his goal: "The guy I felt sorry for was the fellow [Barilko] beat, Gerry McNeil. He had done a terrific job for us. In 11 playoff games he didn't have a bad one. Even in the last one that we lost to Toronto he was outstanding and the fans at Maple Leaf Gardens knew it because they gave him many ovations."[30]

One of the things my father used to say about the 1951 Final was that "you didn't always win when you played your best." It begs the question: what is preferable—to play one's best or to win? There is no easy answer. Individual achievement is all very well, but hockey is a team sport and with it comes all the positive aspects thereof, chief among which is the fact that members of a team win and lose together. Many in Canada today, and elsewhere, still grow up with the dream of winning the Stanley Cup. McNeil had that dream, and it was still unfulfilled. The other thing that helped ease McNeil's pain was the fact that he now had a baby daughter, born the same day that Barilko scored his goal. Over the years he and his family could not discuss Barilko without mentioning Karen, and over the years the father-daughter love easily eclipsed any significance that could have followed from a Stanley Cup win in '51.

In covering the Final for *The Globe*, Jim Vipond would allude to my father's coolness in waiting for the offensive player to make the first move,[31] something that is particularly important for small goalkeepers who cannot rely solely on size to block shots. The observation was consistent with earlier assessments of McNeil's style. One thing that could easily be deduced from the Barilko goal was the need for goalies to stay on their feet, especially when they can't control the rebound.

I began this chapter with the suggestion that part of the Barilko mystique has to do with the famous Turofsky picture which hung prominently for years in the middle of the west-end lobby of Maple Leaf Gardens, just feet away from that dressing room where the Canadiens had to swallow their defeat (see fig. 20). My father was often asked to autograph copies of Nat Turofsky's picture for fans, and it bothered him only a little. A second photographer, Michael Burns, was positioned on the west side of the ice, and he captured the event a millisecond later and from the side opposite to Turofsky. A smile is emerging on Barilko's face, so the victory is probably just registering in the defenceman's mind. As for McNeil, one can only see the back of his head. Both pictures appeared in *The Globe* the next day.[32] However, there is nothing

Fig. 20 The picture that has launched a thousand comments. 21 April 1951. (Photo by Nat Turofsky. *Globe and Mail*, Apr. 23, 1951, 20. Subsequent publications are too numerous to itemize.) Reproduced by permission of Imperial Oil – Nat & Lou Turofsky.

special in their first public formats. Both shots are trimmed, which has the effect of emphasizing the Barilko-McNeil duel, and the players are all labelled, as is the puck (with an arrow) in Turofsky's. The Burns photo has the prominent position at the top of the page with a large title, "It's the Goal That Paid Off on Another World Hockey Title for Toronto." (Canada Post used this image in its commemorative stamped envelope to honour the Toronto Maple Leafs' seventy-fifth anniversary.) Turofsky's sits inauspiciously just underneath. There is nothing here that hints at the notoriety that would eventually attach itself to the latter picture in the decades ahead—nothing to explain why this would be a picture to launch a thousand comments. Andrew Podnieks correctly draws our attention to what makes Turofsky's so memorable as sports still-photography: that it captures the exact split second after the puck has entered the net yet before the goal has registered on the faces in the crowd.[33] It might be argued that the Burns photo captures the same essential moment, a split second later; however, the puck is not clearly visible.

THE GOALIE IN THE BARILKO PICTURE

This precise timing cannot be attributed to another well-known picture of a defenceman scoring a Stanley Cup overtime goal. I'm referring, of course, to Ray Lussier's image of Bobby Orr airborne in 1970 against St. Louis (and the subject of another book by Andrew Podnieks).[34] Selected for inclusion in *SI*'s fiftieth-anniversary issue, Lussier's shot is probably better known among Americans than Turofsky's.[35] It is worth noting that the puck is still suspended in the mesh in Turofsky's picture, while in Lussier's it has already come back out of the net and lies in the crease. Orr's airborne position is celebratory—i.e., the fact that he has scored has already clearly registered. In fact, it is worth noting that Lussier himself didn't think the photo would be printed because the puck had already exited the net.[36]

Another noteworthy detail about Turofsky's picture is that one can count four Leaf skaters in the frame (Barilko, Watson, Meeker, and Gardner) and only three Canadiens (Johnson, Bouchard, and Richard). Had the Habs gained control of the puck, they would have outnumbered the Leafs two to one going the other way. Barilko was taking a real gamble and could have ended up the goat instead of the hero. Still photography freezes the moment but tells us nothing about what happened just before, or just after. Growing up and seeing the picture, I often wondered to myself. What happened exactly? How did my father end up back in the net?

There have been several narrative descriptions of the goal. One of the most detailed, and I believe accurate, is by Kevin Shea in his biography of Barilko.[37] Actually, the description Shea uses is by Paul Patskou, who is responsible for finding the footage of the goal. What is interesting about the Patskou narrative is how it attempts to capture some kind of *truth* or full version about what happened, based on what remains unknowable from viewing the moving picture. Another description is by James Duplacey and Charles Wilkins in their book *Forever Rivals*.[38] The one aspect of the sequence that remains a mystery is how Watson's shot ended up bouncing to the right of the Canadiens' goal. Although Patskou follows Duplacey and Wilkins in suggesting that it hit Butch Bouchard's skate, there is no way to be certain about this detail. My father confirmed that the shot never hit him or got to the net, so it would appear that Duplacey and Wilkins are right. I once asked my father what he thought of checking with Butch Bouchard, and I can recall vividly how he and my mother just laughed. "Sure, I can ask Butch, and he would probably respond with something like, 'What, half a century later, you're trying to blame me for the goal?!'"

It was simply a moment in the careers of several players, a moment determined by innumerable circumstances too mundane to be of any interest to any but those fascinated by Turofsky's picture. Reviewing the footage of the goal, which I have done now countless times, gives one a better sense of what happened.[39] The Leafs simply stormed the Montreal end and pressed successfully for the winning goal. That is all we know, and all we need to know. Forget the fact that hundreds of details could be cited from regulation time that determined any of the previous four goals or that thwarted all kinds of close chances for an earlier winning goal. History follows a very narrow and precise path, and in our retrospective glance, that path does not change.

The cultural significance of Turofsky's picture is reflected in the fact that it was selected for inclusion in Kingwell and Moore's compilation of twentieth-century photographs entitled *Canada: Our Century* (it would be one of nine hockey pictures in the collection).[40] With an exception or two, the other eight photos constitute a virtual who's who of hockey culture in Canada:

1) Foster Hewitt giving a hockey broadcast in 1923.
2) Lester Patrick, the manager of the New York Rangers, replacing his injured goalie in 1928.
3) Jimmy Orlando bloodied after a fight on November 7, 1942 (erroneously said to be from April 1944; see Chapter 1).
4) Maurice Richard on the occasion of the riot in March 1955—although it must be said that the photo is not related to the riot.
5) Bobby Hull pitching hay on the family farm.
6) Gordie Howe on a poster after scoring his 1,092nd point in 1960.
7) Paul Henderson scoring the winning goal against the Soviets in 1972.
8) Wayne Gretzky raising his first Stanley Cup in 1984.

Podnieks remarks of the picture of Barilko scoring his famous goal that it is "quite likely the most reproduced Turofsky image at the Hockey Hall of Fame,"[41] which has over nineteen thousand hockey photos in its Turofsky Imperial Oil collection. Its popularity from the 1960s onward is due to Barilko's tragic story, the fact that the Leafs have not won a Stanley Cup since '67, the large Leaf fan base around the HHOF, and, of course, the picture itself. Similar to how Bobby Thompson's pennant-winning home run (also in 1951) has been called "the shot that was heard around the world," due to its overseas radio broadcast (i.e., "the Giants win the pennant, the Giants win the pennant"), so Barilko's feat, manifest in Turofsky's image, is ubiquitous in pictorial histories of hockey. As far as the theory of the spectacle is concerned, we can

THE GOALIE IN THE BARILKO PICTURE

easily identify MacAloon's festive frame and Turner's threshold moment—time is suspended between the game action, or the goal, and the registration of that action by the players and fans.

We have already noted the depth of field and detail that sports photographers could achieve with the Speed Graphic camera (its 4″×5″ negative is technically large-format) when used with the powerful strobe lights mounted on the mesh or retaining glass. These features were lost with the adoption of 35-mm that became the norm in much sports photography in the latter part of the twentieth century. Moreover, during this same period the still action-shot lost its exclusive status of being the only visual record. The moving images of television and film improved and became dominant. We remember Barilko's goal with the still image, Bobby Hull's fifty-first goal in 1966 as a visual sequence, and Paul Henderson's as footage plus voice-over (i.e., Foster Hewitt's "*They score… Henderson!*"). It might even be argued that the 1940s and '50s were the golden age of sports photography at least as far as infiltrating the popular media was concerned.

The success of *Sport* magazine was largely attributable to its rich pictorial layouts, and just as colour was making its way into the major motion picture, so it was with popular magazines. Reflecting this transitional period, a typical layout featured a lush coloured item among the standard black and white photos. The same visual formula seems to have been responsible for the popularity of *Life*, only in *Sport* it was scaled down from the large 14″×10.5″ size to what would become the magazine industry standard of 11″×8.5″. When Henry Luce began his rival publication *SI* in 1954, not only did he imitate this pictorial strategy, but he had actually tried to buy out *Sport* and its name.[42]

In any case, McNeil's full-page colour portrait appeared in the 1951 February issue of *Sport* to illustrate a general article on NHL goaltenders (see back cover).[43] Although the actual item lacks a credit for the photographer, this Rockwell-like image must surely be the work of Ozzie Sweet, famous for his staged portraits of athletes. Sweet's work has appeared on an estimated eighteen hundred magazine covers.[44] When it came to professional hockey, Sweet seemed particularly fond of the red sweater (McNeil, Richard, and Plante for Montreal, Howe for Detroit, and Hull for Chicago), usually framed with a dark background. The predominance of red isn't surprising, given that colour's associations in Western culture with anger, passion, love, and danger. Red's attention-drawing property and consequent universal use to denote warning as in the fire truck or stop sign also come into play here.

Unlike the spontaneity in the work of action sports photographers like Turofsky, Peskin, and Kilpatrick, Sweet carefully composed his photos. This kind of representation is often used for the popular sports card that was marketed to children, but Sweet's work is more in the line of classical portraiture. McNeil looks to the left; his expression is unusually calm, his features delicate. He leans with his arms crossed on the crossbar of a net; his goalie gloves and stick visible at the bottom. Four years later Sweet would do a similar portrait for McNeil's teammate Maurice Richard, and this 1955 image is much more familiar in the popular imagination of hockey fans. Benoît Melançon has compared its composition to *The Martyrdom of Saint Sebastian* by Luca Giordano, and the comparison is valid given the saint-like veneration accorded some professional athletes (like Richard for Quebecers born prior to 1960).[45]

Two factors make hockey photos of Turofsky's time distinctive: one is technical, the other historical. First, the grey-scale composition imparts an imaginary nostalgia, an otherworldliness that we associate with the mid-twentieth century. (By "we," I refer to a 2015 viewer; this imagined otherworldliness will probably be different a half century from now.) Looking at pre-1950 photos, one can easily forget that previous generations did live in a world of colour. A number of experts have attempted to account for the differences in our experience of the black and white (i.e., grey-scale) and colour photo. Free of any noise from the colour palette (Josh and Ellen Anon speak of a "visual intensity" that colour conveys), grey-scale has the effect of emphasizing all non-colour aspects: detail, framing, composition, depth.[46] Woodward reminds us of how journalism retained a snobbishness about black and white film, how colour film wasn't deemed trustworthy (he notes how even Lussier's 1970 image of an airborne Orr was originally shot in black and white). The second aspect is purely historical: the lack of face masks or helmets gives greater access to the facial expressiveness of the individuals depicted. We read and feel Barilko's reckless hope, McNeil's desperation. Similarly, when HD television came to sports, commentators pointed to the new wonder of being able to read the faces of football players through the mask.[47]

My father was asked several times if the Barilko goal haunted him. Although he did think that hockey people were more obsessed with it than he was, he did periodically express a desire to escape the Barilko mystique. Needless to say, it was Kilpatrick's shot of my father stopping Gordie Howe that hung for decades in our home, not Turofsky's. Like the professional athlete who just wants to "go fishing"—that is, get away from an ever-scrutinizing public—McNeil did want to get away from the Barilko hounds who otherwise knew very little about him or the '51 playoffs.

The Rocket, ironically, relished the solitude of fishing, almost as much as he enjoyed the public spectacle of competition. Perhaps it's just about finding something different to do. Fishing trips were popular among hockey players of Barilko's time, and this isn't only because the fishing season opened when the hockey season came to an end. "Goin' fishin'" was then what it still is for many, an escape from the everyday routine.

However, there was one fishing trip in the early 1950s that was no escape from the public eye. A professional film company was hired to shoot a group of hockey players having a grand time at O'Connell Lodge on Lac-des-Loups. Four Canadiens were chosen as subjects: Gerry McNeil, Elmer Lach, Maurice Richard, and Doug Harvey. The players and crew were flown to the location. McNeil remembered donning the expected plaid flannel shirt, grabbing a pole, and casting in the lake.

The crew got it all, but they soon grew impatient. "Okay, we're all set; now this would look a lot better if you guys could reel in a few." The players took this comment as a criticism of their professional sportsmanship and were not amused. Somebody did get a small trout after about ten minutes, but the crew chief just got sarcastic, "Great, now maybe you can catch something bigger than a minnow."

The fish simply weren't biting that day and so the production crew and players were transported to a nearby hatchery where there was sure to be more action. A photograph was taken of the players as they stood on a pontoon with their Algonquin guide (see fig. 21). The clothes, the plane, and the setting make it a great "era" shot, but ironically the tension, from which fishing is supposed to be an escape, can be read in the faces. Mac has a cigarette in his left hand; like many of his generation, he had picked up the habit casually. Many years later he would pay the price. Neither Doug nor the Rocket look happy about the situation. Infuriated at the director's repeated complaints about not getting any decent-sized fish, Richard would eventually refuse to co-operate and didn't even make it into the final cut of the movie.

In the end, *Angling Around* did get made and, since fishing was supposed to be an escape, it is perhaps fitting that the subjects (sans Richard) are never even identified as professional hockey players.[48] A VHS version of the film was sent to Mac by Jeff Klassen of Reel One In in the 1990s—some fifty years after the film was made. The Quebec

Fig. 21 An Algonquin guide stands on the pontoon of a plane with three members of the Canadiens: Gerry McNeil, Doug Harvey, and Maurice Richard. Lac-des-Loups, circa 1951. (Photographer unknown.) Copyright unknown.

setting is what really interested the fishing company, since the second and third segments feature fishing in Cuba and Chile respectively, the full title being *Angling around the Americas*. In any case, in the film it is Elmer who lands the fish; Mac casts out but reels nothing in, and Harvey snags one only to see it get away. The Rocket is nowhere to be seen. Seething back at the lodge perhaps? Unlike Barilko, at least McNeil and company got to laugh about their "fishing" trip at O'Connell Lodge for years afterwards.

A week after losing to the Leafs, McNeil signed his 1951–52 contract with the Canadiens that reportedly made him "among the high salary performers in the game." Frank Selke told the press, "Gerry is today the best in the business as far as we are concerned and his play in the play-offs proved it beyond a doubt. He outgoaled Sawchuck [sic], Broda, and Rollins at every turn. Losing out in our bid for the Stanley Cup was a

THE GOALIE IN THE BARILKO PICTURE

bitter pill to swallow but we think that we have found something more valuable than the Stanley Cup ever was or ever will be."[49] Despite the overstatement here, which leans toward the ridiculous (what could be more valuable to a professional hockey club than the Stanley Cup?), McNeil felt good to know that management had such confidence in him, that his job was secure.

For the rest of his life, he remained proud of how he played against the Leafs in that Final series, and proud to have been part of the only playoff series in which every game went into overtime. Even when he was billed as "the goalie in the Barilko picture," my father had a clear sense of having played a necessary role in the sports drama, of having transcended the competitive world that others assumed he still inhabited. He tended to use such opportunities to remind people of his 218-minute shutout streak against Detroit in the Semifinal. He would also talk about how much his daughter Karen meant to him over the half century since that night. I suspect that his peace with the Barilko goal also had more to do with what my father accomplished in the ensuing few years—his greatest NHL thrill was yet to come.

1   The story is well known. There have been two books devoted to it. See Kevin Shea, *Barilko: Without a Trace* (Bolton: Fenn, 2004); and John Melady, *Overtime Overdue: The Bill Barilko Story* (Trenton: City Print, 1988). When Red Burnett retired in 1975 after forty-four years in the sports department of the *Toronto Star*, he said that "Bill Barilko's goal [was] his greatest memory." See Red Burnett, "Barilko's Goal My Greatest Memory," *Toronto Star*, May 3, 1975, B1.
2   I published an article on this subject. See David McNeil, "The '51 Stanley Cup: A Spectacle of Sudden Death Overtime," *Textual Studies in Canada* 12 (1998): 5–18.
3   The first round series between Chicago and Phoenix in 2012 began with five overtime games but wasn't decided until game six, which ended in regulation time.
4   I know there have been attempts to change the nomenclature (i.e., "sudden death" to "sudden victory") but I seriously doubt if the latter will be adopted.
5   A detailed description of Barilko's heroic play is given by Al Nickleson, "Blocked Richard Sizzler: Barilko Saved Leafian Bacon," *Globe and Mail*, Apr. 12, 1951, 18.
6   These facts are taken from Brian McFarlane, *Stanley Cup Fever: 100 Years of Hockey Greatness* (Toronto: Stoddart, 1992), 113–14. This is a brief narrative history of the Stanley Cup Playoffs.
7   For the details of Game One, see Jim Vipond, "Leafs Shade Canadiens in Cup Opener, 3–2 . . . ," *Globe and Mail*, Apr. 12, 1951, 19; and Elmer Ferguson, "Leafs Win Cup Opener 3 to 2 in Overtime," *Herald, Montreal*, Apr. 12, 1951, 1, 24.
8   The caption reads, "This One Did It!" *Globe and Mail*, Apr. 12, 1951, 1.
9   Ferguson, "Leafs Win Cup Opener," 1, 24; Jim Vipond, "Leafs Shade Canadiens," 1, 19.

10 Red Burnett, "Credit McNeil's Magic for Carrying Leafs to Overtime," *Toronto Star*, Apr. 12, 1951, 24.

11 See Dave Stubbs, "A Slice of Netminding History," *Gazette* (Montreal), Mar. 27, 2004, 1, A2, A3.

12 Mike Leonetti, *The Game: Hockey in the Fifties* (Vancouver: Raincoast, 1997). Leonetti published two more Barkley collections: *The Game We Knew: Hockey in the Sixties* (Vancouver: Raincoast, 1998) and *Hockey in the Seventies: The Game We Knew* (Vancouver: Raincoast, 1999). As these titles suggest, Leonetti locates a nostalgic appeal in Barkley's work.

13 This picture was republished in 2006. See Dave Stubbs, "Portraits of Courage Frozen in Time; Photos of Habs Goalie McNeil Reveal NHL's Joy and Pain," *Gazette* (Montreal), June 19, 2006, C2.

14 See *The Jacques Laperriere Auction* (October 21, 2008), Classic Auctions, 90, catalogue. Lot #527. The Classic Auctions website indicates that McDiarmid's painting sold for $656.

15 McNeil's comments and those by Dick Irvin are quoted by Ferguson, "Gist and Jest," *Herald, Montreal*, Apr. 12, 1951, 25.

16 "Movies Show That Chadwick Erred in Disallowing Mortson's Goal in Opener against Habitants," *Globe and Mail*, Apr. 16, 1951, 23.

17 Jim Vipond, "Richard's Overtime Score Sinks Leafs, 3–2," *Globe and Mail*, Apr. 16, 1951, 23. All details from this game are taken from Vipond's article.

18 Jim Vipond, "Leafs Edge Canadiens, 2–1, in Overtime Duel," *Globe and Mail*, Apr. 18, 1951, 15.

19 Vipond, "Leafs Edge Canadiens," 15.

20 Ibid.

21 Ibid.

22 *Standard, Montreal*, Apr. 21, 1951, 11.

23 "It's a Girl at the McNeils." Unidentified newspaper clipping in family scrapbook.

24 "Backstage in Sport." Unidentified newspaper clipping in family scrapbook.

25 Al Nickleson, "Leafs Could End Hockey Spectacle with Win Tonight," *Globe and Mail*, Apr. 21, 1951, 19.

26 Nickleson, "Leafs Could End," 19.

27 All facts related to Game Five are taken from Jim Vipond, "Barilko's Goal Sinks Canadiens, 3–2 …," *Globe and Mail*, Apr. 23, 1951, 21; and Al Nickleson, "Cup Aftermath: Defeat Not Easy for Great Habs," *Globe and Mail*, Apr. 23, 1951: 20; and Baz O'Meara, "McNeil Magic Fails to Keep Habs in Stanley Cup Hunt: Leafs Artillery Blasts Out Overtime Victory—Canadiens Yield Lead in Last Minute of Third Period—McNeil Marvellous," *Montreal Daily Star*, Apr. 23, 1951, 29.

28 O'Meara, "McNeil Magic," 29.

29 Nickleson, "Cup Aftermath," 20.

30 Geoffrion and Fischler, *Boom Boom*, 28.

31 Vipond, "Barilko's Goal," 21.

32 See *Globe and Mail*, Apr. 23, 1951, 20.

33 Andrew Podnieks, *Portraits of the Game: Classic Photographs from the Turofsky Collection at the Hockey Hall of Fame* (Toronto: Doubleday, 1997), 62.

34 See Andrew Podnieks, *The Goal* (Toronto: Doubleday, 2004).

35 See *SI*, Apr. 26, 2004, 104.

36 This piece of information is provided by Howard Berger, "Catching History by Accident," *National Post*, May 10, 2000, B12.

37 See Shea, *Barilko: Without a Trace*, 153–55.

38 James Duplacey and Charles Wilkins, *Forever Rivals: Montreal Canadiens and Toronto Maple Leafs* (Toronto: Random House, 1996), 114.

39 Andrew Hunter's installation exhibit "Up North: A Northern Ontario Tragedy" included a five-minute loop of footage from Game Five that included the end of regulation time and the overtime. I watched it repeatedly in 1998 at the Kamloops gallery, and the experience did not clarify anything with respect to the Barilko goal. My father and I subsequently received a tape from the Hockey Hall of Fame with the same footage. "Up North" exhibited at the Tom Thomson, McMaster, Winnipeg, and Kamloops Art Galleries in 1997–98. My father and I used to joke that there would soon be a musical based on the Barilko story.

40 *Canada: Our Century* (Toronto: Doubleday, 1999), 276. The other eight pictures are on pages 145, 155, 235, 289, 320, 321, 379, and 431. It should be noted that the Turofsky shot of a bloodied Jimmy Orlando was taken in November of 1942 (not 1944).

41 Podnieks, *Portraits of the Game*, 62.

42 For the story of how Henry Luce was willing to pay MacFadden Publications $200,000 for *Sport* magazine just so he could use the name, see Richard Hoffer, "A Great Year for Sports… And a New Sports Magazine," *Sports Illustrated 50*, 28, 35.

43 Reproduced on the back cover of this book. See *Sport*, February 1951, 19. The credit line reads, "exclusively by International."

44 See Bruce Weber, "Ozzie Sweet, Who Helped Define New Era of Photography, Dies at 94," New York Times, Feb. 23, 2013. http://www.nytimes.com/2013/02/24/sports/ozzie-sweet-who-helped-define-new-era-of-photography-dies-at-94.html?pagewanted=all&_r=0.

45 See Benoît Melançon, *The Rocket: A Cultural History of Maurice Richard*, trans. Fred A. Reed (Vancouver: Greystone, 2009), 85–86.

46 For black and white versus colour photography, see Josh and Ellen Anon, *See It: Photographic Composition Using Visual Intensity* (New York: Focal Press, 2012), 98–100. For their comments on red and its associations, see p. 87.

47 Robert Willox, director of marketing for content creation at Sony Electronics, comments: "In the old days, the cameras could barely penetrate the shadows under the helmets, so the players all looked like Darth Vader. Now because of HD, you not only can see the sweat on their faces when watching at home, you see their state of being, which brings a whole new emotional level to viewing the game." See Ken Freed, "ABC Sports Prepares for HD Super Bowl XL," TV Technology, accessed May 31, 2006, http://www.tvtechnology.com/features/news/2006.01.25-n_abc.shtml.

48 Angling Around the Americas (Columbia Film, 1952).

49 "McNeil Signs: Selke Says Goaler Now Super Star Salary Earner," *Montreal Daily Star*, Apr. 28, 1951, 16.

5 Playing Through

PROFESSIONAL ATHLETES MUST PLAY THROUGH ALL KINDS OF adversity. Sometimes they are thrust into a controversial situation over which they have no control, sometimes there are personal problems that are distracting, sometimes they must endure physical pain, and sometimes they must overcome a crisis in confidence. Whatever form the adversity takes, the athlete may be motivated not by some inner need to prove oneself, but by a felt obligation to perform come hell or high water. Overcoming adversity can be a positive experience, but the price may be costly.

Ironically, it was McNeil's great goaltending during the 1951 playoffs that led to his first difficult situation in the 1951–52 season: his selection to the Second All-Star Team over the Vezina-winning Al Rollins. Under the new format for the 1951 game, a poll of sportswriters and sportscasters voted for the ten starting positions on the First and Second Teams.[1] The coaches of the '51 Stanley Cup finalists, Joe Primeau of the Cup-winning Leafs and Dick Irvin of the runner-up Habs, were responsible for selecting alternatives. Surprisingly, Rollins didn't make either the First or Second Teams; these positions went to Sawchuk and Rayner. Primeau had to make his selections from the four American-based teams, and so he chose Lumley from Chicago as the alternate goalie. Irvin had to select from the two Canadian-based teams. He didn't hesitate to call upon his own man, McNeil, over the Vezina-winning Rollins, which drew considerable attention.[2] Al Nickleson of *The Globe and Mail* pointed out that this would be the only All-Star game in which the Vezina winner did not dress, an oddity to be sure.[3] Ever controversial, Irvin apparently gave the following justification: "We'll see how McNeil does with a good team in front of him. I know he is much better than Rollins and, besides, I want the best players on my team. I don't consider Mr. Rollins a very good goaler."[4]

The game was played at Maple Leaf Gardens, so the air was thick with controversy. Was Irvin getting a dig in at the team that beat his for the Stanley Cup? Perhaps, but the whole thing could backfire in his face if McNeil did not live up to the billing. As for McNeil, he couldn't control any part of it. What went through his mind at the Royal York luncheon is anybody's guess, but he certainly had reason to be concerned. He knew he could depend on Bouchard and Harvey for defensive support, but what about all the Leafs on the second team: Thomson, Kennedy, Smith, Mortson, Bentley, Watson, and Sloan? Would any Leaf have an incentive to backcheck? If Irvin was sending a message, then maybe the Leaf players would do something to answer it. McNeil knew that players could leave a goalie out in the cold, make him look terrible if they wanted to. Ultimately he would have to fall back on a goaltender's resolve and ability to stand alone. He had to put aside the mental baggage and simply do his best.

Unlike the friendly, no-hitting encounters of today, the All-Star game of the early 1950s was a seriously contested affair with all kinds of physical checking. The entire Leaf team was planning to come in from their St. Catharines training camp to watch the game in '51. None of the Leafs was voted to the First Team (there were three voted to the second team and three more selected by Irvin), even though they won the Stanley Cup.[5] Irvin did express hope that Bill Barilko would make a miraculous appearance,[6] but that was not to be. Needless to say, the evening was full of tension, and, scheduled to play the second half, McNeil had plenty of time to sit on the bench and think about all the consequences if he didn't perform well. The most important, of course, would be that Irvin himself wouldn't hesitate to let Mac know that he let his coach down, embarrassed him in front of the entire NHL brass. It was becoming clear to McNeil that superlative play only created more pressure to deliver. Maybe it would have been better not to have been chosen.

The first unsettling moment came in the dressing room. The Second Team was assigned to the regular Leaf room which was managed by Tim Daly. As the players were suiting up, Daly accosted Dick Irvin in the passageway: "We don't allow children in the dressing room when the players are getting ready. There is some kid sitting in there, maybe a friend of yours or of one of the players. Whoever he is, get him out of there."

Irvin went into the room with Daly to see who had his son with him. "What kid are your talking about?" he asked after inspecting the area.

"That kid over there."

"Why that's our goaler Gerry McNeil," answered Irvin.[7]

The misunderstanding could hardly have inspired confidence. After the ceremonial introductions, the game got underway. Howe scored on Rayner in the first; it would be the only goal to be scored by a "voted" player.[8] The Second Team tied it up just before the midway point of the

PLAYING THROUGH

second period. Then Johnny Peirson, the Bruin who would become McNeil's Nemesis, put the Firsts back in front. McNeil knew that he could not afford to give up another, especially anything soft. He didn't. His Canadiens friend Ken Mosdell scored the nicest goal of the evening in the third to knot the game again, and it ended 2–2. The First Team outshot their opponents 28 to 17, so Al Nickleson attributed the tie to the "great goaltending" by Rayner and McNeil. Ted Lindsay was the "bad man" of the evening, although it must be admitted that he was elbowed in the face by Kennedy. His cross-check on Richard seemed unprovoked, however, and when Richard tapped him back on the shoulder, it looked for a second as if a fight would break out. Early in the third, Richard rode Howe into the end boards and the two went down struggling. According to Ferguson, Howe got up and snapped, "What's the matter with you? This is only an exhibition game." To which Richard replied, "With me, it's a hockey game."[9] The best thing about the tie was that nobody lost any pride. McNeil could return to Montreal knowing that he did not embarrass his coach.

The same format was followed in the 1952 game. This time Sawchuk was voted to the First Team (his stellar play in 1951–52 including the playoffs made this a no-brainer) and Jim Henry to the Second. Henry's choice was based on a 2.52 goals against average for the regular season (2.41 playoffs). McNeil's corresponding 2.34 and 2.01 were better, but an argument could be made that Boston gave up more shots. In any case, Rayner was chosen as the alternate for the First Team, and McNeil for the Second. Sawchuk, however, had to go the distance as Rayner couldn't play due to an injury. He turned away 19 shots, and was only beaten on a rebound in the third that Richard banged home. Henry played only the first half but was tested 21 times (an indication of the superiority of the First Team); Marty Pavelich beat him just before he was replaced by McNeil, who came in and stopped all 10 shots sent his way. However, the game was not really a success, "a listless contest that drew few cheers" from only 10,600 fans at the Olympia.[10]

McNeil played in the All-Star game again in 1953, but because of a change in format (i.e., Stanley Cup champions from the previous spring versus All-Star team) his selection was not subject to any commentary. This time, however, he played the entire game and gave up two goals, both to Wally Hergesheimer. The first came with McNeil's team down a man, the second with his team down two men. His five-year-old son Ronnie was sitting near the passageway to the dressing room and screamed down to his father while the latter exited after the first, "How did you like that one, Dad?" Sawchuk turned in another great performance at the other end since his side was outshot 31 to 20. Kelly and Olmstead got into a good fight at the beginning of the third, and Richard scored to make it close. The Forum crowd of over fourteen thousand produced the largest gross gate of over thirty thousand dollars (one third of which went to the players' pension fund).[11] For reasons which will become clear later, this was McNeil's last All-Star game. According to Rauzulu's Street (an Internet source of sports statistics), of goalies who have played a minimum of two All-Star games, McNeil has a 1.49 GAA, second only to Gilles Villemure's 0.68.[12] When I mentioned this statistic to a friend, the response was, "no way a goalie could ever get that with the offence displayed in the All-Star game today," and "but things are skewed because nobody takes it seriously." The penalties and fights make it clear enough that they took the game seriously in the early 1950s, but, granted, things have changed.

Another substantial difference between the NHL in McNeil's time and the present day is that most people now know the league only from television broadcasts and highlight reels. We will defer discussion of the first CBC telecast until Chapter 7 and the news clip until Chapter 8. Suffice it to say that few people had access to these. Few people owned television sets in the early 1950s and only the last period was broadcast (later this would increase to the last two periods, and finally, the entire game). News clips were largely restricted to people who paid to see feature films in movie theatres. For those who could not see games live or afford the ticket prices (steep for the time, although nowhere near the astronomical amounts of today) there was the radio or newspaper the next day. The radio voices of the Habs were Charlie Harwood, Doug Smith, and Michel Normandin.[13]

It was my father's impression that only a small proportion of the fan base nowadays can actually afford to attend games; those that do are often "clients" or business associates being entertained rather than fans. This corporate crowd has hardly any understanding of the game, let alone passion for it, which only encourages team owners to step up the artificial atmosphere. Laser lights, blasting music, dry ice, and mascots all add up to one pathetic attempt to manufacture what, for my father, is an excitement that used to be generated by the game itself. A huge screen now directs the crowd to make noise, which remarkably is still possible even with all the electronic, computerized sound effects that drown out chants or cheering. In the early '50s there may have been an organist, perhaps one dedicated fan with a trumpet leading cheers, and many more ready to break out in another spontaneous rendition of *Les Canadiens sont là*.

There were other distractions in McNeil's career during the 1951–52 and 1952–53 seasons. A game against the Leafs on October 30, 1951, was played in front of royalty, Princess (soon to be Queen) Elizabeth and Prince Philip the Duke of Edinburgh. The Princess shook hands with the team captains before the game, and Butch Bouchard was dripping with nervous perspiration. The royal couple, looking rather young, sat between William Northey, President of the Canadian Arena Company, and Mayor Houde; unlike their official hosts, they actually appeared to be enjoying the action.[14] McNeil's roomie "Busher" Curry rose to the occasion and notched a hat trick—the only one of his career—and the Habs dumped the Rangers 6–1. In Baz O'Meara's words, McNeil, in a bit of a slump of late, "reclaimed his old wizardry."

Concern for family either at the game or sick at home was another distraction. Once Teacy was hit with a puck and had to be taken to the Forum clinic. Then there were the reporters who were eager to learn anything from anybody who might speak to them—like a precocious child. Eddie McCabe casually inquired of the five-year-old Ronnie what he liked most about the game, and the little guy answered that his greatest thrill was seeing the attendants water the ice between periods (this was the time before the Zamboni)! As for his father, Ronnie wasn't impressed: "Why can't he skate like the other players?"[15]

By far the greatest distraction for McNeil in the late fall of 1951 was the illness of his mother, who was suffering from terminal cancer. Her condition was known publicly, and one Saturday night as the team was hurrying to catch a train somebody called to say that Rose Ann (Dyotte) McNeil had passed away. McNeil broke down in tears. After a few moments, somebody phoned his family in Quebec City and discovered that the call had been a hoax.[16] When his mother did pass away on a weekend McNeil continued to play: a win in Detroit on Monday and then a shutout against Chicago on Tuesday, where he again cried in the dressing room between periods. From Chicago McNeil flew back to Montreal and took the train to Quebec to attend the funeral. He declined to take time off to recover but travelled back to Montreal to face Toronto that night. Impressed by his courage and dedication to the team, the Habs stymied the Leafs, allowing them only 15 shots. Ferguson wrote: "And when the game was over, it wasn't around the goal scorers that the players gathered. It was around McNeil shaking his hand and pounding him on the back."[17]

Another major distraction a few weeks after his mother's death was a crisis involving his daughter, Karen—the child born the day of Barilko's goal—who became seriously ill. Her temperature reached a critical point and she was rushed to the hospital. On another road trip with the team, McNeil got the news on the phone and was told that they might lose her. He flew home from Boston to be at her bedside. After she stabilized, he flew back out to Detroit to rejoin the team, calling home a number of times a day for updates.[18] As anyone in a situation like this knows, the feeling of helplessness is overwhelming. Fortunately, the fever broke and Karen recovered. As for McNeil, the world had somehow changed. More conscious of what he had, of what he enjoyed, he was also more conscious of the precariousness of life, of what he could lose. While McNeil seemed to take team-commitment to a questionable extreme, those close to him knew that not only did his family mean much more to him than the game, but that there was a sense of the latter having already robbed him of "quality time." He missed Halloween costumes, birthdays, and Sunday dinners and knew that he couldn't make them up. The moments were gone forever.

McNeil was often asked what it was like to play without a mask. He responded by pointing out that it was the norm at the time, as it was to drive without seatbelts. "Nobody really gave it much thought, like using cellphones today." Precaution is a mindset that follows disaster. The risk of injury was always there, and rather than reduce the risk with extra protection, it was more common to suppress the fear of injury, which could only detract from one's performance as a goaltender. Watching footage of his play later in life, however, he was amazed at how vulnerable his face was if he had gone down in a scramble. McNeil was there when Jacques Plante, the man who finally insisted on using a face mask, first expressed his desire to use the extra protection. Dick Irvin's response was immediate: "You'll never be a goalie if you're afraid of the puck."[19] Although no sane person would want to stand in there today without a mask, there's some sense in the comment. A goalie cannot be afraid of the puck hitting him if his essential job is to get in front of it. Perhaps shots weren't as hard or high in the 1950s as they are today, but goalies did routinely throw themselves down on the ice or fall, in which case their exposed face was right in the action, as illustrated in a picture that Kilpatrick took of my father (see fig. 22). Injury to the face or head area could come from a stick or skate as well as the puck.

Kilpatrick's photo was taken in the early 1950s at the Detroit Olympia and given to my father, as was the one of my father and Howe (see Chapter 3). While the latter was always displayed somewhere in our home, the former had been stuffed in a storage barrel, where it lay, buried and forgotten, for almost half a century. I remember helping my

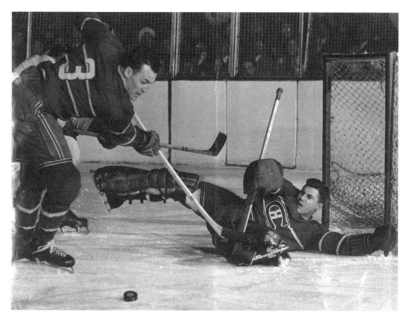

Fig. 22 Goaltenders did go down to block shots, thus exposing their faces to severe injury. Detroit Olympia, circa 1951. (Photo by James "Scotty" Kilpatrick.) Copyright unknown.

father sort through some family junk in a condo locker that was just a sectioned-off area in an underground garage. After filling a half-dozen garbage bags, we finally got to the barrel, the contents untouched in decades, and pulled out what looked like a discarded piece of cardboard that was folded in half. I opened it and Kilpatrick's image suddenly came back to life. Mesmerized by its unusually large size (11″ × 14″) and detail, we stared at it for quite some time. I have used the image in promotional posters for a class I teach on hockey literature; it is also the background to all the PowerPoint presentations I make. I have also framed and sold about a half dozen actual-sized reproductions (entitled "Before the Mask") with Kilpatrick's history on the back at charity auctions. For over ten years, if you googled "Kilpatrick, McNeil, Bouchard" you would have pulled it up on the Internet. Needless to say, the image has now been viewed by thousands of people, and it came so close to being thrown away with so much family junk. How many other photos or artifacts are not rescued?

I spent hours restoring the image with Photoshop. The fold line was relatively easy to eliminate; the damage to the left side—Butch's backside and leg—much more difficult and time-consuming. However, I feel it might be better to reproduce it here with all its historical scars, especially the fold line clearly visible running down the middle (fig. 22). It serves as a symbolic paraline between the lost world of that moment at the Olympia and the recovered view now evoking all that was—the players and the fans and the Olympia (now all gone). The original print bears "*The Hockey News*" on the back, but I have not found the photo in any *THN* issue from this period.

The more general debate in hockey over protective equipment centres on whether it is justified given the nature of the sport or whether it encourages irresponsible behaviour. Nobody would question the importance of goalies wearing masks today, but their use has certainly made "high" shots more part of the game than they were before the mask. It makes sense that all players wear full facial protection (cage or visor), but the counter-argument you will hear is that such things only encourage high-stick play. Should all goalies wear a neck protector like Patrick Roy? Ideally yes, but my father and I agreed that there was a trade-off between protection and a host of other things like mobility, comfort, and excitement. One also had to consider probability. Serious head injuries can occur in a variety of ways, but few would advocate that everybody walk around with bike helmets 24/7. The degree of risk is just not high enough. The protective glass and net that surround all NHL rinks today is probably a good thing, but at some point we lose some of the thrill of being close to the action. Otherwise the game would be played in a bubble by players encased in armour. Having said that, he and I also agreed that the risk of pucks or sticks or skates being deflected up into the upper-body area was enough to warrant the full visor.

"But do fans want to see the players' faces?" I asked him once, not really sure how I felt myself.

He paused before responding, "With a few exceptions, hockey players aren't that pretty to look at." Then he looked to my mother for support, "Right, Teacy?"

"Yeah," she answered, "they usually have more scars than teeth."

Goalies are often hurt in practice when they face hundreds of shots. One of my father's more serious injuries occurred during a team scrimmage at the Forum. The Forum in the early '50s had a loudspeaker that hung over the north-end net.[20] Many times when he found himself standing underneath it, McNeil would wonder nervously about how securely it was fastened to the roof. He could only spot a few wires, and they didn't seem very thick. In any case, there was a scramble in front of the net and my father only remembers getting hit with something awfully hard. When he came to minutes later, he apparently complained that what he feared had come to pass—i.e., the speaker system had finally fallen on him. The trainer quickly got McNeil to the hospital; Floyd Curry's skate had caught McNeil right in the temple and part of it was embedded. A surgeon removed the material, stitched the wound, and allowed my father to rejoin the team. As he tells it, "In a couple of days, I developed a small-sized horn on the side of my forehead and it was mighty sore. I was shipped back to the hospital. X-rays proved a sliver of Curry's skate was still in my head. They took it out, sewed up the gash with 10 more stitches and I was ready to get back into action."[21] It was the 1951–52 season, and my father never missed a game.

To say that NHL goalies of this era were tough is an understatement. Glenn Hall played in 502 consecutive games between 1955 and '63, a record that nobody believes will ever be broken, but he was so nervous before and during games that he frequently had to throw up in the dressing room. The man they call Mr. Goalie humorously summed up his reputation: "I'm always known for the streak and for throwing up."[22]

McNeil's worst injury came in a game at Maple Leaf Gardens on October 29, 1952. There was a lot of interest in the game because Maurice Richard was only two goals short of 324, the mark set by Nels (Old Poison) Stewart for the most goals scored by anyone in the history of the NHL. Olmstead opened the scoring for the Habs, and then Richard streaked down the right wing and beat Harry Lumley to the left. This left him one shy of the record. A few minutes later there was a scramble in front of the Canadiens' net. Ron Stewart got a low shot off, and when McNeil dove to stop it, the puck hit him flush in the face.[23] McNeil went to the clinic at the Gardens for attention, and a patch was placed on the impact area. The medical staff, of course, did not know that not only had the bone been shattered but it also had been displaced. The injured goalie was shaking; he asked for a cigarette. Dick Irvin was offered the services of a couple of substitutes to finish the game: Ed Chadwick from St. Michael's College and Johnny Henderson from the Toronto Marlboros. Even Jacques Beauchamp, sports editor for *Montréal-Matin,* who had considerable amateur experience, was willing to replace the injured goalie, but McNeil insisted on returning. This act of quixotic courage would eventually prove to be costly.

McNeil was numb with shock when play resumed; it wasn't long before Hannigan drifted in, faked a pass and slipped the puck between his legs. Everyone was focused on Richard, and he didn't keep the audience waiting long. While McNeil felt his face getting puffier by the minute, the Rocket gathered up the puck and scored number 324. The

Fig. 23 Gerry McNeil plays an entire game after having had his cheekbone shattered in the first period. Maple Leaf Gardens, 29 Oct. 1951. (Photo by Harold Barkley. Reprinted *Gazette* [Montreal], June 19, 2006, C2.) Reproduced by permission of "Harold Barkley Archives."

Toronto fans gave him a standing ovation, and the referee Red Storey retrieved the puck for the superstar right winger. The first period ended with the Canadiens holding a 3–1 lead. By the beginning of the second, it was apparent that McNeil was in serious trouble. His right eye was swollen shut and the puffiness even extended to the left side of his face, impairing the vision out of his "good" eye. According to Irvin, who was interviewed by Ferguson after the game, McNeil said that he "[could]

PLAYING THROUGH

see perfectly." "I'll be okay out there. Don't worry."[24] The truth was that the pain was so intense that his teeth began to ache; meanwhile, the Leafs scored three unanswered goals in the period to take the lead. The teams exchanged a pair of goals in the third before Kennedy scored into the open net.

After the game McNeil admitted that he shouldn't have gone back in, and Dick Irvin blamed him for the loss. "If I had known … just how badly McNeil was hurt, I never would have allowed him to go back. … McNeil's eye cost us four goals. Armstrong threw a shot from the blue line … and Gerry didn't even make an effort to stop it. And when he didn't turn to pick it out, I knew that he hadn't seen the shot at all."[25]

There were all kinds of telegrams and letters for Richard in the dressing room, but Richard ignored them for the moment to berate Irvin. "What do you mean, you didn't know if he could see? Just look at his eye, it's obvious he can't see." Hal Barkley got a picture of McNeil's face immediately after the game (fig. 23), and it appears to support Richard's assessment. McNeil appreciated how the Rocket came to his defence, but for the rest of his life he would also chuckle about the absurd nature of the epistemological argument—i.e., over who was capable of, and responsible for, seeing exactly what. McNeil shouldn't have lied about his vision; Irvin should have realized that his goalie was half blind. As it was, the reporters crowded around the Rocket, and one even asked Irvin if he had told his star to hold off scoring the record-breaker until the team got back to the Forum. Irvin claimed that he wanted to punch the reporter in the nose for posing such a stupid question.[26]

Don Sabo has written about masculinity and the "pain principle" in sports: "Boys are taught that to endure pain is courageous, to survive pain is manly."[27] He argues that the pain principle is a fundamental part of a patriarchal system (e.g., Judeo-Christian), insofar as the father "has the right to inflict pain" and that the inflicted should, ideally, "take it."[28] While this mindset certainly seemed to be part of the ethos surrounding professional hockey in the 1950s, I cannot say that my father necessarily demonstrated what Sabo describes as the two main effects of the pain principle in sports: 1) limited emotional expression; and 2) rechannelled rage.

For the purpose of elucidating the present example, John M. Hoberman's *Mortal Engines: The Science of Performance and the Dehumanization of Sport* may be more applicable, since Hoberman notes how detrimental drug therapy can be for athletes whose desire to compete outstrips the physical limits of their bodies.[29] I cannot but think that this was the case with my father when his cheekbone was shattered and later in his career. However, Hoberman sounds the alarm with regard to enhanced performance based on long-term steroid use, not so much with the single painkiller episode to get an athlete through a specific injury. Somehow managing the physical signals that we experience, be it pain or mental pressure, is key to an overall state of health and happiness. While our knowledge about the specifics of how the human body functions has increased, the interaction of the physical and the mental is an extremely complicated mechanism. In tracing the history of scientific research on sport performance, Hoberman notes how Dr. Fourcault published his theory of temperament in 1858 and how the "nervous" type "did not refer to fragile or fearful personalities. . . . [but] a vibrant nervous system that poured energy into the limbs."[30] According to this theory of temperament, the same system that was responsible for my father's excellent reflexes may have also produced his high anxiety.

Hector Dubois, the Canadiens trainer, applied ice packs to McNeil's face on the long train ride back to Montreal. When the train arrived at Windsor Station, McNeil went for X-rays at the Western Hospital. Teacy hurried to meet him there and was directed to his room. Her heart sank when she entered only to discover somebody else in the bed. The staff at the counter confirmed the room number, and when she returned she realized—in horror—that the grotesquely swollen face actually belonged to her husband! Friends calmed her down, and she learned from the doctor that an operation was necessary to reposition the bone.[31] It was scheduled for the next day. McNeil was given the room reserved for Dickie Moore, who was to have an operation on his knee.

That night Gerry actually returned with Teacy to their semi-detached home on Borden Avenue in Montreal's west-end community of NDG (Notre-Dame-de-Grâce). Since the importance of keeping good relations with the press was something that she knew all too well, Teacy couldn't refuse the request of a reporter and photographer to visit the house the next morning before Gerry left for his operation. Still, the irony was not lost on her as she changed into a nice skirt and stylish top and hunted for Gerry's leopard-skin pyjamas. David Bier, one of the most important press photographers for the Canadiens in the 1950s, was there to get a picture of the wounded recuperating in the domestic comforts of home. Gerry, tucked under the covers, is being attended to by Teacy; 18-month-old Karen sits on top to his right. The child looks at her father's swollen face in wide-eyed wonder; her parents meet her gaze. With the painkillers doing their work, an operation and recovery lying ahead, Gerry feels completely at ease. Dr. Gordon Young, the club

PLAYING THROUGH

physician, said that McNeil would not see action for a period ranging from two to six weeks.[32]

That Saturday night McNeil missed his first game since taking over from Durnan in March of 1950. The extent of the injury meant that the Habs had to find a long-term replacement. Jacques Plante, the goalie for the Royals, was available for a three-game lease, but if the Canadiens kept him for more than three games, he would have to turn professional. In any case, using Plante was what the Canadiens decided to do. Irvin did not like Plante's habit of wearing a toque, George Vézina style, or wrapping a towel around his neck; nor was he keen on Plante leaving his crease as much as he did. But this plan seemed to be best; Hal Murphy, a goalie with Sainte-Thérèse of the provincial league, was brought up to the Royals, and Plante to the Canadiens.[33] Then the picture, so beloved by the Montreal press, appeared in the paper—the regular goalie, McNeil, in his civvies in the dressing room to congratulate the substitute, Plante, who pretends to be inspecting Gerry's cheek (see fig. 24).[34] A very similar picture featuring Durnan and McNeil was published when the latter took over in March 1950.[35]

Plante's debut as an NHLer was successful. He won two of three games and only gave up four goals (his official GAA was 1.33). However, nobody was really taking notice of McNeil's young replacement. All attention focused on Richard. *Life* magazine deemed the eminent event important enough to dispatch its best sport photographer Hy Peskin to Montreal where he stayed a week in hopes of getting a picture of the record-breaking goal. Dick Irvin, Jr., remembers being next to Peskin on the catwalk as the photographer got into position for one of his classic stadium-profile shots (see Chapter 2).[36] By Peskin's third game, other markers emerged as possible subjects, like Elmer Lach's two hundredth goal, which Peskin did capture; unfortunately, he had to reload his camera and missed Rocket scoring number 325, which happened less than a minute later. Such are the pitfalls of event photography. Needless to say, there was no record-breaking hockey story in *Life,* and so the NHL missed an important publicity opportunity.

That same night Hal Murphy was pressed into NHL service, since McNeil still wasn't ready and Plante had played all three allowable games. What a difference a week makes—from the Sainte-Thérèse junior team to a Saturday-night assignment with the Canadiens at the Forum! After a rough start—Montreal fell behind 3–0 to Chicago—the Canadiens came back and posted a 6–4 win. Murphy's story was overshadowed by the Rocket's record. Looking back over the numbers of Gretzky and Howe, one might say that the Rocket's mark of 325 was

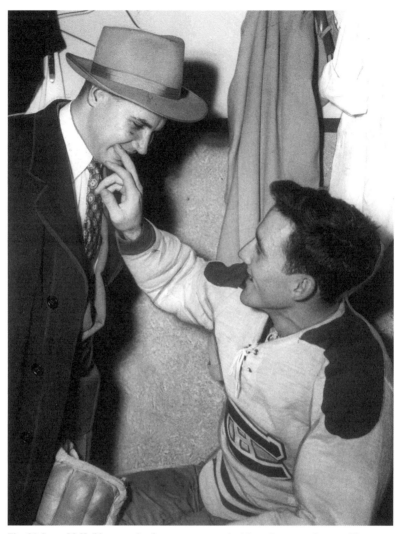

Fig. 24 Gerry McNeil has words of encouragement for his replacement Jacques Plante, who inspects Gerry's cheek. Montreal Forum, Nov. 7, 1952. (Photographer unknown.).

modest, but time does strange things to how we might view a record. Unbeknownst to any that night, Hal Murphy would not play another game in the Big Time league. His all-time performance as an NHL goalie went into the books, and would forever remain, a perfect 1-0-0.[37]

So McNeil returned after missing only four games. The solid performance by Plante could have been an incentive, but the fact was that

PLAYING THROUGH

McNeil had healed enough, felt rested, and wanted to get back out on the ice. There were things to accomplish. Irvin claimed he was glad to see his regular goalie return. Despite the winning record in Mac's absence, he remarked, "we've been lucky."[38] The comment might have been designed more to reduce Plante's ego than boost McNeil's.

Paul de Saint-Georges featured McNeil in a weekly "Les Canadiens chez eux" column while the goalie was recuperating at home on Borden Avenue.[39] His popularity with the fans was noted, as were his good looks. More important, however, it was pointed out that Gerry and Thérèse, while raised in English schools in Quebec City, were fluently bilingual. Gerry's father, Pierre (Pete) McNeil, still worked for Anglo Pulp and Paper and lived in Limoilou where Gerry grew up. Golf, fishing, and gardening were listed as Gerry's hobbies; the first and the last he would continue for the rest of his life. It was remarked that he lived in a west-end community along with other members of the Canadiens: Johnny McCormack, Elmer Lach, Kenny Mosdell, Doug Harvey, and Floyd Curry. The players and their wives and children were said to be one group.

Some years ago, I happened to be by myself in Montreal on a Saturday night and I drove to the old neighbourhood on Borden Avenue. I stood on the sidewalk and looked around in the glow of the streetlights. It was startling how immediately familiar certain markers were: the sloped and curved driveway (impossible to get up on my tricycle), the hill in front of the semi-detached house, the steeple of Saint Monica's in the distance. There were two huge differences; a canopy of leaves cast comforting shadows over much of the scene and everything seemed to be on a much smaller scale. I looked up at the walls of the house and felt a Proust-like, infantile sense of place and déjà vu. I imagined the long tense nights my parents suffered every playoff spring and the moments of play at other times of the year. I knew that much of what I was experiencing was fuelled by the Kodak films my father took in the late 1950s. I thought about the press who had probably stood on the exact same spot that I was standing.

McNeil's face healed nicely, but questions were raised about how the injury might affect his play. Fear can develop with experience. As goalies become more aware of how vulnerable they are in certain situations (e.g., playing with a numb hand or weak knee), they are more likely to become apprehensive about their ability to perform well. Furthermore, this awareness can be heightened through injury. Bill Durnan seemed to have suffered this fate. Any player can develop fear, but goalies, whose job it is to get in front of the puck, are especially prone.

The fearless also tend to be the naive. For his part, McNeil did not show immediate repercussions from the cheekbone injury. In two January wins against the same Leafs, he gave up a single goal.[40]

Playing well breeds confidence, and confidence makes one play better. Conversely, when one loses confidence, performance often deteriorates. Despite the cheekbone injury, McNeil went on to have his best NHL season, posting 10 shutouts and a 2.12 GAA.[41] He had a reputation for slow starts, steady improvement, and sensational finishes. In fact, *The Hockey News* did a full-page story the previous season on how McNeil had struggled back from his less-than-spectacular pre-Christmas play.[42] Len Bramson remarked how the goalie had to live up to his amazing play in the '51 playoffs: "It is also no secret that too often he was being compared with the McNeil that put on the greatest exhibition of goalkeeping ever seen in the playoffs."[43] The article was accompanied by a picture of him having been hit in the face by another Leaf player (Watson) and the subtitle reads, "He Got Up and Played." McNeil's greatest weakness as a goalie was said to be "his slowness in getting up off the ice after making a stop." Bramson noted how he continued to play while his mother was dying of cancer and also when his daughter was seriously ill. Bramson also pointed out that the Canadiens had lost no less than eleven games by one goal; so when the Habs weren't winning, McNeil was keeping them close.[44]

The mental aspect of sport has received a lot of attention recently. Every team has its sport psychologist whose job it is to make sure that the athlete is in the best state of mind to maximize performance. Managing stress and visualizing positive outcomes are two common practices. In the 1950s, this aspect of an athlete's preparation was usually handled by the regular coach, and Dick Irvin was infamous for playing all kinds of mind games with the other teams as well as with his own players. Sometimes athletes will find themselves having to play through a stretch of below-par individual or team performances. Sometimes they will have to endure a lack of success that is the direct result of running into stiff competition or an opposition that just happens to be peaking. This latter situation arose when the Habs met the Wings in the Cup Final for the first time in NHL history in 1952. The Montreal faithful were hoping for a repeat of the '51 Semifinal when the Habs beat Detroit in six, but this time the Tricolore ran into the amazing goaltending of Terry Sawchuk.

In an odd twist to the regular format, the '52 Stanley Cup Final opened in the city of the second-seeded Canadiens (Games Three, Four, and Five, if necessary, were scheduled for the Olympia). While the Habs were coming off a tough, seven-game series against the Bruins, the Wings knocked off Toronto four straight and hadn't played in nine days. Still, Detroit had a few key injuries. Red Kelly would play but with a brace on his wrist, which was said to be 80 per cent.[45] Leo Reise didn't make the trip to Montreal, having sustained a deep cut to his ankle in practice. Unlike the year before, the Detroit press wasn't predicting an easy Cup win. Paul Chandler's headline story in the sports section of *The Detroit News* touted the series as the first Detroit-Montreal Final and featured a pair of pictures: McNeil on the left and the Rocket on the right. Ted Lindsay looked forward to a rematch with the team that eliminated them the previous spring. "I haven't forgotten they put us out last season. I like the idea of being able to give them a little dose of medicine."

After a scoreless first, the second period of Game One began with the first mishap. Doug Harvey got tangled with McNeil and both fell over an already prone Dollard St. Laurent. When the puck came out to Tony "Mighty Mouse" Leswick, all he needed to do was lift it over the sprawling players into the net.[46] Then Leswick scored again at the eight-minute mark of the third on a blazing forty-eight footer that was screened in front. This time it was Butch Bouchard who backed into McNeil, making it impossible for the goalie to get in position to make the save. Montreal pulled within one when Tom Johnson scored two minutes later. Then with what appeared to be less than a minute left in regulation time (the official timer, C. L. Lane from New York, had announced, "One minute remains in this game"), Irvin called McNeil to the bench for the extra attacker. Bob Goldham gained control of the puck and sent it to Sid Abel who, in turn, passed to Lindsay. Lindsay carefully hit the open net from about twenty-five feet out. With the score now 3–1, the timer seemed to allow the clock to run an extra sixty seconds (a twenty-one-minute third period?). Nevertheless, the result remained the same—a Habs loss on home ice.

Detroit reporters were not impressed by the performance of their team, with the exception of Leswick and Sawchuk. Chandler wrote that the Production Line, in particular, was "terrible." Irvin was quoted as saying, "if Detroit plays that poorly again, we'll win the series." Richard had a strong game, but Sawchuk thwarted every opportunity.[47]

The Canadiens really needed Game Two, and they dominated the first period. At one point they had a two-man advantage for a minute and forty-one seconds but were unable to beat Sawchuk, who was aided by Lindsay, Kelly, and Woit. With less than five minutes left in the opening period, Leswick sent a pass in the direction of Pavelich streaking in on the left wing. The man known as "Sabu" took a swipe at the puck, and it slid along the ice into the open side of the net.[48] Montreal tied it up less than three minutes later when Boom Boom Geoffrion fired from the blue line and the puck deflected off a couple of bodies and ended up behind Sawchuk. Lach got credit for the goal. Early in the second, Harvey was penalized and Lindsay controlled the puck behind the Canadiens' net. He decided to just flip it in front, and when he did, the puck hit Bouchard in the chest as the big defenceman charged in to help. Bouchard then collided with McNeil and both players, along with the puck, ended up in the cage. The Canadiens seemed to fade in the second, victimized perhaps by the fatigue from the previous series. However, led by the Rocket, they did threaten again in the third but were unable to score. The game ended 2–1 for the Wings. Sawchuk stopped 17 shots to McNeil's 27.

The sense of competition between the two teams was fiercely bitter. The Wings complained about the aggressive stick work by Richard. Pavelich indicated that the cut on his forehead was courtesy of the Rocket, and Howe claimed that Richard knocked his tooth out with a high stick. Dollard St. Laurent received a scraped eyeball in a collision with Howe and did not make the trip to Detroit. Terry Sawchuk and Dickie Moore also had a running feud that went back to Game One when Moore interfered with the goalie as he was clearing the puck behind the net. Sawchuk took a swipe at Moore's knees, a sensitive spot, with his stick. The two exchanged verbal threats after the game.[49] In situations like this, it is incumbent on the players to focus on the game; worrying too much about "getting the other guy" or being targeted by the opposition can only distract from the key objective of winning. The NHL of the 1940s and '50s was easily more violent than it is today, but the fighting and stick-swinging didn't receive the media attention it now does.

The task for the Canadiens going into the Olympia for Game Three was to get to Sawchuk. Both Richard and Geoffrion, the biggest guns for the Tricolore, had yet to score in the series. Things did not go well for much of the first two periods. Montreal continued to look tired; three of their four regular centres (Reay, McCormack, and Mosdell) were out of the lineup. Detroit, on the other hand, looked like a team hitting its stride. Toward the end of the second, Paul Meger got no less than four shots away from close range; Sawchuk blocked them all.[50] Unlike the Canadiens, the Wings were able to capitalize on their chances. When Harvey was sent off for two minutes for tackling Lindsay early in the game, Howe worked a give-and-go with Stasiuk and then got around

MacPherson and blasted a shot past McNeil. Abel's interference in front went unnoticed.

Playing from behind again, the Habs needed a break but didn't get one. Instead, McNeil had to endure one of the most humiliating moments in his career, when Lindsay, at mid-ice, hoisted the puck high into the air toward the Montreal end. Mac watched it twirling in the air and moved out to catch it before it hit the ice. "It hit right in front of me and took a crazy bounce... to the top corner of the net." Irvin called it the softest goal "since Jack Shill lofted one past Turk Broda the year Chicago won the Stanley Cup."[51] However, he still had confidence in his goalie: "I don't blame Gerry at all. He played well enough to win." Howe scored again in the third on a rush with Abel, whom he used as a decoy, then backhanded the puck low, short-side. After the game, McNeil sat dejectedly and stared at the floor. His teammates were showering, but he hadn't moved to take off his uniform or remove his pads.

Richard sounded bitter when he commented on the Wings' good fortune: "Sawchuk is their club. Another guy in the nets and we'd beat them. They're just lucky. They don't work—they just shoot the puck— they're lucky."[52] Dickie Moore, the rookie who had only been with the team since Christmas, predicted four straight wins by the Canadiens. Nobody took him seriously, and Montreal was on the brink of being swept in the playoffs for the first time. Conversely, Detroit, with one more victory, could become the first team to win the Cup in eight straight games.

Hockey can be a game of momentum, and sometimes a team can ride it all the way. Richard was penalized in the first. Delvecchio and Wilson fought for possession, and eventually they shoved a pass to Prystai who fired home a shot from about twenty feet out. Halfway through the second period, a blue-grey mass was tossed from Section 10; it landed on the ice and appeared to have several legs approximately a foot long. It was an octopus, the first of hundreds that would be thrown onto the Olympia ice in the ensuing decades—an allusion to the eight-game sweep, but also meaningful, as Chandler notes, in the general sense of "an organization with many branches through which it maintains a hold on others."[53] Late in the second Prystai set up Skov, who scored low to the corner. More of the same in the third. Prystai poked the puck from Meger and took it one hundred and thirty feet down ice before beating McNeil cleanly.

Playing out the last ten minutes was painful for the Canadiens. Desperate to at least break Sawchuk's second consecutive shutout, they failed to come close. Defeat burned like salt in a wound. Finally, the bell sounded and they made a merciful exit off the Olympia ice. Lach, Richard and Irvin did not stop to shake hands with the winners.

A few weeks later, McNeil and Meger escaped to Florida to forget it all. They got a tee time at a local golf course and headed for the first fairway. The course starter had warned them that they would be matched up with another twosome. Fine, anything to play a round. When they approached the starter's booth, they could hardly believe their eyes. There, waiting, were Ted Lindsay and Red Kelly! Stunned, they turned around and left the course without even bothering to ask for a refund of their green fees.[54]

The incident that best exemplifies an athlete's commitment to playing through adversity is the famous goal that Richard scored against the Bruins to win the 1952 Semifinal and earn the right to face the Wings. Some have called it the best goal ever scored in the playoffs. Physical injury seemed to play a major role in the series as a whole, individuals had to "suck it up" and the respective teams had to adjust for lost players. First, Maurice Richard was battling a serious groin pull during the 1951–52 season. Eventually it became necessary to send him to Florida for six weeks where he couldn't be tempted to get on the ice. The only treatment for his condition was rest. When Richard got back to Montreal in mid-March he said that he didn't feel much pain, just enough to know that something was wrong. The Habs were in second place with Toronto just three points back. They played a decisive game on March 20th in Toronto, and the Canadiens came away 3–0 victors. It was McNeil's fifth shutout of the season.[55]

A few days later a story appeared in *Le Petit journal* entitled, "Gerry McNeil, le 'Canadien' oublié [forgotten]."[56] With the playoffs approaching, reporters were looking for some newsworthy item about the team, and Desjardins decided to focus on McNeil's low profile. Gerry's fluency in French was noted, and he was quoted as saying, "*Si je suis oublié du public, je me console en pensant que je ne suis pas oublié de mes coéquipiers, qui savent bien me protéger.*" Although the statement is just another example of locker-room banter, it also reflects something that my father believed more widely about how his career, coming as it did between the Hall of Fame performances of Durnan and Plante, was largely forgotten by subsequent writers. It bothered him *just slightly* that most hockey people knew him only as the goalie on whom Barilko scored his famous goal, because he felt that he always had the respect of his teammates. What your teammates thought about you mattered more than what reporters, or fans, or even coaches might think. Bouchard facetiously mentioned how Gerry seemed to steal all the publicity in the playoffs the year before, and the comment was made that McNeil was known for his post-season exploits. Desjardins then asked my father what was the most important aspect about playing goal, and my father responded by emphasizing speed—the ability to read a situation and have confidence in your reflexive movements. He expressed admiration for Howe's hard and precise shots, which could be aimed for either corner (*"Il lance très fort, avec précision, des deux côtés."*). Dick Irvin then entered the dressing room and ironically it is said that *"le Renard Gris… n'a que des éloges pour son cerbère bilingue: 'Il est bon pour dix ans dans la NHL.'"* I assume that the reporter was translating for the Grey Fox. So much for French in the Quebec workplace during the 1950s. In any case, as we shall see, Irvin's endorsement statement could hardly have been more ironic.

Late in his life my father was often asked if there were French-English tensions among players and management during his time with the Canadiens. He always answered no, that francophones and anglophones got along perfectly well, but that there was a perceived "western" contingent on the squad that could make anybody east of Winnipeg a little nervous. Most of the so-called "fringe" players were from the West (Lorne Davis, Eddie Mazur, Bud MacPherson, Paul Masnick, Paul Meger), and, of course, Dick Irvin himself came from Regina. He seemed to think "West" when it came to signing on those role players who didn't play a key part of the lineup.

Richard's groin pull could still be felt when the '52 playoffs opened. Nevertheless, the Rocket scored twice in the opening game at the Forum and the Habs won 5–1.[57] Pentti Lund, added to the Bruins roster in place of a flu-stricken Fleming Mackell, scored the lone Boston goal. Game Two saw Geoffrion score a hat trick and McNeil post a shutout as the Canadiens won 4–0. Mosdell tallied the other marker for the Habs before he went down in a collision with Ed Sandford and suffered a double fracture to his lower right leg.[58] It had been a rough year for Mosdell as well; he was just feeling strong again after suffering a broken shoulder the previous December. Back at the Garden, the Bruins bounced back and dumped the Canadiens 4–1 but suffered some significant injuries of their own: Kryzanowski's eye was swollen shut, Peirson had a big egg on his forehead inflicted by Bouchard, Labine had a welt across his face and a swollen nose.[59] The Bruins then tied the series by taking Game Four 3–2. Among the wounded were a couple of players with knee problems: Hal Laycoe, a star in Game Three, was injured when he was crushed into the boards so hard that the glass panel popped out (it fell on Garden cop Chris Curtin and knocked him out).

Dickie Moore had his left knee frozen so he could continue. If it wasn't injury, it was illness. Fleming Mackell felt sick all afternoon but dressed for the game anyway and ended up scoring the winner.[60]

Irvin apparently told his veteran players, "produce or else" before Game Five, but "Sugar" Jim Henry led the Bruins to a 1–0 victory to put the Bruins up 3–2 in the series. Tom Fitzgerald of *The Boston Daily Globe* rated 75 per cent of Henry's 31 saves as "spectacular".[61] The hard physical play continued. Milt Schmidt decked Moore with a body-check late in the first, and the stretcher was brought out. Fortunately, Moore got off the ice with nothing more than a serious bruise, but the hits were adding up. The Canadiens were clearly hurting, as well as facing elimination. The Bruins emerged from their sleepers at North Station the next morning to find a line of fans and photographers waiting. Irvin, forever feeding lines to the press, remarked that his fellows were already making golf and fishing plans. Rather than staying at the Hotel Manger at North Station as they did on the first trip to Boston, the Habs moved to the Kenmore "solely to get the players away from distractions right in the center of activities."[62] Much of this distraction was said to be the hundreds of "zealous" Montreal fans who were following the team.

For the first time in three years, there was a sellout at the Garden for hockey.[63] The crowd had plenty to cheer about early as Schmidt and Chevrefils teamed up on a pretty passing play that Schmidt finished with a twenty-five footer, waist high into the net. Then Creighton put the Bruins up 2–0 when he finished another series of passes with a good shot past McNeil. The Habs got one back in the second when rookie Ed "Spider" Mazur whacked home a rebound. Injury then came into play in the third. Harvey fired a close-in shot at Sugar Henry and nailed him right in the nose. The game was delayed as medical attention was given the Bruin goalie whose eyes were so watery he couldn't see. Eventually he returned to the net but had little chance to get over the blow as Richard picked up a loose puck off Schmidt's stick and skated in to fire home the tying goal.

The Garden crowd came back to life as the Bruins dominated in overtime. Mackell set up Woody Dumart and Eddie Sandford and for a second it looked like Boston would take the game, but the Canadiens defenders were able to keep the puck out. The Bruins continued to press until seven minutes into the second overtime when Harvey went end to end and fired the puck off Henry's chest. It went up into the rafters and hung there—a moment of suspended action—then fell right before Paul Masnick, another rookie, who swept it behind Henry for the winner. Only twenty years old, Masnick was flown in from Cincinnati especially for the game.

With Henry's broken nose, the Bruins did not feel good about going back to Montreal. The story of Richard's famous end-to-end rush and goal in Game Seven is well known.[64] With the game tied at one apiece, he had just run into Schmidt when he himself was levelled by a solid bodycheck from Leo "The Lion" Labine near the end of the second period and cut for six stitches. Whether he received the cut directly from Labine's stick or when he crashed into the boards is uncertain, for Richard would say only that "everything went black." Despite leaving a deep blood stain on the ice, the Rocket managed to come to enough to head for the clinic under his own power. Just before the end of the period, Richard emerged from the south-end passage of the rink; for a split second the crowd was surprised, then it erupted into a thunderous ovation as Number Nine skated to the Canadiens' bench.

The goaltending that night was great at both ends. McNeil made a sensational catching save off Mackell when the Bruins forward had split the defence in the third. Twice he robbed Sandford in the first, once while flat on his back. Then there was another diving stop off Mackell, and a third block on Sandford in the second. Henry pulled off his own heroics, blocking shots by Johnson, Mazur, and Bouchard.

McNeil had a good view of the beginning of the play that led to *the* goal. The Bruins were pressing; behind the net Dumart passed out for Sandford but Bouchard leaned down and got the tip of his stick on the puck, deflecting it to Richard, who immediately started up the right wing. McNeil didn't know that it was Quackenbush who moved over to face the Rocket. In any case, he could see the fake to the inside that Richard made and then the familiar wide stance that marked his skating style. Just as he seemed trapped in the corner, Richard cut to the centre and ripped the puck past Henry. McNeil saw the red light go on and then heard the Forum explode. He could taste victory. The Bruins, however, weren't finished yet. The longer it took the maintenance crew to clean up the debris, the more nervous McNeil got. Schmidt and company gave it one last try, pulling Henry for the extra attacker. Reay got control of the puck and shot it through Schmidt's legs for the insurance goal.

David Bier's picture of the teams shaking hands after the game was published in the *Herald* April 9, 1952; in the middle of the frame are the two goalies. Both seem to be smiling, but the shot is taken from such an angle that only Henry's face is visible. Moreover, what is odd is that McNeil and Henry appear to be the same height. Sugar Jim was at least two inches taller than my father. Much more memorable are Roger

Saint-Jean's pictures of the same event. Saint-Jean, the photographer for *La Presse,* was able to frame pairs of opposing players congratulating each other. In the most famous of these, a black-eyed Henry bows and looks up at the bloodied and bandaged Richard who stares back intensely as if he is unable to drop the competitive spirit. In shooting the popular film, *The Rocket,* director Charles Binamé conceived an entire scene around this picture.[65]

It makes sense that filmmakers working on sports subjects from this era would manufacture a series of moving pictures around a famous still image. Something very similar was done with the Neil Leifer's famous shot of Ali standing over Sonny Liston in Michael Mann's 2001 film of the boxing legend.[66] There are still images that have embedded themselves into the collective memory of sports' greatest moments, and filmmakers are naturally drawn to them when they build their stories. It might be argued that film scenes like these actually celebrate the power of photography in our culture's sense of history. Even the not-so-famous photos from this era can be discovered by researchers and form the basis for a scene or shot in a film. When Martin Scorsese uses a shot of Cathy Moriarty playing Vikki LaMotta at ringside in *Raging Bull,* I cannot help but think he had seen Hy Peskin's photostory on the spectating wives (Vicki LaMotta and Edna Mae Robinson) referred to in Chapter 2. The hair and dress are all too similar. Time, of course, changes everything, but I wonder if future generations will revere the still image as we do—simply because the moving image is now more than often the designated visual record. Will walls of the future be decorated with video screens as opposed to the framed photo? There is something special about the picture frozen in time—something that encourages us to contemplate and reflect in a fashion that doesn't happen when things are in motion. We pause to look deeper and wider.

When one realizes that Saint-Jean's shot was taken just after the famous goal, one gets a sense of the grace and dignity being displayed by Henry. Saint-Jean got his own version of McNeil and Henry shaking hands, and this shot is the one that hung in my family's rec room until well after I left home (see fig. 25); here Henry seems to tower over my father. Henry's smiling expression is the same, but unlike Bier's shot, this one also shows my father's face clearly. His eyes make direct contact with his opponent's. Their gaze communicates mutual respect and an unspoken understanding about being netminders in situations such as this—the pressure of a seven-game series. Henry obviously had the good character and ability to rise above the meaner level of the game. For many years I wondered why I found the image so

PLAYING THROUGH

Fig. 25 Gerry McNeil and Sugar Jim Henry shake hands after Game Seven of the Semifinal. Montreal Forum, April 8, 1952. (Photo unconfirmed by Roger Saint-Jean.) Copyright unknown.

fascinating, and I think it is because it is impossible to distinguish winner from loser. That observation might be made of many such postgame, player-to-player congratulatory lines, but genuine moments of sportspersonship are truly rare and fleeting. We seldom manage to demonstrate such reverence for the game itself.

The photo was displayed in our home almost as prominently as the Howe photo I described in Chapter 3. Then around 2002 my father was invited to an autograph session that was billed "Goalies of the Original Six." Chuck Rayner and Jim Henry were supposed to be in attendance. By this time the Saint-Jean photograph was in my possession; in fact I had hung it up in my office at the university. It initiated several discussions about hockey and my father's career. In any case, my father thought it would be a good idea to take it with him to the session to get Henry's signature. As it turned out, Henry wasn't well enough to make the trip to Toronto; the man organizing the event said that he would see Henry and offered to take my father's photo with him. That was the last we saw of the photo. It would have been lost forever, if my father, careful man that he was, had not made a copy of it first.

This book is dedicated to the players from my father's era who are not in Hockey's Hall of Fame, players like Sugar Jim Henry, Jimmy Peirson and Ed Sandford, Tod Sloan and Sid Smith, Metro Prystai and Tony Leswick, Wally Hergesheimer and Leo Reise, Lee Fogolin Sr. and Gerry Couture. Henry fought back from a serious burn injury suffered in a fire at his Kenora lodge. Peirson had four 20-plus-goal seasons with the Bruins. Sandford played in five consecutive All-Star games from 1951 to '55. Sloan was a solid forward who got shipped to Chicago for helping in the effort to form a players' association. When Smith retired in '57, only three active players had more goals. Prystai scored twice in the Cup-clinching game that saw Detroit sweep the '52 playoffs. "Mighty Mouse" Leswick, a pesky forward, was instrumental in winning three Stanley Cups with the Red Wings. Having lost two fingers in a punch press accident, "Hergy" made the NHL against the odds and scored thirty goals in the 1952–53 season. Reise was a dependable defenceman who played with three NHL teams. Fogolin could throw a tremendous bodycheck and was great at blocking shots. Couture was another defensive specialist.[67] All had a part in NHL history, all figured in the careers of more famous players and all had contact with my father.

So the Habs prevailed in the first round and were off to the Final again. In the dressing room after the handshaking, the Rocket collapsed into sobbing convulsions.[68] There is little to be gained from romanticizing the exploits of athletes who risk greater injury when they remain in a game. Today, neither the Rocket, who had probably suffered a concussion, nor Henry, recovering from his broken nose, would have played in that final period of Game Seven. That they did without suffering further injury was due to their good fortune. Henry, however, wasn't so lucky three years later when he took a puck to the face that effectively ended his NHL career.[69]

1   The format for the first four such games consisted of the Stanley Cup winner playing an All-Star team (1947–50). In 1951, the First Team was made up of the best players from the four American franchises, and the Second Team drew from the two Canadian teams. The league decided to go back to the original format in 1953. The game was played just before the start of the regular season up until 1967, when it was moved to mid-season. Proceeds from the games went toward a pension plan for the players. See Herb Zurkowsky, "All-Star Game," *Gazette* (Montreal), Feb. 3, 1993, C5–C6, C11–C13.

2   See Len Bramson, "Irvin Cuts Down Rollins, Puts Wee Gerry in his Spot," *Hockey News,* Oct. 6, 1951, 5.

3   Al Nickleson, "NHL's Modern Greats at Gardens Tonight," *Globe and Mail,* Oct. 9, 1951, 20.

4   Quoted by Bramson, "Irvin Cuts Down Rollins," 5.

5   Nickleson, "NHL's Modern Greats," 20.

6   Quoted by Bramson, "Irvin Cuts Down Rollins," 5.

7   The incident is recorded by Ferguson, "Gist and Jest," *Herald, Montreal,* Oct. 10, 1951, 20.

8   Al Nickleson, "Feuding Season Opens Early as Dream Teams Draw, 2–2," *Globe and Mail,* Oct. 10, 1951, 16.

9   Quoted by Elmer Ferguson, "Richard, Howe and Lindsay Feud as All-Star Game Ends in Draw," *Herald, Montreal,* Oct. 10, 1951, 20. Despite his comment here, Howe was in the first All-Star Game fight two years before (with Gus Mortson of the Leafs).

10   "Pavelich, Richard Score as All-Stars Draw 1–1," *Gazette* (Montreal), Oct. 8, 1952, 20.

11   "Record Crowd Sees All-Stars Strike Early," *Gazette* (Montreal), Oct. 5, 1953, 24.

12   See Rauzulu's Street, http://www.rauzulusstreet.com/hockey/nhlallstar/allstar recordsplayer.html/, accessed June 16, 2004.

13   See Dick Irvin, "Writing and Broadcasting," in Diamond, Total Hockey, 117. Unfortunately, there are few archival recordings of the CBC broadcasts prior to 1960.

14   See Baz O'Meara, "Presence of Royalty Embellishes N.H.L. Hockey History," *Montreal Star,* Oct. 30, 1951, 33–34.

15   Eddie MacCabe, "McNeil Finds Son Is an Iconoclast," [publication, date, and page number unknown]. Article in author's family scrapbook. Eddie MacCabe worked as a sportswriter/editor for the *Ottawa Journal* and the *Ottawa Citizen,* but this article does not seem to have appeared in those newspapers in October 1953, at least not in the final editions.

16   This according to Ferguson, "Gist and Jest," *Herald, Montreal,* Jan. 4, 1952, 23.

17   Ibid.

18   This story is by Len Bramsom, "Records Show McNeil Main Reason for Habs Climb into 2nd Place," *Hockey News,* Mar. 15, 1952, 7. The *Globe and Mail* reported that McNeil returned to Montreal with Richard, who was suffering a groin injury; see Feb. 6, 1952, 13.

19   When Plante took over for my father for three games in November 1952, Irvin wouldn't even let him wear a toque, let alone a mask.

20   McNeil related this story to Matt Jackson, sports editor of the *Rochester Times-Union* (see the issue for Mar. 12, 1959, 46) eight years after it occurred. He also shared it with me on a few occasions.

21   Quoted by Matt Jackson, "Cut, Bruised, Battered, But McNeil Loves It," *Rochester Times-Union,* Mar. 12, 1959, 46.

22 Quoted by Pat Doyle, "That's Hall, as in Hall of Fame," *Gazette* (Montreal), Jan. 26, 2005, C8.

23 See "Habs Lose to Leafs—McNeil Hurt," *Herald, Montreal,* Oct. 30, 1952, 16; "Rocket Ties N.H.L. Goal Record," *Gazette* (Montreal), Oct. 30, 1952, 19; and Len Bramson, "Habs['] First Bad Break Big Break to Gerry's Battered Cheekbone," *Hockey News,* Nov. 8, 1952, 2. Jacques Beauchamp, who offered to replace McNeil himself, also covered the story. See "Gerry McNeil, victime de son courage," *Montréal-Matin,* Oct. 31, 1952, 30, 32; and Jacques Beauchamp, *Le sport c'est ma vie* (Montreal: Quebecor, 1979), 85–87.

24 Quoted by Ferguson, "Gist and Jest," *Herald, Montreal,* Oct. 31, 1952, 26.

25 Ibid.

26 Ibid.

27 Don Sabo, *Sex, Violence & Power in Sports* (Freedom: Crossing Press, 1994), 86.

28 Sabo, *Sex, Violence,* 87. While I am writing about a 1950s mindset, others have argued that this ability to take pain remains a fundamental part of hockey. See Philip G. White, Kevin Young, and William G. McTeer, "Sport, Masculinity and the Injured Body," in *Men's Health and Illness: Gender, Power, and the Body,* ed. Donald Sabo and David Frederick Gordon (Thousand Oaks: Sage Publications, 1995), 158–82.

29 John M. Hoberman, *Mortal Engines: The Science of Performance and the Dehumanization of Sport* (Toronto: Macmillan, 1992).

30 Hoberman, *Mortal Engines,* 165.

31 These details were supplied by my parents who, years later, could see some amusement in the gruesome story.

32 The pictures appeared with three different stories; see "Plante to Replace McNeil, Out for At Least a Month," *Herald, Montreal,* Oct. 31, 1952, 23; "Avant le départ de McNeil pour l'hôpital," *Montréal-Matin,* Oct. 31, 1952, 32; and Bramson, "Habs['] First Bad Break," 2.

33 "Murphy to Guard Nets for Royals," *Gazette* (Montreal), Oct. 31, 1952, 22.

34 The original glossy has markings that suggest it was published in a newspaper on Nov. 8, 1952, but I have yet to find it in any Montreal paper.

35 See *Herald, Montreal,* Mar. 10, 1950, 23. The caption reads, "Bill Durnan, in civvies, beams on his substitute goaler, Gerry McNeil, who relaxes with a cigarette after the battle." Marking the passing of the torch, so to speak, at the goaltender position was so much part of the hockey photographer's agenda that a picture was even published of Plante shaking hands with McNeil when the latter arrived in time to replace Durnan (see Chapter 2). George Whittaker, "McNeil Helps Habs to Hold Onto Third Spot," *Montreal Daily Star,* Mar. 8, 1950, 27. This caption reads, "Gerry McNeil shakes hands with Jacques Plante his successor in the Royals nets. McNeil replaced the ailing Bill Durnan in the Canuck cage on Saturday and did a workmanlike job. Plante was standing by in case McNeil didn't get here on time."

36 Irvin, Jr., *Now Back to You,* 57–58.

37 See "Hal Murphy," in Podnieks, *Players,* 611.

38 "Gerry McNeil Back Thursday," *Gazette* (Montreal), Nov. 11, 1952, 18.

39 Paul de Saint-Georges, "Gerry McNeil... figure pitoyable," *Samedi-Dimanche,* Nov. 8, 1952, 33. The "pitiful" designation was because of the damage that the cheekbone injury did to McNeil's face.

40 These were 2–0 and 4–1 wins on January 21st and 22nd respectively.

41 Diamond, *Total Hockey,* 1677–78.

42 Len Bramson, "Records Show McNeil Main Reason for Habs Climb into 2nd Place," *Hockey News,* Mar. 15, 1952, 7.

43 Ibid.

44 Ibid. Four games were lost 2–1; two 1–0, and five 3–2 losses.

45 The details in this paragraph are from Paul Chandler, "First Detroit-Montreal Meeting in Final," *Detroit News,* Apr. 9, 1952, 49.

46 Paul Chandler, "Tony and Terry Triumph For Wings…," *Detroit News,* Apr. 11, 1952, 25–26. All details in this paragraph are taken from this article.

47 Chandler, "Tony and Terry Triumph," 26.

48 Paul Chandler, "Wings Lead Series 2–0 in Easter Parade: Bouchard is 'Goat,'" *Detroit News,* Apr. 13, 1952, 2.1–2. All details in this paragraph are taken from this article.

49 Paul Chandler, "Fair Game," *Detroit News,* Apr. 13, 1952, 2.2.

50 Paul Chandler, "Hockey Can End as Base Ball Starts: Wings on Verge of Being First to Win Stanley Cup in 8 Straight…," *Detroit News,* Apr. 14, 1952, 21–22. All details in this paragraph are taken from this article.

51 Quoted by John Walter, "They're Just Lucky: Richard, Irvin Agree on Wings' Breaks," *Detroit News,* Apr. 14, 1952, 21.

52 Ibid.

53 Paul Chandler, "Wings Acclaimed the 'Greatest Team': First to Sweep to Hockey Championship; Prystai, Sawchuk Take Night's Bows," *Detroit News,* Apr. 16, 1952, 55–56.

54 My father told me this story a number of times. Tommy Ivan, the Wings coach, also tells it to Carroll, "Playing the Field," *Gazette* (Montreal), Apr. 17, 1954, 8.

55 *Montreal Star,* Mar. 20, 1952, 41. A picture of McNeil accompanied the article and carried the title "The Kid Was Hot."

56 Maurice Desjardins, "Gerry McNeil, le 'Canadien' oublié," *Le Petit journal,* Mar. 23, 1952, 61. All details in this paragraph are from this article.

57 Dink Carroll, "Habs Blast Bruins 5 to 1; Richard Scores Two Goals," *Gazette* (Montreal), Mar. 26, 1952, 15; and Tom Fitzgerald, "Richard Leads Canadiens to 5–1 Victory Over Bruins," *Boston Daily Globe,* Mar. 26, 1952, 8.

58 Dink Carroll, "Mosdell Bags First Goal, Breaks Leg," *Gazette* (Montreal), Mar. 28, 1952, 23; and Tom Fitzgerald, "Geoffrion Scores Three Goals as Canadiens Win, 4–0: McNeil Stars in Nets…," *Boston Daily Globe,* Mar. 28, 1952, 18.

59 Baz O'Meara, "Two Quickies Tainted, Mackell Provides Fire," *Montreal Star,* Mar. 31, 1952, 41; and Herb Ralby, "Laycoe Gives Canadiens Cause to Regret Trading Him," *Boston Daily Globe,* Mar. 31, 1952, 14.

60 Dink Carroll, "Mackell Scores Winner; Curry Counters Twice," *Gazette* (Montreal), Apr. 2, 1952, 18; and Herb Ralby, "Mackell Was Ill in Afternoon, but Felt Great at 10:30," *Boston Daily Globe,* Apr. 2, 1952, 27.

61 Tom Fitzgerald, "McIntyre's First Goal in 15 Games Wins for Bruins, 1–0," *Boston Daily Globe,* Apr. 4, 1952, 36. All details in this paragraph are taken from this article.

62 See Tom Fitzgerald, "Surging Bruins Eye Series," *Boston Sunday Globe,* Apr. 6, 1952, 46.

63 Tom Fitzgerald, "Bruins Lose, 3–2, in Second Overtime," *Boston Daily Globe,* Apr. 7, 1952, 1, 6; and Elmer Ferguson, "Habs Overtime Win Ties Bruin Series," *Herald, Montreal,* Apr. 7, 1952, 1, 26. All details in this paragraph and the following one are taken from these articles.

64 Elmer Ferguson, "Habs Eliminate Bruins," *Herald, Montreal,* Apr. 9, 1952, 1, 32; and Tom Fitzgerald, "Canadiens Score 2 in Third Period, Oust Bruins 3–1," *Boston*

Daily Globe, Apr. 9, 1952, 11. It is also worth noting that Richard's comeback was an important sequence in the 2005 film *The Rocket* (director Charles Binamé) in which Roy Dupuis plays Richard.

65 Charles Binamé, dir. *The Rocket* (Toronto: Alliance Atlantis, French 2005; English 2006). The National Film Board (NFB) of Canada did a documentary on Richard in 1998 that is also called *The Rocket.*

66 See Chapter 3 for a discussion of the photo, taken at the end of the second Ali vs. Liston fight (May 25, 1965) and chosen for the cover of *SI*'s special issue "The Greatest Sports Photos of the Century." For Leifer's comments on the photo, see *The Best of Leifer* (New York: Abbeville Press, 2001) and his interview with Larry Berman and Chris Mahar "An Interview with Neil Leifer," Jan. 8, 2002, http://bermangraphics.com/press/leifer.htm.

67 These portraits are taken from Podnieks's *Players* and Diamond's *Total Hockey.*

68 Ferguson doesn't mention this in his original article on the game (see note 64), but the story is well known. Dick Irvin, Jr., relates it in *The Habs: An Oral History,* p. 86. Irvin quotes Ferguson as saying, "That beautiful bastard scored semiconscious."

69 Podnieks, *Players,* 347.

6 The Comeback

MCNEIL'S MOST SUCCESSFUL YEAR IN THE NHL WAS 1952–53, despite the fractured cheekbone that happened at the end of October which kept him out of the lineup for four games. A main team objective for the season was to increase goal production, and there is a fine balance between paying attention to defensive fundamentals and being a threat offensively. While every goalie knows the value of a back-checking forward who may not break up the first play but makes sure that there are no second chances, most would also agree that falling back into a defensive shell usually spells disaster. Sometimes the best defence is a consistent offence, and it is easy to defend your net when the play is in the other end.

McNeil was stellar in the regular season, posting 10 shutouts.[1] The 10-shutout mark stands as a level of excellence, something like the fifty-goal season for forwards. What made McNeil's shutouts noteworthy was that four of them were close games, two ending in 0–0 ties and two more 1–0 wins. Giving up a goal in any of the first two would have meant a difference of two points, one point in the latter. Another four were only 2–0 scores. The sole blowout was an anomalous 9–0 annihilation of the Red Wings at the beginning of the season—one of Sawchuk's rare off nights. Otherwise, one could say that when McNeil was perfect in blocking everything thrown his way, it was because he had to be. This observation fits with his comments about the stellar play of José Théodore when the latter won the Most Valuable Player Award in 2002. McNeil remarked that Théodore had to play in several very tight games, a situation that keeps a goalie sharp.[2] Lopsided scores do not bring out the best athletic performances, let alone enthusiastic fans.

Elmer Ferguson was aware of these factors when he wrote about McNeil's shutout mark in his column and made a case for his being awarded the Hart Trophy for the Most Valuable Player.[3] A week or so before the end of the regular schedule, Jack Adams was widely quoted as saying that he would pick Gerry McNeil over Terry Sawchuk for the All-Star team: "I thought it wonderful the way McNeil played when his mother died, or when his baby was under the cloud of death."[4] The

McNeil for the Hart Trophy campaign was picked up by the French press in Montreal.[5] Another feature of the 10 shutouts was that two of them came in December at the Olympia. When Marty Pavelich scored against McNeil the next time the Habs were in Detroit (January 18th), it ended McNeil's Olympia shutout streak at 139:28—not bad considering that the Wings, as expected, led the league in scoring with 225 goals. After McNeil's playoff performance of the year before, Detroit fans had to respect the small goalie from Montreal.

In any case, the Habs hoped for better offence in 1952–53. On the eve of the regular season, Dink Carroll interviewed Dick Irvin, who predicted that the Canadiens could finish first if they could reach the 85-point mark.[6] Detroit had 100 points the year before, 22 more than the Habs, who finished with 78, but much of that margin came from the fact that Montreal could only manage two wins in twelve games against Detroit. "I figure that all we have to do this season to finish first is break even in our games against Detroit," said Irvin. There were specific concerns. Nobody knew if the Rocket, who played in only forty-eight games in 1951–52, would be able to regain his top form. Nobody knew if Dickie Moore's knees would hold up.

Going further with his prognostications, Irvin said that if the Habs could score 225 goals (i.e., 3.21 goals per game) while giving up only 150, they should win the league championship and McNeil the Vezina.[7] Montreal would go on to score a total of only 155 goals, but they still finished second. They allowed only 148 goals (GAA 2.11), but McNeil would not win the Vezina (Detroit gave up a meagre 133). Breaking it down to an individual level, Irvin was looking to Richard for fifty, Geoffrion for forty, twenty from Curry, twenty-five from the centres, and ten from defencemen. Two weeks into the campaign Carroll came back to the subject of Irvin's predictions. The Habs had played six games and scored eleven times for an average of less than two goals per game. There was talk of getting the "boards" out again—an allusion to Irvin's shooting drill that gave players practice in hitting the top and bottom corners where most goalies had trouble.[8] For all the attention that has been paid to the great Montreal goal-scorers like Richard, Lach, Geoffrion, and Moore (with justification), the Habs were a poor offensive threat in the early '50s. Their goals for (GF) from 1951 to '53 went from 173 up to 195 and then way down to 155.[9]

The lack of a solid scoring punch was something that Irvin continued to address. In early December *The Hockey News* ran a story on McNeil being in the thick of the race for the Vezina, and it reproduced the goalie's version of a conversation he had just had with Theresa:

THE COMEBACK

"How do you like that," laughed Gerry McNeil. "I go home after the morning practice and the wife tells me we're going shopping. Oh no we're not, I tell her because I've got to go back and practice this afternoon. A few of the boys weren't hitting the net this morning.

"'We'll [sic] that's great,' she tells me. 'If you'd practice right in the morning you wouldn't have to go back in the afternoon.'

"So what can I do? May be [sic] it would be better if I let those guys score goals on me in the morning, eh?"[10]

The story closed with reference to McNeil having kept a cardboard box full of pictures of goalies. Along with the pictures was a newspaper clipping that reproduced Lynn Patrick's famous words, "A fellow doesn't have to be crazy to play goals but it helps." McNeil's reaction to Lynn's statement reflected how confident he felt about his game at the time of the interview: "Patrick may be right ... but I wouldn't trade jobs with any other athlete. Not the way I'm going now."[11]

The fall of 1952 would become a milestone in the history of the NHL, since it saw the beginning of televised games on the CBC.[12] The first of these was the French broadcast on October 11th from the Montreal Forum. A digital reproduction of the beginning of this broadcast (originally a kinescope recording) was made available at CBC's online archive around 2008, but few people would have seen this recording since the actual broadcast itself more than a half century earlier. We hear the dulcet voice of René Lecavalier, *"directement du Forum de Montréal,"* and see—yes, see—Gordie Howe take a shot on Gerry McNeil, who deflects the puck toward the corner. Thanks to Paul Patskou, my father and I got to see this clip in the 1990s. Although he was generally aware that televised broadcasts started while he was with the Canadiens, he had no memory of the first telecast, nor could he remember ever having met somebody who did see it. With the control we now have over digital video, we have fallen into the habit of rewatching and reusing. The initial CBC broadcasts started at 9:30 PM and essentially covered only the third period; later in the 1960s, of course, this was moved up to 8:30, which usually meant the end of the first period (in 1952 Toronto games started at 8:30 PM). There was no replay or slow motion.[13] Commentary and commentators were kept to a minimum.

Few people had televisions in Montreal in 1952, so the majority still experienced the NHL aurally via radio. Hence the voices of Michel Normandin and Doug Smith would remain a part of the Canadian consciousness along with Foster Hewitt, of course, even more so than I believe more recent play-by-play announcers. Unlike 1952, when the television audience only got to see part of the game, telecasts now often have pre- and post-game segments, a consequence of the luxury of having so many broadcasters and hence air time. These segments now consist of three to four panellists—usually all male former players with a few well-known commentators—who are placed in a glittering electronic set that resembles a pinball arcade. My point here is that the panels of suits, along with special segments like "Coach's Corner," seem to command more and more of our electronic arena. Yes, there always was a "colour commentator," perhaps a Dick Irvin, Jr., to interject observations, do an interview, report on a behind-the-scenes story, but I would argue that sixty years has seen this commentary (which we might understand as part of MacAloon's "festive frame") expand. Media personalities are better known than most of the players. In fact, the gargantuan monster that is the NHL on television—running from early October to June on multiple channels most nights (and the days now marked by repeated "highlight" segments)—clearly spills over into MacAloon's "spectacle frame," which comes with a nagging sense of doubt: Is this too much?

The most important regular season game in 1952–53 was the last one at the Olympia. For at least a week, all the talk around the league was about the prospect that Gordie Howe would tie and perhaps surpass Richard's record of fifty goals in a single season, which the Canadiens star had set back in 1944–45. With three games remaining, Howe had 47. The Wings were playing the Bruins at home and everybody was anxious to see Gordie get the record so that he could relax a little before the playoffs. Howe streaked down the middle of the slot unguarded; Lindsay hit him with a beautiful pass and number forty-eight was in the net. Wilson made a similar play to set Howe up in the third for goal number forty-nine.[14] At that point there wasn't a person in the Olympia who would have bet against Howe setting a new record. In fact, Howe almost got number fifty a few minutes later. Playing all kinds of extra shifts, Howe dug the puck out from behind the net and passed to Lindsay in front. Normally, Lindsay would have just fired it home, but he noticed Howe all alone at the other side of the net, so he tried a return pass. Howe could see number fifty already, but the puck hit Hal Laycoe's skate and deflected away.[15] Despite scoring twice, Howe was disappointed about the one he missed when the game ended. He slumped at his stall, looking more than a little fatigued. Still, if he continued to get 13 shots per game, his chances of matching or surpassing the Rocket's mark were better than even odds.

The Wings travelled to Chicago for a Saturday night game. Things looked good for Howe early as he got 2 shots: "Fogolin deflected the

THE COMEBACK

first one[,] and [g]oalie Al Rollins stopped the next one."[16] Desperate for their first playoff berth in six years, the Hawks had a strong game, winning 4–3, and Howe was held off the scoring sheet. Ironically, the Chicago team was coached by Sid Abel, an ex-Red Wing. This result set the stage for the last game at the Olympia and Howe's last chance at fifty. Both clubs were proud enough not to want to end the season with a pair of losses (Montreal had lost 2–1 to Boston the previous night). Hence what should have been a pressure-free game—the outcome would not change the team standings—was just the opposite, for McNeil at least, and perhaps, Richard. The other Canadien directly involved was Bert Olmstead, who was given the task of checking Howe. Olmstead would have to play a lot of minutes because Howe was sure to be double-shifted until the record fell.

The Habs took a 1–0 lead in the first period when Meger dished to Geoffrion, who got a short breakaway and made good.[17] The Wings tied it up early in the third on a forty-foot screen shot by Red Kelly that deflected in off Metro Prystai. The goal was credited to Kelly, which would have given him twenty for the year and a fat bonus, but the stellar defenceman, in a classy move, went over to the scorekeeper and had it officially awarded to Prystai.[18] Nobody, however, was paying any attention to the score. All that mattered was whether Howe could get a goal. Coach Tommy Ivan had him playing a shift on defence in between his regular shifts just to increase his opportunities. The strategy might have backfired in the same way that going to a "short bench" too early can backfire—your best players become too exhausted to play well. Howe ended up playing thirty-two and a half minutes but only managed 5 shots on goal (another 4 went wide). His best chance came halfway through the third when he shook Olmstead and slipped right in on the Montreal net. Firing from about fifteen feet out, he watched as McNeil dove across the crease and made a sensational save.[19] It would probably have been the game winner as well as number fifty. The clock wound down to a minute left—then thirty seconds. Dollard St. Laurent rode a Wing into the boards and was sent off. The fans suddenly came alive for one last effort with the man advantage. They chanted for Ivan to pull Sawchuk for a sixth skater, but he resisted. The faceoff was inside the Montreal zone. Controlling the draw, the Canadiens dumped the puck out to centre; Harvey draped himself over Delvecchio, which prevented the Wings from bringing it back in.[20] It was over.

My father never mentioned stopping Howe's bid for a fifty-goal season when I was growing up. I must have overheard something about it once, because when I was older I had a vague memory of a conversation in our home in which the subject came up. It wasn't until I was forty or thereabouts that I looked up the newspaper coverage of that game in March of '53, and then I asked my father why he never mentioned it before. His answer was roughly, "It isn't nice to be seen taking something away from one of the truly great players." While my father never spoke about the event, I do remember how the Kilpatrick photo of him kicking out a shot from Howe (see Chapter 3) had always hung on the den wall. I know now that the picture wasn't taken during the 1951 playoffs, since Howe was still wearing the protective headgear then (having suffered his serious concussion in the 1950 playoffs). In the final analysis, Howe just seemed to lack that explosive energy that was responsible for so many of the forty-nine goals he did score, and part of that had to do with the checking of Olmstead. "Goose" McCormack also deserved praise as the centreman who made sure that Delvecchio wasn't allowed to set up his right winger. Since 1952–53 was not a year for goal production as far as Montreal was concerned, it seemed fitting that it would end with a great defensive effort by the entire team. In a not-so-classy move, Dick Irvin stepped out onto the Olympia ice and raised Richard's hand in the "and-still-champion" gesture, an act that drew loud boos from the Detroit fans. Back in the dressing room, McNeil went over to Richard and said, "Well Rock, he'll have to start over at one."[21]

The team that did surprise the league with their offence in 1952–53 was Chicago. Rejuvenated under Sid Abel, the Black Hawks led the league in the first few weeks and ended up finishing fourth, which meant that they would face Montreal in the Semifinal. Things went well for Montreal in the first two games, which the Habs won by scores of 3–1 and 4–3. Perhaps the team was a little overconfident on the trip to Illinois. They lost Game Three at the Stadium 2–1, but there was no panic in the Montreal camp.

Game Four was scheduled for two days later. The paid attendance was close to 16,500, and the crowd was at the Stadium not only to make noise but to have fun. The atmosphere was wild and unruly. Everything got tossed on the ice: coins, cards, peanuts, bolts, hats, shoes—even a toupée! One fan managed to throw a lighted cigarette down Tom Johnson's sweater. Another nailed him in the head with an egg (had it been hard-boiled it probably would have knocked him out). A turnip narrowly missed Elmer Lach. At one point toilet-paper streamers trailed behind a few players.[22] As far as the game itself was concerned, the home fans had something to cheer about (fig. 26). After Bert Olmstead scored a power-play goal to put the visitors up 1–0, the

Fig. 26 Gerry McNeil makes a save off Jack McIntyre. Chicago Stadium, early 1950s. (Photographer unknown.) Copyright unknown. The mascot name for the Chicago franchise was officially the "Black Hawks" (two words) until 1985. Black Hawk was a Sauk leader in the nineteenth century.

tide changed.[23] The Hawks got the equalizer early in the second when Mosienko beat McNeil on the short side. The Canadiens argued that George Gee was offside, but the goal stood, much to the delight of the Stadium crowd. Al Rollins was spectacular at the other end, making great saves off Geoffrion and Curry in the third. Then Vic Lynn took a shot that deflected off MacPherson and ended up behind McNeil. McFadden scored into the empty net when McNeil was pulled for an extra attacker and that was that.[24]

Suddenly the series was tied, but it felt even worse. The Black Hawks had all the momentum going back to Montreal; they knew that they could play tight defensively and hold off the Montreal attack. The first period of Game Five back at the Forum might have been the most horrendous of McNeil's NHL career. Four minutes in, Fred Hucul looped a shot from outside the blue line that took a funny bounce—right over McNeil's stick—and ended up in the net.[25] All of a sudden McNeil felt panic tingling through his body. His mouth seemed to go dry. This couldn't be happening, but it was. A couple of minutes later Bill Mosienko fired from about ten feet and caught McNeil frozen. Down 2-0, the Habs never recovered. The period was just half over when Mosienko broke in again; this time he drew McNeil out and left the puck in the crease. Gus Bodnar, following the play, was there to knock it over the line. Every Hab at that point realized that the season might soon be over.

The teams exchanged goals in the second. Objecting to some of Chadwick's calls, the Montreal fans took their turn throwing debris on the ice. Michel Normandin, the public announcer, appealed for them to stop and was roundly booed. The third was a wild affair. Tom Johnson made it 4-2 with about five minutes left, but that was as close as it would get. With less than two minutes to go, Vic Lynn got into a fight with Paul Meger and was sent to the dressing room. As he headed down the passageway, he was hit by an irate fan who was then chased by the rest of the Chicago players. The siren sounded, and Chicago was convinced that they were on the verge of an upset. Coach Abel was beaming, "We have a hotter attack, a stiffer defense and a goaltender no club in this league can match." Al Rollins, traded to Chicago from the Leafs, stopped 26 shots, including a sensational save against Richard, who would have brought the Habs to within one if he had scored. Elmer Ferguson noted how Rollins's performance was so superlative that it earned an applause from the Forum fans and then repeated the belief that hot goaltending can steal a series.[26] There were complaints about the officiating in the Canadiens' dressing room and a general sense of gloom.

During the same discussion in which my father commented on José Théodore's 2001-02 performance, he recalled his feelings during that series against Chicago. "A couple of untimely mistakes and I felt shattered." My father had lost before, but never because of his own poor play. This time he felt that the loss was his fault. What he didn't remember was that he did make seventeen saves in that first period, twelve more in the second. He might have been flat for a couple of the goals, but the entire team was flat. Dink Carroll quoted Irvin on how the goalie had asked to be replaced by Plante after the game: "[McNeil] said he felt he wasn't helping the team. If they lost, he'd feel personally responsible for the fellows mising [sic] out on the money."[27] In today's world of multi-million-dollar salaries, it seems silly to talk of being responsible for the guys missing out on "the [prize] money", but in the early 1950s, the prize money represented a much larger percentage of a player's earnings for the year. Nerves and waning confidence obviously had worn my father down despite his excellent regular season performance.

What a difference a few bad games can make. Perhaps there is no factor more important in sports than being able to push one's game with the belief that only good things can follow. Conversely, to feel doubt about one's game is sure to impact negatively on performance. The fear of failure has a paralytic effect; one becomes tentative and reaction time slows down. Athletes must constantly fight a mental struggle as well as the physical one. Moreover, there is little one can do to avoid a turn from good to bad. There almost seems a natural equilibrium that operates among teams or between players. One side gets the upper hand and is able to maintain a psychological advantage for a time, but then a freak accident or turn of events causes some reverse in momentum and the other side takes over. One sees this in several sports: shifts in shooting percentage in basketball, of "winners" in tennis, of a pitcher who has been cruising along only to get shelled in a late inning. A collateral truism in sport has to do with the upset—the underdog who suddenly believes that he or she can win, and the favoured player or team who suddenly senses that defeat is coming to swallow them up. The question is, what is to be done in such situations?

Irvin waited until the last minute before Game Six in Chicago before confirming that Jacques Plante, up from Buffalo, would start. Later he told Dink Carroll that he made the move in part because Gerry asked him to, that his first choice would have been to stick with the goalie who got them there.[28] Irvin had apparently given Plante the nod late that afternoon at the Hotel LaSalle. Afterwards the young replacement would admit that he was so nervous that he had trouble doing up his skates.[29] Nevertheless, Montreal went on to win 3–0. Plante's playoff debut was perfect.

Chicago Stadium was unique in that the team dressing rooms were in the basement. McNeil, who watched the game in his civilian clothes by the bench, had to make his way through the throngs of fans to the stairs located behind the net. He caught up to Plante halfway down on the stairs and embraced the goalie: "It worked, Jacques, it worked."[30] Although changing goalies happened very rarely and almost always due to injury, McNeil knew that the strategy could give a team a lift. He also thought back to the game in Toronto when his cheekbone was shattered, his stubborn insistence that he could continue contributed to the team's ultimate loss. This situation was different—there was nothing wrong with McNeil physically—but his instincts told him a change would be positive. It was.

However, it is a popular belief among coaches that all athletes should demonstrate a willingness to compete at all times. If players start to feel any doubt, they had better quash it quickly. When the playoffs were over, Irvin was quoted as having referred to McNeil's "crack up."[31] Dink Carroll made a comparison to Durnan's decision to step down in the 1950 Semifinal with the Rangers.[32] On the train back to Montreal, the Canadiens listened to Game Six of the Detroit-Boston series on the radio. The Bruins finished off the Wings 4–2, so for the second time in three years the highly touted Detroit team got bounced in the Semifinal. Plante was certainly good enough on Saturday to get the start again on Tuesday.

Monday's practice, a brisk affair given what was at stake, took the decision out of Irvin's hands. McNeil threw his right skate out to block a shot from Richard, a shot that was so hard it collapsed the boot casing in the ankle area.[33] So much for taking it easy on goalies during practice! The netminder was immediately taken to the hospital. Although the X-rays were negative, it was determined that there was ligament damage in addition to the severe bruising. Told that he would probably miss at least a week, McNeil was given crutches and allowed to attend the game Tuesday night. A huge weight seemed to be lifted from his shoulders. It was no longer a matter of not being confident; he was physically unable to play. On the Montreal goalie situation, Sid Abel commented, "Plante can't be better than McNeil."[34]

The Hawks flew to Montreal for Game Seven. The press box contained the Boston broadcast team of Johnny Crawford and Fred Cusiak, eager to see whom the Bruins would face in the Final.[35] The hero of Game Seven was the lanky rookie from the Victoria Cougars, Eddie Spider Mazur, who scored twice as the Habs won 4–1. Periodically, Plante could be seen wandering from his net to play the puck, an innovative feature of his style and one for which he would become famous. However, Forum fans, seeing the technique for the first time, seemed to go into apoplectic shock whenever the goalie left his crease.

According to Ferguson, McNeil, hobbling around on crutches, was the welcome committee in the Canadiens dressing room afterwards.

> *"You played a great game, Jacques."*
> *"I don't know," said Plante. "That goal scored by that little fellow, Mosienko you call him? Maybe I should have stopped that."*
> *"You were swell," said McNeil. "We're in the Stanley Cup Finals now."*
> *"You're a nice guy, Gerry. If I can do as well as you, I'll be happy."[36]*

While Ferguson's fictionalized dialogue may now seem overly warm, there is no evidence to suggest that it is inaccurate. Ferguson himself then draws attention to this very personal and emotional exchange by implying that "these little side-plays, these incidents that a lot of folk consider unimportant" are just the opposite—they are easy to miss when the dressing room is full of well-wishers and what Ferguson calls "sudden friends." He writes that, despite the crowded room, the players know who the "old friends" are. Having been in countless such situations over many years, the veteran sportswriter captures and saves a pocket of history that has been missed by hockey historians since. Most people writing about my father's place between Durnan and Plante want to manufacture stories of frustration and loss, yet my father himself never remembered it that way. He genuinely respected and admired Durnan; he genuinely believed Plante could help the team.

It is interesting to note that in all four of Montreal's wins the Habs scored either three or four goals, and in the three games they lost, they could manage only two twice and one once. Comments by Lach and others suggested that the truly outstanding netminder of the series was Al Rollins, who made a point of shaking hands with both Plante and McNeil at the end of the game. To the press the Chicago goalie said simply, "It was a good series, but it is all over now."[37]

Banking on the likelihood that everything he says will get back to his own players, Irvin spouted self-deprecation to the press:

> *We'll be lucky if we score a single goal against Boston in the Stanley Cup finals. Lynn Patrick has devised the best defensive system ever seen in hockey and I don't think we have the team to cope with it. The Bruins might knock us out in four straight games. We have only tired old men to send into the fray along with four rookies. It's not a bright prospect.*[38]

For his part, Lynn Patrick, lounging on a chesterfield in the lobby of the Sheraton-Mount Royal, responded casually, "I predict a long, hard series." Then the real questions and answers were fired about.

> *"Who will check Maurice Richard?" Patrick was asked.*
> *Patrick laughed. "Who will check Eddie Sandford?" he countered briskly.*
> *"He's the hottest guy in hockey right now with six goals in six playoff games."*[39]

When told of Patrick's comment, Irvin dropped the posturing, "Who is Patrick trying to kid? Sandford has been in the league six seasons and has scored only sixty-four goals, an average of about ten a season. I'm not worried about who's going to check him. I've got a bigger worry than that. I've got to find a way to get a low-scoring team past the greatest defensive system in hockey."[40] Consistent with his pre-season observations, this assessment revealed what was really on Irvin's mind.

The truth is that Irvin had reason to be worried. In the fourteen games between the teams during the regular season, the Bruins had won nine, the Habs three, and two ended in ties. Sugar Jim Henry, the Bruins goalie, had shut out the Canadiens on four occasions. The last one, a 5–0 win at the Garden on March 5th, effectively ended McNeil's chances for the Vezina. That game saw Johnny Peirson score twice.[41] Peirson just seemed to have McNeil's number. In fact, my father would laugh and say that he "kept Peirson in the league." Once he admitted to me that he often felt the memory of going down in some goalmouth scramble against the Bruins, only a second later to see the puck behind him in the net, and then a minute later to hear the following words on the PA system: "Boston goal by Johnny Peirson, assisted by..." This scenario became a recurring nightmare—in the scramble his arms would always be pinned down and he would never see Peirson score, only hear it announced later. "Boston goal, Peirson." Any second thoughts about having asked to be replaced were countered by the fact that Plante got the job done. If my father had played Game Six, his team might not have made the Final. Plante, for his part, was gaining confidence and feeling more comfortable. At one point he remarked to the press that "Gerry is a great goaler but his size is a handicap. He's so small that he has to move twice as fast as me to cover the same area."[42] Success does have a way of releasing the braggart, but Plante's cockiness would not last.

The Habs won the opener 4–2. They peppered the Boston goalie, Sugar Jim Henry, with 33 shots. It wasn't a bad performance by Henry, who played even though he was dreadfully sick with the flu.[43] In contrast, Dink Carroll wrote that Plante could have tended goal in the second period from a rocking chair as the Bruins could manage only 2 shots on net (18 for the game).[44] It was a good thing, because the Canadiens goalie had been injured himself toward the end of the first, when he went down hard stopping a shot from Laycoe. The Bruins played poorly, perhaps experiencing a natural letdown after ousting the Red Wings, perhaps missing their leader Milt Schmidt, who fell on the end of a skate blade against Detroit and wasn't dressed.[45]

McNeil had to get used to being a spectator. As his ankle began to heal, he had to wonder if he would ever get back in the net. Game Two showed that Irvin might have been right with his comments. The Bruins were able to thwart the Montreal attack while scoring four goals of their own and winning 4–1. With the split in Montreal, the Bruins felt confident going back home. Game Two also saw the regular Bruin netminder, Sugar Jim Henry, twist his ankle when he got his skate caught in a rut. "Red" Henry, no relation to Sugar, had to replace him. This marked the first time in history that two substitute goalies faced each other in the Stanley Cup Final. But this wasn't the end of it. Not long after coming in, Red Henry was cut on his upper left arm by a skate in a goalmouth scramble. For a moment it looked like Lynn Patrick would repeat the history that his father, Lester Patrick, made twenty-five years earlier in the same building when as the coach of the Rangers he replaced an injured Lorne Chabot in a Stanley Cup game against the Montreal Maroons. Red, however, got stitched up and continued to play.[46]

Later Irvin would say that in his opinion, McNeil would have stopped at least two of the four Boston goals. My father once told me that he had the opposite disposition to Plante's—that Jacques would blame the team for a loss, while he would blame himself. "You last longer with Plante's attitude." However, on the train to Boston, Selke and Irvin discussed the situation and the former sounded ominous. "The trouble with Jacques is that he can't stand prosperity," said Selke. "I'm afraid we'll have to do something."[47]

Elsewhere on the same train Mac and Bill Head, the team physiotherapist, dug out my father's skate from the equipment bag and figured that a hole could be drilled through the boot to allow a painkiller to be administered at the bench. This was necessary as the painkiller would wear off before the next intermission. There was no question that my father was eager, if not physically ready, to go back in. If anything, the ankle injury took his mind off his debacle against Chicago. All his energy was focused on getting comfortable physically—the mental part of the game quickly disappeared, and there wasn't time to stew about things. The special overnight train arrived at North Station at 9:20 AM. Game Three, the third straight sellout at the Garden, was that night.

The next day a picture of McNeil kicking out a shot by Milt Schmidt was on the front page of *The Boston Daily Globe*.[48] Underneath, the headline read, "Bruins Defeated, 3–0, by Montreal, McNeil." Irvin was quoted on the inspiration that a hockey team can find with the return of a key player: "It makes all the difference in the world to the team to have a major league goaltender in their net."[49] As mentioned above, confidence sometimes comes mysteriously from within; at other times it can come from seeing a teammate back in the play who has a history of solid performances in clutch situations. The last time the Canadiens won at Boston Garden was December 21, 1952, when they took the game 4–3 with Jean Béliveau scoring two goals in his brief stint with the Habs that year. Boom Boom Geoffrion provides an insider's account of McNeil's comeback game:

> To a man we all loved McNeil. What we didn't know was whether or not he was over the nervousness that made him pull himself out of the last game against Chicago. . . .
>
> If Gerry had butterflies you would never have known it by the way he played. Gerry was reassured by Tommy Johnson's goal in the first period and that's all he needed. He gave Boston nothing and Paul Masnick got two more goals in the second and third periods. We played our butts off for McNeil. It looked as if we had booby-trapped all the lanes going toward our goal. If we had done that all winter McNeil probably wouldn't have had any problem with his nerves.[50]

However, it was the Montreal press who enthused about my father's gutsy performance: "The most warming sight of the entire hockey season was Gerry McNeil's comeback in the Garden here last night. No one knew just what the future held for Gerry after his nervous crack-up in the Chicago series."[51] Carroll went on to quote Irvin on what happened at a team meeting and on the pressure my father played under:

> We had a meeting of the players and I asked Gerry if he thought he could help us. . . . He looked eager and he said, "I'd sure like the chance." If he had shown any hesitation, whatever, I wouldn't have risked it . . .
>
> Before the last period he had difficulty getting up to the rubbing table. . . . He has tremendous courage.

Carroll then commented:

> Dick then went back to review some of the obstacles Gerry had overcome in the last few seasons. His mother was critically ill when the club was on a long road trip and he worried about her all the time. She died and he flew home for the funeral, and then returned to take his place in the nets. His baby daughter also fell ill and he was on the long distance telephone four or five times a day, but he stayed in there despite the pressure and acquitted himself well.
>
> Then he was hit with a puck . . . in Toronto Maple Leaf Gardens and suffered a shattered cheekbone. One eye was swollen tight shut, but he insisted on finishing the game. . . .
>
> I wasn't too surprised at that little crack-up he had in Chicago. There were 25 games during the regular schedule during which we scored exactly one goal

or less. The pressure on the goalkeeper is terrific when he's trying to protect a one-goal lead. It wasn't just the pressure of the playoffs that made his nerves buckle momentarily. It was that plus all that had gone on before.[52]

Today journalism attempts to sound more scientific; goalies are said to "succumb to the pressure" rather than experience "crack-ups," a term that implies a freakish inadequacy to cope. What Irvin did not say out loud but was probably thinking is that alternating McNeil and Plante, or getting them to compete for the Number One job, might be the best way to manage the netminding position. He did let slip that he thought "[McNeil] will have to fight his way back to the nets."[53] Although the Habs outshot the Bruins 31 to 18, McNeil was called upon to make four sensational saves, two off Sandford (someone was still needed to check this guy) and others off Réal Chevrefils and Leo Labine.[54]

Game Four was a Tuesday night. Oddly enough, Irvin wasn't available to the press, and there was a lot of press in town. At an NHL luncheon, President Campbell revealed that the Final was being covered by more reporters from different parts of North America than ever before (i.e., thirty reporters and radio staff).[55] He pointed to the increased attendance in Boston and Chicago (in fact, the last playoff game at the Stadium between the Canadiens and the Hawks set a new league record) as proof that the game was growing in the US market—an issue that would dog the NHL for at least another half century. *The Boston Daily Globe* had assigned two reporters to the Final: Tom Fitzgerald, who filed stories primarily for the morning edition, and Herb Ralby, who did the same for the evening edition. Readers were getting two updates a day on the Bruins' injury situation. (In our online world, we tend to forget that many dailies published morning and evening editions during the twentieth century.) Noticeably absent from the luncheon was Dick Irvin. Rumour had it that, having shifted his poultry interest from pigeons to chickens, the outspoken coach was in Providence looking at some Rhode Island Reds. Meanwhile, Sugar Jim Henry had received "whirlpool bath treatments," and team physician Dr. Thomas Kelley announced that there had been "considerable improvement."[56] With Red Henry filling in admirably, the goaltending issue seemed mute for the Bruins anyway.

This situation changed with Game Four. Just before the opening faceoff, the Canadiens skated one by one up to McNeil to give him encouragement and signal that they were ready to repeat the defensive effort of the previous game.[57] That didn't happen. What did happen was that Montreal broke out of its lethargic offence and scored seven goals, including a hat trick by Richard.[58] With the Canadiens leading 5–3 and about three minutes left in the game, Patrick decided to pull his goalie for the extra attacker and the strategy seemed to work. Buzzing all over the Habs, the Bruins seemed to get all kinds of chances, especially Creighton and Peirson. Desperate for a break, McNeil skated to the bench, ostensibly for equipment repairs but also for another shot to his ankle. If the Bruins kept this pressure up, it was just a matter of time. Suddenly, he felt a little jittery under the cheers of the Garden fans. They knew that their team had the Habs on the run, and they had waited a long time to see the dominance that the Bruins had during the regular season. Bill Head did give McNeil another treatment, and the goalie made his way back to his crease.

Ralby interviewed the goalie afterwards: "'I did fall on my ankle,' he admitted, 'But the Bruins were putting on the pressure and I wanted to cool them off. Actually I didn't need the treatment. My ankle hurt a bit, but not too bad.'"[59] Tom Fitzgerald, the other *Boston Globe* reporter covering the series, clarified the treatment that McNeil received: "While Dr. Gordon Young supervised the proceedings, Bill Head the club physiotherapist applied a needle to the area, but he explained after the game that the needle merely penetrated the goalie's boot as he applied a freezing spray of sulphuric either [ether?] to the area around the ankle."[60] Forty years later McNeil viewed the Briston Film footage of his skate to the bench and could hardly believe what he saw. Unable to recall the details with absolute certainty, he thought he got a novocaine shot and suggested that Head may not have told the truth to the Boston reporters for fear of being reprimanded for not following usual procedure. In any case, the Bruins had to take chances to keep the pressure on and things backfired. Montreal scored twice more.

At this point, Sugar Jim, seemingly impressed by my father's painkiller performances, told Ralby that he was ready to go back: "Henry feels that if McNeil could do it there is no reason why he can't. He's a real team man and he figures it's worth a chance. If he can play without the ankle being frozen, all the better, but if they have to resort to that he's willing."[61] His intention, of course, was to give the Bruins a lift. The next day Tom Fitzgerald ran a story with the heading, "Jim Henry Vows to Play Tonight," and the subtitle "Patrick Bans Freezing of Goalie's Ankle" spoke directly to the issue of playing with a painkiller: "We're not going to permit any freezing of that ankle," the coach [Lynn Patrick] said. "We don't treat our players like that. It isn't worth it.... This is a man we are counting on heavily to help us next season. If he had the ankle frozen, there might be further serious damage, and he wouldn't be aware of it because there would be no pain."[62] Wise words.

THE COMEBACK

Much has been written about how males have historically been taught to endure pain as part of being masculine (see Chapter 5). This mindset certainly seemed to be part of the ethos surrounding professional hockey in the 1950s, and we now accept the fact that "sucking it up" often means that emotional energy is rechannelled elsewhere. A player might endure the pain at practice or during games, only to come home and abuse his wife or children. McNeil was never guilty of such behaviour, but it would be naive to think that he got through the stressful episodes in his career without any negative consequences. Patrick's comments quoted above remind us of the long-term risk that is taken when we artificially numb our pain, that pain is the clearest message the body sends regarding any damage it has sustained. As implied in Chapter 5, my father's excellent reflexes, so crucial to his success, may have been part of an acutely developed, and hence vulnerable, nervous temperament that caused his confidence crisis in Chicago.

Although neither team was in a position to win the Cup on Tuesday night, Lord Stanley did make a public appearance in a corner of the tiny Garden lobby. Shipped from Detroit, the Cup sat there is all its glory for the Boston fans to admire.[63] Their team, however, was now down 3–1 and the series was headed back to Montreal. McNeil had felt good on the train back home before, but this time things were a little different. So close to the big prize, he found it hard not to toss and turn in his berth. Scoring seven times on the Bruins was certainly a boost, and if that happened again the Cup was as good as won. The only problem was that McNeil could not recall his team ever having two consecutive big scoring games. Never. It was more likely that the next time out would see few goals. Things could still go wrong. They shouldn't, but then Hucul shouldn't have scored in Chicago.

McNeil was right about the Habs not scoring many goals the next time out. It would take at least one to win, and if they scored only one, he would have to be perfect. But this was way too much thinking. Just play the game. Crowds of people gathered outside the Forum on Sainte-Catherine Street all day on Thursday. While the players were getting ready for the opening faceoff inside, Sergeant Marcel Roy of Station 10 oversaw the arrest of six men outside for scalping tickets—a $2 ticket was selling for $16, a $1.75 ducat for $10.[64] This was the Big Time in 1953.

As promised, Sugar Jim was in the Boston net, and the game quickly evolved into a goaltending duel.[65] Henry used his size well and was always in good position. McNeil mastered the art of eliminating rebounds; all shots were either caught in his trapper or steered into the corner. The first period saw McNeil make great stops off his nemesis Peirson and then Creighton. Meanwhile Henry robbed Olmstead and got lucky when Eddie Mazur just missed a rebound on a shot from Richard. There were some spectacular bodychecks. Hal Laycoe nailed Geoffrion early in the game, and Boom Boom never regained his stride. The Forum did erupt when Paul Masnick banged home a rebound off a shot from Dollard St. Laurent, but the goal was quickly waved off by Bill Chadwick who ruled that it came just after the end of the period. When Dickie Moore went off for holding early in the second, the Montreal defensive unit, led by Harvey, thwarted the power-play attack, and the Bruins failed to record a shot on net.

In the third, the Rocket had two good chances to repeat the heroics of the 1952 Semifinal, but Henry stoned him. In the last minute the Boston goalie also turned back a hard shot by rookie Lorne Davis. McNeil, meanwhile, made a couple of fine saves off Leo Labine and Hal Laycoe. Milt Schmidt had an opportunity to break the scoreless spell, but he missed the net. Overtime. On the first shift, McNeil made a routine save and then Henry lunged to stop a shot by Eddie Mazur. The puck went behind the Boston net where Richard wrestled with the defence for control.

The 1953 playoffs were the first to be televised by the CBC. Footage of the winning goal has survived and has been easily available in CBC's online digital archive. (While there is no guarantee that it will remain so, there are enough copies floating around the Internet.) I have viewed it several times, and what it shows is that Schmidt desperately tried to move the puck up to the left wing. Unfortunately for him and the Bruins, he moved it right to Elmer Lach, and the veteran centre from Nokomis, Saskatchewan, wasted no time in redirecting it at the Boston net. Good thing, because a Boston player immediately took him out of the play. The shot seemed to catch Henry a little unbalanced; the mesh behind him bulged. The red light went on. It was only 1:22 into overtime; the crowd had just settled itself back in. The Canadiens had won the Stanley Cup!

A select few would have seen the goal when it happened on the CBC broadcast (as mentioned earlier, few people had televisions), and if they did, the experience would have felt more like seeing it live. The moment came and passed as it did for those in the Forum. No replay, no slow motion, no overlaid analysis or commentary. The former two would be at least another decade away. The cameras remained rolling forever in the present, in tandem with the post-game reality. And yet for those lucky enough to have access to those moving pictures, they must have seemed magical. Fortunately, we cannot know how impoverished our experience of an electronic reproduction is until the future shows us something better.

The Forum roared and shook so loud that those outside felt the ground move under their feet. The next few minutes were a whirl. First, it was the Rocket, for once the person not to score the Big Goal, making straight for his centreman and leaping hard into Elmer's arms (Roger Saint-Jean, the photographer from *La Presse,* captures the moment in his famous picture), the pair about to fall to the ice in an embrace. Years later Saint-Jean would tell the story behind the photo. As with Ray Lussier's famous photo of an airborne Orr, the picture was taken during the first overtime period, always a strategic challenge for photographers who are often set up in the opposite end (i.e., the offensive zone for the home team during the first and third periods). Saint-Jean had to make his way to the other end of the rink if he was to capture a goal by the Habs in the first overtime. He got a view of the Boston net, but without a seat he had to watch helplessly as a man stood in front of him just as Lach was about to shoot. He heard the cheers while seeing nothing but the back of the man's coat. However, a second later, with his flash still charged and ready to fire, an opening miraculously appeared in front of him. He pushed the shutter button just as Richard and Lach jumped into their embrace, the image now part of the collective memory of the Habs aficionados. While the set shot can appeal to our artistic sensibility, especially in the hands of an Ozzie Sweet, it is the spontaneous action shot that we value the most in sports photography. In Saint-Jean's photo, one notices a series of V (as in victory) patterns: the sticks of Richard and Lach, the fans with their outstretched arms on the opposite side.[66]

What happened next I only know from the CBC footage, newspaper coverage, and my father's rather poor memory. The rest of the team, including my father, join Richard and Lach on the ice; they are soon followed by the coach, trainers, and handlers. Hugging teammates, Elmer being mobbed, fans climbing over the boards and onto the ice, the debris raining down. All through it, the ear-splitting cheers. Elmer complaining about the Rocket hitting his nose; "You did it, Elmer, you did it!" In their delirium, the Rocket and others carried Lach to the bench. At first Sugar Jim Henry didn't move from his crease; Quackenbush, who screened him on Lach's shot, offered consolation. After a few moments, the Bruin netminder slowly made his way over to congratulate McNeil. At one point the Canadien goalie was kept from joining his teammates as a number of Bruins surround him and extended their hands. Both

Fig. 27 Canadiens hockey team after winning Stanley Cup, 1953. Montreal Forum, April 16, 1953. (Photographer unknown. Gazette [Montreal], Apr. 17, 1953, 23.) Reproduced by permission of Library and Archives Canada/*The Gazette* [Montreal] fonds/PA-142658.

teams mingled uncharacteristically in a general mélange. Eventually, Mac was hoisted up by Floyd and Doug and carried on their shoulders.[67] Later a group of other players did the same with Irvin. When the Cup made its appearance on the ice, all the Habs pushed in around it childlike as if it wasn't real until you actually touch the thing. I see my father move toward the silver, but the crowd of players and fans seem to cut him off. The footage never shows him actually making contact with the Cup; it does show him, seemingly put off by the chaos, turning away. Now, of course, it is customary for every player to hoist the Cup.

The euphoria didn't subside as Clarence Campbell, himself on crutches, made the red carpet presentation: "On behalf of the National Hockey League and personally, it gives me great pleasure to present this grand old trophy to Captain Butch Bouchard and to congratulate the Canadiens on winning their sixth Stanley Cup Championship."[68] The Forum erupted again. Butch thanked the fans in French and English, then paid tribute to his teammates. More back-slapping and embracing.

Then the team picture (fig. 27). McNeil in the right front, between Frank Selke and Hector Dubois; Butch and the Rocket on the left; in the middle Dickie Moore and Billy Reay, drunk-happy youth and age, holding on to each other.[69] All are standing with fists raised. The ecstasy of victory on every face. The Cup itself is in the extreme left side

THE COMEBACK

of the frame—far from the players. These on-the-ice victory pictures are now expected and have become routine rituals. While a spontaneous, of-the-moment look distinguishes them from the official team picture that follows the game, a careful composition formula still operates insofar as all team members and officials are included with either their Olympic medals or the Stanley Cup in front. The best in sports photography, like the best in art, always eschews the routine and expected. For spontaneous celebration, it is hard to beat Heinz Kluetmeier's picture of the 1980 "Miracle on Ice," which made the *SI* cover March 3, 1980, and is reproduced in *Sports Illustrated 50: The Anniversary Book.*[70]

Watching the footage of the playoffs and the winning goal with my father sometime during the 1990s was truly memorable. While he may have seen the goal once or twice on television, he didn't recall it with any specificity. He couldn't remember if he had thrown his stick and gloves into the air (that subject will come up again in Chapter 8). My father did remember looking up into the crowd, searching for my mother. Nothing seemed complete, he said, until he connected with her, but at first he couldn't be sure if they were able to spot each other in the melee. It had been almost ten years since he first stepped out on the Forum ice (seven years since the Canadiens last won the coveted trophy). Between games and practices with the Royals and the Canadiens, he had logged hundreds of hours in this arena. So many times he stood and heard its dark, cavernous corners echo with the sounds of shots, at ice level the stroking of blades, the cackle of men at play. Now the entire space was bright and sang loud with climactic joy. Years later he would have ample opportunity to savour winning the Cup in a perfect 1–0 overtime game on home ice, to bask in the glory of knowing that his name was engraved on Lord Stanley, to be part of what would become the greatest Cup-winning franchise. Hours later the official photo would be taken of the team with the Cup (fig. 28). At the time, however, there was only the celebration of the moment. A sixth Cup for Montreal (i.e., the sixth as part of the NHL, seven total); the Leafs still led with seven wins (five of the last nine). We pondered this a moment in the family study, and then my father said that he believed he did pick out Teacy and some of the other wives; she seemed to be crying—he remembered that and a Forum usher trying to protect the wives from the pushing crowd. My mother does not remember crying or a pushing crowd; now almost fifty years later she remembers feeling tremendous relief, like a hundred pounds of weight taken off her back.

In my mind's eye, I reconstruct the minutes after the on-ice Cup presentation. My father finds himself back in the bedlam of the dressing

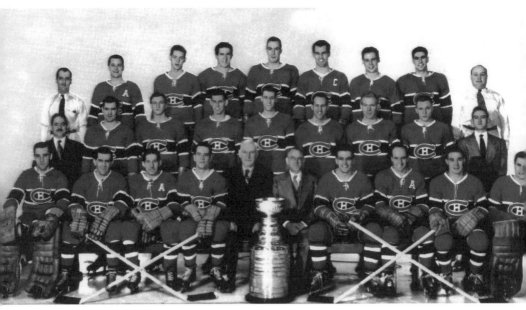

Fig. 28 Official team picture of the Montreal Canadiens, Stanley Cup Champions 1953. Montreal Canadiens, 1952–53. (Photo by David Bier.) Reproduced by permission of Club de hockey Canadien Inc.

Front (left to right): Jacques Plante, Maurice Richard, Elmer Lach, Bert Olmstead, Dick Irvin (Coach), Frank Selke (Managing Director), Bernie Geoffrion, Billy Reay, Paul Meger, Gerry McNeil.
Centre: Camil Desroches (Publicity), Calum Mackay, Dickie Moore, Dick Gamble, Ken Mosdell, Floyd Curry, Lorne Davis, Paul Masnick, Frank P. Selke (PR)
Back: Hector Dubois (Trainer), Doug Harvey, John McCormack, Ed Mazur, Bud MacPherson, Émile Bouchard, Tom Johnson, Dollard St. Laurent, Gaston Bettez (Asst. Trainer)

room. The reporters and other well-wishers are squeezing in around Richard and Lach. Toe Blake appears, and there are more pictures taken of a reunited Punch Line. "Busher" Curry boasts about his grand slam, now having won the Memorial, Allan, and Stanley Cups. McNeil, sitting in his usual spot, is happy to be left alone. Irvin shakes hands with each player and sits next to him. "Coaching is strictly for the birds," he says, "I don't want any more of it."[71] Knowing his obsessive interest in poultry, everyone laughs. More seriously, Irvin remarks that it was the best game of the series, "real playoff hockey." Then a reporter asks McNeil about his ankle injury. He smiles, "I certainly can't feel anything wrong with it just now."[72]

THE COMEBACK

1   These were 9-0 (vs. Det.) in Mont., 2-0 (vs. Bos.) in Bos., 3-0 (vs. Chi.) in Mont. 0-0 (vs. Det.) in Det., 2-0 (vs. Det.) in Det., 2-0 (vs. Chi.) in Chi., 1-0 (vs. Tor.) in Tor., 0-0 (vs. Bos.) in Bos., 2-0 (vs. Tor.) in Tor., and 1-0 (vs. Chi.) in Mont.
2   Dave Stubbs, "McNeil's Win Only Part of Story," *Gazette* (Montreal), May 7, 2002, E3.
3   Ferguson, "Gist and Jest," *Herald, Montreal,* Mar. 11, 1953, 19.
4   Quoted by Ferguson, "Gist and Jest," *Herald, Montreal,* Mar. 9, 1953, 17. See also note 3. Dink Carroll also refers to this comment, *Gazette* (Montreal), Apr. 2, 1953, 18.
5   See Robert Desjardins, "Pourquoi pas le trophée Hart à notre Gerry McNeil?" *Le Petit journal,* Mar. 1, 1953, 84; and Jean-Paul Jarry, "McNeil mérite le trophée Hart," *Monde Sportif,* Mar. 29, 1953, 3.
6   Carroll, "Playing the Field," *Gazette* (Montreal), Oct. 9, 1952, 20.
7   Ibid.
8   Carroll, "Playing the Field," *Gazette* (Montreal), Oct. 24, 1952, 22.
9   The year-end totals cited here are from Diamond, *Total Hockey,* 74.
10 Vince Lunny, "Gerry Gets into Thick of Vezina Trophy Race by Thinning GA Record," *Hockey News,* Dec. 13, 1952, 5, 15.
11 Lunny, "Gerry Gets into Thick of Vezina," 15.
12 For a description of the early years of CBC hockey broadcasts, see "Habs to Televise Only 3rd Periods of NHL Contests," *Globe and Mail,* Oct. 10, 1952, 22; Scott Young, *The Boys of Saturday Night: Inside Hockey Night in Canada* (Toronto: Macmillan, 1990), 80-102; and "Hockey Night in Canada," The Museum of Broadcast Communications, accessed July 26, 2007, http://www.museum.tv/archives/. The website for the archive is currently being upgraded.
13 There is a claim that in 1955 Gary Retzlaff made a kinescope recording of a goal and aired it seconds later. However, regular replays did not become a feature until the early 1960s.
14 Marshall Dann, "Lindsay Gives Howe a Big Boost toward Goal Record in 6-1 Romp: Gordie Gets No. 48, 49, One Short," *Detroit Free Press,* Mar. 20, 1953, 23.
15 Harry Stapler, "Help-Howe Result: 49," *Detroit News,* Mar. 23, 1953, 49-50.
16 "Hawks Lead Red Wings," *Detroit News,* Mar. 22, 1953, Part 2.1.
17 For accounts of the game, see "Canadiens, Red Wings Play to 1-1 Draw; Gordie Howe Fails in Bid for 50th Goal," *Gazette* (Montreal), Mar. 23, 1953, 20; "Gord Howe Fails in Bid to Equal Scoring Mark as Red Wings Tie Habs," *Globe and Mail,* Mar. 23, 1953, 18; Marshall Dann, "Canadiens Stop Howe, 'Win' 1-1 Tie with Wings" *Detroit Free Press,* Mar. 23, 1953, 33. All details about this game are taken from these articles.
18 Dann, "Canadiens Stop Howe," 33.
19 "Gord Howe Fails in Bid to Equal Scoring Mark as Red Wings Tie Habs," *Globe and Mail,* Mar. 23, 1953, 18.
20 "Gord Howe Fails," 18.
21 According to Bert Olmstead, Irwin, *Habs: An Oral History,* 94.
22 See Ferguson, "Gist and Jest," *Herald, Montreal,* Apr. 1, 1953, 24; and Carroll, "Playing the Field," *Gazette* (Montreal), Apr. 7, 1953, 20.
23 See Dink Carroll, "Black Hawks Even Round with Canadiens by 3-1 Victory," *Gazette* (Montreal), Apr. 1, 1953, 25; and Vince Lunny, "Hawks Nip Canadiens," *Herald, Montreal,* Apr. 1, 1953, 1, 24.
24 All details in this paragraph are taken from Carroll, "Black Hawks Even Round," 25; and Lunny, "Hawks Nip Canadiens," 1, 24.
25 Dink Carroll, "Chicago Beats Canadiens 4-2 to Take Playoff Lead," *Gazette*

(Montreal), Apr. 3, 1953, 17; and Vince Lunny, "Hawks Seek Clincher Over Habs Tonight," *Herald, Montreal,* Apr. 4, 1953, 12. All details about this game are taken from these articles.

26 Ferguson, "Gist and Jest," *Herald, Montreal,* Apr. 4, 1953, 13.

27 Carroll, "Playing the Field," *Gazette* (Montreal), Apr. 6, 1953, 18.

28 Ibid.

29 This is according to Ferguson, "Gist and Jest," *Herald, Montreal,* Apr. 6, 1953, 21. Ferguson quotes Plante as having said the following:
    I didn't think I could make it.... My hands started to shake so much that I could hardly adjust my pad straps. I didn't dare talk to anybody because I thought my voice would break. It wasn't until I got out on the ice that I calmed down. Then I stopped a couple—one of them a tough one—and the players came rushing around to say atta boy and I was all right. I never expected this would happen but I guess such things can only happen with a great team like the Canadiens. If I never play another game behind them it will be enough of a thrill for a lifetime.

30 Quoted by Ferguson, "Gist and Jest," *Herald, Montreal,* Apr. 6, 1953, 21. Another headline read, "Gerry Praises Plante's Play," *Gazette* (Montreal), Apr. 6, 1953, 18.

31 Quoted by Carroll, "Playing the Field," *Gazette* (Montreal), Apr. 14, 1953, 18.

32 Carroll, "Playing the Field," *Gazette* (Montreal), Apr. 6, 1953, 18.

33 See Vince Lunny, "Irvin Pat on Habs for BIG Hawk Game," *Herald, Montreal,* Apr. 7, 1953, 16; and "Jacques Plante to Stay in Goal against Hawks," *Gazette* (Montreal), Apr. 7, 1953, 20.

34 Quoted in "Jacques Plante to Stay," 20.

35 The Bruins ousted the Red Wings in their Semifinal. Dink Carroll, "Canadiens Rout Hawks 4–1 to Reach Stanley Cup Final," *Gazette* (Montreal), Apr. 8, 1953, 21.

36 Quoted by Ferguson, "Gist and Jest," *Herald, Montreal,* Apr. 8, 1953, 25.

37 Quoted by Carroll, "Canadiens Rout Hawks 4–1," 21.

38 Quoted by Vince Lunny, "Irvin, Patrick Agree It's Boston's Series," *Herald, Montreal,* Apr. 9, 1953, 16.

39 Ibid.

40 Ibid.

41 Ibid.

42 Quoted by Carroll, "Playing the Field," *Gazette* (Montreal), Apr. 14, 1953, 18.

43 "Bruins Lose First Game to Canadiens: Henry Turns Out Brilliant Stint in Nets Despite Attack of Flu," *Boston Daily Globe,* Apr. 10, 1953, 1, 30.

44 Dink Carroll, "Habitants Get Jump on Bruins," *Gazette* (Montreal), Apr. 10, 1953, 24.

45 "Schmidt Returns to Bruins: Reay May Miss Game," *Gazette* (Montreal), Apr. 11, 1953, 8; "Schmidt Able to Compete Saturday, Doctor Believes," *Boston Daily Globe,* Apr. 10, 1953, 30.

46 Herb Ralby, "Bruins Coach Ready to Go into Nets If Both Henrys Were Unable to Play," *Boston Daily Globe,* Apr. 12, 1953, 44.

47 Conversation reported to Carroll, "Playing the Field," *Gazette* (Montreal), Apr. 14, 1953, 18.

48 Tom Fitzgerald, "Bruins Defeated, 3–0, by Montreal, McNeil," *Boston Daily Globe,* Apr. 13, 1953, 1.

49 "Canadiens' Goalie Plays in Pain, Has Ankle Frozen 3 Times in Game," *Boston Daily Globe,* Apr. 13, 1953, 6.

50 Geoffrion and Fischler, *Boom Boom,* 57.

51 Carroll, "Playing the Field," *Gazette* (Montreal), Apr. 14, 1953, 18.

52 Ibid.

53 Quoted by Carroll, ibid. This comment might explain his treatment of McNeil in the Stanley Cup Final the next year (see Chapter 7).

54 Herb Ralby is credited with two stories on McNeil playing with his injured ankle. See "Canadiens' Goalie Plays in Pain, Has Ankle Frozen 3 Times in Game," *Boston Daily Globe,* Apr. 13, 1953, 1, 6; and "Gritty McNeil, Defying Ankle Injury, Inspires Canadiens in Win over B's," *Boston Daily Globe,* Apr. 13, 1953, 12.

55 Tom Fitzgerald, "Rival Goalies Uncertain for Fourth Stanley Cup Game: J. Henry, McNeil Status Doubtful Until Tonight," *Boston Daily Globe,* Apr. 14, 1953, 9.

56 "Hub Cup Hopes Riding on Sugar Jim's Return," *Montreal Daily Star,* Apr. 14, 1953, 31.

57 This gesture is captured by the Briston Film of the 1953 NHL playoffs.

58 Dink Carroll, "Richard Nets Three Goals as Canadiens Whip Bruins 7-3: McNeil Big Factor in Victory: Habs One Game from Cup," *Gazette* (Montreal), Apr. 15, 1953, 20; Tom Fitzgerald, "Richard Gets Three Goals, Canadiens Belt Bruins, 7-3," *Boston Daily Globe,* Apr. 15, 1953, 1, 14.

59 Herb Ralby, "Sugar Henry Set to Play Whether Ankle Heals or Not," *Boston Daily Globe,* Apr. 15, 1953, 14.

60 Fitzgerald, "Richard Gets Three Goals," 14.

61 Ralby, "Sugar Henry Set to Play," 14. Ralby refers to "three injections" being administered to McNeil's ankle.

62 Tom Fitzgerald, "Jim Henry Vows to Play Tonight: Hopes to Aid Bruins Keep Hopes Alive; Patrick Bans Freezing of Goalie's Ankle," *Boston Daily Globe,* Apr. 16, 1953, 12, morning edition.

63 "Stanley Cup Arrives, Now Up to Bruins to Keep It in Boston," *Boston Daily Globe,* Apr. 14, 1953, 9.

64 "Scalpers in Action," *Gazette* (Montreal), Apr. 17, 1953, 22.

65 Game details are taken from Dink Carroll, "Fans in Uproar as Veteran Gets Big Goal to Bring Pewter Back First Time Since 1946," *Gazette* (Montreal), Apr. 17, 1953, 22; and Tom Fitzgerald, "Canadiens Beat Bruins, 1-0; Take Stanley Cup," *Boston Daily Globe,* Apr. 17, 1953, 1, 16. Perhaps in recognition of McNeil's stellar performances against the Red Wings, *The Detroit News* reported the Habs victory with a headline that read, "Canadiens Win; Gerry Unbeatable," *Detroit News,* Apr. 17, 1953, 51.

66 These details are from the French Wikipédia entry for Roger Saint-Jean.

67 This detail is shown in the Briston film.

68 "'Didn't See the Puck Go In,' Says Elmer," *Gazette* (Montreal), Apr. 17, 1953, 22.

69 The victory picture appears in *The Gazette* (Montreal), Apr. 17, 1953, 23.

70 All covers can be viewed at si.com. See also *Sports Illustrated 50,* 113. Various embraces of jubilant players dominate the foreground, and an American flag being waved in the stands highlights the background.

71 These details are from Carroll, "Fans in Uproar," 22.

72 Quoted by Ian MacDonald, "Rocket's Crunching Check Tells Elmer Series Over," *Montreal Daily Star,* Apr. 17, 1953, 33.

7 History Repeats

THE 1953 STANLEY CUP MAY HAVE BEEN THE FIRST ON CBC television, but this coverage was not how the majority of hockey fans would have seen their sport in moving pictures. There are two other venues that need to be acknowledged: first, the news clips that often ran prior to the feature in any number of film theatres; and second, the odd professional film that reproduced the action of the game for viewers. What distinguishes these formats is that they were for private or commercial audiences. One had to be in the theatre to catch the newsreel or be invited to a showing of a professional film. These were not films you could view on your own time or in the comfort of your home. Thanks to Paul Patskou, who uncovered some eight hours of coverage featuring my father from the HHOF archives, I have seen three newsreels from the 1952–53 season that include my father.[1] He also appears in Leslie McFarlane's *Here's Hockey* film, which was released in '53 and included coverage of a mid-season match-up between Detroit and Montreal.[2]

The newsreels are approximately four minutes long. They feature audio, of course, as well as video. In fact, the first thing that takes you back to the era is the background music—usually a standard marching-band number from the 1930s or '40s. It strikes an upbeat mood that effectively introduces the spectacle of modern sport. There is a professional voice-over and script; the objective here is to attract any would-be viewer, so there is a certain amount of general information about the sport and league that goes with the reporting of a specific game. The tone is often playful, even when violence dominates the visual register.

A good example might be the "Madison Square Garden Issue 21" clip that covers the Canadiens-Rangers game of March 8, 1953. At one point the commentator says "this looks like war out there," and then casually remarks how an altercation between Maurice Richard and Eddie Kullman results in the former taking his stick and slashing the latter across his helmetless head. The viewer sees Kullman collapse to the ice and crawl away: "Eddie's okay, but he'll need eight stitches to close the wound." The next day *The Globe and Mail* ran the headline: "Richard Konks Kullman."[3]

This clip lacks background music, so one is more conscious of the New York accent of the commentator, who refers to the "Flying Frenchmen of Montreal" and describes how the home team takes an early lead. The clip opens with a view of the MSG marquee—sports entertainment in the Big Apple. Crowd shots are interspersed throughout. Paul Ronty and Wally Hergesheimer are seen skating circles around the Habs. A mock interview of the Canadiens in their dressing room after the second period helps establish the friendly mood. McNeil smiles for the camera and then we see a comic Dick Irvin holding a mute microphone in hand, making fun of Billy Reay's bald head. While the focus of this particular clip is fuzzy, it does have a slow-motion sequence; we get to see a young Harry Howell fire a shot into McNeil's chest protector. With Richard drawing a major penalty for his slash on Kullman, the Rangers come back and win the game, but the commentator is kind to the Habs goalie: "McNeil has been doing spectacular work down there, but he can't stop them all."

A Telenews clip ("Leaders Clash: Play to Tie") describes a January 25, 1953, game between the Habs and Detroit at the Olympia. The teams were battling for first place and had just concluded an evenly fought home-and-home series the week before. Telenews ran a chain of newsreel theatres, none more famous than the downtown Detroit location at 1540 Woodward Avenue, which opened in 1942 and operated until the 1960s when the home television rendered such services obsolete. "Leaders Clash; Play to Tie" runs with some lively band music and includes a goal by Red Kelly when the Canadiens were down two men. Like much of the video footage from the early '50s, the splicing is severe, the camera often shaky, and the viewer doesn't see the actual goal clearly. Another Telenews clip gives us a glimpse of Jean Béliveau playing his third game for the Habs in December of the 1952–53 season (three being the maximum allowed for players still deemed amateurs). Again true to the Telenews format, marching band music blares with the title credit "Rookie Ace Trims Bruins." As in "Leaders Clash," the commentator makes a claim for the largest crowd at the Boston Garden that year. Dave Creighton is seen early on slapping the puck past a sprawling McNeil. What passes for "news" here is not up-to-the-minute, or -hour even, but something that stretches over days. My father himself remembered seeing such clips every Saturday afternoon at the matinee. In this sense, our voracious appetite for the update now regulates all but the immediate to the psychological dustbin of history (read the live countdown on the screen tickertape). In the day of the newsreel, the pressure of the moment could last a week.

If there is one thing these clips convey, it is that my father played in the style made familiar by the likes of better-known goalies like Gump Worsley or Johnny Bower. These relatively small men routinely threw themselves maskless and face first into the fray of swinging sticks, up-ended skates, and flying bodies. I distinctly remember viewing these clips with my father sometime during the 1990s. I was fascinated to catch a glimpse of a world that came before me and featured my father; he was bewildered to witness his own abandonment committed some forty years in the past and said more than once, "I can't believe I dove right into the goalmouth scramble like that." Foolhardy, brave, reckless—take your pick.

Another aspect of this "moment" that could last up to a week was that news clips of the 1940s and '50s were experienced largely in a public domain, the theatre to be exact. Our engagement is now decidedly more personal or individual, unless we are watching with a group of friends at the sports bar. We can make a similar observation with regards to the professional film. Leslie McFarlane's *Here's Hockey* (1953) is remarkable for being an early expression of what would become the standard and ubiquitous pronouncement on the sport as an integral part of Canadian nationalism. One can locate all the elements of the myth about hockey and Canadian society in this ten-minute film: the importance of the local hockey community, the minor hockey associations, the minor leagues that feed the NHL, and of course, the spectacle-business that is the modern NHL. McFarlane, of course, is famous for being the father of Brian McFarlane (who himself had a long career as a hockey broadcaster) and for being "Franklin W. Dixon," the author of the *Hardy Boys* series for young readers. *Here's Hockey* is a National Film Board of Canada masterwork for its time (available on their website), beautifully shot and put together. Framed around a senior game in small-town Anywhere in Canada, we go to the minor associations, to the junior ranks, to the blossoming career of Jean Béliveau, and finally to the NHL. All aspects of the game are included, especially the involvement of the fans or parents, or both, the cost of equipment, the preparation of rinks (both the slick artificial ones versus their natural counterparts with their primitive boards and fresh air), the media frenzy for the Big-Time games, right down to the gargantuan ticket prices and salaries of the professionals. One need only follow the same topics and update the statistics to reflect the sport for a contemporary setting.

One could say much more about any of these subjects, but two details in particular stand out for me. The first is the rink attendant who quickly paints a perfect faceoff circle, with a free but steady hand. One has to think that the frames per second were increased to avoid boring the viewer; the result is something that looks miraculous. Cut from the actual surface to the play board and follow the drawing hand of Punch Imlach, who outlines a drill to a group of Marlie juniors. The second detail is the success with which McFarlane and his crew capture the speed of the game, which can look so unnaturally slow or fast in any newsreel. McFarlane knew how to get some close shots, both on-ice during a drill and game action from just beyond the boards. We see the Marlboro juniors come to a spectacular stop at centre ice and send up a gigantic spray of snow; we see game-action collisions only a few feet away and are amazed to see the players survive the contact.

In just ten and a half minutes, *Here's Hockey* hits all the standards for a professional sports film. We catch glimpses of those wonderful interiors of what were the shrines to the sport: the distant and all-inclusive shots of Maple Leaf Gardens with its high, mansard-style ceiling and close end stands, the Quebec Colisée with its distinctive convex roof that had the look of a gigantic tin shed, and the old Montreal Forum, its darkness punctuated by the view-obstructing pillars. The Colisée was constructed so that a whole city could enjoy the magic of Jean Béliveau, the film's featured player-subject. Hence, it is only logical that the viewer gets to see this very magic in two spellbinding, slow-motion sequences as the Quebec Ace star first fakes out the goalie, and then in a reversal of time, dekes out the defencemen to get to the goalie. All this comes in a marvellous sharpness through McFarlane's lens.

McFarlane's NHL game features the Canadiens and Red Wings at the Forum on a Saturday night (January 17, 1953, to be exact). It begins in the Habs dressing room, and after a brief view of some players, I see the back of my father pulling on his Number One jersey. There is Dick Irvin wearing the same plaid jacket that he will wear in New York almost two months later—a kind of subdued Don Cherry look. (Being black and white, the film must be subdued in terms of colour intensity.) As my father leads his teammates out to face the Red Wings (a ritual he would always appreciate—*the goalie leads the team*), I catch Richard giving my father a pat on his butt with his stick—an example of the priceless minutiae that only the moving picture can capture. We see an anxious crowd pour through the turnstile, a group of women getting Richard's autograph (their elegant dress disqualifying them as early versions of the "puck bunny"). We see the old veteran in the crowd, one Newsy Lalonde who can recall the game when there were only seven players on a team and few substitutions. Soon we are in the middle of a whirl of players. Dollard St. Laurent tries a fake at the blue line and gets flattened. Lindsay and Richard duel one another and go recklessly into the boards; Olmstead works hard to get the puck out of his zone; tall Bud MacPherson and tiny Tony Leswick tangle cartoon-like in front of my father. Howe, referred to by the commentator as "Gordon" (I have never heard Gordie Howe called "Gordon"), pounces on a rebound and lifts the puck over my father who is again on his stomach, face first in the scramble. Tom Johnson, the defenceman, arrives a split second too late. The game ends in a 1–1 tie. The film closes with the senior hockey frame, a home team win, and the words, "Our goal, our team, our town, our game."

McNeil spent the summer of 1953 much as he did other summers while playing with the Canadiens. He sold cars for the Mongeau Buick dealership at the corner of Amherst and de Maisonneuve. He played handball at the MAAA (Montreal Amateur Athletic Association), and he took time to visit family back in Quebec City. Winning the Cup was great, but as with many successes, it came with a price: the expectation that it would be repeated. True, the Canadiens had gained ground on Detroit ever since '51, but now anything less than finishing first would be a disappointment. Nevertheless, he couldn't change the situation; he could only do his best. Irvin expected his players to report to camp at a certain weight, and McNeil with his slight build could not afford to put on extra pounds. One of the primitive techniques used to get down for a weigh-in was to carry a paper cup around and spit into it at every opportunity.

The 1953–54 season was going well for Mac until he injured his ankle on February 11th in a brawl-filled game at the Stadium in Chicago. Pete Conacher crashed into the small goalie and pinned him against the goalpost in such a way that he sprained his ankle.[4] With two and a half minutes left in the game, Bodnar and Johnson were sent off with incidental minors and ended up in a fist fight in the penalty box. When some fans from behind the Chicago bench got involved, the ushers raced in to break things up. Anybody who thinks that NHL violence has gotten worse since the Original Six era would be appalled at some of the things that occurred in the 1940s and '50s. After a break, McNeil came back to finish the game, but the ankle swelled up overnight and there was no way he could play on it. To this point in the season, he had a 2.15 GAA and 6 shutouts. The big difference was the number of wins: 28 wins in fifty-three games as opposed to only 25 in sixty-six games the previous year, the difference no doubt attributable to the increased goal production (forty more than in 1952–53).[5] There was no question, however, that Plante was capable of filling in for McNeil, so he was summoned from the Buffalo Bisons and met the team in Toronto. Plante played so well—a 1.59 GAA with 5 shutouts[6]—that Irvin continued to use him for the last seventeen games of the season (with those figures he would have been crazy to do otherwise). McNeil could have pressed to be put back in but he held off. Why? My father once told me that it was because he believed the team didn't need him: "Plante was doing a great job; playing for the Habs was never about yourself. You did what you felt was best for everybody." To demonstrate his support of Plante and team loyalty, McNeil would even give up "his Lower No. 1 train berth to his substitute."[7]

The injury gave McNeil time to think about his career and life in general. He had been a professional hockey player since he was seventeen, had played six years with the Royals, one with the Mohawks in Cincinnati, and almost four full seasons with the Canadiens. Having tried a few things, like selling cars, in the off season, McNeil now began to give serious thought to what he would like to do with his life after hockey. NHL players enjoyed a certain celebrity in Montreal and Toronto, but for those who disliked public scrutiny or the pressure of the Big Time, the experience was not 100 per cent positive. For McNeil, life as an NHL goalie was beginning to feel rather unbalanced—his mind couldn't get away from the rink. He started to have trouble sleeping.

Detroit commanded the league during the regular season but was suspect in the post-season. Eager to make amends for their Semifinal exit against Boston the year before, the Wings came out flying and took the Leafs in five games. The Canadiens were equally impressive as they swept the Bruins in four straight. This set up another Montreal-Detroit Final, one that everyone expected to be closer than their showdown in 1952.

Although Plante's wandering style had given fits to many Canadiens fans the year before, at the end of the 1953–54 season W. R. Wheatley gave a detailed description of how the team had not only adjusted to his style but was taking advantage of it.[8] The day before the Final began Plante missed practice at the Verdun Auditorium due to indigestion or possibly the flu.[9] Rumours started that McNeil would play the first game in Detroit, but Jake recovered in time. It was clear that he had taken over the Number One position. Elmer Lach was another player who couldn't find his way back into the lineup. The Wings took Game One 3-1 on some great goaltending by Terry Sawchuk and returned to their Toledo hideaway.

Meanwhile the Habs tried to regroup. There was talk of benching the entire Mosdell-Olmstead-Richard Line, which had been held pointless

HISTORY REPEATS

thus far in the post-season. More mind games from Irvin. Irvin, of course, didn't bench the Rocket, but he did shuffle lines. It was now Richard-Masnick-Mazur. Richard responded by scoring two goals, both on the power play, as the Habs turned the table on the Wings and came away with their own 3–1 win. In fact, all of the scoring thus far in the series had been with the man advantage. After the game some angry fans tried to storm the referees' room, and the police were called in to restore order. A sixty-year-old Frank Selke got into the fray when he ripped up a sign that read "Rocket Richard Stinks" and challenged some young boisterous Wing fans.[10] The win proved costly for the Canadiens as Harvey wrenched his knee and Béliveau suffered a charley horse. Neither was able to play the next game. The train ride home was marked by a discussion of the officiating, which arguably went in favour of Detroit in the opener with Chadwick, and of Montreal in Game Two with Red Storey in charge.[11]

The Canadiens practised on Thursday and McNeil injured his finger, so that put to rest the question of who would start.[12] The first two periods of Game Three belonged to Detroit, who went up 3–0 and coasted to a 5–2 win. Both of Montreal's goals came from defencemen (Johnson and St. Laurent), which says something about the scoring power of their forwards. Dink Carroll wrote that "Jacques Plante was mediocre, possibly because of Harvey's absence."[13] The game was a scrappy affair on several fronts. Near the end, Johnson and Lindsay squared off but the officials got between them. Several fights broke out in the crowd and the police were called in to restore order: playoff hockey at the Forum. Game Four was lost when Plante allowed Johnny Wilson's lob shot from forty feet to dribble off his glove into the net.[14] Meanwhile Sawchuk was brilliant at the other end and racked up another playoff shutout. The Wings got an empty-net goal and won 2–0. Lach was back in the lineup, as were Harvey and Béliveau. Desperate to find some offence, Irvin had Tom Johnson centring a line between the Rocket and Mazur.

Back to Detroit. That meant quick cab rides from the Forum to the Westmount Train Station, where police would be on hand to keep the teams separated and the fans at bay. On the train was Ken McKenzie, an NHL publicity man, charged with looking after the Stanley Cup. He did not know if he would have to return with it, but given the responsibility of looking after the trophy, he almost wished it to be over that night. As the train neared Detroit, Irvin told McNeil that he was starting in the "do or die" Game Five.[15] Elmer Ferguson has a different version; he claims that the coach didn't mince words, "Are you ready to go out and fight for your job as a major league goaler, or are you ready to give up[?]" McNeil's reply apparently was "Certainly I'll play. Tell Hector (the Canadiens trainer) to get my pads and stuff ready. I'll be there."[16] The players didn't know until they saw his equipment laid out in the dressing room. For the first time in his career, McNeil asked the team physiotherapist Bill Head for a "rubdown." He felt exhausted after the warm-up but attributed it to nerves and not having played in two months.

When the playoffs were over, Dink Carroll reported in his column that both Selke and Irvin wanted to go with my father earlier in the playoffs but didn't because he wasn't asking for the opportunity.[17] It seems that my father wasn't sure that he could do any better than Plante and remained silent: "Gerry was thinking of his teammates ahead of himself." Selke apparently told him, "Gerry, there's such a thing as being too unselfish.... This is your job and I want you to fight for it." Obviously the strong endorsement McNeil had from the management in 1951 and '52 had waned somewhat. There were two guys on the scene now, and the Canadiens wanted to see them compete for one position.

Irvin was very much the hands-on coach despite all his talk to the press about the "unseen hand" determining the outcome of the games thus far. In addition to replacing Plante with McNeil, he substituted Paul Masnick for Goose McCormack, and Gaye Stewart for Calum Mackay.[18] Almost like an omen of things to come, it was Tony Leswick who gave McNeil some anxious moments in the first, shooting just wide once, and losing control of the puck while in close another time. Leswick got another opportunity in the third when Pavelich sent him in the clear, but McNeil came up with a sensational save. The Montreal goalie then stopped Johnny Wilson when the Wings had the man advantage.[19] Regulation time ended with the score 0–0.

Early in the overtime Gordie Howe unleashed a one-timer off a great centring pass from Delvecchio, but McNeil dove across, "stopped the puck with a daring thrust of a pad and smothered the rebound" just as Howe got there.[20] Vince Lunny quoted the great right winger: "It was one of the best I ever fired.... I thought this is it. When that puck hits the net, the Cup is ours. I'll never know how Gerry stopped it."[21] The Olympia crowd, showing their Hockeytown class, actually applauded.[22] A few minutes later Mosdell tried to get around Bob Goldham. When Goldham checked him closely, Mosdell spun around and in one motion fired a backhand that caught Sawchuk by surprise. Off the post and into the net.

There are two video reproductions of the highlights of the series. (The remnants of a third cover Game Six only.) One is an unidentified newsreel that is marked by a fuzzy focus, some shakiness, and a background buzz. No music. The players look slow and awkward. Harvey, with his damaged knee, is seen falling on a couple of occasions. The slapshots of Richard and Geoffrion seem weak. In another foreshadowing moment, Tom Johnson knocks a puck out of the air with his hand and then carries it out of the zone. The camera also catches him whacking Delvecchio across the head. The Detroit centreman curls up on the ice as his teammates mill about. Johnny Wilson is depicted getting a number of clear opportunities. What is truly valuable about the clip is that it includes Howe's great chance during the overtime. It suggests that nothing was slow about the game. Delvecchio has the puck to my father's left; suddenly he turns and sends a pass to Howe on the opposite side—the left wing. Somehow my father manages to move quickly to his right and block the one-timer. Howe, being right-handed, had a lot of net to shoot at. What is also noteworthy is that Richard, who is skating right with Howe, fails to get any piece of the play. Mosdell's winner is as unusual as the print reporters made it out to be. The centreman had been turned around so his back was to Sawchuk. The backhand doesn't catch the Detroit goalie off guard so much as it just catches the far corner of the net. My father enters the mob of players quickly to congratulate his friend Kenny.

The second video reproduction of the 1954 Final was done by Briston Films, a Montreal company. In fact Briston had produced promotional films for the league featuring the Final in 1952 and '53. More on Briston in a moment. For now I will just say that neither the unidentified newsreel nor the Briston film record what happened to my father a few seconds later—something my father would never forget. Laughing with his teammates as he got off the ice, Mac was confronted by Irvin: "Swipe that smile off your face. Every stop you made, you made the wrong way."[23] McNeil, perhaps responding to the pressure, took the criticism to heart. He promised himself then and there that when the playoffs were over he would not play another game under Irvin. Clearly, Irvin was trying to keep McNeil and Plante on edge, playing one off against the other in the belief that the extra competition would be motivational. He actually told the press that he considered using both goalies for five-minute segments.[24] However, he misread McNeil's competitive spirit. Willing to do anything for his teammates, Mac was not willing to accept any additional tension. He didn't need it. In fact, he had been thinking that his life had become much too tense. At some point he needed to get away; maybe that point was coming sooner rather than later. When my father told me about Irvin's remark, I could tell that he still felt the sting of the criticism as if it had happened yesterday. I also sensed that he had carried the emotional baggage of the incident with him for forty years.

The press was once again uniformly positive about my father's play. Dink Carroll wrote that "the brilliant comeback of Gerry McNeil proves that he still owns a working ticket in the Goalkeepers Union."[25] In the meantime, there was Game Six back at the Forum. Unfortunately, home ice had mattered very little between these teams in the playoffs. The first period was wide open with good chances at both ends, but it ended scoreless.[26] The Canadiens came out extra strong in the second and tallied three unanswered goals. The first was a blast by Boom Boom Geoffrion, the man who has been credited with developing the slap-shot.[27] Knowing that my father had faced Geoffrion's shots in practice, people often asked him what it was like. I remember that he would respond cautiously. "As soon as you see that backswing, you can get set and come out to cut down the angle, which doesn't give the shooter much of a target." These discussions became even more pronounced when Bobby Hull popularized the shot during the '60s and the phrase "Bobby Hull winding up" was the most exciting thing in hockey. The slapshot has a special attraction insofar as it is the fastest element in what is considered the fastest of team sports. It epitomizes the speed of the game itself. However, my father always had more respect for the sniper who could look "to pass" and fire a quick snapshot at the opposite corner. "It's often about fooling the other guy as opposed to sheer power."

The other two goals were by Floyd Curry, who scored twice on one shift, the second goal coming after he tried unsuccessfully to get to the bench for a substitution! The only goal by the Wings was the result of an inglorious pileup in the Habs' crease. Gaye Stewart and Tom Johnson backed right into McNeil and knocked him into the net. Everybody expected the whistle. Instead, Storey skated to the official scorer. The puck had apparently crossed the line. The Canadiens, feeling confident, didn't even bother to protest. With the outcome already determined, the third period became a little dull. A loud hoot went up when a bag of peanuts was tossed onto the ice during a break in the action. The ushers and police ejected an elderly man with a bright yellow cap.[28] In the end, it was another great performance by Mac, who stopped 33 shots (13 in the third) to Sawchuk's 25. A picture ran in *The Gazette* the next day showing the Habs leaving the ice after the game.[29] Despite Irvin's reaction in Detroit, McNeil can be clearly seen smiling as his teammates congratulate him on another solid performance.

However, in the dressing room it was clear that the goalie was still feeling the effects of all the pressure. According to Lunny, Mac sat in the dressing room and "his hands were shaking like those of a nervous hold-up man on his first big job[,] and the sweat rolled down his lined face in tiny rivulets."[30] Gaye Stewart sat next to him and joked, "You ought to be playing defense—the way you shoved me around when I tumbled into the net with you on that goal... all my fault darn it!"[31] According to Andy O'Brien, McNeil tried to laugh, but what came out sounded more like a sob. Unable to talk, Mac was given a cigarette and he then headed to the anteroom in an attempt to unwind. Since his return two games ago, he had faced 56 shots, and the only puck to have gotten by him was due to a pileup of his own players. O'Brien estimates that "five would have been goals on any other goaler." The reporter claims to be "awed" by the "effort under such strain" and concludes, "As long as I write sport, McNeil will be part of what I mean when I speak of hockey's Big Time."

In any case, there is approximately three minutes of primitive footage of Game Six that may well be the remnants of a professional project gone wrong.[32] Some of the close-ups are very dark, and some of the views of the ice are overexposed. There are some set sequences of both goaltenders and also both benches. While McNeil is only five foot seven, the crossbar is only four feet high so his body does tuck neatly underneath. Granted, a really tall goalie can cover the vertical space on his knees; the only problem then is moving to actually block a shot. What this remnant of a film captures is Geoffrion's spectacular slapshot goal. We get a flash of whirling action, the goal, and the crowd celebration as the cameraman closest to the ice turns to shoot a bank of frenzied fans. Geoffrion, however, lies in a heap and looks like he'll have to be carried off on a stretcher. At this point, even a photographer is seen scurrying across the ice. Seconds later we see the Canadiens bench go wild: 2–0. (Frequent shots of the scoreboard tell the viewer exactly what's happening.) Then comes goal number three by Curry. Although we don't see the Detroit goal, we do see McNeil scramble comically on top of a couple of his defencemen to find the puck. The unidentified newsreel does capture the Detroit goal. Never did two players combine (literally) to make things impossible for their own goalie! Skating backwards, Stewart clips Johnson and both players fall down; not only does the pair take McNeil's feet out from under him, they push him to the back of the net and pin him there. The puck somewhere underneath this pile finds its way into the net.

The Briston Film comes closest to the professional quality of McFarlane's *Here's Hockey*.[33] A flourish of orchestral music strikes the upbeat and lively mood. The tone is light and positive; this is a general promotional tool for the NHL with Molson along as a sponsor. The league, its playoff structure, and its elaborate system of player development are all emphasized, as is the speed and excitement of the game itself. Some effort has been made with the script and there is a pattern and variety in how each game sequence is presented. We get panoramic views of each city, including the Detroit River and NHL headquarters, which is said to be the Sun Life Building sitting hugely and elegantly in the middle of the island of Montreal, a powerful reminder of the British Empire. (An exaggeration of sorts—to be exact, the NHL rented some office space in the building.) We see the Olympia marquee and the Forum on Sainte-Catherine Street. We get mute interviews with groups of players and front-office personnel that are meant to be friendly; the players break into smiles as they answer questions and are made to look over their shoulders. As with McFarlane, there is an excellent use of slow motion, which must have seemed miraculous to the sports fan of the era. Then there are details that just amuse: the rink attendant at the Olympia who sits between opposing players in the penalty box wearing what appears to be a circus-like military uniform with bright labels and visor, the chicken wire at the Olympia that makes the venue look so low class and dingy, the perfectly shabby dressing rooms, the referees in solid grey and no stripes.

As far as the play action goes, there are things to be learned from the film. Johnny Wilson had a quick shot. For the small Tony Leswick, think a combination Martin St. Louis–Tie Domi. Some of the forgotten Montreal forwards did make meaningful contributions: Eddie Mazur and Paul Masnik. Delvecchio and Howe were an earlier version of Gretzky and Kurri. Nobody could stickhandle like Jean Béliveau. For the defence, Harvey was as solid as they come, but the real pass-maker and general was Red Kelly. Tom Johnson and Dollard St. Laurent were capable of end-to-end rushes. As for the goalies, McNeil and Sawchuk played extremely well; Plante not so much.

There is a special aura about Game Seven, especially when it comes in the Finals. While many focus on the five straight Stanley Cups that the Habs would go on to win in the late 1950s, the first half of the decade was easily more exciting. Nobody really challenged the Canadiens during their five-straight run, and when they won the last of those Cups in a sweep in 1960, Doug Harvey summed things up nicely: "Well, when you win 4–0 and win in four games and after four Cup titles you don't get too excited."[34] Aside from '52, every Final series in the early 1950s was closely fought. And so for the second time McKenzie had to pack up Lord Stanley and travel to Detroit.[35] The only difference was that this time he knew

HISTORY REPEATS

he would not have it in his possession on the way back. There was talk in the media about Irvin's use of four lines compared to only three by the Wings. There were 15,791 people crammed into the Olympia—the largest crowd to ever see a hockey game in Detroit. Scalpers could get seventy-five dollars for a pair of tickets, but the more common price was fifty. A number of fans made the trip from Montreal and Toronto, hoping to get tickets; many had to settle for watching the game on television in a hotel or bar.[36] The CBC broadcast Game Seven to several Canadian cities.[37]

The Wings looked to settle things early. They were all over the Canadiens. McNeil was tested by Pronovost who broke in all alone (see fig. 29); then Lindsay just missed on a nice pass from Howe.[38] The break for the Canadiens came when Curry fired from forty feet; Sawchuk, partially screened by Olmstead, got a piece of it but not enough. Montreal took a 1-0 lead into the second, but Detroit continued to press. Masnick was sent off for hooking; Delvecchio passed back to Kelly, who fired a screen shot just off the ice that found the corner. The goal rallied Detroit and they pressed even harder. Johnny Wilson had an excellent chance to put the Wings up, but he couldn't beat McNeil.

The Canadiens came to life somewhat in the third. Moore hit a post, Curry's shot was blocked by Goldham, and Gaye Stewart's attempt was turned away by Sawchuk. Then, late in the period, Richard fell to the ice, lost his stick, and saw the puck right next to him. In front was the gaping open, Detroit cage. The urge was irresistible; Rocket knocked the puck into the net with his hand.[39] Unbeknownst to him, Eddie Mazur was right behind. Had Rocket just left the puck alone, Spider would have undoubtedly whacked it in. Referee Chadwick immediately signalled "no goal"—the correct call. The unidentified newsreel shows Mazur throwing his arms up in despair. It is as ironic as anything can be that Richard's will to win actually robbed Montreal of the Stanley Cup! Irvin was the only one to comment publicly on the incident when he said, "The real turning point came when Richard threw the puck, when Mazur might have knocked it in legally."[40] It is a playoff moment that Richard biographers have ignored, probably because it doesn't contribute to the legend of the Rocket.[41] However, the incident does suggest that passion can have negative consequences, that Number Nine for the Tricolore was human and fallible. Considering all the playoff games that he won for the Canadiens, his teammates easily forgave him. Just before the end of regulation time, Gilles Dubé lobbed the puck toward the Montreal net. It took an odd bounce, and—horror of horrors—went through McNeil's pads. Fortunately for the Habs, the puck rolled just wide of the net. Overtime.

Fig. 29 McNeil makes a first-period save off Marcel Pronovost. The picture is auto-graphed by McNeil and Dollard St. Laurent, the defenceman trailing the play. Detroit Olympia, April 16, 1954. (Photographer unknown.) Copyright unknown.

Early in the extra period Howe set up Lindsay who shot on McNeil but couldn't beat him. Soon after the puck came to Leswick in the cen-tre-ice area. Leswick just fired it at the Montreal net on a shift change. Doug Harvey eyed the disk in the air and tried to knock it down with his glove to start a counterattack. Perhaps his mind was too much on the counterattack. In any case, the puck hit higher on his glove than he anticipated, flipped up, then over McNeil's shoulder and into the net. A moment after the red light came on, the Olympia tension, building all evening, detonated into cheers and screams.

McNeil was devastated. For a second or two he could not move, could not believe that the Cup had been lost. Then, as the roar of the crowd settled in, as the Detroit players and fans spilled wildly onto the Olympia ice, he started the long skate to the other end of the rink, to the visiting team's exit. He left the ice with his teammates, none of whom waited to congratulate the Wings. In fact, the vanquished were led off

HISTORY REPEATS

by Harvey himself, who had never shaken hands with the opposing team since McNeil made his playoff debut in 1950. Asked later what it was like, McNeil replied hyperbolically, "It felt like the end of the world."[42]

This lack of sportsmanship on the part of the Canadiens drew criticism.[43] My father and I discussed the incident and the general subject of festive behaviour in such situations several times. In his defence, Mac maintained that the Detroit players got so caught up in their own celebration that it was just too painful and awkward for the Montreal team. Harvey would stand by his belief that it was unreasonable to expect him to go from an all-out-war mode to a genuine congratulatory gesture. It was too hypocritical. While I concur that the handshake can be more pro forma than sincere, and one can say this about all levels of sport, it sometimes does involve a true rising-above-the-game that reflects the ideals of sport. For that reason alone, it should be adhered to.

As a theatrical performance, sport constantly shows us the tension between spontaneity and ritual. Today, the spontaneous celebration is usually restricted to an immediate reaction after scoring, and then players will go down the entire team on the bench bumping fists ever so lightly. While allowing for the spontaneous, I feel that overdoing the celebratory sends the wrong message: "Look at me; I'm such a lousy player that I never expected to score." Somebody once reminded me that after most of his many goals, Bobby Orr would nonchalantly skate right back to his defensive position for the faceoff at centre ice. Just business as usual. How intimidating was that! (Well, even he had to make that famous horizontal jump through the air when his overtime goal won the Cup in 1970.) My father and I agreed that the glove-bumping is more ritualistic trouble than it's worth, and we kept hoping the practice would disappear. (A dozen or so years later and it's unfortunately still with us.) Also, if a hockey team wins anything in overtime today, forget about it; nobody's going to be bumping fists. Some players like to butt helmets. Whatever.

It must be admitted that those who have just lost the Stanley Cup must somehow suffer the moment, while the winners do their thing. Having watched the NHL in the last few years, I can say that this aspect of the game has truly come a long way from the bitter, personal animosity of the early 1950s. A losing team is called upon to suck it up and endure the on-ice hoopla of the winning team, whose exuberance can easily become excessive. I've always thought that since the overtime game could easily have gone either way, a winning team should tone it down, realizing that their margin of victory was slim. Usually, just the opposite happens; the pent-up emotions come flooding out. Perhaps this was what irked the '54 Habs so much. The Wings and their fans were overdoing the celebration. Nevertheless, they would have done the same. Professional sport demands the spectacle of a decision, and those involved should not allow emotions to result in excessive behaviour. These are games after all, even if adults are playing them, and every effort should be made to keep a sense of perspective and balance.

Among those who complained about the Canadiens' exit was Leswick himself, the guy who most liked to antagonize the opposition with his persistent checking. In the Montreal dressing room, there wasn't much said. As he had done after the Barilko goal, McNeil wept and wished he could somehow, magically, disappear. As he had many times before, Dink Carroll praised the little goalie's performance: "It was Gerry who held Canadiens up in that final game. For the first two periods the Red Wings had far more of the puck than the Habitants, outshooting them 25 to 10. . . . Summarily, as far as we are concerned, this series belonged to Gerry McNeil. He made us choke up."[44] McNeil did speak to the press. He had the puck in his sights and would have blocked it easily if Harvey had left it alone: "It's real hard luck . . . to lose a great series and an overtime game on that kind of a shot, but I guess that's the way a lot of close games are decided. There's no one to blame and no excuses to be made, unless you call it bad luck."[45] The irony was that he could hardly blame Doug, because Harvey was easily the best of the Canadiens' defence. Who else to bat a puck out of the air but somebody who had the chance to play professional baseball?

My father was unequivocal about this whenever I put the question to him: "Who was the defenceman that you had the most confidence in, the guy who made you feel good whenever he came onto the ice?"

"Harvey," he replied. "Harvey was so good, so dependable and tough, that forwards would often just get rid of the puck to avoid him.[46] They wouldn't even try to get through. Doug had his man covered 99.9 per cent of the time. You could always count on Doug."

Game Seven—brimming in paradox. Such is the fascination of sport.

Gerry McNeil announced his intention to retire a few days later. The English press ignored the announcement, suggesting that they were obliging the Canadiens management, who wanted to pretend that their goalie was just upset and acting capriciously. Leave the guy some space; he'll come around. Andy O'Brien didn't mention a "retirement" or "replacement," but in his final tribute to my father's performance during the Final, he wrote as follows: "In almost 190 minutes of sustained

HISTORY REPEATS

playoff pressure, Gerry gave up only one earned goal. If there is anything to the rumor that [the] Canadiens plan a change between the posts, they'll have to do a lot of looking to better that record."[47] But Jacques Beauchamp, a French journalist my father always had tremendous respect for, did run the story in *Montréal-Matin,* and *Le Petit journal* did publish an open letter from Amateur Hockey to the goalie asking him to stay with the club.[48] The truth was my father was serious; he had promised himself he would not play another game for Irvin and he would keep that promise. Exits are hard to plan, and sometimes harder to execute, but just like the entrance, they form the other end of the narratives we construct about professional athletes. Keeping Turner's notion of liminality and the spectacle of performance in mind, we are especially interested to know how they got there, and how they left.

A parade of visitors came to 4700 Borden Avenue that spring to talk my father out of his decision: Harvey, Irvin, Selke, to name a few. My mother remembers how Doug Harvey, in particular, sat in the living room and, after listening to my father, said he would play no matter what. "And he did," she added with a kind of sad retrospective look in her eyes. That look was for all that had happened to Doug both on and off the ice since that spring. He would go on to all those trophies (the Norris, the Stanley Cups) and a Hall of Fame career. He would also struggle with alcohol and a bipolar disorder.[49] Doug Harvey's funeral, which I attended with my father, was probably the saddest Canadiens-related event I have ever been involved with, much worse than the Richard funeral when my father served as a pallbearer. It was especially sad because of the acute and palpable family grief for what did not happen for Harvey off the ice or after Harvey's playing career had ended. Having met Doug Harvey's daughter, Nancy, in college and knowing something of the family's troubles, I felt deeply sympathetic for those who were left behind, those who suffered so many sleepless nights worrying. Anybody who has lived with an alcoholic loved one knows that anxiety; it cuts through any sense of peace or normalcy.

Professional athletes have lives and families beyond the sports they play, and the needs related to these are crucial in deciding whether to play or not to play. Too often we overlook an athlete's need to develop other professional skills that will determine success off the ice or court or field. Too often we miss what other family considerations are sacrificed to accommodate the career of a professional athlete. I would even argue that the mega-salaries of today do not compensate for these sacrifices: how much money would you give up to see your child in a school play or Halloween costume, to be there for extended family dinners on Sunday, to be there when a child or parent is sick? It is impossible to put a price on such moments.

There is another photo from the box of hockey-related memorabilia that sat for years in our basement which relates to this subject of "to play or not to play." It features my mother Teacy (see fig. 30). She is sitting at the Forum in an elegant dress and with a cigarette in hand. (Another reason not to wax nostalgic about the Original Six era—these "hockey shrines" were full of smoke.) Her neighbourhood friend Thérèse Audette is on her left (players were given two tickets for each game, and my mother was usually in attendance). There are a number of other people scattered about in surrounding seats. My mother's eyes are anxiously fixated on something to the right of the scene. When I asked her about the shot, my mother told me that it had been taken after the game. While everybody else in the frame wears a kind of relaxed, time-to-go smile, exactly what one would expect when the entertainment has come to an end, my mother looks a bundle of nerves, as if she is about to be executed. The expression on her face speaks volumes about the pressure felt by a family member in such situations. Unable to work out the tension (or unable to absent herself, as my father liked having her there), she must sit and suffer. The end of the game should have brought some

Fig. 30 While a number of fans are smiling and ready to leave, Theresa McNeil, Gerry McNeil's wife, remains nervously smoking in her seat. Montreal, Forum, early 1950s. (Photographer unknown.) Copyright unknown.

HISTORY REPEATS

relief, but there is no sign of it on her face. A few years ago I remember feeling sympathy for Jeff Reimer's mother, who was at the AC Centre to watch her son in the playoffs against Boston; ironically, the tension she was feeling was so intense that she had to cover her eyes whenever the Bruins threatened. The fact that there is something absurd about getting so worked up about what is essentially "just a game" only makes the whole experience worse. Your head tells you that you should relax; your body tells you that that will be impossible.

Charles Binamé's film *The Rocket* includes a scene in which Richard's wife Lucille expresses her apprehension about joining the wives in the stands to watch games at the Forum. She is concerned about keeping up with the other wives, who seem to appear regularly in new and elegant dresses. As the Rocket grew in stature in the 1940s, this concern must have waned, but the tensions associated with just watching the games obviously didn't. Game days were in some ways harder on my mother than my father, who was pampered with a pre-game steak and nap. Just as there are all kinds of unique aspects about the goaltender's position, so there are unique pressures felt by the goaltender's family. A woman who was the mother of a goalie in minor hockey once told me that if her son happened to have a poor game, she avoided all the other parents on the team. The adage "you win or lose as a team" only goes so far. Goalies can make or break a team's success, and their families are helplessly taken along for the ride. I remember my father telling me that it was natural to strive for success, but that a great performance didn't let you off the hook. Ironically, it only brought more pressure to repeat it. And so it follows with the goalie's family. Worse, as a spectator, the only action a family member can take is to pray that one's loved one isn't the goat.

There is another scene in Binamé's film that depicts Irvin attempting to get more out of his players by demeaning them: "Richard, people say you're a waste of money." Jacques Beauchamp, who was closer to the players than any other journalist (see Chapter 1), supports this view as he recalls Irvin remarking, "Béliveau, you are a million-dollar flop."[50] It seems that he was using the same tactic with his goalie. The Canadiens' general manager, Frank Selke, did talk my father into coming back, and he signed a contract that summer, only to reannounce his retirement after a few days of training camp. The *Herald* front page for September 27th reads "McNeil Quits Hockey"; to the right and in smaller print is news about a natural disaster: "Death Toll 1,550 in Jap Typhoon."[51] It just so happened that this was the same day that Ted Williams announced his retirement from baseball. The sports section ran the headline

"McNeil Quits, Says Nerves Forced Move" above "Williams Retires For Good."[52] However, the newspaper accounts differ from what my father recalled. He did not remember reporting to training camp. The Canadiens would have been reluctant to accept my father's decision since at the very least they could have traded him and received something in return. There were rumours in the press that McNeil would be dealt to another club. My father always maintained that he was not interested in playing for anybody else; what he wanted to do was begin a "normal" life—to get up in the morning and go to a job that didn't have such life-or-death pressure about it.

An article by Montreal reporter Vince Lunny ran in *The Hockey News* in June 1954; it predicted that the Canadiens would attempt to use both McNeil and Plante the following season.[53] Citing the circumstances surrounding Durnan's retirement and a number of other NHL netminders who had or were having difficulty with nerves, Lunny argued that alternating goalies might be a way to prolong a goalie's career. He claimed that if Durnan had been relieved when he was nursing an injury and didn't have to carry the pressure of performing night-in and night-out, he may well have continued playing. The same was possibly true for McNeil who, according to Dick Irvin, had "cracked under the pressure in the last two seasons." But it seemed to be too late to rescue McNeil. Perhaps in an effort not to see Plante go the same way as his predecessors, Irvin and Selke remained committed to a two-goalie system for 1954–55. They brought in Charlie Hodge for fourteen games.

McNeil's decision was not just about Dick Irvin. The account given by Boom Boom Geoffrion in his autobiography supports my father's version of events (i.e., that he never did report to training camp) and also alludes to the real issue:

> *The big surprise of training camp in September 1954 was the man who wasn't there—Gerry McNeil. One of the best I ever had the pleasure of playing with, Gerry stunned everyone by announcing his retirement at the age of 28! "I'm through with hockey," McNeil said. "And I don't intend to change my decision." He went on to explain, "I have a nervous temperament and I want to do something that involves less worry. I want to be able to spend more time with my family."*
>
> *What shocked me was that Gerry was doing this when he was right at the top of his game in his goaltending prime.[54]*

Vince Lunny reiterated his comparison to Bill Durnan: "When his nerves became as taut as trout lines he quit right in the middle of the 1950 playoffs. So history repeats."[55]

No other goalie in NHL history has been involved in three overtime Stanley Cup games, let alone three in four years. Moreover, many of the goalies who began their careers in the 1940s or early 1950s, when the substitute did not dress, had problems with nerves: Durnan, Sawchuk, and Hall to name a few. There is no question that the position of goaltender (or goalkeeper in soccer) carries with it the pressure of knowing that the slightest misjudgment could be disastrous for one's team.

Baz O'Meara ran an interview with my father in *The Star* and pointed to my mother as the one who encouraged my father to retire—something which my mother did not deny when I asked her about it in the summer of 2001.

> *Gerry McNeil confirmed The Star report carried in the final edition on Saturday that he is retiring from hockey because of "pressures." By these, he means the nervous tension associated with playing a long schedule, his wife's anxiety over injuries he has suffered and the feeling that he couldn't do himself justice this year.*
>
> *"I am well enough, but I found the going rough in practice. I found I couldn't sleep again. I want to live a normal life so I am quitting with regret because I will miss the game a lot," he said.*
>
> *... "Did the presence of Jacques Plante around as alternate goalie worry you in any way?" he was asked.*
>
> *"Not a bit. Jacques is a fine fellow. He has his work to do. I had mine. The only thing is that I felt I couldn't do full justice to myself and the club under the conditions. By that I mean the conditions affecting me, not the conditions of the club....*
>
> *I have been well treated, I had a good contract but things were going to be mentally rough though physically I am all right. My wife doesn't want me to play. So I will take less money and try to make my way in business.... I won't reconsider my decision as I did last time...."*
>
> *Gerry had been talked back into accepting a new contract against the wishes of his wife. The latter is said to have pleaded with him not to "renew his contract." The persuasive powers of Frank Selke changed his mind in July, but business and wife pressure prevailed this time or has until next press time at least.[56]*

The interview does suggest that my father did not feel "ousted" by Plante, that he bore Plante no ill will; it also reveals that he was content to take my mother's advice over that of his teammates and the Canadiens' management. While the portrait of my father in the O'Meara article borders on the negative cliché of the "wife-whipped" husband, the text itself, when examined closely, represents the desire of a professional athlete who genuinely wishes to get away, "to live a normal life," and whose wish happens to coincide with his wife's desire. Moreover, this latter interpretation agrees with my own sense of the relationship that my parents had in fifty-seven years of marriage. Never did my father indicate that he wanted to play longer for the Canadiens; never did he direct any resentment toward my mother for encouraging him to step down.

Two and a half years later, my father told a Rochester reporter that he didn't want to divulge exactly what had happened in the spring of 1954: "I'd rather not discuss that.... They call it nerves, so let it stay that way. Other factors were involved but never brought out, so I won't be the one to make them public."[57] Many of the Habs who retired under Selke had mixed emotions. While still feeling an intense loyalty for the club, they did not always appreciate the post-retirement treatment they received from management, which sometimes made them feel like old circus animals rather than people. My father recalls Selke, exasperated at the prospect of losing a perfectly good asset to nerves, yelling at him in the summer of '54, "You can't retire—we could trade you!" Such is the nature of professional sport; the athlete is a commodity. But the truth was that he could retire. The "other factors" to which my father refers really consist of the conflict he had with Dick Irvin. As for his nerves, he revealed to Trent Frayne in March 1955 that he kept replaying certain shots in his mind: "After every game, through the season or playoffs, I'd toss and turn in bed half the night, playing the game all over again. When I fell off to sleep around three or four in the morning, I'd dream about it."[58] While not the only factor, emotional stress was definitely a key element.

My father spent 1954–55 running a new FINA gas station at the Dorval traffic circle near the Montreal airport. Ironically, as he drove back into the city with his old friend Jimmy Galbraith estimating the weekly profits, their own vehicle ran out of gas! An omen that McNeil was not cut out for the car service industry? Whatever he did manage to calculate that day, the reality of the situation was that there wasn't much money to be made. And so the falling out with Irvin and Selke was not the end of his professional hockey career. In the summer of 1955 *The Globe and Mail* reported that McNeil had been approached by the Canadiens management; he was considering a comeback but would not "play if he had to beat out Plante" and that "he wanted no part of former [c]oach Dick Irvin's two-platoon system in which goalies were alternated during a game."[59] McNeil returned to play for the Royals in the fall of 1955 and he led them to the QHL crown that spring.[60]

Meanwhile, Dick Irvin's tenure with the Canadiens was itself coming to an end. He had run-ins with Dickie Moore, Béliveau, and finally

Richard. Selke knew who was dispensable, and Irvin soon found himself headed back to Chicago, where he had coached years before. When Toe Blake took over as coach, he too came to visit at 4700 Borden Avenue and offered my father a contract that would give him as much money as he would make with the Canadians but would allow him to play wherever he liked. One option was Rochester (an AHL franchise was established in 1956), and my father thought that it would be good to get out of Montreal and join his friend Skippy Burchell with the "Amerks." Blake wanted to keep my father as a backup to Plante, and this arrangement suited my father. From a strictly professional point of view, this was a great situation—you played your sport for the same money but with much less pressure.

When "Jake's" asthma started acting up in the fall of '56, Mac was content to return to the Tricolore for an eight-game stint. Although he wasn't so ego-driven to want to battle Plante for the job of Number One, he was always ready to step up when *les* Canadiens needed him. It turned out to be something of a farewell tour of the Original Six arenas, which included a close win at Toronto, a pair of losses to the league-leading Bruins, a pair of wins over the Rangers (one involving quite a brawl at the Gardens), a split in a home-and-home against Detroit, and a final loss at Chicago. Both games in the split with Detroit were lopsided, the Habs winning on home ice 6–2 and the Red Wings roaring back at the Olympia 8–3. The drama of their past close encounters had vanished. It had been Sid Abel's night six years earlier when McNeil made his debut at the Olympia; this night he would have to endure the ovation for Ted Lindsay, who notched his three hundredth. The loss at Chicago Stadium brought back that difficult Semifinal series of '53. One of the last goals McNeil gave up was to his lifelong friend Kenny Mosdell, who had been traded to the Hawks the previous spring. For Mosdell, it was the next-to-last goal he would score in the NHL. Officially, my father was part of the Stanley Cup–winning team of 1956–57, but his face in the team photo tells the real story. His expression is older, more serious, and almost cynical—nothing like the smiling youth of '53.

McNeil played for the Amerks in the 1957–58 and 1958–59 seasons. Life in the AHL in the latter part of the 1950s and into the 1960s was characterized by one fear and one hope. The hope was to play in the NHL, a hope which McNeil, of course, had already realized. Hence, press stories about my father while he played for the Americans had a definite nostalgic angle. This was the professional athlete in the twilight of his career. One such piece in the *Rochester Times-Union* recalled his

218-minute playoff streak and was accompanied by a picture of my father and me as a two-year-old (see fig. 31).[61] The original photograph hung in our home all the while I was growing up, and it now hangs in my home. I'm dressed in a plaid jumpsuit with a bow tie. I'm also leaning on a tiny stick, sawed off for my size, in the classic hockey-portrait position. I stare into the camera with my father crouched down next to me. My expression is all serious joy as only a toddler can muster. I am definitely co-operating for the photographer. My father unfortunately has his eyes closed but is otherwise smiling. His cigarette pack is visible in his shirt pocket; life in Rochester seems to agree with him. Over the years I associated my pose with that of a defenceman ready to take a pass back at the point. I don't know why that is so, but I suspect it has something to do with the fact that defence was the position I played and that I have always found that there was a special relationship on, and sometimes off, the ice between goalies and their defencemen. And so the picture is about a father and son, about mutual support, and of course, about hockey.

My parents always spoke fondly of their two winters in Rochester. They decided to keep the house in NDG, where they returned in the spring, and to rent a cottage near Quebec City to be near their families for part of the summer. This obviously meant a lot of moving. My mother remembers telling me one April that "we were going home," by which she meant Montreal. My response was, "What home?" Since my older brother and sister were now of school age, my parents wanted to be more permanently settled. Staying in professional hockey was not helping, so my father started telling the press that he planned to retire (for real this time). There are many families of professional athletes who live rather nomadic lives. This isn't necessarily bad, but many people prefer putting down roots in a chosen location. And so when McNeil arrived in Rochester for his second season, he let it be known that he thought it would be his last.

His love of family and security was given a quick jolt, however. His routine for home games included leaving his crease as the linesman checked the net to chat with Robbie Lempert, a fifth grader at Brighton School, who was in a wheelchair.[62] Robbie came to every game and had mailed McNeil a trophy that summer that was inscribed "Rochester's Friendliest Hockey Player." It was the home opener and Robbie wasn't there, so my father asked the usher how he could thank the little guy. The usher said, "Didn't you know Robbie died a little while ago?" Robert Lempert had passed away of leukemia a few weeks before. His parents had said that Robbie loved the Amerks and especially

Fig. 31 Father and son pose for the photographer. (Photographer unknown. *Rochester Union-Times*, Dec. 27, 1957, 28.) Copyright *Rochester Union-Times* (defunct).

liked how McNeil always "took time to chat with him before games." McNeil earned a $100 savings bond from Lou Perlman for being voted the "club's most popular player by the fans."[63]

The great fear of AHL players in the 1950s and '60s was to be traded to Eddie Shore's Springfield Indians. Anybody interested in the zany antics of Shore should simply look at the relevant chapter ("The Siberia of Hockey") of Don Cherry's book *Grapes*.[64] One of Mac's best games in his two years with Rochester came against Cherry and Shore's Indians on the night of February 15, 1959.[65] Stricken with tonsillitis, McNeil had a fever of 102° F. Nevertheless, he stopped 36 shots and led the Amerks to a 5–1 victory. Asked during the first intermission whether he wanted the doctor to look at him, McNeil apparently responded: "We've only got a one goal lead. I'm too busy to be examined."[66] His hand turned out to be as hot as his head.

Mac was spared the ignominy of being traded to Shore's team; in fact, wanting to end his career back in Quebec, McNeil went back to the Royals (now in the Eastern Pro Hockey League) for what he assumed would be his last year. Jacques Beauchamp, who also alluded to McNeil's dispute with Irvin,[67] made it clear that his desire would be to finish as a professional in Quebec City, but the Canadiens, who still owned his rights, were reluctant to let him go. After being struck with a shot to the mouth in a game in Sault Ste. Marie, McNeil required surgery to repair five broken teeth. By now Plante was wearing a mask in the NHL, and so McNeil followed suit.[68] Better late than never. The Royals ended up winning the EPHL crown by beating the league-leading Sudbury Wolves in Games Six and Seven in Sudbury. A familiar pattern is discernible—McNeil leads his team further in the playoff than is expected. The small guy always played big when something was on the line.

After the 1959–60 season, McNeil again announced his retirement. However, the Canadiens finally released him and he signed his last contract as a professional hockey player with the Quebec Aces in 1960–61. The kid from Limoilou had returned home. When the Aces travelled to Rochester for the first time that fall, Tom Ward wrote an article for the local paper that carried the headline "Owners Won't Let McNeil Retire."[69] It reiterated that the goalie's intention was to hang up his skates after his second season with the Amerks.

I once asked my father a question that had been on my mind for years: "Dad, do you think you would have stuck with the team that went on to win five Stanley Cups in a row if Harvey had knocked that puck out of the air and taken it down the ice to score the winner?"

"Yeah, maybe," he answered with little enthusiasm. I could sense that he had pondered the question himself and had decided that whatever joy might have come with a longer stint with the Canadiens was more than offset by the memory of what it was like to try and live a life with your stomach in a nervous knot. Later I realized something else: if my father had not retired in the fall of '54, I probably would never have been conceived.

HISTORY REPEATS

1   MSG Issue 21, Newsreel of Montreal Canadiens versus the New York Rangers, New York, Mar. 8, 1953; "Leaders Clash: Play to Tie," Telenews: Montreal Canadiens versus the Detroit Red Wings, Detroit, Jan. 25, 1953; and "Rookie Ace Trims Bruins," Telenews: Montreal Canadiens versus the Boston Bruins, Boston, Dec. 21, 1952.

2   Leslie McFarlane, dir., *Here's Hockey* (Montreal: Briston Films, 1953).

3   *Globe and Mail,* Mar. 9, 1953, 19.

4   "Plante Replaces Injured McNeil in Montreal Goal," *Globe and Mail,* Feb. 13, 1953, 22.

5   These statistics are from Diamond, *Total Hockey,* 74, 1677–78.

6   Diamond, *Total Hockey,* 1690.

7   This detail from Andy O'Brien, *Standard* (Montreal), Apr. 19, 1954.

8   W. R. Wheatley, "Wrist Operation Paid Off for Plante," *Gazette* (Montreal), Apr. 2, 1954, 20.

9   "Hab Goalie Ill, Fails to Appear at Practice; McNeil May Play," *Gazette* (Montreal), Apr. 3, 1954, 5.

10 W. R. Wheatley, "Habs, Wings Resume Tonight; Harvey Doubtful Starter," *Gazette* (Montreal), Apr. 8, 1954, 13.

11 Carroll, "Playing the Field," *Gazette* (Montreal), Apr. 8, 1954, 13.

12 Carroll, "Playing the Field," *Gazette* (Montreal), Apr. 10, 1954, 8. All details about Game Three are taken from this article.

13 Dink Carroll, "Wings Strike Early, Jolt Habs 5–2," *Gazette* (Montreal), Apr. 9, 1954, 23.

14 Pat Curran, "Wilson Scores Soft Goal… Wings Win 2–0," *Gazette* (Montreal), Apr. 12, 1954, 25. The headline in the *Herald* read "Plante Misses Softie from Wilson to Give Wings Easy Win at Forum," *Herald, Montreal,* Apr. 12, 1954, 20. All details from Game Four are taken from these articles.

15 According to W. R. Wheatley, "Canadiens, Red Wings Plan No Big Changes," *Gazette* (Montreal), Apr. 13, 1954, 20.

16 Quoted by Ferguson, "Gist and Jest," *Herald, Montreal,* Apr. 12, 1954, 21.

17 These comments and Selke's are quoted by Carroll, "Playing the Field," *Gazette* (Montreal), Apr. 19, 1954, 20.

18 All details related to Game Five are taken from Dink Carroll, "Mosdell's Overtime Goal Beats Wings 1–0," *Gazette* (Montreal), Apr. 12, 1953, 23.

19 David Bier's photo of this save was published on the front page of two Montreal dailies: *Herald, Montreal,* Apr. 12, 1954, 1, under the headline "McNeil Accepts Challenge"; and *Montréal-Matin,* Apr. 12, 1954, 1. The caption for the latter includes the statement, "[McNeil] était en grande forme et a fourni une magnifique exhibition."

20 Vince Lunny, "Mosdell Saves Habs from Elimination: McNeil Was Never Sharper," *Herald, Montreal,* Apr. 12, 1954, 17. Howe is quoted by Dink Carroll, "I shot from 10 or 12 feet out and the puck went right where I wanted it to go, but McNeil made a terrific save…. The rebound came right out on my stick, but I was in too deep and I couldn't do anything except shoot into his pads." See "Playing the Field," *Herald, Montreal,* Apr. 13, 1954, 20.

21 Quoted by Vince Lunny, "McNeil in Nets for Big Game against Wings," *Herald, Montreal,* Apr. 13, 1954, 19.

22 This detail is from Brian Kendall, *Shutout: The Legend of Terry Sawchuk* (Toronto: Penguin, 1997), 108.

23 Irvin's comments were related to me by my father.

24 This comment was made to Wheatley, "Canadiens, Red Wings Plan," 20.

25 Carroll, "Playing the Field, "*Herald, Montreal,* Apr. 13, 1954, 20.

26 Details from Game Six are taken from "Canadiens Clip Wings 4–1, Force 7th Game in Detroit; Victory Happy Helpmates Salute Gerry McNeil," *Gazette* (Montreal), Apr. 14, 1954, 25; and Vince Lunny, "Habs Force 7th Stanley Cup Game," *Herald, Montreal,* Apr. 14, 1954, 18, 22.

27 The nickname "Boom Boom" is meant to represent the double sound of the stick on puck and then puck on boards. Non-hockey people hearing the name for the first time often think it's a reference to a stripper.

28 "Short Shots from Forum," *Gazette* (Montreal), Apr. 14, 1954, 23.

29 *Gazette* (Montreal), Apr. 14, 1953, 25.

30 Vince Lunny, "Habs Force 7th," 18.

31 Andy O'Brien, *Montreal Star,* Apr. 14, 1954, 61. All details in the rest of this paragraph are from this article.

32 This unidentified newsreel is in the HHOF research archives.

33 The credits list four cameramen: Leo Thompson (who seems to be with the company into the 1970s), Ross McConnell, Jack Bristowe, and Bill Street. Tom Foley, who would go on to *Hockey Night in Canada,* does the narration.

34 Quoted by McFarlane, *Stanley Cup Fever,* 136.

35 "Short Shots from Forum," *Gazette* (Montreal), Apr. 14, 1954, 23.

36 According to Dink Carroll, "Wings Cop Stanley Cup on Leswick's Overtime Goal," Gazette (Montreal), Apr. 17, 1954, 8. In his regular column, Carroll estimates that there were five hundred Montreal fans in Detroit for Game Seven, see "Playing the Field," *Gazette* (Montreal), Apr. 17, 1954, 8.

37 This detail from "Canadiens, Wings Do or Die for Stanley Cup Tonight," *Gazette* (Montreal), Apr. 16, 1954, 16.

38 This action is captured by both the unidentified newsreel and the Briston film of the 1954 NHL Final.

39 This action is also clearly depicted in both the unidentified newsreel and the Briston film of the 1954 NHL Final.

40 Ferguson, "Gist and Jest," *Herald, Montreal,* Apr. 17, 1954, 13.

41 Nor is it mentioned in Binamé's feature film, *The Rocket,* where it might easily have contributed to the Irvin-Richard feud that is so pronounced.

42 Quoted by Dick Irvin, Jr., *Habs: An Oral History,* 111. My father's comment has been quoted repeatedly over the years.

43 See "Leswick Chides Habs for Evading Handshakes," *Herald, Montreal,* Apr. 17, 1954, 11; and "Wings Whoop It Up in Room after Game," *Gazette* (Montreal), Apr. 17, 1954, 8. Dink Carroll offers a mild criticism of the Canadiens, see "Playing the Field," *Gazette* (Montreal), Apr. 19, 1954, 20. Gaye Stewart had been quoted as saying that the Habs management prohibited their players from shaking hands, but this statement was quickly denied by Stewart and the Habs. See "Stewart Denies Remark," *Herald, Montreal,* Apr. 20, 1954, 19.

44 These comments came a couple of days later, with a better sense of perspective; see Carroll, "Playing the Field," *Gazette* (Montreal), Apr. 19, 1954, 20.

45 Quoted by Ferguson, "Gist and Jest," *Herald, Montreal,* Apr. 17, 1954, 13.

46 My father also expressed this opinion in a 1970 interview. See Roland Sabourin, "McNeil: Un pro hors pair durant toute sa carrière," *Le Soleil,* Dec. 12, 1970, 33. His view reflects popular opinion. See Red Fisher, "The Best Defenceman of His Time: Doug Harvey Had the Uncanny Talent of Either Speeding Up a Game or Putting the Brakes on It," *Gazette* (Montreal), Jan. 26, 2005, C1, C4.

47 Andy O'Brien, *Montreal Star,* Apr. 19, 1954, 19.

48 Jacques Beauchamp, "McNeil prendrait sa retraite," *Montréal-Matin,* Apr. 20, 1954, 21. In later articles and his 1979 book Beauchamp would go on to identify a conflict with Irvin as being the real reason for McNeil's retirement. See note 67 below and Beauchamp, *Le sport c'est ma vie,* 118. Robert Desjardins, "Gerry, reste avec les Canadiens pour nous!" *Le Petit journal,* Apr. 25, 1954, 80.

49 See Brown, *Doug Harvey Story.*

50 Beauchamp, *Le sport c'est ma vie,* 118.

51 "McNeil Quits Hockey," *Herald, Montreal,* Sept. 27, 1954, 1, 20.

52 See *Herald, Montreal,* Sept. 27, 1954, 20.

53 Vince Lunny, "Hockey's Goaltenders Have Toughest Job in Sport," *Hockey News,* June 1954, 5.

54 Geoffrion and Fischler, *Boom Boom,* 70.

55 Vince Lunny, "McNeil Quits, Says Nerves Forced Move," *Herald, Montreal,* Sept. 27, 1954, 20.

56 Baz O'Meara, "McNeil Confirms Puck Retirement," *Montreal Star,* Sept. 27, 1954, 34.

57 Quoted by George Beahon, "In This Corner," *Rochester Democrat and Chronicle,* Nov. 7, 1957, 44. In the same column, Beahon makes a direct allusion to McNeil's feud with Irvin when he brings up the subject of the '54 retirement: "Sources say McNeil and the late Dick Irvin, then Montreal coach, were incompatible."

58 Quoted by Trent Frayne, "Why Big-League Goalies Crack Up," *The Thrill of Victory: Best Sport Stories from the Pages of McLeans'* (Toronto: Viking, 2003), 27.

59 *Globe and Mail,* May 10, 1955, 18.

60 The Royals were now part of the Quebec Hockey League (QHL), a professional version of the senior team that operated in the 1940s.

61 *Rochester Times-Union,* Dec. 27, 1957, 28.

62 This story and Gerry's retirement plans were reported by Dave Ocorr, "About a Boy, His Hero and a Trophy," *Rochester Times-Union,* Oct. 14, 1958, 34.

63 See Hans Tanner, "Amerks Nip Hershey in Home Finale, 3–1," *Rochester Democrat and Chronicle,* Mar. 17, 1958, 21.

64 Don Cherry and Stan Fischler, *Grapes: A Vintage Age of Hockey* (Toronto: Prentice Hall, 1983).

65 Hans Tanner, "Amerk Skaters Club Springfield, 5–1; Goalie McNeil Stars Despite Illness," *Rochester Democrat and Chronicle,* Feb. 16, 1959, 22.

66 See "Icicles," *Rochester Democrat and Chronicle,* Feb. 16, 1959, 22.

67 Jacques Beauchamp, "Le sport en général," *Montréal-Matin,* Sept. 11, 1959, 36: "On se souvient que McNeil a déjà abandonné le hockey, soit à la fin de la saison 1953–54, après avoir eu une violente dispute avec le défunt Dick Irvin."

68 Graeme McMurray, "Royals Unbeaten in Last Five…," *Gazette* (Montreal), Mar. 7, 1960, 19.

69 Tom Ward, "Owners Won't Let McNeil Retire," *Rochester Times-Union,* Oct. 28, 1960, 38.

The Hockey Sweater

MUCH OF WHAT I HAVE LEARNED ABOUT MY FATHER'S HOCKEY career has been gleaned from general histories of the sport and the biographies of other players (e.g., Harvey, Geoffrion, Barilko, Howe). Most of these are rather positive about my father's play; occasionally, it is implied that the overtime loss of 1954 precipitated his retirement. For example, after recounting my father's solid play against the Red Wings, Roy MacSkimming in his "unauthorized biography" of Howe follows up on my father's hyperbolic comment on that loss, "It's like the end of the world," with the sentence, "On that note he retires from hockey while the Red Wings and their lovers party long into the night."[1] Sport narratives delight in emphasizing the ecstasy of winning and the agony of losing, but the really interesting material goes beyond this simple binary. More recently, Howe himself remembered the '54 Final in a way that is more generous as far as my father is concerned: "Trying to find a spark, Dick Irvin benched Jacques Plante for Gerry McNeil. He hadn't seen much action in a while, but he was so sharp you couldn't tell. He turned out to be the edge the Habs needed and they took the next two, to even the series at three games apiece."[2] Sixty years later, Mr. Hockey, whose career achievements went far beyond encounters with a single goalie, has the magnanimous perspective.

The purpose of this chapter is to touch on Gerry McNeil's post-hockey life as a Canadiens alumnus and to examine how his career has been represented in the literature of the sport. Thus far we have relied on the day-to-day journalism that was concurrent with the playing career; now we will review how hockey historians and writers have shaped what we remember about the NHL mid-twentieth century. We will also come to some conclusions about the difference between experiencing the NHL in the time of McNeil versus that of today.

My father's hockey career, much less his NHL statistics, was rarely the subject of family discussions when I was growing up (we knew he had won a Stanley Cup and had figured in some famous overtime games, but that was all). However, in the last decade of his life his career did become a research interest of mine and, as a consequence, my father addressed it more than I remember him doing prior to that. From a distance of decades gone by and emotional investments long over, he was proud to talk about his years as a professional hockey player with his grandchildren and others. Evidence of the athletic exploits of the latter hung with his own on the den wall. For many years my peewee trophy sat next to his replica Stanley Cup on the mantelpiece. He was always eager to offer an opinion on a player or team, and watching games with him was always enjoyable. Unlike many others, my father was often reluctant to find fault: "The pace is so fast out there that committing yourself to one thing might end up looking silly, but it could just as easily turn out wrong had you done something else." Slow-motion replays exaggerate the sense of there being much more time than there is to make a decision. Perhaps remembering his own NHL days, he tended to cheer on the smaller, less well-known goalies.

My first discussion with my father about his NHL career stats came after a friend had dropped off a copy of *Sports Illustrated* in the late 1990s that had a story on an all-time list of modern-day goalies.[3] My father was proud of his 2.36 NHL career average, which had him tied for third before the 1997–98 season. Only Ken Dryden at 2.24 and Martin Brodeur at 2.25 had better averages at the time the article appeared (Brodeur would finish in 2015 with a 2.24 over a remarkable 1,266 games!). The list included only those who had played at least two hundred games, and the rest of the names read like a who's who of goalies: Bill Durnan also at 2.36, Jacques Plante 2.38, Dominick Hasek then at 2.40 (he would finish with a 2.20), Glenn Hall 2.51, Johnny Bower and Terry Sawchuk 2.52, and Bernie Parent 2.55. One assumes that an updated list would have to include Patrick Roy and perhaps Eddie Belfour, yet their NHL net GAA are 2.54 and 2.50 respectively. All of these goalies have had longer careers, but none would match my father's playoff GAA of 1.89. It is perhaps worth noting that although my father's record put him third on the list, the *SI* article itself makes no mention of him (all of the other names are immediately recognizable to knowledgeable hockey fans). When one checks a complete list (not just "modern" goalies), my father's playoff average ranks ninth, and the two "modern" goalies with better records are names that one might not expect to see—Braden Holtby (as of this writing still playing for the Washington Capitals) and Patrick Lalime.[4]

While my father is usually remembered for being the goalie on whom Barilko, or Leswick, scored their famous Stanley Cup–winning overtime goals, there is a piece of Canadian literature that features him in what must have been his happiest moment as a professional athlete. I refer to Wayne Johnston's 1990 novel, *The Divine Ryans* (which was

THE HOCKEY SWEATER

made into a film), and the moment right after my father realized he had won the Stanley Cup with a shutout overtime performance. As we have seen, this was April 16, 1953, Game Five of the NHL Final. Wayne Johnston fictionalized the event in his novel only because he wanted to anchor one of his characters as having been in Montreal circa April 1953. You'll have to read the novel if you want to know why. Blending fiction with fact, Johnston has a character in the novel at the final game who claims to have grabbed a puck kicked into the crowd by the Montreal goalie. The puck, identified as one that was "deflected into the stands by Canadiens goalie Gerry McNeil," serves as a family heirloom, and the son searches a photograph (in one of the many illustrated histories of hockey) of McNeil apparently taken just after Lach scored to see if he can find his father's face in the crowd.[5] While only a "few faces" were unobstructed or in clear focus, the depth of field required to see "the Montreal zone" with my father and *any* individuals in the crowd behind him would obviously have owed itself to a Speed Graphic (with flash).

Johnston, whose fiction fascinates for how it draws on history, maintains that the photograph on which he based this scene (a kind of *ekphrasis*) actually exists. Perhaps; in any case I have failed to find it, despite being on a search similar to Johnston's narrator.[6] In fact, I have scoured scrapbooks, microfilmed newspapers, and used bookstores without turning up Johnston's photo. I suspect that Johnston simply conflated the so-called facts of that game with another picture of another goalie to serve the purpose of his novel. My father doesn't remember throwing his stick, which is what he is apparently doing in the photograph, but the photos that do exist of the on-ice celebration show him without a stick. So we don't really know. Footage of the game indicates that the puck did go over the boards during the first minute of overtime, but this was near the Canadiens bench. The father in the novel records the exact game time when McNeil apparently deflected the puck over—1:03 of overtime, or "nineteen seconds" before Lach fired home the winner.[7] According to the scoresheet that appeared in *The Gazette,* Lach's goal did come at 1:22, or nineteen seconds later, so Johnston is accurate in that respect.

It doesn't matter, of course. What does matter is that Gerry McNeil's perfect game has a place, albeit small, in Canadian literature. Johnston, himself, seemed touched that his story of a boy trying to connect with his father had actually served as an occasion for me and my father to enjoy how fiction had inadvertently immortalized what must have been one of my father's happiest moments. And somehow I find it fitting that the photograph that enables this intersection of fiction and history remains, for me at least, an imaginary one.

Johnston's novel, like DeLillo's *Underworld,* dramatizes the cultural importance that attaches itself to sports memorabilia—e.g., a puck from the last minute of the last game in the 1953 Stanley Cup Final, the baseball that Bobby Thompson hit in 1951 for a pennant-winning home run. These novels may well register a shift that has come with an increased sense of the spectacle of sport and its commercialization. We crave the relic that somehow puts us in touch with a time that is nostalgically idealized. I have a friend who happened to come into possession of a stick that Maurice Richard used during the 1953 season. He kept it for many years, knew its every little mark, its weight, its feel. He ultimately offered it to one of the popular auction services and fetched a nice sum for his children's college fund, a move that I admire as wise and noble.

My father's gear sat in a dusty green bag in our basement for at least two decades, more like discarded tools than anything relic-like. (Why green I don't know—a colour of his last team, the Quebec Aces?) Every once in a while I would poke around inside. I remember the large, blue Canadiens pants (one could tell by the red strip on the side) that seemed reinforced and had a special sheen. The heavy black jock—much more professional-looking than my own. The face mask he adopted just before the end of his career. I recall that he always had his goalie skates tied with a strap to the appropriate leg pad and would not allow anyone to undo them. The catching glove was such a lovely black leather. Then there was the felt padding that was worn on his shoulders with what seemed to be extra pieces sewn in, the thin crusty chest protector that he had since 1943. In fact, I remember the specific musty smell of sweat-seasoned leather that emanated from the bag whenever its zipper was opened—smelling the equipment was a palpable connection to the past. The remnants of the bag are now with my nephew, who is himself a goaltender.

At five foot seven and 155 lb. my father didn't look like a natural goaltender. He wasn't ambidextrous like Bill Durnan, and he didn't leave his crease to handle the puck like Jacques Plante, but he came to play, and play he did, especially in the playoffs. Harvey and company did not succeed in talking my father out of retirement in the summer of 1954. The official NHL record reads that Gerry McNeil "DID NOT PLAY" the 1954–55 season; well, he certainly wasn't playing hockey. As mentioned at the end of the last chapter, chances are that I would not have been conceived in February of 1955, as I was, if my father had continued playing. Both my older siblings were, like many children of professional hockey players, spring babies. I haven't done a systematic study, but I believe one would bear out this hypothesis. Whenever I ponder the "what might have been" had my father not retired in '54, I wonder whether my own existence owes something to the fact that he did.

Like many ex-professional athletes who capitalize on their public image, McNeil pursued a career as a sales representative during the 1960s. He tried a number of different things ranging from wood products to insurance. Being an NHL goaltender may not have been easy, but neither was finding the right business opportunity. Preoccupied with making a living, Mac had little contact with his former teammates. One of my fondest memories of my father dates from this time. It was a late weekday afternoon in early November, my birthday circa 1962. I was playing road hockey with my friends when my father came out of the house with what looked like a hockey net. The object had a shiny chrome frame and a white mesh—it was marvellous! Nobody had ever seen such a thing! The first road hockey net to appear in Quebec City; no more snow-pile goalposts or arguments about it being "in" or not. Soon there were kids coming from distant neighbourhoods asking to join our game. In the half century since that day, those hockey nets have become a ubiquitous part of the Canadian landscape from St. John's to Vancouver Island to Rankin Inlet. That Friday night my father said to me that maybe, just once, we could take the net down to our rec room so he could check it out. For the next half hour or so our rec room became the Montreal Forum and then Chicago Stadium. My father was the goalie, of course. We were having a great time working up a sweat until "Bobby Hull" took a slapshot that sent the tennis ball off the back wall and right between my mother's head and a lampshade. My father even as a senior enjoyed play.

Early in the 1960s he was asked to be a special guest on the French CBC to select the three stars. He took me with him to Montreal and we stayed at the Mount Royal Hotel. Around six o'clock in the evening we went down to the lobby, where my father knew the visiting team would be gathering. Sure enough several members of the Toronto Maple Leafs were there. I still remember shaking hands with a smiling Terry Sawchuk, seeing the scars on his face, and thinking that this guy looked like Frankenstein. I can't remember what he said to me, but he was friendly. I now know through a number of biographers and the poetry of Randall Maggs that the scars could be said to be visible representations of the trauma he endured. My father's face in contrast wasn't disfigured with scar tissue.

For an eight-year-old kid going to his first NHL game, the walk down a neon-lit Sainte-Catherine Street to the Forum was ecstasy. As we got closer to the rink, the sidewalk became more crowded, then there were the sounds of street vendors. Our seats were up in the second tier, close to the broadcast booth. You can see from photos and film clips that the second tier of the pre-1968 Forum was very dark; it was also a very steep drop to ice level. My father had to leave for an intermission interview, and an usher was supposed to watch me. All I remember is being surrounded by a crowd of loud and boisterous adults. I was frightened. As late as the 1960s, the NHL arena was a place for adult entertainment. I believe the Habs won a close game 3–1.[8]

Although McNeil had little or no contact with the Canadiens management at this time, he did get involved with a group of former players to form the Quebec Oldtimers. They would practise on Friday nights and play a game against the Montreal Oldtimers for charity. Later Mac would join the Montreal Oldtimers himself and do a couple of European tours, then a return to the Detroit Olympia. All games were for charity, but soon after a number of the guys started playing Oldtimer games for a percentage of the gate. Dollard St. Laurent told me that he believed he made more money as an Oldtimer than he did in the NHL.

It was around this time that I learned about my father being scored upon by Barilko. It would often come up at family get-togethers when the talk would turn to my father's career or to the ritualistic (remember when…) baby tales. Somehow we started believing that my father had received a death threat on the Saturday when Karen was born—a mysterious caller contacted Dad at the Royal York Hotel, "Make sure you lose the game tonight or else you'll never see your new baby." Losing the game a few hours later could then be construed as my father opting for his baby daughter over the Stanley Cup. Karen, who has a tremendous sense of humour, loved to tell the story. However, the truth was that no such threat was ever made. Both my parents confirmed the story as being fictitious, "but you all seemed to enjoy it so much we didn't have the heart to tell you."

In 1968 McNeil became a sales representative with Thomas Adams Distillers, a subsidiary of Seagrams. He also cheered for St. Louis, with former Canadiens like Harvey and Moore in their lineup, against the Habs in the Cup Final that year. He spoke fondly of all the defencemen who played in front of him (Harvey, of course, Butch Bouchard, Dollard St. Laurent, "Bud" MacPherson) with one exception—Tom Johnson. At some point after all of these players had retired, it was suspected that Tom Johnson, who went on to a successful head office career with Boston, had ratted on his Hab teammates to management—e.g., who broke curfew. "We knew we had a mole among us but never could figure out who it was." In any case, the Original Six league was now a thing of the past.

Promoted to sales manager in 1972, McNeil moved the family back to Montreal (although by now Ron and Karen were out on their own). The Forum, extensively renovated in 1969, was no longer recognizable as the same building. It wasn't until Ron Corey made efforts to welcome alumni back to the Canadiens family that McNeil and others would feel welcome at Canadiens games or events. One night my father took me inside the alumni room at the Forum and we chatted briefly with Toe Blake about the club's "problems." I remember it being a meaningless game against a poor opponent, but it didn't matter to Blake. He was incensed about the performance of a certain line—so upset that I thought he was going to have a heart attack right there.

As a child, I remember my father not as a goalie but as a sales manager who was always ready with a lesson in how to bargain for goods. "You have to find something about the item you don't like. Make something up if you can't find anything. Like, 'I really wanted a blue Oldsmobile, not a red one.' That forces the guy to come down in his price." I vividly remember having an occasion to put this stratagem into practice when I needed to buy some used hockey socks from the skate sharpener. "That will be three dollars." I responded that I really needed the dark "away" colour, so I wouldn't pay more than two dollars. This wasn't true. It was the white, home sock that I needed. He smiled and said that it was my lucky day, that he had some brand new dark socks and they were five dollars. When my father found out he was not going to get any change back from his five-dollar bill and that I was for some reason holding a second pair of dark socks, he immediately went over to the skate sharpener himself. Before long the skate sharpener and my father were laughing, and my father eventually came away with the right colour. Deceit, I realized, could get you into trouble.

His brief but spectacular NHL career might not be well known, but Gerry McNeil is well remembered by those whose connections to the league go back to the Original Six era. Bobby Hull, for instance, recalled to a family friend how excited he was when the Canadiens visited his home town of Pointe Anne (just east of Belleville, Ontario) in the early 1950s.[9] He had a clear memory of standing in awe behind the steel mesh that rattled and banged as the Habs fired a barrage of pucks at "the little guy." By the time I was old enough to take an interest in the NHL, Hull had become a superstar, and I was a devoted Black Hawks supporter. My father could hardly feel betrayed, since his own cheering for the Habs was rather subdued during the '60s. Nevertheless, I do wonder how he felt about his son's enthusiasm for the Golden Jet (Hull's nickname) and Chicago Stadium, the building where Mac had suffered his humiliating debacle twelve years before. Dad, however, got the last laugh, especially in Game Seven of the 1965 Final when the Habs took control of the contest by scoring three unanswered goals early. He teased me mercilessly as I broke into tears and retreated behind my chair, unable to watch my Indianhead heroes go down in defeat. I was mature enough to handle the 1971 and '73 losses like an adult at least, and I believe my father actually felt sorry for me.

Like many players, my father had problems adjusting to life after hockey. One of his problems was dealing with his alcoholism, which he was able to do despite being employed in the spirits industry. I suppose when a professional career reaches a climax at age twenty-six, there is a tendency to seek out anything that might help in escaping the long denouement that your life inevitably becomes. Gerry lost his charm quickly when he was intoxicated, and despite some low moments, it has always amazed me that my affection and admiration were never permanently diminished.

During the mid-1960s my father had been drinking in Quebec City and rear-ended another car. When the driver of the other vehicle got out to inspect the damage, he recognized the person who had hit him as a former NHLer and local celebrity and offered to settle the incident on the spot if my father only agreed to pay for the repairs. My father, with an exaggerated sense of doing the "right thing," insisted on calling the police. The driver clued into my father's condition and reiterated his willingness for a gentleman's agreement. Gerry, blind to his good fortune, was having none of it. When the police arrived they also recognized my father, and when the other driver repeated his offer, they let my father go home in a cab. Obviously, this kind of thing doesn't happen any more (and it shouldn't), but I think it was common for the time. It represents how poor our decision-making is when under the influence. It also reflects my father's good fortune that nothing really tragic occurred as a result of his inability to handle alcohol.

The worst that did happen may have been the painting of our new house when our family moved to Quebec City in 1960. Dad had arranged to paint the house with some of his hockey buddies, and they had gotten into the beer. Things then went downhill fast. Soon guys were painting the window panes and making a general mess of things. When the real estate agent dropped by to see how things were going, my father merely tossed some money at him and told him to see that it was cleaned up. My father never really made much effort to hide his faults, and I think this made him easier to love. His pretenses routinely crumpled, but he always had a dignified way about him.

However, the alcohol-related incident that has haunted me ever since it occurred is probably typical for family members in similar situations. I was working in downtown Montreal during a summer in the 1970s, and I would routinely drive to and fro with my father, whose office was at De Maisonneuve and Stanley. One day I met him at the parking garage and didn't realize that he was intoxicated. If he kept his mouth shut he could fool you for a few minutes. We got into the car and he proceeded to drive west on the Ville-Marie Expressway. I soon realized from his speech and erratic steering that he was drunk. Since we were already speeding along in traffic, I didn't think that I could insist that he allow me to drive. I should have. An angel must have been guiding us, because we did make it to the West Island without killing ourselves or, worse, somebody else. Still, on the exit ramp he misjudged the distance between our bumper and the motorcyclist in front, and we touched his back wheel. Although it wasn't serious (the motorcyclist just gave us a dirty look), it could have been, and I can remember how my heart jumped with fear. Disaster was a slip away.

I have to think that recognizing the burden problem-drinking places on loved ones is the strongest incentive to reform. They say that you take it one day at a time; well, I still remember how one day of sobriety became two, then a week, a month, soon a year and then a decade, then close to three decades. It may not have been a perfect shutout, but it was a great act of love, for my father did not hide the fact that he gave up alcohol for us. In sport as in life, and fairly or not, we are often judged by our last outing. In this respect, Mac had reason to be proud, and it was such a pleasure when from time to time we told him how great it was. So we were able to enjoy many holiday and birthday celebrations, because Mac was content to sip his Diet Pepsi while watching the rest of us indulge.

The second major obstacle that McNeil overcame was homophobia. Ron, his eldest son, had asserted his sexual preference in unequivocal terms at the age of sixteen. It couldn't have come as a complete surprise—this was the boy who had said that the best thing about watching a game at the Forum was seeing the men water the ice in between periods, the boy who ran around with a number of girlfriends, who could imitate a woman's voice on the phone with ease. Nevertheless, Mac didn't respond in a positive manner. He ordered Ron to his room, where he could stay *until he changed his mind*. Our house was full of arguing while I continued to play with friends and, like many children, didn't exactly pretend nothing was wrong but carried on as if that were the case. I have an image of my father from this time leaning on a kitchen counter and simply staring into an ashtray. My mother and brother were yelling at each other behind a closed door. Having come upon him unnoticed, I quickly retrieved what I was there for and left.

For years, my parents seemed to behave as if they hoped their son would somehow get over being gay—would grow out of it. Then one of those life-changing accidents occurred, one that involved both alcohol and homophobia, to turn this situation around, and I was at the centre of it. It was just after Christmas 1970, and I was watching television with my older sister and brother; my father, having overindulged in some festive cheer, had gone to bed. I proceeded to get into an argument with Karen about some political issue and ended up saying something so hurtful she broke into tears and headed for her room. My brother went to comfort her, and the noise woke my father who, thinking that Ron had caused Karen's distress, proceeded to attack my brother physically. We went from watching television to a complete family breakdown in a matter of minutes. Realizing that I was the cause of it all, I simply grabbed a coat and left the house. By the afternoon of the next day my father was desperate to locate me, so he appealed to my brother and his partner for help. For Ron that marked the point at which my father finally accepted his homosexuality. Ron then tracked me down at a local shopping centre. Although you probably would never have found Gerry McNeil leading the gay parade, he would eventually take pride in how accomplished his eldest son was. Ron, now Shannon, was always welcome in the McNeil home, and Shannon's partner, Gérald (which just happened to also be Gerry's real name), was always considered a true son-in-law. The conversion was enough to give hope to anyone who thinks that people cannot change for the better.

Whatever celebrity my father had as a retired NHL goalie, he carried it well. It was common enough for the two of us to be in a store or on our way somewhere and for some stranger to suddenly stop my father, "Gerry, *comment ça va*?" You could count on losing at least ten minutes with every encounter, and they were always amiable. I would inevitably get asked if I played hockey, and if I was a goalie like my dad. Up until I was fourteen I'd answer "yes" to the first question, and always "no" to the second. Mostly my father would carry the conversation about kids, the NHL, and life in general. I'd get impatient. Afterwards I'd ask him, "Who was that?" and he'd reply, "I can't really remember, but I think somebody introduced us at a restaurant some years ago." I was constantly amazed at his performances of civility for such strangers.

While working in an office during the 1970s, I was introduced to a woman as "Gerry McNeil's son." That was common enough as I grew up, but what was unusual this time was what she would reveal to me later when we happened to be alone. She described herself as having been a member of a group of "girls" who followed certain hockey players rather closely back in the late 1940s and early '50s. "We were mad about your father; we thought he was so attractive—those eyes—and we'd wait outside the Forum for him," she mused wistfully. All I can remember is that she used the plural "we," that she seemed lost in a flashback moment, and that I didn't want to hear any more. I never brought the matter up with my father.

In 1983 McNeil received an NHL Milestone Award for his 28 regular-season shutouts. He was ambivalent about the rise in player salaries, admiring the strong stand taken by the Players Association, but wondering how the league could still operate in the black. He was temporarily set against the NHL and many of the younger players when a pension surplus, owed the players from his era, was held up in the courts for years. "Some of the old boys could really use a few extra bucks right now, and these greedy guys don't have enough already?" Carl Brewer, who led the fight on behalf of the players, suddenly became a hero in McNeil's eyes. Bob Pulford, the NHLPA representative who had originally signed away the rights to the surplus, was vilified.[10] (Pulford, of course, would be well looked after by Bill Wirtz, the owner of the Blackhawks and long-time president of the Board.) Even some ex-Habs, like Bob Gainey, were said to have taken the owners' side, and McNeil would not soon forget it. Yet even through the worst, he rarely missed games on TV. Like many others, my father considered himself a solid fan of the game but could not name one player from the visiting team.

Mac retired from Seagrams in 1991 and looked forward to wintering with some of his old Canadiens pals in Florida. Some of his former teammates succumbed to health problems or passed away. Floyd Curry, his roomie, took care of Toe Blake when Toe fell victim to Alzheimer's; then Floyd himself was stricken by the same disease. When the dark, cold days of Canadian November set in, Mac would pack the golf clubs in the car and head south with Teacy, eventually meeting up with the Lachs or Mosdells, the Rocket and Lucille in places like Panama City Beach. He could always be counted on to take his turn rising at 4:00 AM to drive over to the course to secure a tee time for himself and Elmer. I remember how even in his seventies, Mac would display his competitiveness on the golf course and pull off clutch shots just when he needed to. The Rocket didn't like golf because, as Mac used to say, he had trouble getting a birdie on every hole. So he tended to hang out with Kenny. No doubt the group had many opportunities to reminisce about the battles with Lindsay and Labine as the sun set over the gulf.

Early in the 1990s the Canadiens presented sweaters to a number of the Oldtimers. Since Number One had been retired for Jacques Plante, my father was presented with Number Thirty, which was the last number he wore when he replaced Plante in 1956. They were authentic NHL jerseys (1990s not 1950s authentic) and they were beautiful—the darks, that red so familiar, and the crest conveying such tradition. My father's hung in his closet for years. When I asked him about it, he admitted that he was a little disappointed about the Number Thirty. "Jacques was a great goalie, may he rest in peace," he said, "but I was Number One before Plante." True enough, he had played most of his NHL games with Number One before Plante. "No problem," I said, "I'll get it changed." And I did. To everyone in our family he was Number One, and I remember how he smiled when I held it up for him.

McNeil was a regular at the annual golf tournaments: Dickie Moore's, Toe Blake's, and the Canadiens'. He felt it was his "civic" duty as an alumnus to participate in such events, even if his knee ached badly or the weather was lousy, because the purpose was to raise money for some charity. The usual format would call for three, or sometimes just two, wealthy individuals to be matched up with one or two former players. In 2001 a special challenge between former Leafs and Habs was organized at a course near Toronto. Unfortunately it was scheduled for a couple of days after 9/11; the airlines still weren't flying, so there was a chance that the whole thing would have to be cancelled. The Montreal players decided to rent a bus and make the trip there and back without staying over. Hotel expenses would only cut into the amount of money that would be donated. I can remember my father saying that it had been an exhausting yet satisfying day; the long bus ride reminded many of the players of the fun they once had on those long train trips.

At the dinner for another golf tournament, Mac was seated with Jocelyn Thibault, the former Canadiens goalie, and Ron Corey, who attempted to bring his two table guests together by describing Gerry's heroics during the 1951 playoffs. My father recalls how Thibault eyed him (a short septuagenarian with a gimpy knee) suspiciously and then looked baffled. "He must have thought that Corey had gotten too much sun—no way this guy could have played in the NHL, let alone starred." The incident struck Mac as so funny that he laughed up tears as he recounted it.

One by one he saw the Original Six arenas either fall to the wrecking ball or be themselves "retired": first the old Madison Square Gardens, then the Olympia, Chicago Stadium, Boston Garden, the Forum itself, and Maple Leaf Gardens. He found it hard to watch hockey in the Molson (now Bell) Centre with its laser lights, pounding music, and flashing scoreboard. So much artificial excitement interfered with the real drama on the ice. We often spoke about how professional hockey had changed over the course of our lives. It was at these times that I remember how my father could sound downright poetic or even philosophical.

"Remember, years ago, the magical moment before the beginning of an important game when the ice would glisten with a fresh flood. There'd be this buzz in the crowd, and then if you happened to be sitting close enough to the ice, you'd hear the first scratches of the referee's skates, before the teams came on. At the first sight of a team colour, the crowd buzz would turn to a roar or boo and then suddenly that white surface would fill with two sets of opposing colours."

"Yeah, even I'm old enough to remember that."

"As a goalie, you were the first player to get out on that brilliant, unmarked ice, and there was always something special about it. Something that suggested a fresh beginning. Arena hockey is unique in how you can get that feeling at the beginning of every period…"

"It's like that Bauer TV commercial that shows a player getting onto a clean sheet with the voice-over 'What will you write?'"

"Enough to make you forget that there are a finite number of floods in a playing career."

"What will you write?"

My father knew that I was collecting material to write about his career and he was conscious of trying to help me. I now appreciate how he tried so hard to be accurate and honest about what he could remember. More often than not, he'd simply admit that he couldn't recall a detail, but the general picture he knew well. "Can't remember where we liked to eat in New York, but wherever we went the bill was always split evenly."

Over the years Quebec newspapers would periodically run a retrospective feature on my father's short but brilliant NHL career; these usually appeared at playoff time when a young goalie had burst on the playoff scene: Ken Dryden, Steve Penny, José Théodore.[11] History repeating itself. My father traded on his ever-diminishing celebrity to bolster business contacts, yet he also gave time to all kinds of charitable causes. For a number of years I remember my father making yearly Christmas visits to the Veterans' Hospital in Senneville. Once he returned home visibly shaken up and told us that many of the patients he saw had no idea who he was. "But they seemed so happy to have a visitor, you felt you had done a good thing just touching their hand."

Like all of us, he did fear growing old. One by one, Mac saw many of his hockey buddies get hit with the usual ravages of time. Harvey's body could only take so much abuse, cancer caught up with Jimmy Galbraith, and Kenny Mosdell suffered a stroke. Only Elmer Lach seemed to go on without the physical problems others were experiencing. For months, it was known that the Rocket was very sick.[12] Everybody was prepared for his passing, but not for the public display of solemn respect by so many Quebecers and others that followed.[13] It was as if a whole generation was nostalgically mourning its own passing.

I remember calling my father from Edmonton when I first learned that the Rocket had passed away. He seemed to be taking the news okay, but as the grief swelled in the next few days and he was asked to be a pallbearer, the momentous nature of what was happening staggered him. His phone did not stop ringing as reporters from all over sought his comments. "My voice is hoarse, and I'm going to go crazy from repeating the same thing over and over." Among the other pallbearers were Elmer Lach, Dickie Moore, and Kenny Mosdell, three of his closest friends, "Butch" Bouchard and Jean Béliveau, two more he could call teammates (Ken Reardon had retired before my father took over from Durnan).[14]

Special visitation arrangements were made for the Rocket to lie in state at the Bell Centre. Dignitaries paid their respects, but what was more impressive were the thousands of Quebecers who wanted show their appreciation for not only the hockey player but the man who had stood up for French Canadians. It did not go unnoticed that five of the eight pallbearers had anglophone names (McNeil, Moore, Reardon, Lach, and Mosdell), but my father, born in Limoilou, whose mother was an Acadian from Northern New Brunswick, was fluently bilingual and always managed to straddle the English and French communities.[15] All eight felt as one—one group of teammates, the elders, so to speak, of the Canadiens' family. At the centre of the crowd and solemn dignity, they were as perplexed as anybody as to why such a public spectacle of affection was being expressed for a hockey player. Politics could never take away from a bond of friendship that went back a half century.

THE HOCKEY SWEATER

The procession through the streets of Montreal, with all those limos, and the funeral service in Notre-Dame Basilica seemed like something for a head of state, not a professional athlete. My father emerged from the day only to reflect on it all again by seeing the coverage on television and in the print media. When it was over, he and my mother came to Halifax for a visit. We watched recordings of the funeral and pored over the newspapers yet again, agreeing in the end that the political and cultural dimensions of the event were larger than we could grasp. "I shook hands with a lot of politicians who, I know, couldn't have cared less about hockey," Dad said. It was around this time that my father prepaid his own yet-to-come funeral (his and my mother's). As mentioned, my father had an uncanny ability to anticipate and prepare for the future: "I can see it coming."

Still we both sensed that there was something fitting about the grandeur of the scale insofar as it reflected the importance of the game, of national heroes, and of the glory that was the old NHL. My father was happy to have played his minor role. On the other hand, he would often remark whenever yet another writer or filmmaker contacted him about the great Rocket or Plante that there were a number of other guys that deserved some recognition. "Not to take anything away from the Rocket, but we were very much a team." The next year Tony "Mighty Mouse" Leswick passed on, then Chuck Rayner, then Sugar Jim Henry. In the past year alone (2014–15) we have lost Béliveau, Dollard St. Laurent, Marcel Pronovost, Gus Mortson, Leo Reise, Elmer Lach, Bert Olmstead, and Dickie Moore. The human connection to the world I have described in this book exists largely beyond the living. We keep in touch through the relics of memorabilia, the pictures (still and moving), the sounds, and the literature.

So what exactly is different about how we experience the NHL today from my father's time? We have seen how MacAloon's idea of frames and Turner's emphasis on liminality (i.e., the turning point) inform our understanding of what makes sports photography and modern sport itself spectacular. There are other commentators whose theories for understanding how a sport like hockey operates as a cultural spectacle veer toward the negative. Lewis Mumford may have been the first twentieth-century commentator to attempt to account for a mechanical role of what he referred to as "mass sport" in society or to its status as "spectacle": "sport in the sense of a mass-spectacle . . . comes into existence when a population has been drilled and regimented and depressed to such an extent that it needs at least a vicarious participation in difficult feats of strength or skill or heroism in order to sustain its waning life-sense."[16] Mumford also argued that "sport, which began originally, perhaps, as a spontaneous reaction against the machine, has become one of the mass-duties of the machine age," that "mass sport" is a "profit-making mechanism."[17] How odd do we feel in the arena when we catch ourselves staring at the scoreboard representation of the live action before us? Attend a political convention and witness how the audience watches the huge video image rather than the live, albeit now diminutive, figure.

The answer to the difference in how the NHL was experienced mid-twentieth century as opposed to now may be best explained if we tweak Walter Benjamin's understanding of the relationship between mechanical reproduction and art. The necessary tweak is to substitute sport for art: "what withers in the age of the technological reproducibility of the work of art is the latter's aura."[18] "Aura" gets defined as "a strange tissue of space and time."[19] What withers in our age of digital reproduction and mobility is the unique nature of passing through one moment and one place—the Montreal Forum on the night of April 16, 1953—to see and hear and feel the overtime victory as a single experience. "Aura" has the vague sense of religiosity about it that easily slips through our fingers while our secular grasp is more intent on possession, the desire to hold that moment forever. This idea may sound like I'm pressing too far into philosophical reflection, but I sincerely believe it is at the heart of what has changed about much of our everyday reality, not just how we experience an elite sport.

Another question—what is the role of sport literature in the reproduction? Words are not multimedia, but all the writing that is done about sport may be understood as part of MacAloon's festive frame (first the game, then ritual, then the festive, then spectacle). And once we recognize that criticism is part of this festive atmosphere, then we can account for the popularity of the controversial in the literature. So the aesthetics of artistic narrative is overlaid on a game; we love the conflict, not just in the oppositional nature of sport itself, but in the stories we entertain ourselves with. We can celebrate and criticize simultaneously. Nostalgic and commercial spectacle still dominates the popular histories of hockey, what Tom McSorley calls "an avalanche of coffee-table hockey books published at Christmas."[20] And characteristic of much of the writing about the celeb industries, including sports, hockey books tends to be lavishly illustrated.[21] The bulk of this material falls into the popular categories of personal or pictorial histories, especially of the stars or team dynasties.

THE HOCKEY SWEATER

Michael McKinley's *Hockey: A People's History*[22] is the most recent effort in the general area. The book, however, was meant to accompany the CBC's ten-part (i.e., ten-hour) special which exhaustively traces the sport from a Canadian perspective—a film that attempts to do for Canadian hockey what Ken Burns did for American baseball. In the age of multimedia marketing, the book serves as a kind of accessory to the main product. Like most hockey books, it was launched in the fall to coincide with the new season on the ice and to feed into the Christmas gift-giving just around the corner. Comparing media is beyond my scope, yet it is worth noting that, as far as the still image is concerned, there isn't much difference between film and print, except that the viewer's experience of the latter involves more control and leisure, and these engage the imagination. One tends to view the printed image or pore over the text as long as one wants. While the experience of reading has itself been romanticized vis-à-vis film or television, it is important to remember that spectacle involves sound and that sound may be more crucial than the visual in how the whole affects the audience. Music, verbal chants, game and crowd noise are all part of how one experiences hockey, and this is usually part of its dramatic representation (note the sound effects in Tomson Highway's play *Dry Lips Oughta Move to Kapuskasing*). McKinley and Burns use voice-overs effectively when filming still shots. However, something special can be said for what Keats called art's "unheard melodies" in reference to a picture of a flute-player on an urn. The imagined sound can tease us out of thought and delight more exquisitely than our awkward reconstructions.[23]

Hence it isn't surprising, therefore, that this factor itself becomes part of the written record. David Gowdy entitled his 1989 hockey anthology *Riding on the Roar of the Crowd,* and he borrowed the expression from Marshall McLuhan, who was apparently quoting Maurice Richard: "Sport, as a popular art form, is not just self-expression, but is deeply and necessarily a means of interplay within an entire culture. Rocket Richard, the Canadien hockey player, used to comment on the poor acoustics of some arenas. He felt that the puck off his stick rode on the roar of the crowd."[24] This interplay is similar to Turner's two-way process of reflection and critique. When Hugh MacLennan wrote a 1954 article on hockey for *Holiday Magazine,* he paid special attention to the sounds of the ritualistic warm-up in a way that only a fan and sharp listener could:

> *With the warm-up come the familiar sounds—the ring and snick of skate blades and the special noises made by the puck. Against the goalies' pads*

the puck hits with a heavy thud: in close stickhandling it clucks: when it strikes the crossbar of the goal it gives out a loud clang; it makes a flat crack against the broad blade of the goalie's stick, and when it misses the goal and hits the boards it sends a reverberating bang through the whole arena.[25] [my emphasis]

The transference of sound into the written word paradoxically offers an artistic rendering to be savoured in the comforts of silence.

MacLennan's essay offers a number of insights into a 1954 NHL game at the Montreal Forum (i.e., on this night Gerry McNeil faces Terry Sawchuk), but MacLennan also makes it clear that this is not his first NHL game at the Forum. Despite the historical specificity, he also captures a timeless sense of hockey's elegance. MacLennan was not the only major writer to be commissioned or assigned in the 1950s to cover hockey in the hope that something profound may find its way into the record. William Faulkner's "An Innocent at Rinkside" (January 1955), which constitutes one of *SI*'s first treatments of ice hockey, is another such item, and seeing the MSG game through the eyes of an "innocent" often lends an aesthetic touch to what is overlooked and commonplace. Faulkner is struck by "the vacant ice" and then by the figures that move with so much "motion, speed" like "weightless bugs which run on the surface of stagnant pools"—an expression that echoes Eliot's Prufrock or maybe Conrad's Marlow.[26] These "larger-format" moments offset the player or team narratives that attempt to engage with specialized knowledge and statistics, the insider's information that overshoots popular interest. Commenting on Faulkner's hockey essay, Hamblin notes how the author finds something claustrophobic about the smoke-filled arena.[27]

But the popular writing on hockey (as with all sports) is all about insider information, usually served up with little documentation and poor indexing. Stan Fischler produced dozens of such books over the last thirty years, and now the role seems to have been taken up by Andrew Podnieks, who seems intent on matching the former's output.[28] Many publications seem designed merely to merchandise celebrity or capitalize on fan allegiance; the two longest-standing Canadian franchises have numerous books of all kinds devoted to them—the easy gift for Dad who just happens to be a Leafs or Habs fan. More substantial histories or biographies, incorporating cultural critiques and scholarly apparatus, have been published by Douglas Hunter and Stephen Brunt.[29] Brunt's *Searching for Bobby Orr* not only pits the Boston star against his agent, Eagleson, but also traces the history of the

NHL in the greater context of professional sport in North America—expansion westward, the founding of player associations, and collective bargaining. Similarly, *Gretzky's Tears* tells the story not only of one particular trade but of the attempt to sell ice hockey to the southern United States.

It is sometimes difficult to separate the wheat from the chaff. Don Cherry's first book *Grapes*[30] contains a certain raconteur charm, especially in the chapters about Eddie Shore, which probably owe much to Stan Fischler who had written on Shore previously. This raconteur charm is at the heart of male sports culture. It is the essential discourse of beer-league locker rooms; guys love to tell and hear entertaining stories about sports ("Did you hear the one about Yogi Berra?"). However, in the three subsequent Cherry books the charm starts to wear very thin. The stories lack substance and the books start to read like self-parodies. As for the *Coach's Corner* segment of HNIC, as much as one might want to bemoan the lack of depth in what is spoken, Cherry seems to understand two important yet simple truths about sports commentary and television: 1) controversy sells; and 2) what you see matters.[31]

The insider's reflective and critical commentary is well represented by Ken Dryden's *The Game,* which otherwise follows the quotidian account of a late 1970s Canadiens season with its routines and rhythms. There are some wonderful passages in this well-received book on goaltending, and I would have to say that my own personal favourite has to do with Dryden's pre-game superstitions, which have everything to do with trying to control the *un*controllable. However, Dryden's book has caused considerable confusion among hockey historians who have tried to match up Dryden's account with specific games. One never questions the essential truths, but it would have been nice to have a note about fictional licence. There are a number of studies of hockey's goaltenders, most of which fall into the popular or pictorial categories.[32] This past year has seen two more personal accounts—Clint Malarchuk's and Grant Fuhr's. Malarchuk, of course, is famous for having his carotid artery severed in a goalmouth scramble.

It is commonly suggested that goalies are different from other hockey players, moody individuals who must be a bit crazed to do what they do. Gary Genosko deconstructed an advertising campaign for a new skate that was based on this cliché.[33] The skates make the shooters so good that a number of top goaltenders have gone insane—something similar to McNeil's "crack-up." A more intellectual and literary exploration of a goalie's psychology is offered by Randall Maggs's poetry collection, *Night Work: The Sawchuk Poems,* which tries to capture something of the troubled goalie's career. As for a fictional account of a netminder, one can turn to the main character of Paul Quarrington's *Logan in Overtime*; the novel has its amusing moments but offers little insight into hockey's loneliest of positions.

One of the most memorable reviews of a hockey book was Mordecai Richler's praise for George Plimpton's *Open Net,* which documents Plimpton's experience as an undercover rookie goalie at a Boston Bruins training camp. Published in 1986, the review includes Richler's negative impression of literature on the sport, "that still unfortunately small shelf of literate hockey books."[34] A veritable avalanche of good and bad has followed. Richler admires how Plimpton captures the raconteur in Don Cherry and repeats a gem on the torturous nature of the position *à la* Jacques Plante: "Imagine yourself sitting in an office and you make an error of some kind.... All of a sudden, behind you a bright red light goes on, the walls collapse and there are eighteen thousand people shouting and jeering at you, calling you an imbecile and an idiot and a bum and throwing things at you, including garbage."[35]

My father often told his own version of the same ordeal. When a goalie makes a mistake, the opposing team usually scores. The play stops.[36] The red light and celebration of the opposition emphasize any subpar performance; this doesn't happen for the forward who fails to backcheck, or even the defenceman who neglects to cover a man in front. My father was self-conscious about this sense of public embarrassment and always talked about it later when we discussed the difficulties of playing the position. The spectacle of defeat that is the goaltender has been a favourite in sports photography (the easy, after-the-fact still), as seen in Larry Downing's picture entitled "The loneliness of the losing goalie"—a shot of Edmonton netminder Tommy Salo surrounded by the hats tossed on the ice in celebration of the scorer's hat trick.[37] Barkley's photo of my father skating away from a line of celebrating Leafs in the Final of 1951 (see fig. 18 and pp. 106–108) is another example.

My father also believed that there were no secrets to success, that luck always played a role and that there were always factors over which you had no control—a deflection, a screen, a jostle. The other aspect that he emphasized consistently was that the context meant everything. With a comfortable lead in a game or series or the standings, the pressure is not nearly as intense, and emotionally it is much easier to endure a sudden bad break. However, when there is more on the line, the pressure increases and more attention is paid to the goalie's every

THE HOCKEY SWEATER

move. McNeil's stress as the Habs goalie clearly exceeded what Plante would have to endure, and may have also been marginally worse than Durnan's. On the other hand, McNeil would also attribute the development of sharp reflexes to pressured situations. At least it was so for him—the greater the stakes, the better the performance.

Perhaps the best post-career interview my father gave was the one he did for Douglas Hunter when the latter was preparing his section of *A Breed Apart* on Jacques Plante. (Once again, my father comes up in the shadow of another figure.) Jacques, of course, had passed away in 1986, and so Hunter tried to get a sense of the goalie by talking to the man he replaced, Gerry McNeil. Everything my father is recorded as having said rings true. On the subject of his own self-criticism versus Plante's self-confidence, McNeil remarked, "A goal was never his fault—it was the defenceman's fault. It was a great way to go to sleep. I was the opposite. I would figure if I did it this way or that way, I could have stopped it."[38] On leaving the crease, he is quoted as saying, "[Plante] defied the principles. If I went out of the net, they got after me. With him, it was okay."[39] Finally, my father had a front-row seat to Plante's efforts to wear a face mask: "If I'd worn one . . . they would have sent me home."[40] I heard variations on these statements all through my life.

Moreover, there is also a definite nostalgic sensibility in much of the writing on hockey, including some of Roy MacGregor's work and Mordecai Richler's Barney Panofsky.[41] A common theme is that the game has somehow been corrupted over time, and this impression smacks with romantic or sentimental nostalgia that needs to be deconstructed. There is a fair amount of writing that sees hockey as a means of tracing family history, like David Adam Richards's *Hockey Dreams,* a text that wonderfully brings to life the significance of the sport for the average boy growing up in small-town northern New Brunswick.[42] Again, the liminal moments are emphasized; hence the extended debate on the birthplace of hockey and all the rhetoric about the death of hockey (not dead but more urban, more organized, and more expensive). Various claims for the origins of hockey continue to play out and are well documented in the latest book on this subject, Jean-Patrice Martel's *On the Origin of Hockey.*[43] Playing within a game-model itself, analysts are not content with one unified history of the sport—there can only be one winner, one birthplace. At the other end, there have been two different analyses of our national game that are entitled "The Death of Hockey."[44] Given the sport's ongoing popularity in Canada and Europe (and now the US), we might, in the spirit of Mark Twain, characterize these reports as "premature."

If conflict can be said to be integral to an engaging narrative, then the same is true for sport itself. In 1961 Roland Barthes wrote the text to a film entitled, *Le sport et les hommes,* an NFB project with Quebec writer Hubert Aquin. The leitmotif of the film became, *Qu'est-ce que le sport?*/What Is Sport? Barthes's answer seems to be conflict, which can become spectacular as it is suggested in the opening sentences:

> *Of all sports-loving countries, Canada is one of the most often frozen, yet of all 'pedestrian' sports ice hockey is the fastest: sport is this specific power to transform each thing into its opposite. And it is in this renewed miracle that a whole country participates, by its crowds, its press, radio, television: behind the scenes, before the combat, however fierce, there is the physical relation of a country and its inhabitants.*[45]

Out of the dead of winter is born the passionate sport of hockey, and not just for participants but for a whole country.

It is commonplace to think of hockey as part of the Canadian national identity, something that actually crosses the French-English-Aboriginal divides. In a *Globe and Mail* review article, Bruce Dowbiggin poses the question, "How has this unique symbiosis of sport (i.e., hockey) and psyche (Canadian nationalism) been reflected in the literature?"[46] Richards's memoir points to how hockey serves as a factor in constructing individual, regional (i.e., the Miramichi), and national identities. As players mark their lives by the sport, so do communities associate themselves with local junior teams.

A related topic, as far as Canada is concerned, is the *perceived* take-over of professional hockey by American or corporate interests or how the purity of the sport has been lost to the entertainment industry. "When Gretzky went to LA / My whole nation trembled / Like hot water in a tea cup when a train goes by," writes the poet John B. Lee.[47] The truth is that American interests have always dominated professional hockey on this continent. Furthermore, John B. Lee is just one of many poets who have embraced the game since Al Purdy first did so in the 1960s. Stephen Scriver, Robert Harrison, and Matt Robinson all have collections devoted to hockey.[48] Since we cannot do better than mention a few of these works, interested parties would do well to begin with Jason Blake's wide-ranging, critical study *Canadian Hockey Literature*.

It is not surprising that Canadian playwrights would use the sport to represent a political struggle much larger than a game. In Rick Salutin's play *Les Canadiens,* hockey is a structural metaphor depicting the history of French-English tension. Tomson Highway's powerful and evocative *Dry Lips Oughta Move to Kapuskasing* depicts the formation of a women's hockey team, the Wasy Wailerettes, that is representative of the dignity and strength in the struggle of any marginalized group (gays, Aboriginals) against a dominant power.[49] The David and Goliath myth (or Darlene and Goliath) drives much of the dramatic engagement of sports literature.

While the connection between sport and nationalism goes back to the ancient Greeks, hockey, in particular for North Americans, has provided moments of national pride (e.g., wins over the Soviets by Canada in 1972 and the US in 1980). Sportswriters like to distinguish between North American and European styles, even though the European leagues now include many North Americans and vice versa. Bobby Clarke's famous slash to the ankle of Valeri Kharlamov, which took the Russian star out of the '72 series, seemed to solidify the "rough" image of the Canadian game.

Then there are a slew of conferences (both academic and professional) that address the culture surrounding hockey and the game itself. I have only touched on some of the better literary examples of this festival, but there is so much more—the songs, the films, the TV shows, and the artwork (visual, installation, etc.). I actually try to cover all of these subgroups in the class I teach in sports culture, and it all spills over into popular media. For at least a decade advertising has hammered home the association of beer and hockey in the Canadian identity.

Among other general themes or topics is the long-standing issue of violence in hockey. As David McGimpsey argued almost twenty years ago, hockey's image as a violent sport is probably at the root of why the Canadian literary and academic community has not embraced it as the literary and academic community did baseball in the United States.[50] The McSorley-Brashear and Bertuzzi-Moore incidents gave rise to a plethora of editorials on the "state" of the game and what should be done to encourage skilled players rather than goons. The representations of violence that surface repeatedly in fiction and poetry no doubt contribute to this image; that the image may be deserved perhaps explains why other writers attempt to counter it with sentimental images of pond shinny.

There is some indication that things have changed since McGimpsey's 1997 article, that the literary community is now more accepting of hockey literature—its quality as well as its quantity. In March 2008, Paul Quarrington's *King Leary* would win the 2008 CBC Canada Reads competition hosted by Jian Ghomeshi; it was picked over works by Mavis Gallant and Timothy Findley. First published in 1987, *King Leary* was only known to those already familiar with the literature that deals with Canada's national sport. Ghomeshi, who is now known for his own brand of violent recreation, used the "contest" playdown format (something similar to the playoffs of sport) to initiate discussion about what makes good art. Quarrington's novel is roughly based on the life of King Clancy and does a credible job of recreating the nostalgic engagement with bygone era (i.e., professional hockey in the first half of the twentieth century).[51]

Now that hockey novels aren't automatically dismissed as not being serious fiction more attention may be given to those published in the last decade that have attempted to capture a quintessential *Canadianness* with a hockey story. The one that I personally find does the best job of this is Robert Sedlack's *The Horn of a Lamb,* a wonderfully moving story about a man who suffers a serious brain injury as a junior player.[52] Not only does Fred Pickle manage to carry on living with a strong sense of personal dignity and charm, he also succeeds in registering his profound protest against the move of the Winnipeg Jets to the American south. Now that the Jets are back, one wonders if Sedlack will produce a sequel. Despite the uplifting comic sensibility of *The Horn of a Lamb,* Sedlack reminds us that the excitement of hockey is linked to the fact that it can be a dangerous and violent game. Of course, this is a commonplace observation in hockey literature, and debates over the appropriate policy for monitoring the physical aspect of the game remain a perennial fascination with hockey journalists.

Periodic violence erupts naturally out of another aspect of our national sport: toughness—and my father was always clear on what he thought true toughness was: the ability to take a hit. At this point in our discussion Doug Harvey's name would often come up. "Some guys coming into the league didn't know that Harvey had been a Canadian Champion Boxer in the navy. If they made the mistake of taking on Harvey, they weren't apt to repeat it." He admired how Harvey never lost his composure and how he insisted on settling scores himself. He remembers how one night Harvey was given a dirty hit by a Bruin late in the first period. During the intermission Doug was slumped over in pain. A few of the guys offered to "take out" the culprit, but Harvey was adamant, "No, leave him for me." Nothing happened until the third period. Then the Bruin in question was going around the Canadiens' net with the puck; my father watched him disappear on the right and expected the play to come out on the left. However, nobody came out the other side. After a second or two, my father took a quick glance behind; Harvey was slowly skating away and the Bruin lay in a heap.

THE HOCKEY SWEATER

All the great goal-scorers of my father's era—Howe, Richard, and Lindsay—and of the next generation—Hull, Esposito, and Bathgate—fought their own fights. Although there were always a few goons in the league, my father played before it was standard practice to have so-called tough guys protect the so-called skilled players: for every Gretzky, a Semenko. The skilled players were tough players; they had to be. The movement toward specialized roles (certain players are expected to score, others, to fight) had a distorting effect on the game. With their staged fights and what some naively refer to as the "code," the goons were taking hockey in the direction of professional wrestling; fortunately, they seem to be disappearing. The true hockey fan wants to see the skilled players, as evidenced by the popularity of the Olympics. It is sad but true that there was a popular subgenre of hockey literature devoted to "Bad Boys"; several instalments under this title appeared in the 1990s. Fortunately, we have moved beyond the naive glorification of the hockey goon (despite the apparent commercial success of the film *Goon*) and can be thankful for the Pulitzer Prize journalism of John Branch, whose book *Boy on Ice* (2014) recounts the decline and tragic death of Derek Boogaard.[53]

Professional hockey also has image problems with unscrupulous or corrupt owners and agents, who may now merit the title of the sport's new Bad Boys. The "exposure" commentaries on such figures constitute another part of the negative narrative (at their extreme, closer to a demonization) that offsets the idealization of shinny or quality time with Dad (e.g., part of this very book) or "Canada's Game." There is an ugly redneck streak in NHL ownership that goes back to the racism of my father's day and lived on in people like Harold Ballard. There are also agents, like Alan Eagleson, who might be accused of having taken advantage of the naïveté of players. The case of Mike Danton and his relationship with David Frost suggests that the exploitation of youth and parents is a real danger in junior hockey.[54] The lure of "making it to the NHL" can make any unsuspecting person vulnerable, and of course, the real cancer in all this business is due to the gargantuan sums of money that are at play.

Sexual abuse is another sore on the sport. Here are the really *bad* Bad Boys of hockey. Incidents of rape (players of young women, coaches of players, etc.) have received national attention and certainly do not help hockey's image. Whether this is more of a problem in hockey as opposed to other sports is an open question. However, as far as the spectre of evil is concerned, there is plenty to offset the more romantic associations that many Canadians have with hockey.

Other controversial topics may be less sensational but more prominent in how they affect young players and involve fundamental rights. Should girls have the option to play on boys' teams? Are gay young men welcome in the hockey dressing room? What can be done to make the sport more affordable for more young people? Hockey may be the most expensive sport after equestrian competitions or motor-racing. In addition to the costly equipment that must constantly be replaced as children grow bigger, there are ice rentals and away tournaments. Participation is great, but forcing our youth to play year-round ("because that is the only way to excel against others") may be detrimental. There was a time when one put one's skates away in the spring and explored other sports, a time when one's love of hockey was experienced anew every fall.

Consequently, my father, like many players from his era, spent a lot of time answering questions about the state of hockey today as opposed to the days of yore. It is easy to see how the game has changed: players are bigger; they shoot harder; the equipment is better; the game is mass-marketed; women are now playing; professional players are well represented by the NHLPA and the Hockey Players Association (for AHL and ECHL players); and so on. The key question is whether hockey has changed for the better or worse. While there are improvements one can point to (technical and financial, although "big" money also creates other problems), the spirit of the game remains the same (speed, finesse, collision).

Mac never pushed his own sons to be goalies. Ron agreed to put on the gear once, and we have a picture of him in an Amerks uniform kicking out a shot. But he showed no interest in goaltending, or in hockey for that matter. I started as a goalie but quickly found that I enjoyed being a skater more, and so I played defence. I still play defence, where one's reaction time is so important, and where special relationships develop between goalie and defensive partner. What I found magical about hockey as a youth, what truly distinguished the game from all others, was the magic of skating, of being able to move so quickly and smoothly. Those sharp crossover strokes, the tight turns and skilful pivots front to back to front. I still remember how impressed I was with Jimmy Galbraith's backward crossovers when I saw him play as an Oldtimer. Add to this magical motion a puck that can itself travel over one hundred miles per hour, the ability to control that puck at the end of a stick, the art and socialization of teamwork—and the result is that wonderful game of winter. And now with roller hockey, the same magic can be experienced on wheels in sunny California (ice-skaters beware the stopping technique of in-line skates). There is an excitement about the speed of hockey that thrills and is accentuated by the danger of body contact or the cannonading shot, or, as captured in the melodic voice of Jane Siberry, the "breakaway, breakaway, breakaway".[55] Like many Canadians I love this game, and watching it isn't bad either.

It hasn't been a continual love affair. Because hockey is played with a stick and sometimes out-of-control egos, it will have its violent outbursts. As a teenager, I noticed that the girls I was becoming interested in were not interested in hockey as much as they were in peace and love. When I turned away from hockey and switched to basketball at the age of fourteen, my father had no comment. There was no need to live out his dream through his offspring. However, Mac was happy to see his first grandson, David, play goal; a few years later he enjoyed watching his second grandson, Nicholas McIntyre, play forward. He paid equal attention to the athletic exploits of his granddaughters. The tape that was left in his VCR was of Kathleen winning a provincial basketball championship; the screen saver on his computer featured Vanessa after placing first in a cheerleading competition. On his den wall was a picture of Tricia running the last leg of the 100 × 4 relay.

Gerry wore his Stanley Cup ring proudly, and appreciated the interest I took in researching his career. Soon I knew more about specific games and statistics than my father, and I'd kid him about it: "Dad, you must have witnessed Elmer Ferguson and Dink Carroll murder somebody, because I cannot believe how much they praised you in their columns" (fig. 32). Reading drafts of the first few chapters, he approved of this book and was a good proofreader ("It's *Paul* Bibeault; not Phil").

Many of the individuals I would love to have interviewed were no longer available; they had either passed away or had recollections that were extremely fuzzy. However, I do remember my father getting me to phone Elmer Lach, who was there from the beginning and who remained an active friend. He confirmed what he had said at the time about scoring the Cup winner in overtime in 1953: "I didn't see the puck go in the net." He then started making some general remarks. "You know it was a real tough series that went seven games."

I suspected he had confused the '52 Semifinal with the Final of '53, which was only five games, and I made the mistake of suggesting as much. "Yes, Elmer, I think you might be thinking of the previous playoff year."

There was this silence on the other end followed by a sharply worded question: "Were you there? I was f___ing there! I don't think you were even born yet."

Fig. 32 My father and I pose for a picture in the kitchen. Family photo, circa 2001. Photo courtesy of the author.

I had to admit that this fundamental truth was on his side. I listened while he cursed me for asking for his opinion only to challenge what he said.

I could see my father out of the corner of my eye; he could sense that something had gone wrong. When I was able to hang up, he simply said, "I forgot to warn you that you don't want to get on Elmer's bad side because he can really strip a piece off of you."

"Thanks Dad."

My father's only complaint about my manuscript was the overuse of the name McNeil—he wasn't comfortable being the centre of attention. Asked about what accomplishment made him most proud, he said there wasn't one but that he was proud his children had done well.

I remember my father always being on the lookout for schemes designed to dupe him, and on occasion he could combine this sharpness with his love of pranks. Near the end of his life, Mac received a package in the mail containing several poorly reproduced pictures of the old Forum. The letter enclosed purported to be from some grandmother with an odd name who claimed to want to give her thirteen grandchildren a token of her love—the token would be a picture of the old Forum autographed by a member of the Canadiens. The letter contained careful instructions not to personalize the autograph—just an autograph, please, for all fifteen grandchildren. My father counted, and

THE HOCKEY SWEATER

there were as many as twenty pictures in the package. Mac was aware enough to sense something funny about the request; he was convinced that "grandma" was really some charlatan selling hockey memorabilia on eBay. So he took the time to write on each picture with his blue-ink pen (special for signing pictures), "You have a nice grandma," and gleefully sent the pictures back in the stamped envelope.

Mac could be happy with little—watching the planes fly over Lac Saint-Louis from his apartment window, his indoor parking space, his morning newspaper. One of his last hockey thrills occurred in March 2004 when Dave Stubbs arranged a meeting between him and the then-current Canadiens goalie, José Théodore, the purpose of which was to give the two a chance to compare equipment a half century apart. David and Alanna Barkely drove to Ottawa with the pads and spent the day with their grandfather. Théodore felt the wafer-thin leather of my father's chest protector in amazement, "I wouldn't play road hockey in this." McNeil's pads were at least two inches narrower, shorter, and considerably heavier, especially when they were wet, which was all the time from October to April. The story ran in *The Gazette* and was picked up by the *National Post*.[56] It featured a picture of Gerry sitting with José in the Canadiens dressing room. While the family was pleased to read the story, especially Dave Stubbs's final sentence ("It matters little that the birthdays of two men are separated by 50 years when their careers are joined by one sweater"), they would also express concern at how much weight Gerry seemed to have lost.

Gerry meantime was making arrangements to move himself and Teacy to an apartment complex that provided some nursing care. Stricken with Parkinson's, Teacy was having trouble getting around and Gerry felt he couldn't leave her alone. He wasn't able to play much golf. Around Christmas 2003 he started coughing up blood (he should have "seen this coming"). The years of smoking had finally gotten to his lungs, but he kept it to himself, wanting to avoid the hospital as long as possible. He complained about forgetting things.

"Me too," I would respond, trying to make him relax. I assured him that I'd help with the move in July. "By the way, do you remember that big guy who played defence for Chicago, Number Four, I think? He had some kind of animal nickname."

Pause.

"Moose Vasko. There's a lot to move or get rid of."

And so there was.

On April 17th he enjoyed celebrating his 78th birthday with his family; Karen brought lobsters. The night the "Richard: The Legend" exhibit first opened at the then Museum of Civilization was the night we knew something was seriously wrong with Dad. He and the usual group of Rocket-era teammates were invited to the opening by the curator, Sheldon Posner. Mac and Teacy planned to drive up to Ottawa with the Mosdells. Despite getting lost occasionally, my father was a dependable driver. However, on this April day he got off the main highway and took hours to get back on the right road. When they finally did pull into the Museum's underground parking garage, the opening had just finished and everybody was going home. Nothing to do but get back in the car and hope for a better return to Montreal. Again, I tried to reassure my father that navigating the downtown area of the nation's capital was challenging enough for anybody, but it was clear that he felt the defeat ("poor Kenny and Lorraine, stuck in that car for hours") and knew that circumstances were closing in. A few days later, he would fall in a parking lot. Unable to walk, he could not avoid the hospital any longer. What started out as lung cancer had spread to his brain. Mac spent the last weeks of his life at Saint-Luc's hospital in Montreal. He received calls (one from Gordie Howe) and visits from friends and family.

The brain tumour was in the frontal lobe. It caused him to feel euphoric, which was a blessing, and it robbed him of his short-term memory, which was probably good for him but hard on us. Typically, he would forget about his "terminal" condition and say something upbeat like, "As soon as I get out of here, I'll call and get us a tee time." I would have to remind him that he was dying and there would be no more tee-offs. It's bad enough to see a loved one get that news once, but we had to see my father relive it daily as he forgot what was said to him the day before. My mother's Parkinson's dementia also robbed her of her short-term memory; so we would have to remind her of my father's terminal condition as well. My parents had made it to their late 70s without any major medical problems, but that streak had ended.

Despite being in pain, Gerry was only concerned about Teacy and had nothing but praise for his caregivers. Feeling particularly euphoric one day, he asked the nurse to send "his compliments to the chef"! Assuming he was being sarcastic, the nurse glared back at him. Later she realized that my father was serious and apologized. There was a problem with the reception on his bedside television, so I brought him an old, scuffed-up transistor radio from home. At least he could listen to baseball games in the evening, and later he told me that he found it relaxing. It was fitting that in terms of media we had retreated to radio.

My father was rather cynical, a big believer in conspiracy theories. As a child, I remember begging him to send away for a toy advertised on the back of a cereal box, and he would just say that "it was all a racket," that what I'd actually be sent would be about one one-hundredth the size of the picture. He was right. As I sat with him in Saint-Luc's, I thought that he was right about the big picture as well. Love brings us into the world, and we have no control over it. Then love makes hostages of us all, and we can't control that either. It certainly feels like a conspiracy.

Since Mac had been looking after Teacy, Teacy had to be moved into a new home when he was hospitalized. A week later she fell down the stairs, and all I could think about was that if Gerry had been there he would have made sure to be right behind her. He would have had it covered. Teacy's condition deteriorated in another Montreal hospital. For a couple who had been together since the age of twelve, the separation was hard. They would manage a few phone calls but did not see each other again.

I wish I could say that Mac didn't suffer; he did. One day had been particularly bad, and as I was leaving he held my hand again and said, "Thanks for coming." It seemed grotesquely funny at the time, and he sensed this and managed a smile before adding, "I really mean it." Since they ended up being the last words I would ever hear my father say, I have decided to remember them in the greatest possible sense— as in, "I'm glad I got something out of my 'DID NOT PLAY' season." Some months later I discovered that something very similar was said by Jonathan Franzen's dying father.[57] The coincidence is indicative that such absurd utterances are probably common. May the grateful be fast-tracked to heaven.

On the morning of June 17th, Shannon called the rest of the children to gather at the hospital. I arrived next, then Donna and finally Karen, the daughter born on the day of the Barilko goal. The vigil continued all afternoon and through the evening. Mac had been pumped up with painkillers. Donna and Karen took turns carefully wiping their father's brow with a cool face cloth. Midnight came; a hush seemed to fall on René-Lévesque Boulevard. About twenty-five minutes later, in the balmy quiet of a Montreal summer night, my father died.

Dave Stubbs wrote two tributes for Gerry, the second and more personal carries the subheading, "'He never got the credit he deserved,' says former teammate Bernie Geoffrion." Perhaps, but those who were close to him knew he was content with what life had given him. One person who attended the funeral was Gerry Courteau, McNeil's neighbour from 11th Street in Limoilou and senior hockey opponent. Allan Schofield from the Saint-Fidèle bantam team was there and remembered his childhood friend as an active boy. *Les Canadiens sont là*: Dickie Moore, Butch Bouchard, Ken Mosdell, and Léo Gravelle. From the Royals: Gerry Plamondon, Tod Campeau, Howard "Rip" Riopelle. On this day, Mac the prankster, was remembered as a loving father and husband, and a goalie you could count on to be his best when it mattered most.

1   Roy Macskimming, *Gordie: A Hockey Legend* (Vancouver: Greystone, 1994), 128.

2   Gordie Howe, *Mr. Hockey: Gordie Howe, My Story* (Toronto: Viking, 2014), 125.

3   Michael Farber, "Kid Glove," *Sports Illustrated*, Oct. 6, 1997: 81.

4   "Complete NHL Statistics," Quanthockey, accessed May 6, 2015, http://www.quanthockey.com/nhl/records/nhl-goalies-all-time-playoff-goals-against-average-leaders.html.

5   Wayne Johnston, *The Divine Ryans* (Reprint Toronto: Vintage, 1998), 152.

6   I had the opportunity to ask Wayne Johnston if the picture really existed after a reading he gave at Frog Hollow Books in Halifax (Sept. 22, 1999). He claimed that it did, but I have never seen it.

7   Johnston, *Divine Ryans*, 152.

8   I cannot be absolutely certain, but I believe this was Game Two of the 1964–65 Semifinal.

9   Bobby Hull related this story to John Kruspe in February 2006.

10 This story is told in Bruce Dowbiggin, *The Defense Never Rests* (Toronto: Harper-Collins, 1993).

11 See Jacques Beauchamp, "Gerry McNeil demeure actif," *Montréal-Matin*, Dec. 15, 1966, 70; Roland Sabourin, "McNeil: Un pro hors pair durant toute sa carrière," *Le Soleil* (Quebec City), Dec. 12, 1970, 33; Ed Conrad "Sudden Death Playoff Hockey Old Hat to Canadiens," *Gazette* (Montreal), Apr. 26, 1976, 14; Marc de Foy, "Gerry McNeil: Le hockey des années 50, c'était 'ben l'fun.'" *Dimanche* (Quebec City), Feb. 15, 1976, 34–35; Paul Patton, "Where Are They Now? Gerry McNeil, Hockey," *Globe and Mail*, Mar. 26, 1986, D5; Jean-Paul Sarault, "Vous souvenez-vous de Gerry McNeil?" *Journal de Montréal*, Feb. 26, 1986, 84; Jacques Beauchamp, "McNeil Was Penny of '51," *Sunday Express*, Apr. 15, 1984, 34; Jacques Arteau, "Gerry McNeil," *Le Soleil* (Quebec City), June 11, 1993, S3; Dave Stubbs, "McNeil's Win Only Part of Story," *Gazette* (Montreal), May 7, 2002, E1, 3; and "A Slice of Netminding History," *Gazette* (Montreal), Mar. 27, 2004, front page, A2–A3.

12 See Neil Stevens, "No Reunion Now for Habs of '50s," *Gazette* (Montreal), May 20, 2000, G2.

13 Richard's death and funeral were front page news in all Canadian daily papers at the end of May 2000. It would be pointless to try and list all stories, but the two English-French Montreal dailies ran "Maurice Richard: August 4, 1921 – May 27, 2000," *Gazette* (Montreal), May 31, 2000, Special Section, G1–G10; "Requiem for Rocket," *Gazette* (Montreal), June 1, 2000, 1, A8, A9, B3, D1, and D5; and "Merci,

Maurice: Des obsèques empreintes de dignité, d'émotion et de respect," *La Presse* (Montreal), June 1, 2000, A1–A9.

14 The complete group consisted of Gerry McNeil, Ken Reardon, Dickie Moore, Jean Béliveau, Butch Bouchard, Ken Mosdell, Elmer Lach, and Henri ("The Pocket-Rocket") Richard.

15 McNeil, of course, was bilingual, but had sent his children (myself included) to English schools.

16 Lewis Mumford, "Sport and the 'Bitch-goddess,'" in *The Sporting Spirit: Athletes in Literature and Life,* ed. Robert J. Higgs and Neil D. Isaacs (New York: Harcourt Brace Jovanovich, 1977), 260.

17 Mumford, "Sport and the 'Bitch-goddess,'" in Higgs and Isaacs *Sporting Spirit,* 262, 263.

18 Walter Benjamin, *The Work of Art in the Age of Its Technological Reproducibility, and Other Writings on Media,* ed. Michael W. Jennings, Brigid Doherty, and Thomas Y. Levin; trans. Edmund Jephcott, Rodney Livingstone, Howard Eiland, and others (Cambridge: Belknap Press, Harvard UP, 2008), 22.

19 Benjamin, *Work of Art,* 23.

20 Tom McSorley, "Of Time and Space and Hockey: An Imaginary Conversation," in *Pop Can: Popular Culture in Canada,* ed. Marlene Van Luven and Priscilla L. Walton (Scarborough: Prentice-Hall, 1999), 153.

21 My purpose is not to enumerate examples here, but I will mention what remains one of the most exhaustive: Joseph Romain and Dan Diamond, *The Pictorial History of Hockey* (Greenwich, Ct.: Bison Books, 1987), which just so happens to have two sections devoted to goalies—pp. 32–35, 68–73.

22 Michael McKinley, *Hockey: A People's History* (Toronto: McClelland & Stewart, 2006).

23 The first few episodes of *Hockey: A People's History* are full of dramatic re-enactments of players or events from the late nineteenth or early twentieth centuries when actual film footage is non-existent. Simulation rules.

24 This passage forms the epigraph of Gowdy's anthology.

25 Hugh MacLennan, "Fury on Ice," in *Riding on the Roar of the Crowd* (Toronto: Macmillan, 1989), 5.

26 William Faulkner, "An Innocent at Rinkside," in *The Sporting Spirit: Athletes in Literature and Life,* ed. Robert J. Higgs and Neil D. Isaacs (New York: Harcourt Brace Jovanovich, 1977), 164. Ironically, given the motion-stillness paradox, the statement sounds like an echo of Eliot's "patient etherised" or maybe Conrad's "the stillness of an implacable force brooding over an inscrutable intention."

27 Robert Hamblin, "Homo Agonistes, or, William Faulkner as Sportswriter," *Aethlon: The Journal of Sport Literature* 13, no. 2 (1996): 17.

28 One also thinks of Brian McFarlane and Roy MacGregor, both of whom published several hockey books.

29 For an example of Douglas Hunter's best research, see *War Games: Conn Smythe and Hockey's Fighting Men* (Toronto: Viking, 1996).

30 Don Cherry's first book *Grapes* (1980).

31 Cherry is famous for his outrageously colourful suits and controversial comments.

32 The best of these all appeared in the same year; see Denis Brodeur, text by Daniel Daignault, *Goalies: Guardians of the Net* (Toronto: Key Porter, 1995); Douglas Hunter, *A Breed Apart: An Illustrated History of Goaltending* (Toronto: Penguin, 1995); and Dick Irvin [Jr.], *In the Crease: Goaltenders Look at Life Inside the NHL* (Toronto: McClelland & Stewart, 1995).

33 Gary Genosko, "Hockey and Culture," in *Pop Can: Popular Culture in Canada*, eds. Lynne Van Luven and Priscilla L. Walton (Scarborough: Prentice-Hall, 1999), 147–48.

34 Mordecai Richler, "Cheap Skates," reprinted in *Dispatches from the Sporting Life* (Toronto: Knopf, 2002), 147.

35 Richler, "Cheap Skates," 146.

36 See George Beahon, "In This Corner," *Rochester Democrat and Chronicle*, Nov. 7, 1957, 44.

37 See *Art of Sport*, 45.

38 Douglas Hunter, *A Breed Apart*, quoted in *Words on Ice: A Collection of Hockey Prose*, ed. Michael P. J. Kennedy (Toronto: Key Porter Books, 2003), 144.

39 Hunter, *A Breed Apart*, in Kennedy *Words on Ice*, 145.

40 Hunter, *A Breed Apart*, in Kennedy *Words on Ice*, 146.

41 Mordecai Richler, *Barney's Version* (Toronto: Knopf, 1997). As a subject in the novel, hockey—and the Montreal Canadiens team in particular—is one of the protagonist's enthusiasms. It is probably safe to assume that more Canadians are connected to sports as spectators rather than participants.

42 David Adams Richards, *Hockey Dreams: Memories of a Man Who Couldn't Play* (Reprint Toronto: Anchor, 1997).

43 See Carl Gidén, Patrick Houda, and Jean-Patrice Martel, *On the Origin of Hockey* (n.p.: Hockey Origin Publishing, 2014).

44 Bruce Kidd and John Macfarlane, *The Death of Hockey* (Toronto: New Press, 1972) and Jeff Klein and Karl-Eric Reif, *The Death of Hockey* (Toronto: Macmillan, 1998).

45 Roland Barthes, *What Is Sport?* trans. Richard Howard (New Haven: Yale University Press, 2007), 45.

46 Bruce Dowbiggin, "Hockey on Ice," *Globe and Mail*, Sept. 18, 2004, D27. This article appeared on the heels of the 2004 lockout. Annual review articles or general discussions about hockey and the Canadian identity are published at a rate of about one per year in *The Globe and Mail*.

47 John B. Lee, *The Hockey Player Sonnets* (Waterloo, Ont.: Penumbra Press, 1991), 36.

48 For another collection of hockey poetry, see Richard Harrison, *Hero of the Play* (Toronto: Wolsak and Wynn, 1994). There is also a hockey poetry anthology, see ed. Michael P. J. Kennedy, *Going Top Shelf: An Anthology of Canadian Hockey Poetry* (Vancouver: Heritage House, 2005); and a lengthy review article of hockey poetry, see Rob Winger, "'This Combination of Ballet and Murder': Some Thoughts on Hockey Poetry in Canada," *ARC: Canada's National Poetry Magazine* Winter 2004: 60–66, feature article.

49 As a gay Cree, Tomson Highways knows something about marginalization. Genosko appears keen on *Dry Lips* as a literary work that seeks plurality or various subjectivities within hockey culture. See Genosko, "Hockey and Culture," 141, 143. For a good analysis of the politics in women's hockey, see Nancy Theberge, *Higher Goals: Women's Ice Hockey and the Politics of Gender* (Albany: SUNY, 2000).

50 David McGimpsey, "'Rock 'em, Sock 'em, *Terre de Nos Aieux*: Legends of Hockey, Canadian Nationalism and Television Violence," *Aethlon: Journal of Sport Literature* 14, no. 2 (1997): 21–33. For a general history of violence in hockey, see Lawrence Scanlan, *Grace Under Fire: The State of Our Sweet and Savage Game* (Toronto: Penguin, 2002).

51 It must be said that for a novel that tries to recreate another historical period, it contains some problematic elements. Maple Leaf Gardens was erected in 1930 (not 1947), and somebody travelling from Ottawa to New York in 1925 would not have gone by plane. See Paul Quarrington, *King Leary* (Reprint Toronto: Anchor, 2007), 121, 154. On the other hand, Quarrington is accurate with other details like the use of the term "goaler" rather than "goalie" (see p. 66).

52 Robert Sedlack, *The Horn of a Lamb* (Toronto: Anchor, 2004). Other notable works include Richard B. Wright's *The Age of Longing* (Toronto: HarperCollins, 1995), Mark Anthony Jarman, *Salvage King, Ya! A Herky-Jerky Picaresque* (Vancouver: Anvil, 1997), and Bill Gaston, *The Good Body* (Vancouver: Raincoast, 2004).

53 John Branch, *Boy on Ice: The Life and Death of Derek Boogaard* (Toronto: HarperCollins, 2014).

54 Mike Danton was convicted for his involvement in a murder-for-hire plot against his former agent David Frost and sentenced to seven and a half years in prison. Frost, who was a player agent, has been accused of exercising excessive influence over some junior players and their families.

55 Jane Siberry, "Hockey" by Jane Siberry on *Bound by the Beauty,* Duke Street Records, originally released Sept. 8, 1989.

56 Dave Stubbs, "A Slice Of Netminding History," *Gazette* (Montreal), Mar. 27, 2004, 1, A2–A3; and "Bruise Brothers: He Played his Last NHL Game 47 Winters Ago, but Former Canadiens' Goalie Gerry McNeil Shares a Special Bond with José Theodore," *National Post,* Mar. 27, 2004, A17.

57 "Thank you for coming. I appreciate your taking the time to see me." Quoted by Jonathan Franzen, "My Father's Brain," in *How to Be Alone* (Toronto: HarperCollins, 2003), 32.

Epilogue

My father is gone, but a ghostly presence lingers in the physical and electronic debris that remains. A few months after he died, my younger sister was in Ottawa for her son's hockey tournament and took in the Maurice Richard exhibit at the then Museum of Civilization. Suddenly, in the middle of the displays, she heard my father's voice and turned to see him on a video screen describing the Rocket's uncanny ability to position himself between the defender and the puck. It was a recorded interview with the curator of the exhibit, Sheldon Posner, made in the fall of 2003. Posner did the interview in an attempt to learn something about Richard, and from that perspective I don't think it was all that useful. What did my father remember about the so-called greatest goal against Boston in the Semifinal of 1952? Nothing. You had to admire his refusal to make up a story or detail to satisfy the demand. I do remember that in one of his Richard interviews he did convey how the Rocket liked to lead his teammates. If you weren't playing up to his expectations, he had a way of eyeing you in the corridor that said more than any words. Done in the fall of 2003, the Posner interview is a wonderful record of my father in his last year. My siblings and I found it a fitting coincidence that after my father's death the NHL suspended play for a season.

It is now over a decade later. My father was right, as my siblings discovered: there was a lot of stuff, including what might be called hockey memorabilia. The most important were two boxes of scrapbooks, photographs, and miscellaneous items. I used these extensively to complete this manuscript. The scrapbooks, which were kept by my mother, I mused over for hours. (I remember looking at them with my parents periodically when I was growing up.) And so began the long process of consulting microfilm of a number of these newspapers to fill in the gaps. Lastly, I communicated with my father's friends or acquaintances about his life in hockey, at least I tried with those who were still alive.

Collecting certain items in this debris that was part of my father's life has become an issue with me. It began innocently enough when I started obtaining all of his hockey cards on eBay. Then in the spring of 2005, Classic Collections had what it referred to as a "mini auction" of hockey memorabilia. There was nothing of high value as there was for Richard or Béliveau, but rather a piling together of several modest collections and miscellaneous things. There were fifteen items in the Gerry McNeil category, and I recognized many of them from the house. Shannon and I had selected the precious consignment articles and left the rest for my brother to dispose of. Lot number 269 took me quite by surprise: it was reported to be Gerry McNeil's personal scrapbook. I knew it wasn't, because I had those. The only explanation was that somebody else unknown to me and my immediate family kept a scrapbook on Mac, and this one seemed to be even more complete than his own, at least as far as the early years were concerned.

As mentioned in Chapter 2, my father won the Schaefer Player-of-the-Week in his NHL debut. The prize, not surprisingly, took the form of a pewter beer mug. I remembered seeing it around the house as a child—on display in the rec room to be exact. Years later when my parents had moved into a condo, it went missing. Then around 2010, I noticed that it was for sale in one of the many Classic online auctions, one half of a pair of such mugs (the other had been awarded to my father's teammate and friend Kenny Mosdell). (My father and Kenny may well have sold their mugs.) In any case, I made a bid and eventually won the lot. This gave me the opportunity of contacting Lorraine Mosdell, who was still very much alive and about to go on a Caribbean cruise. She gave me the address of her son, who was living in Florida. We exchanged some emails and Kenny's mug was back with his family in time for Father's Day, when it would be hoisted in tribute. As for mine, I use it every Sunday when I have my single beer for the week and pause to remember my father and his hockey past. It serves as a functioning relic, so to speak.

I continue to watch the memorabilia auctions, ready to try and wrestle back more pieces of my father's career. Unfortunately, I missed out what was described as one of his sticks, but when a second became available I managed to retrieve it. It has "McNeil" printed on the shaft and it looks authentic, but I guess there is no way to know for sure. The lot information correctly identifies it as CCM, insofar as I have matched up the visible markings with another stick in what appears to be a David Bier photo of my father (posing in what is probably the Forum before the 1949 renovation). So now, whenever I like, I can take the stick down from the wall and hold it in the same place that my father would have. The act does prompt the imagination.

I wonder whatever became of the silver tray that was presented to him back in 1953 for his Stanley Cup win, but am happy to have his Stanley Cup ring, a special issue that was the work of Ron Corey. Teams didn't start issuing rings until later in the '50s, so sometime during the 1990s Corey arranged for any of the old Habs to get a ring who hadn't received one. My father and Elmer Lach were two such recipients. Truth be told, it tends to stay in the safety-deposit box unless I get it out for special occasions, like every time I teach *The Divine Ryans* in my Sports Literature class (English 2060). Some of my students will start acting like Frodo when the ring goes around the room. I encourage them to slip it on a finger on the understanding that I will not leave the room without getting it back. I remember my father wearing the ring proudly.

When I was reframing the 1957 photo of my father and me (see fig. 31), I realized that it had been mounted on top of an old picture of Mike Karakas, the Black Hawks netminder. The photo was old enough to go back to my father's childhood, when he idolized goalies like Karakas and Frank Brimsek. When my father got his first goalie pads as a Limoilou youngster, it was in part because he was inspired by such images. And so the images of the past get covered over as each generation puts them to new use in the present.

On October 18, 2008, I went to the Bell Centre to see Phoenix against the Habs. I took the metro to Peel Street and detoured through the Mount Royal Plaza, hoping that physical markers would magically produce recollections of my first Habs game in the early 1960s (see Chapter 8). I walked down Peel Street past the Windsor Hotel building where the NHL was born in 1917. Periodically, I glanced over at the Sun Life Building on the other side of Dominion Square, the location of the NHL head office for decades, and it still seemed massive in width. I thought about going past the Windsor Station building to look at where the Queen's Hotel used to be, but there would be nothing to see, so I turned right and arrived at the Bell Centre. It was early. Perfect, because I wanted to look around and absorb all the pre-game street hype.

The Canadiens were celebrating their centenary as a hockey club and there were special events scheduled for the following year. (The club actually began operations in December 1909—more than a year off.) The theme for the year reproduced on a number of banners hanging around the outside wall of the building was "History is played here"— in French, of course. Current players appeared in colour, whereas the greats from the past (the forty-four Habs who are in the Hall of Fame) were reproduced in black and white.[1] The lobby areas of the Bell Centre were full of reminders of the old Forum—wrapped around every cement post was an enlarged photo of the old building on Sainte-Catherine Street.

The Bell Centre box office is a level below ground. From the wickets to the escalator, heading to the arena, there were a number of photographs that had been enlarged on the wall. To the right was Roger Saint-Jean's classic shot of Lach and Richard in their embrace (neither player is recognizable) just seconds after Lach scored in overtime to win the Stanley Cup in 1953. Directly in front was Jacques Doyon's photo of Richard slipping the puck past Sugar Jim Henry a little over a year before (April 8, 1952). Saint-Jean was with *La Presse,* while Doyon worked for *La Patrie.* As I mentioned in Chapter 5, some have referred to Richard's goal, which clinched Game Seven of the Semifinal against the Bruins, as the greatest in playoff history. I made a mental note that my father was the goalie at the other end on both of these occasions—that my father was there for some of the Rocket's greatest moments.

I turned to the right to go up the escalator and noticed a display window in the background to the left. It was meant to represent part of the Canadiens' dressing room at the old Forum. Laid out were vintage uniforms and equipment designed to evoke memories of the best all-time Habs at the six positions (Plante, Harvey, Robinson, Richard, Lafleur, and Morenz). On the wall in the background were listed various years with the team roster. I spotted "G. McNeil" for both the 1950–51 and 1951–52 years.

My seat was 17, row T, Section 105. SportChannel was filming a brief introduction just down to my left as I arrived. The video presentation before the game (which ran some fifteen minutes) featured an action sequence that merged two video streams—one in colour and current, another in black and white and from the past. Players were introduced by being matched up with a historical figure: Kovalev with Richard, Price with Dryden. Ironically, the actual game, when it started, seemed utterly anticlimactic. So wrapped in the nostalgic glow of the past, we cannot avoid being underwhelmed by the present. There was an aura there, I know, but it too had gotten confused with history.

Hours later, with the game in full swing, I noticed the steep bank of spectators rising straight at the De La Gauchetière end. It was an impressive sight. The place was full—21,350 fans, the noisiest of whom seemed to be sitting high up on my left. They produced swells of cheers or jeers as the occasion demanded. Toward the end of the game, they succeeded in getting the whole upper bowl to do the wave. Next to me were a mother and young son; it was his first hockey game. She looked a bit like Madonna and kept texting friends about what was happening. While her thumbs flew over the tiny keyboard, I still found it odd that she passed on at least half the experience to keep in immediate contact with whoever was on the receiving end.

The Habs goalie Price made a few great saves in the first period, which I thought was key, as his team built a three-goal lead. I felt a chill when I saw myself as a single person in that colossal bowl of hockey fans witnessing this spectacular team-ballet of contact and skating. As for the light show, the hostess-led games on the jumbo monitor, and other carefully scripted attempts to keep the entertainment and stimulation constant, I found it all a bit overkill. Too much effort at creating excitement robbed the event of any genuine excitement. Almost. A Hab-finesse player was dealt a dirty hit into the boards, and the blood-lust chants for the goon Laroque brought the crowd to life in the second period. As the fighting started, we were all pulled out of our seats to see how this retaliation would play out. It ended 4–1 for Montreal. The fans were singing and crowding back into the bar and gift shop. Savouring every sensation, I took my time leaving the building. There were inklings of aura, but the feeling was ineffable.

I confess to having felt a little sad when the ring bearing the names of the winning teams from 1941 to '53 was taken off the Stanley Cup and retired into some vault at the Hockey Hall of Fame.[2] In 2017 when the league celebrates its centenary, the names of Maurice Richard, Gordie Howe, and Bobby Hull will also disappear as another ring comes off. Time marches on. I understand that the league cannot add rings indefinitely to the base. My father's Cup win of 1952–53 was the hockey feat of which he was most proud. I said earlier (Chapter 6) that annual awards in sport, including the Stanley Cup, only belong to the winners for a single year. While one might still claim to having one's name engraved on the Cup, that assertion needs some qualification: it will be until the ring on which it appears is retired to the vault with the others.

So the aura surrounding the Original Six (Richard, etc.) is largely gone, as must be the case, and while we amass the photos and news clips and relics that give us a sense of connection, there is no way to get back to the flesh and blood of the past. Nevertheless, a sense of connection is better than nothing, and so we surround ourselves with the stories and pictures that survive. Some are "moving," some "talking," some speak with their wonderfully rich depths of field and historical impact. They comfort us against that empty night beyond the arena and trigger precious memories of those now gone but still in our love.

1 Believing that honoured recognition should be reserved for players, I do not count those who have been inducted in the Hockey Hall of Fame's "builders" category.

2 This fact was reported early in 2007. See Shi Davidi, "Changing of the rings— 1941–53 Cup Winners in the Vault," *Chronicle Herald* (Halifax), Jan. 11, 2007, D6.

Acknowledgements

First, I wish to thank Louis Anctil of Midtown Press for picking up a friendship after forty years and believing in this project; Heidi Petersen, for her help in preparing the manuscript; and Denis Hunter, for designing this book. Second, I would not have gotten far without the help of the Killam Library at Dalhousie (especially Oriel MacLennan, Karen Smith, and all those in the office of interlibrary loans: Kellie Hawley, Marlyn McCann, Shirley Vail, Christine Hatton, Clare Cheong, and Joseph Wickens). The reference department at the National Library and Archives of Canada (LAC) was also helpful in tracing down various microfilmed items, without which this study could not have been completed. Third, there are a number of individuals in various places who lent assistance in various ways: Andrew Podnieks, Thaddeus Holowna, Mike Leonetti, Dave Stubbs, Ian Sutherland, Carl Lavigne, Blaise M. Lamphier, John Kruspe, Mike Wyman, Paul Kitchen, Dick Van Nostrand, Patricia Desjardins, Florence Labelle, and Réjean Houle. I am enormously indebted to Paul Patskou for finding hours of relevant footage at the Hockey Hall of Fame Research Centre, and I thank Craig Campbell for giving me access to the HHOF resources. Earlier versions of this project were presented to the Society for International Hockey Research (SIHR) at the Bell Centre in 2009 and at the "Putting it on the Ice" conferences at St. Mary's University and the University of Western Ontario. I have benefitted from the knowledge of several SIHR members, including Jean-Patrice Martel, Ernie Fitzsimmons, and James Mancuso. Thanks also to Colin Howell of the Gorsebrook Institute and Don Morrow at Western. Richard Harrison, Jamie Dopp, Andrew Holman, Marc-A. Comtois, Michael Quinn, and Benoît Melançon encouraged me along the way. My appreciation extends to all those friends and acquaintances whose oral contributions were instrumental in the writing of this book. Last, and most important, special gratitude to my friend and colleague Ron Huebert who offered comments on a first draft and greatly improved the final one, who understands what it is to be a fan, and with whom I have had the pleasure to play and watch many a game.

List of Figures

Marie-Claire and Butch Bouchard, Elmer Lach, Gerry and Theresa McNeil, Marlene and Bernard Geoffrion, Lorne Davis and his date (?); back to front on the right side: Ken and Lorraine Mosdell, Kaye Lach, Paul Meger's date (?) and Paul Meger, Maurice and Lucille Richard, Doug Harvey. (Photographer unknown. Butch Bouchard's Restaurant [cabaret].) Photo courtesy of Émile "Butch" Bouchard family.

11 (Page 65) McNeil blocks a shot by Dunc Fisher at the MSG, probably sometime in 1950 when Jack Lancien (see sign) was in the Ranger lineup. Note the relaxed poses of the ushers in their white uniforms. (Photographer unknown. MSG 1950.) Copyright unknown.

CHAPTER 3

12 (Pages 74–75) Gerry McNeil kicks out a shot by Gordie Howe. Detroit Olympia, early 1950s. (Photo by James "Scotty" Kilpatrick. *Gazette* [Montreal], May 7, 2002, E3; and *Gazette* [Montreal], Mar. 27, 2004, A2.) Copyright unknown.

13 (Page 81) Ted Lindsay goes airborne over McNeil, who stops the puck to prolong the overtime. Detroit Olympia, March 28, 1951. (Photo by Roy Rash. *Standard* [Montreal], Mar. 30, 1951, 9.) Copyright unknown.

14 (Page 83) "Clipping Detroit's Wings." (Cartoon by John Collins. *Gazette* [Montreal], Mar. 29, 1951, 18.) Reproduced by permission of *The Gazette*/Postmedia Network.

15 (Page 89) Gerry McNeil and Maurice Richard after winning Game Two of the 1951 Semifinal in the fourth overtime period. Detroit Olympia, March 30, 1951. (Photographer unknown. *Montreal Star,* Mar. 31, 1951, 44; and *Detroit News,* Mar. 30, 1951, 57.) Copyright unknown.

16 (Page 92) Dick Irvin, Gerry McNeil, and Maurice Richard after winning Game Two of the 1951 Semifinal in the third overtime period. Detroit Olympia, March 30, 1951. (Photographer unknown.) Copyright unknown.

17 (Page 97) The Canadiens raise bottles of 7 Up (for some reason the NHL's celebratory drink of choice during the 1940s and '50s) after their defeat of the Red Wings in the 1951 Semifinal. (Photographer unknown.) Copyright unknown.

CHAPTER 4

18 (Page 107) Sid Smith and other Leaf players celebrate Smith's overtime goal while McNeil skates off dejected. Star caption reads: "Canadiens' Good Little Goalie Shown Leaving the Ice After He

Was Beaten by Sid Smith's Overtime Goal Last Night at Gardens. Leafs who can be identified, left to right: Klukay, Mortson, Mackell, Smith, Watson, Broda, Meeker, Barilko, Thomson, Sloan and Timgren." (Photo by Harold Barkley. *Toronto Star,* Apr. 12, 1951, 25. Reprinted *Gazette* [Montreal], June 19, 2006, C2.) Reproduced by permission of "Harold Barkley Archives."

19 (Page 114) Gerry McNeil makes the save off Tod Sloan of the Toronto Maple Leafs during Game Four (April 19th) of the 1951 Stanley Cup Final; Floyd Curry is the player attempting to check Sloan. Photo is distinguished by the simultaneous flash of another camera on the opposite side of the rink, which produces a halo effect around Sloan's head. Note also the number of other cameras along the boards. These photographers were close to the action and weren't shooting through protective glass. (Photographer unknown. "Hockey Photo of the Week," *Standard* [Montreal], Apr. 21, 1951, 11.) Copyright unknown.

20 (Page 120) The picture that has launched a thousand comments. 21 April 1951. (Photo by Nat Turofsky. *Globe and Mail,* Apr. 23, 1951, 20. Subsequent publications are too numerous to itemize.) Reproduced by permission of Imperial Oil – Nat & Lou Turofsky.

21 (Page 126) An Algonquin guide stands on the pontoon of a plane with three members of the Canadiens: Gerry McNeil, Doug Harvey, and Maurice Richard. Lac-des-Loups, circa 1951. (Photographer unknown.) Copyright unknown.

CHAPTER 5

22 (Page 137) Goaltenders did go down to block shots, thus exposing their faces to severe injury. Detroit Olympia, circa 1951. (Photo by James "Scotty" Kilpatrick.) Copyright unknown.

23 (Page 140) Gerry McNeil plays an entire game after having had his cheekbone shattered in the first period. Maple Leaf Gardens, 29 Oct. 1951. (Photo by Harold Barkley. Reprinted *Gazette* [Montreal], June 19, 2006, C2.) Reproduced by permission of "Harold Barkley Archives."

24 (Page 144) Gerry McNeil has words of encouragement for his replacement Jacques Plante, who inspects Gerry's cheek. Montreal Forum, Nov. 7, 1952. (Photographer unknown.)

25 (Page 155) Gerry McNeil and Sugar Jim Henry shake hands after Game Seven of the Semifinal. Montreal Forum, April 8, 1952. (Photo unconfirmed by Roger Saint-Jean.) Copyright unknown.

CHAPTER 6

26 (Page 167) Gerry McNeil makes a save off Jack McIntyre. Chicago Stadium, early 1950s. (Photographer unknown.) Copyright unknown.

27 (Page 180) Canadiens hockey team after winning Stanley Cup, 1953. Montreal Forum, April 16, 1953. (Photographer unknown. *Gazette* [Montreal], Apr. 17, 1953, 23.) Reproduced by permission of Library and Archives Canada/*The Gazette* (Montreal) fonds/PA-142658.

28 (Page 182) Official team picture of the Montreal Canadiens, Stanley Cup Champions 1953. Montreal Canadiens, 1952–53. (Photo by David Bier.) Reproduced by permission of Club de hockey Canadien Inc.

CHAPTER 7

29 (Page 200) McNeil makes a first-period save off Marcel Pronovost. The picture is autographed by McNeil and Dollard St. Laurent, the defenceman trailing the play. Detroit Olympia, April 16, 1954. (Photographer unknown.) Copyright unknown.

30 (Page 204) While a number of fans are smiling and ready to leave, Theresa McNeil, Gerry McNeil's wife, remains nervously smoking in her seat. Montreal, Forum, early 1950s. (Photographer unknown.) Copyright unknown.

31 (Page 211) Father and son pose for the photographer. (Photographer unknown. *Rochester Union-Times,* Dec. 27, 1957, 28.) Copyright *Rochester Union-Times* (defunct).

CHAPTER 8

32 (Page 244) My father and I pose for a picture in the kitchen. Family photo, circa 2001. Photo courtesy of the author.

Most of these illustrations are from Gerry McNeil's private collection. Every effort has been made to contact possible copyright holders. Please contact the publisher if you have any information on any of the photographs listed above.

Works Cited

Reference

BROWN, Gene, ed. *The New York Times Encyclopedia of Sports*. Vol. 8, "Professional Hockey." New York: Arno Press, 1979

Total Hockey: The Official Encyclopedia of the National Hockey League. New York: Total Sports, 1998.

PODNIEKS, Andrew. *Players: The Ultimate A–Z Guide of Everyone Who Has Ever Played in the NHL*. Toronto: Doubleday, 2003.

Archival

David McNeil personal collection. T. P. Gorman to Mr. Gerry McNeil. October 6, 1943.

Magazines

Life.
Monde Sportif.
The New Yorker.
Samedi-Dimanche [Radiomonde Limitée].
Sport.
Sports Illustrated [abbreviated *SI*].
The Standard [Montreal weekly].

Newspapers

The Boston Globe.
The Chronicle Herald (Halifax) [also known as *Sunday Herald*].
Detroit Free Press.
The Detroit News.
The Gazette (Montreal).
The Globe and Mail.
The Herald, Montreal [also called *Montreal Daily Herald*].
The Hockey News.
The Indianapolis Enquirer.
Montréal-Matin.
The Montreal Star [also called *The Montreal Daily Star*].
National Post.
The New York Times.
Le Petit journal (Montreal).
La Presse.
The Providence Journal.
Quebec Chronicle-Telegraph
Rochester Times-Union.
Le Soleil (Quebec City).
Toronto Star.

Internet

"The Battle of the Overpass." Review Mirror. The Detroit News. Accessed May 26, 2006. http://info.detnews.com/history/story/index.cfm?id=172&category=events.

"Complete NHL Statistics." Quanthockey. Accessed May 6, 2015. http://www.quanthockey.com/nhl/records/nhl-goalies-all-time-playoff-goals-against-average-leaders.html.

FREED, Ken. "ABC Sports Prepares for HD Super Bowl XL." *TV Technology*. Accessed May 31, 2006. http://www.tvtechnology.com/features/news/2006.01.25-n_abc.shtml. Reproduced at "Radio World." Accessed December 29, 2014. http://www.radioworld.com/article/ABC-Sports-Prepares-for-HD-Super-Bowl-XL/184576.

"Getty Images." Accessed December 23, 2014. http://www.gettyimages.ca/creative/frontdoor/researchservices

"Hockey Night in Canada." The Museum of Broadcast Communications. Accessed July 26, 2007. http://www.museum.tc/archives/. [The website for the archive is currently being upgraded.]

"An Interview with Neil Leifer." Berman Graphics. Accessed December 23, 2014. http://bermangraphics.com/press/leifer.htm.

"Large Format (photography)." Wikipedia. http://en.wikipedia.org/wiki/Large_format_%28photography%29

LINDEMAN, Tracey. "Gerry McNeil's Family Shares Rare Photos of Habs in 1950s." CBC News Montreal. Posted Aug. 10, 2014. http://www.cbc.ca/news/canada/montreal/gerry-mcneil-s-family-shares-rare-photos-of-habs-in-1950s-1.2732557. Accessed May 3, 2015.

Rauzulu's Street. Accessed June 16, 2004. http://www.rauzulusstreet.com/hockey/nhlallstar/allstarrecordsplayer.html.

"Roger Saint-Jean." French Wikipédia. Accessed February 17, 2015. http://fr.wikipedia.org/wiki/Roger_St-Jean.

"Sports Illustrated." *Sports Illustrated*. Accessed December 23, 2014. www.SI.com.

"Sports Shooter." Accessed April 12, 2004. http://www.sportsshooter.com/message_display.html?tid=8831.

WEBER, Bruce. "Ozzie Sweet, Who Helped Define New Era of Photography, Dies at 94," *New York Times*. February 23, 2013. Accessed December 27, 2014. http://www.nytimes.com/2013/02/24/sports/ozzie-sweet-who-helped-define-new-era-of-photography-dies-at-94.html?pagewanted=all&_r=0.

Audio Recordings

SIBERRY, Jane. "Hockey" by Jane Siberry. *Bound by the Beauty*. Duke Street Records. Originally released Sept. 8, 1989.

Films and Newsreels

Angling Around. Columbia film. 1952.

BINAMÉ, Charles, dir. *The Rocket*. Toronto: Alliance Atlantis, French 2005; English 2006.

Hockey: A People's History. CBC Ten-Part Documentary, 2006.

"Leaders Clash: Play to Tie." Telenews: Montreal Canadiens versus the Detroit Red Wings. Detroit: January 25, 1953. HHOF (Hockey Hall of Fame) archives.

MCFARLANE, Leslie, dir. *Here's Hockey*. Montreal: NFB (National Film Board of Canada), 1953.

MSG Issue 21. Newsreel of Montreal Canadiens versus the New York Rangers. New York: March 8, 1953. HHOF archives.

"Rookie Ace Trims Bruins." Telenews: Montreal Canadiens versus the Boston Bruins. Boston: December 21, 1952. HHOF archives.

NHL Playoffs 1952. Montreal: Briston Films, 1952. HHOF archives.

NHL Playoffs 1953. Montreal: Briston Films, 1953. HHOF archives.

NHL Playoffs 1954. Montreal: Briston Films, 1954. HHOF archives and Rare Sports Films DVD.

[Unidentified footage. Game Six of 1954 Final. Montreal. HHOF archives.]

"Wings Upset." Sports Flashes, Telenews. Mar. 28, 1951. HHOF archives.

Print

ANON, Josh, and Ellen Anon. *See It: Photographic Composition Using Visual Intensity*. New York: Focal Press, 2012.

The Art of Sport: The Best of Reuters Sports Photography. London: Reuters, 2003.

BARNES, Simon. Introduction to *Sportscape: The Evolution of Sports Photography*. London: Phaidon Press, 2000.

BARTHES, Roland. *What Is Sport?* Trans. Richard Howard. New Haven and London: Yale University Press, 2007.

BEAUCHAMP, Jacques. *Le sport c'est ma vie*. Montreal: Quebecor, 1979.

BENJAMIN, Walter. *The Work of Art in the Age of Its Technological Reproducibility, and Other Writings on Media*. Eds. Michael W. Jennings, Brigid Doherty, and Thomas Y. Levin. Trans. Edmund Jephcott, Rodney Livingstone, Howard Eiland, and others. Cambridge: Belknap Press, Harvard University Press, 2008.

BLAKE, Jason. *Canadian Hockey Literature: A Thematic Study*. Toronto: University of Toronto Press, 2010.

BORINS, Sara, Mark Kingwell, and Christopher Moore. *Canada: Our Century*. Toronto: Doubleday, 1999.

BRANCH, John. *Boy on Ice: The Life and Death of Derek Boogaard*. Toronto: HarperCollins, 2014.

BRODEUR, Denis. Text by Daniel Daignault. *Goalies: Guardians of the Net*. Toronto: Key Porter, 1995.

BROWN, William. *The Doug Harvey Story*. Montreal: Véhicule Press, 2002.

BRUNT, Stephen. *Searching for Bobby Orr*. Toronto: Knopf, 2006.

———. *Gretzky's Tears: Hockey, Canada and the Day Everything Changed*. Toronto: Knopf, 2009.

CANADA POST. Commemorative Stamped Envelope. Image from the 1951 NHL Final. Toronto Maple Leafs' 75th anniversary.

CHERRY, Don. With Stan Fischler. *Grapes: A Vintage View of Hockey*. Toronto: Prentice-Hall, 1982.

DAVIS, Fred. *Yearning for Yesterday: A Sociology of Nostalgia*. New York: Free Press, 1979.

DELILLO, Don. *End Zone*. Reprint New York: Houghton Mifflin, 1972.

———. *Underworld*. New York: Scribner, 1997.

DENAULT, Todd. *Jacques Plante: The Man Who Changed the Face of Hockey*. Toronto: McClelland & Stewart, 2009.

DOWBIGGIN, Bruce. *The Defense Never Rests*. Toronto: HarperCollins, 1993.

———. *The Stick: A History, A Celebration, An Elegy*. Toronto: Macfarlane, Walter & Ross, 2002.

DUPLACY, James, and Charles Wilkins. *Forever Rivals: Montreal Canadiens and Toronto Maple Leafs*. Toronto: Random House, 1996.

DRYDEN, Ken. *The Game: A Reflective and Thought-Provoking Look at a Life in*

Hockey. 20th Anniversary Edition. Toronto: Macmillan, 2003.

FAULKNER, William. "An Innocent at Rinkside." In *The Sporting Spirit: Athletes in Literature and Life,* edited by Robert J. Higgs and Neil D. Isaacs. New York: Harcourt Brace Jovanovich, 1977, 164–66.

FRANZEN, Jonathan. "My Father's Brain." In *How to Be Alone.* Toronto: HarperCollins, 2003.

FRAYNE, Trent. *The Thrill of Victory: Best Sport Stories from the Pages of McLeans'.* Toronto: Viking, 2003.

FUHR, Grant. With Bruce Dowbiggin. *Grant Fuhr: The Story of a Hockey Legend.* Toronto: Doubleday, 2014.

GASTON, Bill. *The Good Body.* Vancouver: Raincoast, 2004.

GENOSKO, Gary. "Hockey and Culture." In *Pop Can: Popular Culture in Canada,* edited by Lynne Van Luven and Priscilla L. Walton. Scarborough: Prentice-Hall, 1999, 140–156.

GEOFFRION, Bernard, and Stan Fischler. *Boom Boom: The Life and Times of Bernard Geoffrion* Toronto: McGraw-Hill Ryerson, 1997.

GOYENS, Chrys, and Allan Turowetz. *Lions in Winter.* Scarborough: Prentice-Hall, 1986.

GOWDEY, David, ed. *Riding on the Roar of the Crowd: A Hockey Anthology.* Toronto: Macmillan, 1989.

GUTTMANN, Allen. *Sports Spectators.* New York: Columbia University Press, 1986.

HAMBLIN, Robert. "*Homo Agonistes,* or, William Faulkner as Sportswriter." *Athelon: The Journal of Sport Literature* 13, no. 2 (1996): 13–22.

HARRIS, Cecil. *The Black Experience in Professional Hockey.* Toronto: Insomniac Press, 2003.

HARRISON, Richard. *Hero of the Play.* 10th Anniversary Edition. Toronto: Wolsak and Wynn, 2004.

HIGHWAY, Tomson. *Dry Lips Oughta Move to Kapuskasing.* Toronto: Fifth House, 1989.

HOBERMAN, John M. *Mortal Engines: The Science of Performance and the Dehumanization of Sport.* Toronto: Macmillan, 1992.

HOFFER, Richard. "A Great Year for Sports . . . And A New Sports Magazine," *Sports Illustrated 50: The Anniversary Book.* New York: Sports Illustrated Books, 2004, 13–46.

HOWE, Gordie. *Mr. Hockey: Gordie Howe, My Story.* Toronto: Viking, 2014.

HUNTER, Andrew. "Up North: A Northern Ontario Tragedy." Kamloops Art Gallery Exhibit, 1998.

HUNTER, Douglas. Excerpt from *A Breed Apart: An Illustrated History of Goaltending.* In *Words on Ice: A Collection of Hockey Prose,* edited by Michael P. J. Kennedy. Toronto: Key Porter, 2003, 142–49.

———. *War Games: Conn Smythe and Hockey's Fighting Men.* Toronto: Viking, 1996.

IRVIN, Jr., Dick. *In the Crease: Goaltenders Look at Life Inside the NHL.* Toronto: McClelland & Stewart, 1995.

———. *The Habs: An Oral History of the Montreal Canadiens, 1940–1980.* Toronto: M&S, 1992.

———. *Now Back to You Dick: Two Lifetimes in Hockey.* Toronto: McClelland and Stewart, 1988.

———. "Writing and Broadcasting." In *Total Hockey: Official Encyclopedia of the National Hockey League,* edited by Dan Diamond. New York: Total Sports, 1998, 116 –17.

JARMAN, Mark Anthony. *Salvage King, Ya! A Herky-Jerky Picaresque.* Vancouver: Anvil, 1997.

JENISH, D'Arcy. "1946–1955: Selke Builds and Empire." In *The Montreal Canadiens: 100 Years of Glory*. Toronto: Doubleday, 2008, 115–48.

JOHNSTON, Wayne. *The Divine Ryans*. Toronto: Vintage, 1998.

KENNEDY, Michael P. J., ed. *Going Top Shelf: An Anthology of Canadian Hockey Poetry* Vancouver: Heritage House, 2005.

KIDD, Bruce, and John Macfarlane. *The Death of Hockey*. Toronto: New Press, 1972.

KLEIN, Jeff, and Karl-Eric Reif. *The Death of Hockey*. Toronto: Macmillan, 1998.

LEE, John. *The Hockey Player Sonnets*. Waterloo, Ont.: Penumbra Press, 1991.

LEIFER, Neil. *The Best of Leifer*. New York: Abbeville Press, 2001.

LEWIS, Jerry, and James Kaplan. *Dean and Me: A Love Story*. New York: Doubleday, 2005.

LANGFORD, Martha. *Suspended Conversations: The Afterlife of Memory in Photographic Albums*. Montreal: McGill-Queen's University Press, 2001.

LEONETTI, Mike. *The Game: Hockey in the Fifties*. Vancouver: Raincoast, 1997.

———. *The Game We Knew: Hockey in the Sixties*. Vancouver: Raincoast, 1998.

———. *Hockey in the Seventies: The Game We Knew*. Vancouver: Raincoast, 1999.

MACALOON, John. "Olympic Games and the Theory of Spectacle in Modern Societies." In *Rite, Drama, Festival, Spectacle: Rehearsals Toward a Theory of Cultural Performance*, edited by John MacAloon. Philadelphia: Institute for the Study of Human Issues, 1984, 241–280.

MACLENNAN, Hugh. "Fury on Ice." In *Riding on the Roar of the Crowd*. Toronto: Macmillan, 1989, 4 –16.

MACSKIMMING, Roy. *Gordie: A Hockey Legend*. Vancouver: Greystone, 1994.

MAGGS, Randall. *Night Work: The Sawchuk Poems*. London, Ont.: Brick Books, 2008.

MALARCHUK, Clint. With Dan Robson. *The Crazy Game: How I Survived in the Crease and Beyond*. Toronto: HarperCollins, 2014.

MARTEL, Jean-Patrice, Carl Gidén, and Patrick Houda. *On the Origin of Hockey*. Stockholm: Hockey Origin Publishing, 2014.

MCDIARMID, Carleton "Mac." Artistic Reproduction of Hal Barkley April 1951 photo. "Jacques Laperriere" Classic Auction Catalogue, 2008.

MCFARLANE, Brian. *Stanley Cup Fever: 100 Years of Hockey Greatness*. Toronto: Stoddart, 1992.

MCGIMPSEY, David. "'Rock 'em, Sock 'em, *Terre de Nos Aieux*: Legends of Hockey, Canadian Nationalism and Television Violence." *Athelon: Journal of Sport Literature* 14, no. 2 (1997): 21–33.

MCKINLEY, Michael. *Hockey: A People's History*. Toronto: McClelland & Stewart, 2006.

MCNEIL, David. "The '51 Stanley Cup: A Spectacle of Sudden Death Overtime." *Textual Studies in Canada* 12 (1998): 5–18.

———. "The Story of Hockey Photography in the Early 1950s." In *Now is the Winter: Thinking About Hockey*, edited by Jamie Dopp and Richard Harrison. Toronto: Wolsak and Wynn, 2009, 81–95.

MCSORLEY, Tom. "Of Time and Space and Hockey: An Imaginary Conversation." In *Pop Can: Popular Culture in Canada*, edited by Marlene Van Luven and Priscilla L. Walton. Scarborough: Prentice-Hall, 1999, 151–56.

MELADY, John. *Overtime Overdue: The Bill Barilko Story*. Trenton: City Print, 1988.

MELANÇON, Benoît. *The Rocket: A Cultural History of Maurice Richard*. Trans. Fred A. Reed. Vancouver: Greystone, 2009.

MONK, Craig. "When Eustace Tilley Came to Madison Square Garden: Professional Hockey and the Editorial Policy of *The New Yorker* in the 1920s and 1930s."

American Periodicals: A Journal of History, Criticism, and Bibliography 15, no. 2 (2005): 178–95.

MOUTON, Claude. *The Montreal Canadiens: A Hockey Dynasty.* Toronto: Van Nostrand Reinhold, 1980.

MUMFORD, Lewis. "Sport and the 'Bitch-goddess.'" In *The Sporting Spirit: Athletes in Literature and Life*, edited by Robert J. Higgs and Neil D. Isaacs. New York: Harcourt Brace Jovanovich, 1977, 259–63.

PODNIEKS, Andrew. *The Goal.* Toronto: Doubleday, 2004.

———. *Portraits of the Game: Classic Photographs from the Turofsky Collection at the Hockey Hall of Fame.* Toronto: Doubleday, 1997.

QUARRINGTON, Paul. *King Leary.* Reprint Toronto: Anchor, 2007.

———. *Logan in Overtime.* Toronto: Doubleday, 1990.

RAMPERSAD, Arnold. *Jackie Robinson: A Biography.* New York: Alfred A. Knopf, 1997.

RICHARDS, David Adams. *Hockey Dreams: Memories of a Man Who Couldn't Play.* Reprint Toronto: Anchor, 2001.

RICHLER, Mordecai. *Barney's Version.* Toronto: Knopf, 1997.

———. "Cheap Skates." Reprinted in *Dispatches from the Sporting Life.* Toronto: Knopf, 2002, 141–47.

ROBIDOUX, Michael A. *Men at Play: A Working Understanding of Professional Hockey.* Montreal: McGill-Queen's University Press, 2001.

ROMAIN, Joseph, and Dan Diamond. *The Pictorial History of Hockey.* Greenwich, Ct.: Bison Books, 1987.

SABO, Don. *Sex, Violence & Power in Sports.* Freedom: Crossing Press, 1994.

SAINT-CYR, Lili. *Ma vie de stripteaseuse.* Montreal: Quebecor, 2005.

SALUTIN, Rick, and Ken Dryden. *Les Canadiens.* Montreal: Talon Books, 1977.

SCANLAN, Lawrence. *Grace Under Fire: The State of Our Sweet and Savage Game.* Toronto: Penguin, 2002.

SEDLACK, Robert. *The Horn of a Lamb.* Toronto: Anchor, 2004.

SHEA, Kevin. *Barilko: Without A Trace.* Bolton: Fenn, 2004.

Sports Illustrated 50: The Anniversary Book. New York: Sports Illustrated Books, 2004.

THEBERGE, Nancy. *Higher Goals: Women's Ice Hockey and the Politics of Gender.* Albany: SUNY, 2000.

TURNER, Victor. "Images and Reflections: Ritual, Drama, Carnival, Film, and Spectacle in Cultural Performance." In *The Anthropology of Performance.* New York: PAJ Publications, 1986, 21–32.

WHITE, Philip G., Kevin Young, and William G. McTeer. "Sport, Masculinity and the Injured Body." In *Men's Health and Illness: Gender, Power, and the Body*, edited by Donald Sabo and David Frederick Gordon. Thousand Oaks: Sage Publications, 1995, 158–82.

WINGER, Rob. "'This Combination of Ballet and Murder': Some Thoughts on Hockey Poetry in Canada." *ARC: Canada's National Poetry Magazine*, Winter 2004, 60–66.

WOODWARD, Richard B. "Playing with Time." *SI.* April 26, 2004, 75–82.

WRIGHT, Richard B. *The Age of Longing.* Toronto: HarperCollins, 1995.

YOUNG, Scott. *The Boys of Saturday Night: Inside Hockey Night in Canada.* Toronto: Macmillan, 1990.

Index

193n12; first televised Stanley Cup 1953, 179–80, 187; *Hockey: A People's History* (2006), 233; *Hockey Night in Canada* (HNIC), *Coach's Corner*, 235; McNeil selects three stars, 221; replays, 12. *See also* media, radio digital technology (internet), 11, 12, 78, 163, 232, 253

Divine Ryans, The, McNeil fictionalized in, 218-19, 255

Dowbiggin, Bruce (sportswriter), 238

Downing, Larry (photographer), 236

Doyon, Jacques (photographer), 256

Dryden, Ken, 11, 93, 218, 229, 235, 256

Dubé, Gilles, 199

Dubois, Hector, 142, 180, 194, figs. 27 and 28

Dumart, Woodrow "Woody," 38, 152, 153

Duplacey, James, 121

Durnan, Bill, 11, 30, 36, 61, 145, 150, 170, 171, 206, 218, 230, 237; ambidextrous, 220; injured in
(1947), 36-39, 40n4, fig. 7; injured in 1950, 9, 43, 45, 47, 56-57, 143; passes the "torch" to
Gerry McNeil, 64-67, 158n35; remains ahead in 1950 Vezina race, 45-46, 56, 62; shares
netminding duties with McNeil during 1943 training camp, 17-18; signs his first contract
with Canadiens one hour before opening game (1943), 19

Eagleson, Alan, 234, 241

Eastern Pro Hockey League (EPHL), 212

ekphrasis, 51, 219

Esposito, Phil, toughness, 241

fans, 31-32, 47-48, 145, 187, 211; attention to live action in 1950s, 109; Chicago (Stadium), 58
166, 169, 191; "corporate" crowd, 134; depicted (photo, film, newsreels, TV), 50-52, 76,
123, 185n65, 185n70, 185n71, 188, 189, 197, fig. 30; Detroit (and at the Olympia), 86, 113, 162,
165-66, 193, 202; Detroit youths found hiding in Forum, 93-94; dress of, 52-53; Montreal
(and at the Forum), 46, 50, 52, 56, 61, 65, 93, 152, 163, 170, 177, 179-80, 192, 193, 214n36, 256,
fig. 30; "rail birds," 49; Toronto (MLG), 119, 140

Faulkner, William, 234

Ferguson, Elmer (sportswriter), 21, 39, 57, 63, 64, 66-67, 73, 84-85, 89, 99n7, 133, 135, 140,
168, 170-71, 193-94; fictionalizing conversations, 69n50; picks McNeil for Hart Trophy
(1952-53), 161; praise for McNeil, 243

film, 154; *Ali,* 154; *Angling Around* (Habs fishing), 11, 125-26; of Barilko goal, 122; Briston, of
NHL Playoffs, 12, 176, 185n57, 195, 197-98, 214n33; based on photography, 11, 154; of disallowed goal in 1951 Final, 109; family (Kodak), 145; of 1954 Final, 194-95, 197-98; *Goon,*
241; *Here's Hockey* (1953), 187, 189-91, 197; and history, 121-22; *Hockey: A People's History,*
233; McNeil interview (2003), 253; *Raging Bull,* 154; *The Rocket* (dir. Binamé), 50, 88, 154,
160n64, 160n65, 205, 214n41; slow-motion, 188, 190, 198, 218; *Le Sport et les hommes,* 238;
unidentified footage of Game Six, 1954 Final, 197. *See also* media

Fischler, Stan, 234, 235

Fisher, Dunc, 65, 66, fig. 11

Fisher, Joe, 29

fishing, 125-26

Fitzgerald, Tom (sportswriter), 152, 175, 176

Flaman, Fern, 58, 111

Fogolin, Lee, Sr., 156, 164

Forbes, Jackie, 17

Forum, Montreal, 28, 49, 133, 229, 234; alumni room, 223; characteristics in 1940s, 49-50, 57,
138, 179, 181, 190, 198, 222; Hy Peskin at, 50-52

Franzen, Jonathan: his father's dying words, 247

Fraser, Bill (William) "Legs," 24

Frayne, Trent (sportswriter), 208

French, Doug, 28

Frost, David, 241, 251n54

Fuhr, Grant, 235

Gainey, Bob, 227

Galbraith, Jimmy, 26, 28, 29, 31, 42n38, 57, 208, 230, 242, fig. 6

Galley, Andy (Royals trainer), 36, 42n38, fig. 6

Gardiner, Bert, 17, 18, 19

Gardner, Cal, 34, 106, 109, 110, 111, 113, 121, fig. 20

Gazette, The, 196, 245

Gee, George, 86, 167

Genosko, Gary, 235

Geoffrion, Bernard "Boom Boom," 84, 97-98, 111, 112, 113, 148, 151, 162, 178, 217, fig. 28; against Chicago in 1953 Semifinal, 165, 167; with Marlene, 59, fig. 10; on McNeil, 119, 174, 206, 247; origin of nickname, 214n27; plays on "kid" line in 1951, 110, 111; and the slapshot, 195, 196, 197

Giguère, Jean-Sébastien, 94-95

goalies, 151; confidence of, 146, 169, 237; dealing with the unexpected, 40; equipment, 44-45, 87, 245; face mask, 9, 44, 136; fear, 145-46; feeling isolated, 108, 236; hot streak, 92-93; injury, 24-25, 36-38, 108, 138-43, 176-77, 191-92, 193; pressure, 9, 85, 91, 96, 132, 146, 206, 237; reputedly odd or crazy, 163; statistics, 45-46, 94, 134, 218; strategy, 63-64, 85. *See also* Canadiens

Goldham, Bob, 73, 94, 147, 194, 199

Gorman, Tommy, 15, 19-22, 36, 40n1, 40n9, 50

Gowdy, David, 233

Goyens, Chrys, 40n1

Grant, Dunc, 28

Gravel, George (referee), 110

Gravelle, Léo, 47, 49, 54, 248

Gretzky, Wayne, 93, 101n66, 122, 143, 198, 235, 241

Guidolin, Armand "Bep," 46

Habs. *See under* Canadiens, Montreal

Haggarty, Jimmy, 24, 41n34, 42n38, fig. 6

Hainsworth, George, 94

Hall, Glenn, 139, 218

Hannigan, Gord, 139

Harmon, Glen, 47

Harrison, Robert, 238

Hart Trophy, 45, 56, 161-62

Harvey, Doug, 47, 63, 87, 96, 106, 109, 116, 132, 165, 178, 217, 230, 256, figs. 8 and 28; assists on goals, 110, 112, 115; attempts to talk McNeil out of retirement, 203, 220; on the Canadiens five straight Stanley Cups, 198, 212; doles out expense money, 85; the epitome of toughness, 240; fishing, 125-26, fig. 21; hits "Sugar" Jim Henry in 1952 Semifinal, 152; jokes, 84; and the Leswick goal 1954, 200, 202; lives in NDG with other Canadiens, 145; McNeil ranks as the best Canadiens defenceman, 202; on film, 125-26, 195, 198; plays with St. Louis in 1968, 222; plays with the Royals (1947), 28, 29, 31; refuses to shake hands, 117-18, 201-202; troubles and family, 203; with Ursula, 59, fig. 10; versus Red Wings in 1952 Final, 147, 148; versus Red Wings in 1954 Final, 193, 195, 198 ; wins Stanley Cup in 1953 with McNeil, 180. *See also* film, *Angling Around*

Harwood, Charlie (broadcaster, radio), 134

Hasek, Dominick, 218

Head, Bill (physiotherapist), 173, 176, 194

Heffernan, Jerry, 64

Henderson, Johnny, 139

Henderson, Paul, 122, 123

Henry, Gord "Red," 173, 175

Henry, "Sugar" Jim, 231; injured, 156; photos of, shaking hands, 153-55, fig. 25; selected for

1952 All-Star Game, 133; versus Montreal in the 1952 Semifinal, 152–53, 256; versus Montreal in the 1953 Final, 172–73, 175, 176, 177–78, 178–79

Herald (Montreal), *The*, 205–206

Hergesheimer, Wally, 133, 156, 188

Hewitt, Foster (broadcaster), 11, 122, 123, 163

Highway, Tomson, 233, 238–39

Hirschfeld, Bert, 54, 69n40

history: "Battle of the Overpass," 76, 99n14; of hockey, 11, 234–35; oral, 10; relics of 231, 257

Hoberman, John M., 141–42

hockey: in advertising, 235–39; "Bad Boys" of, 34, 240–41; and chance, 236; changes in, 242; conferences, 239; controversy in, 241–42; culture, 239; death of, 237; in drama, 233, 238–39; equipment, 138; goal celebrations, 201; handshake ritual, 117–18, 201–202; images of, 10–11, 122; injuries, 36, 45–46, 71, 98n1, 138–41, 142–43, 145–46, 156, 158n28; international, 49; literature of, 217, 232–36, 237–40; the magic of, 242; and memorabilia, 204, 218–20, 245, 253–55; and momentum, 169; and national identity (Canadian), 238; and nationalism, 239; in the novel (Canadian), 240; origins of, 237; poetry about, 221, 235–36, 238; in popular magazines, 11, 50–52, 54, 79, 123–24, 143, 129n42, 233–34; pregame magic, 229; professional leagues, 40n12; sentimental pond shinny, 239; sexual abuse in, 241; sounds of, 11, 229, 233–34; statistics, 45–46, 134, 143–49, 189, 213n5, 191–92; strategy, 161; terms, 101n58, 127n4; violent image of, 239–41. *See also* AHL; CAHA; ECHL; NHL; QHL; QSHL

Hockey Hall of Fame, The (HHOF), 187, 214n32, 259

Hockey News, The, 62, 71, 79, 113, 138, 146, 162–63, 206

Hockey Players Association, 242

Hodge, Charlie, 206

Holtby, Braden, 218

Houde, Mayor (Montreal) Camillien, 135

Howe, Gordie, 48, 122, 132, 143, 151, 217, 246, 257; against the Canadiens in 1951 Semifinal, 72–73, 86–87, 95, 96, 98; against the Canadiens in the 1952 Final, 148–49, 157n9; against the Canadiens in the 1954 Final, 194, 199, 200, 217; bid for fifty-goal season, 164–66; breaks McNeil's shutout streak, 94; on CBC television with McNeil in 1952 opening sequence, 10, 163; on film, 195, 198; featured in Detroit press, 71; in *Here's Hockey*, 191; Kilpatrick photo of, 73–79, 124, 136, fig. 12; success against McNeil, 61; suffers severe concussion in 1950 playoffs, 63; toughness, 241

Howell, Harry, 188

Hucul, Fred, 167–68, 177

Hull, Bobby, 196, 257; recalls seeing McNeil, 223–24; toughness, 241

Hunter, Andrew, 129n39

Hunter, Douglas, 234; interviews McNeil, 237

Hunter, Ken "Red," 29

Imlach, George "Punch," 190

Indians, Springfield, 211

Irvin, Dick, Jr. (sportswriter), 40n4, 69n51, 164

Irvin, Dick, Sr., 46, 58, 80, 93, 116, 147, 166, 196, 199, figs. 2, 16, and 28; addresses Canadiens' lack of scoring, 162; attempts to talk McNeil out of retiring, 203, 206; criticizes McNeil for smiling, 195; 1953 Cup celebration, 180, 182; demeans his players, 205; depicted in Binamé's film, 205, 214n41; depicted in cartoon, 96; dispute with his own players, 208, 209, 212; goalie substitutions, 36, 66–67, 139–41, 173–75, 193–94, 206, 217; in *Here's Hockey*, 190; impressed by McNeil's play, 17–19, 64–65, 84, 91–92, 151, fig. 16; keeping players on edge, 36, 195; on McNeil allowing a soft goal, 149; on McNeil asking to be replaced, 168; on McNeil's "crack-up," 170, 206; plays "mind games," 71–72, 90, 93, 115, 145, 146, 171, 193; predictions for 1952–53, 162; refuses to allow Plante to wear a face mask, 136; refuses to allow Plante to wear a toque, 143; refuses to shake hands, 150; rooms with goalies

Leonetti, Mike, 108, 128n12

Leswick, Tony "Mighty Mouse," 147, 156, 191, 194, 198, 231; criticizes the Habs for not shaking hands, 202; scores overtime winner in 1953 Final, 200, 218

Lewis, Jerry, 32

Life, magazine, 34-35, 50, 54, 68n27, 78, 123, 143

liminality, 77, 99n18, 123, 203, 231, 237. *See also* Turner, Victor

Limoilou (Quebec City), 15, 37, 145, 212, 230, 247, 248, 255, fig. 1

Lindsay, Ted, 48, 59, 73, 86, 96, 98, 150, 164; animosity toward Maurice Richard, 86, 133, 191; effort to organize NHL players, 86; in *Here's Hockey,* 191; on line with Howe and Abel, 61, 93; on McNeil's luck in 1951 Semifinal, 84; Roy Rash photo of, 80, fig. 13; scores his 300th goal against McNeil, 209; toughness, 241; versus Montreal in 1952 Final, 147, 148, 149; versus Montreal in 1954 Final, 193, 199, 200

literature. *See under* hockey

Locas, Jacques, 29, 35

Lowe, Ross, 84

Luce, Henry, 123, 129n42. *See also Sports Illustrated*

Lumley, Harry, 37, 45, 47, 56, 62, 84, 131, 139

Lund, Pentti, 63, 151

Lunny, Vince (sportswriter), 194, 196-97, 206-207

Lussier, Ray (photographer), 121, 124, 179

Lynn, Vic, 167, 168

MacAloon, John: frame theory of sport, 11, 51, 123, 164, 231-32. *See also* spectacle

MacGregor, Roy, 237, 249n28; ghostwriter for Wayne Gretzky, 101n66

Mackay, Calum "Baldy", 63, 80, 94, 111-12, 194, fig. 28

Mackell, Fleming, 21, 108, 151, 152-53, fig. 18

MacLennan, Hugh, 233-34

MacPherson, Jim "Bud," 73, 84, 87, 96, 106, 109, 110, 112, 115, 149, 151, 167, 191, 222, fig. 28

MacSkimming, Roy (sportswriter), 217

Madison Square Gardens (MSG III), 32, 37, 47, 52, 63, 65, 66, 68n15, 187-88, 229, 254, fig. 11; magazines, 123, 233-34. *See also Life; The New Yorker; Sport; Sports Illustrated; Standard*

Maggs, Randall, 221, 235-36

Malarchuk, Clint, 235

Malone, Cliff, 29

Mann, Michael (director), 154

Maple Leaf Gardens (MLG), 26, 28, 49, 109-10, 117-19, 131, 139, 174, 190, 229, figs. 4, 18 and 23

Maple Leafs (Toronto): at the Mount Royal Hotel, 221; St. Catharines' playoff hideaway, 115; Stanley Cup success, 181;

Marlboro Juniors, 139, 190

Martel, Jean-Patrice, 237

masculinity: and pain, 141-42

Masnick, Paul, 84, 87, 106, 110-111, 151, 152-53, 174, 178, 193, 194, 199, fig. 28

Mazur, Eddie "Spider," 116, 151, 152-53, 170, 178, 193, 198, 199, fig. 28

McCabe, Eddie (sportswriter), 135

McCool, Frank "Ulcers," 37

McCormack, Johnny "Goose," 148, 166, 194, fig. 28; lives in NDG with other Canadiens, 145

McDiarmid, Carleton "Mac": sketch of Turofsky photo, 108, 128n14

McFadden, Jim, 55, 167

McFarlane, Brian (sportswriter), 189, 249n28

McFarlane, Leslie (filmmaker): *Here's Hockey* (1953), 11, 187, 189-91, 197

McGimpsey, David, 239

McIntyre, Horace, 46

McIntyre, Jack, fig. 26

McIntyre, Manny, 25, 35

McKenzie, Ken (sportswriter), 71, 193, 198

McKinley, Michael, 233

McLean, Hugh (referee): altercation with Richard, 88–90

McMahon, Mike, 15–16, 33, 40n1, fig. 2

McNabney, Sid, 84, 86

McNeil, David (son), 21–22, 40n1, 73, 145, 210, 220–21, 222, 227, 242–43, 247, 248n6, figs. 31 and 32; at Bell Centre (2008), 255–57; Black Hawk supporter, 223; collects memorabilia connected to father, 253–54; first NHL game, 221–22; first road-hockey net, 221; precipitates family crisis, 226

McNeil, Donna (daughter), 247, 253

McNeil, Douglas "Dugger", 32–33, 53

McNeil, "Gerry" Gérald, 188, 220; alcoholism, 224–25; Allan Cup win (1947), 22, 26–31; allows weak goal, 149, 167–68; All-Star Games, 131–34; Americans, Rochester with (1957–58 and 1958–59), 208–12; ankle frozen during 1953 Final, 176–77; Barilko scores against in 1951 Stanley Cup Final, 10, 103, 116–17, 124, 218; best NHL season (1952–53), 146, 161–62; bilingual, 19, 145, 150, 230, 249n15; Bing of Vimy, recipient of, 22; born (1926) and raised in Limoilou, 15, 145, 230; celebrates with Richard, 88, figs. 15 and 16; charity work, 230; and childhood friends, 15, 247–48, fig. 1; confidence and lack thereof, 145–46, 168, 177, 237; cynicism, 247; did not play season 1954–55, 220–21, 247; disposition of, 173; in *The Divine Ryans*, 218–22; doesn't push his sons in hockey, 242; equipment, 17, 44–45, 220, 245; family discussions of his career, 217–18; final illness and death, 245–47; Final (1951) versus Boston, 171–82; Final (1951) versus Maple Leafs, 103. 105–13, 127; Final (1952) versus Red Wings, 5.36–45; Final (1954) versus Red Wings, 192–201; first appearance in NHL playoffs (1950), 63–65; first appearance in NHL regular season, 10, 36–37; first NHL contract, 19–21; first NHL training camp (1943), 10, 16–21; fishing, 125–26; forgetfulness, 245; golf, 145, 150, 227–28, 246; grandchildren, 243; on Harvey as best Canadiens defenceman, 202; hobbies, 4.49, 5.31; in *Holiday Magazine*, 234; homophobia, overcomes, 225–26; honeymoon, 31; injuries, 24–25, 71, 98, 138–41, 142–43, 145, 158n32, 170, 191–92, 193, 212; instigates Richard's altercation with McLean, 88–90; invited to the Habs' training camp (1943), 15; interaction with fans, 226–27; marries Theresa Conway (1946), 30; meets Jocelyn Thibault, 228–29; meets José Theodore, 108, 245; mistaken for a child, 132; Mohawks, Cincinnati, with the, 43–44; Morton Junior Aces, 15; nerves, 10, 82, 113–14, 142, 145, 168–69, 207–208, 236–37; in newsreels, 187–89; nicknames, 33; pallbearer at Richard's funeral, 230–31; personal memorabilia, 32, 204; Player-of-the-Week "Schaefer Award," 62, 254; plays during serious family illnesses, 135–36; plays handball in summer, 191; plays Oldtimers hockey, 222; plays rec room hockey with son, 221; plays without a mask, 136; post-hockey, 10, 217, 221, 222–23, 224, 225, 226, 227–31, 237, 242–47; post-NHL life, 10, 208–212; portrait (colour) in *Sport*, 123–24, 129n43, back cover; poses as cook, 96; prankster, 32–33, 72, 244–45; prepays his funeral, 231; presented with a Habs sweater #30, 228; and the press, 19, 31, 38–39, 82, 124, 142, 145, 146, 161–62, 245, 247, 248n11; proud of his children, 244; pulls himself, 168–69; pursued by female fans, 227; pursues a career in sales, 221, 222, 223; receives NHL Milestone Award, 227; released by the Canadiens, 212; replaces Durnan, 10, 36–37, 43, 46–58, 61–62, 66–67; replaces Plante, 173, 193–94, 209; respected by teammates, 150; retirement, 192, 202–203, 208–209; routine, game-day, 33, 57; Royals, Montreal, with the, 22–36, 208, 212; scrapbooks, 108, 253; seems to lose weight, 245; selects three stars on French CBC, 221–22; sells cars, 191; Semifinal versus Black Hawks (1953), 166–71; Semifinal versus Bruins (1952), 151–53; Semifinal versus Red Wings (1951), 71–73, 79–85, 86–88, 91, 91–94, 95–98; shoots family film, 145; shutouts (10) in 1952–53 season, 183n1; shutout streak, playoffs (1951), 10, 93–95; shutout streak, senior hockey (1947), 26; signs his 1951–52 contract, 126–27; on the slapshot, 196; smoking, 80, 210, fig. 21; in *SI*, 218; in *Sport* magazine, 10, 123–24, back cover ; Stanley Cup ring, 254–55; stick of, 254; stops

Howe's bid for fifty-goal season, 164–66; on television, 85, 163; Vezina race (1952–53), 162; unknown Canadiens goalie, 11, 218; views himself in old footage, 189; vows not to play another game under Irvin, 195; wears face mask, 212; wins Stanley Cup, 178–82, 219; winters in Florida with fellow Canadiens alumni, 227; works at the War Assets department, 22

McNeil, Karen (daughter), 142, 146, 161, 226, 245, 247; born on the day of Barilko's goal, 119, 127, 212, 222; seriously ill, 135–36

McNeil, Pierre "Pete" (father), 20, 145

McNeil, Ronald "Shannon" (son), 62, 133, 135, 225–26, 242, 247; announces that he is gay, 225

McNeil, Rose Ann (b. Dyotte, mother of Gerry), 19, 135, 161, 230

McNeil, Theresa (b. Conway, wife of Gerry), 30, 34, 62, 121, 138, 142, 181, 247, figs. 5 and 10; attends games, 31–32, 135, 204, fig. 30; encourages Gerry to retire, 207–208; in labour, 113–14; and the press, 31, 142, 145, 162–63; stricken with Parkinson's disease, 245

McSorley, Tom: on hockey literature, 232

media, 134, 257; art (visual), 82–83, 91, 96, 108–109, 128n14, 129n39; comparison of, 232–33; coverage of the Richard funeral, 230–31; film versus print, 233; history of, 78, 189; newspaper, 38–39, 57, 69n50, 82, 175; newsreel, 72, 134, 187–89; radio, 88, 122, 134, 163, 175, 246; song and sound, 103, 134, 233–34; Telenews, 72, 134, 188; television, 134, 163–64, 178–79, 183n13, 229, 235; television (HD), 129n47; video, 79, 121. See also film; photographs; press; sports photography

Meeker, Howie, 56, 106, 108, 110, 111, 112, 115, 116, 117, 118, 121, fig. 18

Meger, Paul, 59, 84, 110, 111, 115, 148, 149, 150, 151, 165, 168, figs. 10 and 28

Melançon, Benoît: on Sweet's 1955 portrait of Maurice Richard and *The Martyrdom of Saint Sebastian* by Luca Giordano, 124

memorabilia (sports), 32, 204, 220, 231, 245, 253–54

Michaluk, Art, 29

Miramichi, the, 238

Mohawks, Cincinnati, 35, 43–44, 62, 192

Molson: sponsor of Briston film, 198

Montréal-Matin, 35, 139, 203

Moore, Dickie, 142, 148, 149, 152, 162, 178, 180–81, 199, 208, 222, 228, 231, 248, figs. 27 and 28; pallbearer at Richard funeral, 230

Moriarty, Cathy, 154

Morin, Pierre "Pete", 28, 29, 31, 64

Mortson, Angus "Gus," 106, 108, 111, 116, 132, 231, fig. 18

Mosdell, Kenny, 47, 63, 80, 98, 112, 116, 133, 148, 151, 209, 230, 248, 254, figs. 17 and 28; lives in NDG with other Canadiens, 145; and Lorainne, 59, 90, 227, 246, fig. 10; pallbearer at Richard's funeral, 230; scores overtime winner against Detroit, 192, 194–95

Mosienko, Bill, 46, 167, 168, 170

Mount Royal Hotel (Montreal), 171, 221, 255

Mumford, Lewis: professional sport as spectacle, 231–32

Murphy, Bob (sports editor), 85

Murphy, Hal, 143–44

Museum of Civilization (Ottawa): Richard exhibit, 245–46, 253

National Hockey League (NHL): adopts the red line (1943), 19; amateur draft, 21, 41n13; animosity between teams, 86, 193, 201–202; as family entertainment, 53; Final of 1951 only playoff series to have every game go into overtime, 103; head office in Sun Life Building, 198; pension dispute, 227; popularity in US, 175; predictions for 1952–53, 162; racism in, 25, 241; rinks, Original Six, 47–50, 53, 61, 229; on sudden-death overtime, 104–105; the tie (draw), 56, 104; travel (team) in 1950s, 58–59, 69n35, 85

National Hockey League Players Association (NHLPA), 85, 227, 242

National Post, 245

newsreel. *See under* media

New York: 52nd Street in 1940s, 32; Leon and Eddie's, 32, fig. 6; Piccadilly Hotel, 58, 89

New Yorker, The, 54

New York Times Encyclopedia of Sports, The, Vol. 8, 54

NCAA: athletic scholarship, 22

Nickleson, Al (sportswriter), 39, 115, 131, 133; visits the Canadiens dressing room after '51 Cup loss, 118

Normandin, Michel (radio broadcaster and announcer), 134, 163, 168

Northey, William (President, Canadian Arena Company): attends game at Forum with Princess Elizabeth, 135

North Station (Boston), 152, 173

nostalgia, 11, 34, 57, 76, 124, 230, 237

Notre-Dame-de-Grâce (NDG), 142, 145, 210

O'Brien, Andy (sportswriter), 197, 202–03

O'Connell Lodge (Lac-des-Loups), 125–26

O'Connor, Herbert "Buddy," 37, 63–64, 66

Olmstead, Bert, 46, 73, 86, 87, 110, 111, 113, 134, 139, 165–67, 178, 191, 192, 199, 231, figs. 17 and 28

O'Meara, Baz (sportswriter), 39, 82, 84, 90, 99n7, 116, 135, 207–208

Orlando, Jimmy, 32, 34–35, 122

Orr, Bobby, 121, 201, 234–35

overtime (or extra time), 127; hockey compared to other sports, 103–105

Parent, Bernie, 218

Parsley, Al (sportswriter), 18, 95

Patrick, Lester, 122, 173

Patrick, Lynn, 163, 171, 173, 176–77

Patskou, Paul, Society for International Hockey Research (SIHR): expert on early video resources at the HHOF, 121, 163, 187

Pavelich, Marty, 55, 84, 87, 133, 147–48, 162, 194

Peirson, Johnny, 133, 151, 156, 172, 176, 178

Penny, Steve, 229, 248n11

Peskin, Hy (photographer), 50–52, 68n19, 68n20, 78, 124, 143, 154

Petit journal, Le, 150–51, 203

photograph(s), 73–79, 123–24, 154, 166; of Barilko goal, 10, 103, 119–22, fig. 20; basis for feature film, 154; of Canadiens, 98, 180–81, figs. 17, 27 and 28; chance, 113, 143, 179; covered over with generations, 255; discovery, 136–37, 255; family versus public, 73, 77–78, 136–37, 166, 255; fictionalized in *The Divine Ryans,* 218–19; of Gretzky, 122; grey-scale versus colour, 123–24, 129n46; of Henderson, 122; of Hewitt, 122; and history, 76, 124, 137–38; of Howe, 122; of Hull, 122; Kilpatrick's, 76, 78–79, 124, 136–38, 166, figs. 12 and 22; of Lach and Richard, 179; of Lester Patrick, 122; Lussier's of Orr, 121, 124, 179; of McNeil and Durnan, 143, 158n35; of McNeil and Henry, 153, 154–56, fig. 25; of McNeil and Howe, 77–79, 166, fig. 12; of McNeil and Maple Leafs after overtime victory, 4.9–10, 8.45; of McNeil and Plante, 143, 158n32, fig. 24; of McNeil and son, David (author), 210, figs. 31 and 32; of McNeil on front page, 106, 173, 213n19, 251n56; and memory, 32, 59–60, 136–38, 166, 179; red (colour), associations in Western culture, 123; restoration of, 137–38; of Richard and McNeil, 88, fig. 15; of Richard, McNeil, and Irvin, 91–92, fig. 16; of Richard Riot, 122; of Sloan ("halo" effect), 113, fig. 19; staged portraiture, 123–24; of Theresa McNeil at the Forum, 204–205, fig. 30; Turofsky Imperial Oil collection at the HHOF, 122; twentieth-century (Canada), 122; versus video, 79; visual intensity of colour, 124. *See also* sports photography

Piccadilly Hotel (New York), 58, 89

Plamondon, Gerry, 24, 248

Plante, Jacques "Jake," 9, 44, 45, 108, 123, 150, 168, 175, 193, 206, 207,208, 209, 212, 217, 218, 256, fig. 28; announced as replacement for Durnan in 1950, 43; cockiness of, 172; Douglas Hunter on, 237; and Hab goalies, 11; his #1 sweater retired, 228; John Zimmerman's photo of, 52; replaced by McNeil in 1953 Final, 173; replaces an injured McNeil in October 1952, 143-45, 157n19, fig. 24; replaces an injured McNeil in February 1954, 191-92; replaces McNeil in 1953 playoffs, 169-72; Richler's anecdote on, 236; stress level, 236-37; subject of "passing the torch" photo, 158n35; tries to use a face mask, 136; wandering style, 192, 220, 237

This book has been typeset in Utopia, Glypha, and Sport Classic, and printed on Husky paper in Montmagny, Quebec in February of two thousand and sixteen by Marquis Book Printing.